LAMON, Lester C. Black Tennesseans, 1900–1930. Tennessee, 1977.
  320p ill (Twentieth century America series) bibl index 76-49583.
  14.50 ISBN 0-87049-207-1. C.I.P.

Lamon discusses Tennessee's paternalistic white society, which accepted the white man's burden and its blacks who, brainwashed into be-
lieving in their own innate inferiority, existed in a separate social structure.   The underlying problems were "poverty and white control
[which] dulled the enthusiasm of the black masses." While some young
black radicals attempted to break this pattern in the 1920s, the apathy
and ignorance of the masses, along with the accommodation tendencies
of the old guard black leaders, caused them to fail. The notable exception was the Nashville *Globe*, the crusading black newspaper founded
in 1906. Throughout the period, those civil rights organizations that
were either controlled by white Tennesseans or closely associated with
white paternalism met with the greatest success. While generally objective, Lamon's apparent dislike for the accommodation philosophy
shows through, marring his historical perspective. Keeping this in
mind, along with Lamon's sometimes overbearing concentration on detail, *Black Tennesseans* is a valuable study of the foundations of the
early civil rights movement. Specialists will find it useful. Upper-divi-
sion and graduate level.

CHOICE   DEC. '77

History, Geography &
Travel

North America

In process
8-22-77
E
185.93
T3
L35

BLACK TENNESSEANS 1900-1930

Lester C. Lamon, a native of East Tennessee, received his B.A. and M.A.T. from Vanderbilt and his Ph.D. from the University of North Carolina at Chapel Hill, where he specialized in Afro-American history. He has published articles in several journals, including the *Journal of Southern History*, the *Journal of Negro History*, and the *Tennessee Historical Quarterly*, among others. Professor Lamon is now on the history faculty at Indiana University in South Bend.

ट्ठ *Twentieth-Century America Series*

BLACK TENNESSEANS 1900-1930

Lester C. Lamon

THE UNIVERSITY OF TENNESSEE PRESS : KNOXVILLE

ॐ Twentieth-Century America Series

Dewey W. Grantham, General Editor

The support of the
Tennessee Historical Commission
in making this publication possible is gratefully acknowledged.

Library of Congress Cataloging in Publication Data

Lamon, Lester C   1942–
  Black Tennesseans, 1900–1930.

  (Twentieth-century America series)
  Bibliography: p.
  Includes index.
  1. Afro-Americans—Tennessee—History. 2. Tennes-
see—Race question. 3. Afro-Americans—Social condi-
tions—To 1964. I. Title.
E185.93.T3L35   301.45′19′60730768   76–49583
  ISBN 0–87049–207–1

Preface

Seeing Negroes at home rather than at their employment, was like seeing Italians in Italy after having met them only on Bleecker Street in New York . . . . it was a shock to realize Negroes possessed more freedom than a right to somebody else's kitchen, back veranda or rear garden! . . . I felt uncomfortably like a spy.
Evelyn Scott, *Background in Tennessee*

Race relations in Tennessee have never offered fertile ground for historical stereotypes, and black history has appeared incidental. Although blacks have played important roles since the early days of the nineteenth century, they have never exceeded 36 percent of the population. As a labor system, slavery reigned only in the western part of the state, and abolitionism blossomed briefly in East Tennessee. After the Civil War, race-baiting never became the focus of a lost cause as it did elsewhere in the South, and Reconstruction, while psychologically traumatic to many whites, did not challenge significantly Tennessee's traditional racial pattern. As one dominant white faction replaced the other, the newly freed Negroes became loyal Republican supporters, but rarely leaders. Their recognized historical role changed only slightly; their public profile remained low.

The low black profile persisted in Tennessee. Negroes were rarely consulted, frequently abused, and most often ignored. Neglect and limited white awareness continued despite the

v

emergence in Nashville of a cluster of outstanding private black colleges, the gathering in Chattanooga of a large number of black industrial laborers, and the presence in Knoxville of a small, but able, group of black professionals. Blacks were most noticeable in Memphis, a brawling, sometimes booming, commercial city overlooking the Mississippi River. There thousands of black migrants from the Delta cotton lands came together, seeking freedom but instead finding and creating chaos. Except for the violence and crime in Memphis, however, white Tennesseans took little note of their black counterparts; "Niggertown," just like the slave quarters, was a "strange" and "unfamiliar" place, and whites made little effort to increase their awareness.

Throughout the nineteenth century and the first thirty years of the twentieth century, most black Tennesseans lived in rural areas. And in this environment, as Allan H. Spear points out in the conclusion to *Black Chicago*, "Negroes did not really act on their own."[1] Their actions were heavily proscribed by white economic and political control, and black rural residents lived a very inhibited, monotonous, and largely unrecorded existence. Their opportunities for self-expression were limited mostly to the church and, to a lesser extent, the fraternity. Whites took little notice except to demand deference and to market the crops. Black Tennesseans slowly recognized the restrictions of rural life and by 1900 had demonstrated a clear movement toward the cities. Although increasingly segregated and still dependent upon whites, they found that the cities provided greater opportunities for indigenous black expression. The study of Tennessee Negroes in the twentieth century, therefore, focuses more upon the urban centers.

As blacks became more mobile, their visibility increased, and Tennessee's traditional pattern of racial separation took on new intensity. The shadow of Jim Crow lay on the South in 1900, increasing fear, ignorance, and suspicion between the races.

[1] Spear, *Black Chicago: The Making of a Negro Ghetto, 1890–1920* (Chicago: Univ. of Chicago Press, 1967), 225.

White Tennesseans, the enforcers of segregation, were uneasy, and their rising apprehension was more than a response to political demagoguery, to real or alleged racial crime, or even to increased black mobility; it was, largely, a fear of the unknown. Traditional insensibility, reinforced by caste etiquette, had limited the depth of understanding and the range of interracial contact. Even the thought of change was unnerving.

In the face of increasingly overt white restrictions, black Tennesseans, especially those in the towns, were forced to respond. As should be expected of any rather arbitrary grouping of almost half a million people, they reacted to racial constraints in a variety of ways. Some reacted resentfully, calling for a long-delayed black acceptance into the prevailing white system. Most protested at first but then came to accept the accommodating approach exemplified in the public stance of Booker T. Washington. Washington encouraged continued separation and subordination, seeing black advance through self-help. Urban blacks had the opportunity, he felt, to develop their own "system"—their own parallel institutional society. Most white Tennesseans accepted Washington's program because it seemed not to challenge segregation and white supremacy; most black Tennesseans went along with his ideas as being the least likely to cause conflict and the most likely to bring immediate economic gains. Accepting separation, however, did not mean total apathy nor a lack of creativity. Black Tennesseans fought openly and sometimes aggressively for public higher education, and they responded very much the same as their white counterparts to such color-blind social phenomena as the business ethic and the progressive impulse. But the overriding feature of life for black Tennesseans in the early twentieth century was the *separate* community—separated from the recognized white mainstream partly by force and partly by choice. It was a complex society only dimly perceived, if not completely neglected, by contemporary whites.

This book does not pretend to bring to light or evaluate all aspects of its subject. From the time that I first began to think seriously about the past of black Tennesseans, two research avenues opened up. I could either concentrate upon one community—Nashville or Memphis—or I could attempt to deal in more general terms with the whole state. In choosing the latter approach, I have attempted to record and analyze the response of black men and women as they encountered an era of intense social, economic, and legal definition and displacement. In the future, more concentrated and specialized studies should sharpen the historical focus upon black Tennesseans. Not only historians, but psychologists, sociologists, and novelists also offer special tools for further study. Their concern with the individual and his feelings and emotions is vital to a full understanding of life on the "other side of the tracks" of traditional American history. And yet, a broad historical framework of institutional and political events and attitudes provides the essential background for more specific efforts. In another sense, Tennessee offers a uniquely appropriate opportunity for the general approach in that its three grand divisions—East, Middle, and West—present a range of geographic, economic, racial, and historical traditions which in many ways reflects the South in microcosm.

My conceptual view of this study has been that it should determine the position and attitudes of black Tennesseans at the turn of the century and then follow their development and change during the crucial thirty years from 1900 to 1930. Although the focus is soft, I have nevertheless provided several in-depth probes into black activity. The specific discussions are paired with chapters dealing with similar, but general, observations. Chapters VIII and IX, for example, present first a broad approach to the black business experience and then a closer and more detailed look at the development of black financial institutions. Chapters I and II, IV and V, and XII and XIII follow a similar pattern.

Researching and writing black history is not easy in the United States. *Herrenvolk* separatism has left its stamp upon the nation—and upon recorded history as well. If the historian is white, he or she bears the burden of a social and intellectual maturation that rarely includes normal intercourse with black Americans. Whether black or white, the historian inherits the professional handicaps of what Okon E. Uya has described as history "through a white filter"—recorded American history has been white history.[2] Prevailing social values influenced what white historians chose to say about blacks and also accounted for the lack of interest taken by controlling white institutions in preserving the relatively sparse primary source materials of the black past.

Certainly, I have not been able to overcome all of these handicaps; as a white native of Tennessee, I have reflected or encountered most of the biases. Fortunately, however, Mary White Ovington's observation in 1947 that "one cannot go South and be in both the white and the colored world" is not as categorical as it once was.[3] Although all barriers between communities and races have not been removed, and the vision is not unclouded, I have been aided greatly by many black Tennesseans who have made my job easier by sharing their homes and reminiscences with me. Rosa McGhee, a black Chattanooga schoolteacher, introduced me to that city's black history and many of its long-time residents, but during one of my interviews, Dr. J. Monroe Bynes pointed to Ms. McGhee and noted that "there was a time when she couldn't go around with you." Recent social attitudes, therefore, have helped, and blacks and whites do speak more frankly about racial matters than they once did. Much of the damage done by the white filter, however, is irreparable. The preserved record of the nation's black past is often very thin and of questionable quality. Until the 1960s, few libraries were interested in seeking out black manuscript collections and diaries, leaving the record heavily dependent upon sterile government statistics or the alternatingly hostile and paternalistic reporting of the white press. Reconstructing life "within the Veil," therefore, to borrow the words of

[2] Uya, "The Culture of Slavery: Black Experience Through a White Filter," *Afro-American Studies* 1 (1971), 203–9.
[3] Ovington, *The Walls Came Tumbling Down* (New York: Harcourt, 1947), 53.

W. E. B. Du Bois, still presents special problems.[4] Nevertheless, this study does demonstrate that black history is a fertile part
of the nation's past. Black Tennesseans were not simply acted
upon by white society; they created, destroyed, and responded to
national and local stimuli in their own right.

ACKNOWLEDGMENTS

It would be impossible to acknowledge specifically all those
who made important contributions to the research and writing of
this book. Some, however, shouldered heavier burdens than
others. George B. Tindall, Dewey W. Grantham, and Louis R.
Harlan read the entire manuscript during its various stages of
evolution. Their collective store of information and insight and
their perceptive criticisms greatly improved the finished product. More specifically, Samuel H. Shannon shared his knowledge
and research into the early history of black higher education in
Tennessee. In addition, librarians and their staffs have saved me
countless hours of labor and frustration. Rarely did they show
anything but genuine interest and enthusiasm for my repeated
requests for aid. Time for oral research and manuscript revision
was financed by a Summer Stipend from the National Endowment for the Humanities and a Summer Faculty Fellowship from
Indiana University. Without this generous aid those indispensable large blocks of working time would not have been possible.

Permission has been granted to use material which appeared
originally under my authorship in the *Journal of Southern History* (May 1974), *Tennessee Historical Quarterly* (Spring 1973),
Proceedings of the Indiana Academy of the Social Sciences (1974),
and East Tennessee Historical Society *Publications* (1969). The
copyrights for this material rest with these publications, and I am
grateful for their support.

Special acknowledgment should also go to those black high

---

[4] Du Bois, *The Souls of Black Folk* (Chicago: McClurg, 1903), "forethought."

school students in Oak Ridge, Tennessee, who waited outside my classroom one fall morning in 1965. Their requests for greater attention to black history first opened my eyes to this rich, though neglected, field of study.

And finally and most importantly my thanks go to my family who has long nourished my interest in history, my children who learned to respect my clutter of books and notes and to ask less frequently, "when will you be through with your book, Daddy?" and my wife, Beth, an indispensable critic and a possessor of infinite patience and understanding.

Contents

	Preface	*page* v
CHAPTER I.	Black People and a White System	1
II.	Jim Crow Streetcars and Black Protest	20
III.	To Fight, To Switch, or "To Hell With It"	37
IV.	A Respectful Distance Behind	59
V.	One Agricultural and Industrial State Normal School for Negroes	88
VI.	On the Agricultural Margin	110
VII.	"He Will Go Where He Can Live Best"	132
VIII.	Operating in the Black	167
IX.	Bootstrap Capitalism	183
X.	Progressivism—For Whites Only?	207
XI.	Race Relations Under Pressure	231
XII.	A Slight Change in Direction	256
XIII.	In No Uncertain Terms	274
	Conclusion	297
	Bibliographical Essay	300
	Index	309

Illustrations

PHOTOGRAPHS   *following page* 144

Henry Allen Boyd
Robert R. Church, Jr.
Solvent Savings Bank and Trust Company, Memphis
Lincoln League meeting, 1916
First faculty of Tennessee Agricultural and
        Industrial Normal School
Fisk Jubilee Singers
Laborers in Cumberland River freight traffic
Black "roustabouts" at Memphis
Workers in marble quarry near Knoxville
Phosphate miner in Maury County
Black sharecropper
Interior of Roddy's Citizens Co-operative Stores, Memphis
Delivery truck for Roddy's Citizens Co-operative Stores

TABLES

1. Length of Terms of Black and White Schools in
        Counties Having the Largest Black Popula-
        tions, 1928   *page* 78
2. Average Monthly Salaries for Elementary
        Teachers in Tennessee, 1930   86
3. Urban and Rural Death and Birth Rates for
        Tennessee, 1927   137

to BETH

CHAPTER I.

Black People and a White System

"The whites of the South [are] given the alternative," wrote Tennessee's Senator Edward Ward Carmack in 1903, "of recovering their mastery or abandoning their country."[1] Carmack represented a growing number of white Tennesseans who supported an aggressive recovery of complete mastery over the lives of black Americans. Often waving the banner of "progressive reform," these whites generated understandable apprehension in black communities. At the turn of the century, Richard Henry Boyd, a national church leader and black businessman from Nashville, wrote publicly of his fear that, if blacks did not "carefully guard [their] . . . interests," white politicians would "turn the hand backward on the political dial [by] a quarter of a century."[2]

Few Tennesseans, black or white, doubted the reality and even the wisdom of racial separation; a social system, rationalized during a thirty-five-year adjustment to the presence of the freedmen in the state, had clearly established itself on the principles of segregation. The concern expressed by prominent black leaders such as Dr. Boyd originated not in the separateness of the caste system of the South, but in the increasing strictures placed on the subordinate element by the dominant.

Following emancipation, black Tennesseans had held public

[1] Carmack, "The Race Problem," *Olympian* 2 (Oct. 1903), 308, 316.
[2] Dr. R. H. Boyd to his fellow Baptist ministers in Tennessee, March 10, 1900, Citizens Savings Bank and Trust Company Scrapbook, private collection of the Citizens Savings Bank and Trust Company, Nashville.

1

office, ridden on public conveyances, and even attended school with whites. Such experiments, however, had come into direct conflict with the traditional values of the pre-Civil War caste system. As early as 1881 the Tennessee legislature determined that mores and prejudices, alone, would not provide the needed racial distinctions within the state's social, economic, and political institutions.[3] By requiring railroad companies operating in the state to "furnish separate cars, or portions of cars cut off by partition walls" for black passengers, the legislators sought to make explicit the approved role for each race and to give statutory strength to the gospel of separation. Unlike other former Confederate states during the late nineteenth century, however, Tennessee had seemed satisfied that its initial steps toward enforcing segregation would suffice to direct the lives and livelihoods of its biracial population. A stability evolved which, although discriminatory, Dr. Boyd and other blacks could accept.

Black willingness to adjust to existing limitations in 1900 is traceable to a combination of economic, social, and geographic conditions. Most important, a majority of black Tennesseans (and a majority of black Southerners) were rural, and, set apart from communication and contact with less passive and better-educated blacks, they concentrated upon coaxing a subsistence from their small farms or those of their white landlords. Perhaps equally important, however, the state's four-hundred-mile breadth and its two population extremes hindered the unification of black feeling needed to make any effective and safe protest against segregation. Most blacks (48 percent) lived in the western third of the state, and they were primarily (73 percent) in rural areas. Racial relationships in this region reflected the strong white fears and prejudices of the Mississippi Delta and a black submissiveness encouraged by decades of suppression. Ironically, a significantly different economic pattern and ratio of blacks and whites

---

[3]*Acts of the State of Tennessee* (1881), 211. For a discussion of the racially unsettled nature of the affairs surrounding the passage of this bill, see Stanley J. Folmsbee, "The Origin of the First 'Jim Crow' Law," *Journal of Southern History* 15 (May 1949), 235–47.

inspired the same tendency toward black deference in the mountainous eastern third of the state. Although constantly reminded of their inferior position, blacks in this region did not feel so keenly the harshness and degradation of West Tennessee.[4] Only 13 percent of all black Tennesseans lived in the East, and many worked as domestic servants, encouraging black-white relationships based upon paternalism and a minimum of explicit racial hatred.[5] Furthermore, the eastern cities, especially Chattanooga, had considerable industry where blacks could find work; as a result, their standard of living was somewhat higher than that of the sharecroppers of the West. Where fear and a dulling environment held resistance in check in West Tennessee, a desire not to "rock the boat" gave the appearance of reasonable contentment among blacks in the East.

Middle Tennessee offered the greatest potential for black resistance, especially in the Nashville community where, bolstered by the stimulating presence of four Northern-supported colleges and two budding publishing houses, a large class of educated and sensitive blacks prospered. Although relatively free from white economic pressure, even this black elite hesitated to challenge the basic principles of segregation. Educated in church colleges and influenced largely by the fifty-seven black churches in the city, Nashville's black leaders were inclined to put their faith in the hard work and turn-the-other-cheek philosophies of Booker T. Washington, social Darwinists, and the Christian church.

The early movement to establish a legal system of segregation took on new dimensions, however, as the first decade of the

[4] M. W. Gilbert, pastor of Mount Zion Baptist Church in Knoxville, to Mary Church Terrell, Oct. 3, 1910, Mary Church Terrell Papers, container 1; interviews with Mr. and Mrs. J. Herman Daves, July 2, 1970; Carl A. Cowan, June 16, 1970; and George McDade, May 29, 1972.

[5] J. Herman Daves, *A Social Study of the Colored Population of Knoxville, Tennessee* (Knoxville: Free Colored Library, 1926), 6–7; E. Brasher Bailey, "The Negro in East Tennessee" (M.A. thesis, New York Univ., 1947); J. H. Brice, teacher in the Greeneville Colored Schools, to Mary Church Terrell, July 5, 1917, Terrell Papers, container 2.

3

twentieth century progressed. Mastery, as proclaimed by Senator Carmack, implied more than separation. Therefore, the fears of Boyd were justified, and the decade was destined to be a time of further "definition" in Tennessee's caste system. The Maryville College Law of 1901 closed the one remaining loophole that permitted interracial education;[6] the Jim Crow streetcar law solidified segregation on public conveyances in 1905; and politically, the growing "lily white" forces in the Republican party, the increased rigidity of the de facto white Democratic primary, and the trend toward the commission form of municipal government between 1908 and 1913 eliminated blacks from elective office and, in many cases, negated their opportunities for political participation.

Black Tennesseans did not let such developments go unnoticed or even unchallenged, but for the most part they soon accommodated themselves to the new restrictions. Professor W. H. Harrison of Roger Williams University in Nashville set a dominant tone when he advised a state meeting of Negro Baptist young people that "if illegal discriminations are made, we must carry out our allegiance to the state, city, county and town, for God is not dead."[7] Giving spiritual guidance to this public acquiescence was the authoritative figure of Booker T. Washington, who greatly influenced the racial attitudes of the state. Blacks drew comfort from the "Tuskegee ideal" of steady economic advance and hard work, while whites appreciated the conservative preachments of "common sense" and the rejection of specific social and political goals.[8] Washington had performed a miracle at Tuskegee In-

[6] This act prevented private institutions from educating blacks and whites in the same institution. The Constitution of 1870 had decreed absolute segregation in public schools. *Acts of the State of Tennessee* (1901), ch. 7; Robert Hiram White, *Development of the Tennessee State Educational Organization, 1796–1929* (Kingsport: Southern, 1929), 123.

[7] Nashville *American*, June 21, 1901. Speaking to a black audience in Shelbyville, Dr. J. Q. Johnson, presiding elder of the African Methodist Episcopal Church, admitted that Tennessee Negroes had "grievances, but we also have many opportunities. Let us emphasize our advantages and not our grievances at the present time." *Ibid.*, Jan. 13, 1904.

[8] James Carroll Napier to Booker T. Washington, Dec. 28, 1905, Booker T. Washington Papers, container 879. In November 1909, Washington made a nine-day tour of Tennes-

stitute and in 1913 W. H. Lankford of Brownsville wrote Washington, promising that blacks in his area would "lay fast hold of the instruction you shall give us," if only a "Second Tuskegee" could be erected among them.[9] Blacks in the eastern and middle counties sought his appearance at fairs, commencements, educational meetings, and Labor Day celebrations. Not only black leaders, but also the mayor of Murfreesboro and the president of Middle Tennessee State Normal College asked Washington to speak at the Rutherford County Colored Fair in 1912.[10]

Booker T. Washington's emphasis upon black economic solidarity and his encouragement of private enterprise had special appeal in Nashville. In 1903 James Carroll Napier, local politician, lawyer, educator, frequent federal officeholder, and longtime associate of Washington, urged him to bring the annual meeting of his National Negro Business League to the city. In a speech welcoming the convention to the area, John L. Barbour, a black businessman, declared, "if the colored merchant of Nashville is not a success it is not at all due to race prejudice, but is due to his own incapacity." Washington's keynote address ratified this emphasis upon black responsibility and encouraged cooperation with the demands of the white system. Even R. H. Boyd, having accepted the league's vice-presidency, suppressed some of his earlier fears and conceded that white control could have its bless-

see. Traveling between Bristol and Memphis, he spoke to crowds that contained almost as many whites as blacks. In Knoxville on Nov. 19, the mayor, John M. Brooks, greeted Washington with the glowing comment that "It is not often that occasions like this present themselves; not often that Knoxville has the opportunity of greeting a great leader among men." Knoxville *Journal and Tribune*, Nov. 20, 1909. A staunchly Democratic newspaper praised Washington's address in Nashville: "Mr. Washington, himself the greatest black man this country has ever produced and one of the great Americans alive today of any race, was at his very best. He preached industry, frugality, thrift and morality. . . ." Elizabethton *Equity*, n.d., clipping in Washington Papers, container 890.

[9] Oct. 24, 1913, Washington Papers, container 835.

[10] The Reverend H. W. McNair of New Market to Booker T. Washington, June 26, 1913; H. G. Fagg of Knoxville to Washington, Nov. 13, 1913, G. B. Giltner, mayor of Murfreesboro, to Washington, Aug. 9, 1912; Robert L. Jones, president of Middle Tennessee State Normal College, to Washington, Aug. 12, 1912; J. H. Crichlow, elected county official, to Washington, Aug. 10, 1910, all in Washington Papers, containers 832 and 835.

ings for the black communities; leaving public and civic affairs in white hands, the black man could now "concentrate on raising himself economically."[11] This, of course, was at the very heart of Washington's so-called Atlanta Compromise.

In spite of apathy, fear, and Washington's moderating influence, many blacks, especially those under the age of forty, expressed growing dissatisfaction with the increasing discrimination of the segregation system. Each extension of Jim Crow in the early twentieth century met some opposition from black individuals or groups in Tennessee. Although they were the exceptions, the voices of protest and pride played an important role; most of these challenges succumbed to pressure from the white-controlled government and a lack of mass support, but the persistent presence of resistance kept the issue of full citizenship alive among black Tennesseans. And, as with William E. B. Du Bois, the leading national voice of protest, support slowly but surely increased.

Publicity and historical attention have focused most sharply upon measures that restricted Negroes' use of public transportation. In Tennessee this was, indeed, an area of considerable importance; white authorities pushed segregation most insistently, and blacks opposed discrimination most strenuously. In 1901 the legislature considered extending the 1881 Jim Crow law to cover railroad sleeping cars as well as day coaches but yielded to the opposition of the Pullman Company and dropped the idea. Sensitive to public pressure, Governor James B. Frazier decided not to wait for the legislature, and in 1903 he successfully persuaded the Tennessee State Railroad Commission to interpret the existing 1881 statute broadly enough to cover all forms of railroad travel. Blacks protested, particularly the upper-class blacks who had the financial means to use Pullman cars. Both Washington and Du Bois urged their Nashville friends to initiate court proceedings, but they could generate little action. J. C. Napier did

[11] Nashville *American*, Aug. 20, 1903.

6

send a telegram to Pullman President Robert Todd Lincoln, urging him "in the name of your revered father . . . [to] use your great influence to avert this calamity and prevent additional oppression." Napier received no encouragement, and most blacks, failing in their appeals to white authorities like Lincoln and Frazier, adjusted to the new extension of caste restrictions.[12]

Nevertheless, some determined black Tennesseans did take public issue with the failure of railroads to provide the "equal" as much as they emphasized the "separate." Robert L. Mayfield, an enigmatic and ambitious young lawyer, started what was to be a colorful career in the state's courts by suing the Louisville and Nashville Railroad in 1905 for failure to provide him with facilities comparable to those made available to white passengers on a trip from Cincinnati to Nashville. He maintained that the Jim Crow compartment had no lavatory or smoking section. Although admitting the validity of Mayfield's charges, the lower court rejected his complaint, and the state supreme court refused to hear an appeal on the grounds that the discrimination was not "harmful" to Mayfield in that he continued to smoke despite the regulations of the car.[13]

In East Tennessee, a determined young black woman launched a similar charge against the Nashville, Chattanooga and St. Louis Railway in 1907. Taking her complaint to the Interstate Commerce Commission (ICC) instead of the state courts, Georgia Edwards of Chattanooga explained that, having purchased a first-class ticket to Dalton, Georgia, she was forcibly required to occupy unequal facilities without lavatory or towels or smoking compartment. In addition she claimed that black men and women had to share one toilet while there were separate facilities for white men and women. Federal authorities proved to be more

---

[12]*Ibid.*, Feb. 19, 1901. Napier to Washington, Oct. 28, Dec. 11, 1903; Washington to Jesse Lawson, Nov. 5, 1903; Washington to Du Bois, Dec. 14, 1903, Feb. 27, 1904 (2); William H. Baldwin, president of the Long Island Railroad, to Washington, Jan. 7, 1904, all in Washington Papers. Nashville *Globe*, March 27, 1908.

[13] Supreme Court of Errors and Appeals, Tennessee State Library and Archives, Supreme Court *Index* No. 4210.

sympathetic than the state courts. On July 8, 1907 the ICC handed down a ruling in Miss Edwards' favor—reaffirming the "reasonableness" of segregation but declaring that "it by no means follows that carriers may discriminate between white and colored passengers in the accommodations which they furnish to each." Such discrimination, said Commissioner Franklin K. Lane, subjected the passenger to "undue and unreasonable prejudice and disadvantage." The commission then ordered the offending railway to provide the missing facilities in the Negro coach, or to remove the white advantages, by October 1, 1907.[14]

Miss Edwards gained a legal victory and received the public acclaim of many black Tennesseans, but service to black passengers on Tennessee's railways improved very little. The Nashville, Chattanooga and St. Louis appealed the right of the ICC to intervene, and although this appeal was rejected in 1911, federal authorities simply lacked adequate power and will to enforce the decision of their commission.[15]

When segregation was extended to the streetcar systems of Tennessee in 1905, blacks throughout the state attempted to organize protest boycotts. Collectively, these actions became the most widely discussed and by far the most popular "rebellion" against growing caste restrictions in public transportation; every major city in the state experienced some public display of black opposition to the extension of Jim Crow. The reaction of the black communities led to at least one court case and also to the formation of two black-owned transportation enterprises that competed with white streetcar companies for the fares of the black commuters and shoppers.[16] Inevitably, however, lack of capital and in-

---

[14]*Edwards* v. *Nashville, Chattanooga and St. Louis Railway Company*, 12 I.C.C. 247–50; Nashville *American*, July 9, 1907; Chattanooga *Daily Times*, July 9, 1907.

[15] Nashville *Globe*, July 12, 1907; Nashville *Tennessean*, April 16, May 29, 1908; *Crisis* (March 1911), 13; Charles W. Cansler, *Three Generations: The Story of a Colored Family of Eastern Tennessee* (Knoxville: privately printed, 1939), 147; interview with Mr. and Mrs. J. Herman Daves, July 2, 1970.

[16] The court decision upholding the law originated in Memphis and is found in *Morrison* v. *State*, 95 S.W. 494. The two black enterprises were the Union Transportation Company in Nashville and the Transfer Omnibus Motor Car Company in Chattanooga.

ability to sustain mass support in the face of white employer pressure, statutory harassment, and the rigors of walking in winter would doom this uncharacteristically aggressive black "uprising" in Tennessee.

Discrimination in the areas of legal due process and law enforcement elicited a more basic, if less popular, display of black protest. In 1905 Robert L. Mayfield had also challenged the systematic exclusion of blacks from jury service in Tennessee, but he had seen his complaint rejected by the courts with the sweeping and unsubstantiated claim that "the law recognizes no such discrimination." Mayfield let the matter rest, but the question of excluding blacks from juries persisted. In 1906 John H. Early, a white lawyer from Chattanooga, attempted to establish a test case before the Tennessee Supreme Court. Encouraged by blacks and aided by black lawyers, Early appealed the case of *Rivers* v. *State* on the grounds that the "good citizen" requisite for jury duty in Hamilton County had always been interpreted by the jury commission so as to exclude Negroes. In upholding Rivers's conviction of manslaughter, however, the judges dodged the issue of discriminatory justice in Tennessee and instead made their decision on the technical grounds that the competency of the grand jury was not challenged prior to the indictment.[17] As with Mayfield, Early and his friends never attempted another appeal, and de facto exclusion continued.

It was risky for blacks to pursue equitable law enforcement aggressively. Black lawyers who fought legal discrimination too vigorously often found themselves in professional or physical danger from irate white citizens. Robert L. Mayfield knew the

---

[17]*Christian Index*, Oct. 1904; *Rivers* v. *State*, 96 S.W. 956, 957; Chattanooga *Daily Times*, Oct. 9, 1905. The formal statement of Early's argument was that there were many black "householders and freeholders, upright and intelligent . . . and possessing all the qualifications required by law for jury service; yet the jury commission appointed for the county of Hamilton . . . have all the time made up the jury lists for the county of white men only . . . excluded the names of all negroes therefrom, and that the grand jury, which indicted the defendant, was made up exclusively of white men, and the names of all negroes were eliminated and excluded, solely on the ground of their race and color. . . ."

hazards well. Although he claimed graduation from the Howard University Law School, with high honors, this impetuous young lawyer appeared largely self-taught. His behavior as an attorney was unpolished, and his courtroom manner was abrupt and frequently devoid of proper etiquette. His attitude, coupled with his willingness to challenge the white system, resulted in almost constant conflicts with the white judges and white lawyers. Harassment began in 1907 when Criminal Court Judge W. M. Hart agreed to drop dubious bribery charges against him if he would "quit the practice of law in Tennessee." Mayfield refused, was convicted, and then was freed upon appeal to the Tennessee Supreme Court. Mayfield, however, was a careless bachelor, and he left himself open to numerous charges and convictions of disorderly conduct. These mistakes gave the already hostile white bar association grounds for seeking disbarment, and in 1920, after an eight-year battle, Mayfield lost his license to practice law in Tennessee.[18]

Disbarment was a mild reprimand compared to the treatment given Chattanooga attorneys Noah W. Parden and Styles L. Hutchins, the two black lawyers involved in the appeal of Ed Johnson to the United States Supreme Court in 1906. Johnson, convicted of rape, won a temporary stay of execution from Justice John Marshall Harlan, but he was taken from the Hamilton County jail on March 20 and lynched. After much legal wrangling, Sheriff Joseph F. Shipp and five other Chattanoogans were ruled in contempt of court by Harlan and made to serve short terms in the federal penitentiary in Washington, D. C. Enraged whites threatened Parden and Hutchins (a state legislator during the 1880s) with the same treatment given Johnson. Both men moved their families to Oklahoma.[19]

[18] Supreme Court *Index* No. 4210; Nashville *American*, June 1, Aug. 1, 1907; Nashville *Tennessean*, Aug. 1, 1907; Nashville *Globe*, April 30, 1909.

[19] Nashville *American*, March 8, 1906; *Christian Index*, April 7, 28, 1906; *Moon Weekly Illustrated*, June 23, 1906; Nashville *Tennessean*, Nov. 16, 1909; Nashville *Globe*, Nov. 5, 1909; Henry M. Wiltse, "The History of Chattanooga," Vol. II, 164, unpublished manuscript copy in the Chattanooga Public Library.

As the twentieth century began, large numbers of blacks continued to hold minor elective and appointive political offices.[20] By 1910, however, increased white restrictions and the general acceptance of the "progressive" commission system of government in Tennessee's cities caused a sharp drop in their numbers.[21] Although black wards could no longer choose an alderman or a justice of the peace, black political leaders did not forsake the desire to participate in party councils. Their protest against exclusion was complicated by the fact that the Republican party, that haven for black politicians, had recently become infected by a lingering case of "lily whitism." The severity of this infection fluctuated with both national and state politics and at times seemed on the verge of capturing the party organism *in toto*. Black public resistance never completely abated, but it depended heavily upon its leaders. Robert Reed Church, Jr., a wealthy young Memphis businessman, emerged as a black political force in 1912, and by battling continually during the next twenty years he maintained a place for blacks in the Republican party.

Despite the direct confrontation of men and women like Robert L. Mayfield, Georgia Edwards, and Robert Church, formal white repression persisted and solidified. The immediate ineffectiveness of direct protest opened another avenue of black response —self-examination. The conclusions reached after such intro-

[20]Examples include: J. L. Edwards and E. S. Earthman as justices of the peace in Shelby County; Nace Dixon of Clarksville, Joseph M. Trigg and Dr. Henry M. Green of Knoxville, Hiram Tyree, Eugene L. Reid, and Charles Grigsby of Chattanooga, and Solomon Parker Harris of Nashville as aldermen; Green Allen as school director in Carroll County; and several appointments as deputy sheriff in Knox and Hamilton counties. Memphis *Commercial Appeal*, Dec. 4, 1901, Jan. 8, 17, 1903; Clarksville *Leaf Chronicle*, Dec. 19, 21, 1908; Knoxville *Journal and Tribune*, Mar. 8, 1901, Jan. 19, 1908; Chattanooga *Daily Times*, Feb. 21, 1900, Oct. 11, 1905; Nashville *Tennessean*, Oct. 13, 1911; Nashville *Globe*, Oct. 13, 1911; Nashville *American*, Oct. 28, 1904.

[21]Tyree (1911), Green (1912), and Harris (1913) lost their aldermanic seats when the commission system stipulated that all newly designated commissioners were to be chosen at large. Dixon managed reelection in Clarksville in 1908 as "an unusually large number of Negroes voted." Nashville *Globe*, Oct. 3, 1913; Knoxville *News-Sentinel*, Nov. 9, 1969; Gilbert Eaton Govan and James Weston Livingood, *The Chattanooga Country 1540–1951: From Tomahawks to TVA* (New York: Dutton, 1952), 408; Chattanooga *Sunday Times*, July 11, 1937; Clarksville *Leaf Chronicle*, Dec. 21, 1908.

11

spection varied greatly, ranging from the discouragement and submissiveness of Sutton E. Griggs to the selective militancy, racial pride, and self-help of the Nashville *Globe*.

Racial developments in Tennessee had a most devastating impact upon the thinking of Sutton Griggs, a black Texas-born Baptist evangelist and an aspiring novelist. An environmental determinist by conviction, Griggs came to Nashville's First Baptist Church in the closing years of the nineteenth century, convinced that blacks were the racial equal of whites. Seeing a noticeable rise in the influence of the "most vicious white element," this visibly troubled Texan had no one answer for his unfortunate people, but he saw an obvious need for aggressive leadership in standing up for black human and political rights.[22] Such assertiveness, he felt, would awaken the white citizens to the virtues of the black race and discourage the increase of caste restrictions. A gifted orator, Griggs assumed the less suitable role of novelist in an effort to draw his people into action and also to enlighten those whites who seemed most capable of realizing the injustice of the Negro's plight. The first of a series of militant novels was *Imperium in Imperio* (1899). This angry work struck at the violence heaped on blacks in the South, and it was followed in rapid succession by *Overshadowed* (1901), *Unfettered* (1902), *The Hindered Hand* (1905), and *Pointing the Way* (1908). Griggs criticized the accommodationism of Booker T. Washington, and, like Du Bois's *Souls of Black Folk*, *The Hindered Hand* attacked the belief that industrial and manual training would solve the racial problems of the South:

What worker in iron can fashion a key that will open the door to that world of higher activities, the world of moral and spiritual forces . . . ? What welder of steel can beat into one the discordant soul forces of

[22]*Christian Index*, Oct. 15, 1904; S. P. Fullinwider, *The Mind and Mood of Black America: 20th Century Thought* (Homewood, Ill.: Dorsey, 1969), 73–77. For the role played by Griggs in leading local black protest movements, see his opposition to police brutality reported in the Nashville *Banner*, May 18, 1905 and Nashville *American*, May 19, 1905; for his drafting of a set of outspoken resolutions for the state convention of the Colored Baptist Church, see the Nashville *Tennessean*, July 26, 1908.

willing Negroes and unwilling whites, the really pivotal point of the problem? Really pressing is the need of industrial training for our people, but my peculiar case calls for something that must come from Lincoln the emancipator rather than from Lincoln the rail-splitter.[23]

Griggs maintained his adamant stand against discrimination and segregation through the first ten years of the century. He participated prominently in the Niagara Movement and, at first, supported the formation of the National Association for the Advancement of Colored People (NAACP).[24]

The literary efforts of this Baptist firebrand, however, won little notice among the black masses in Tennessee. Financially embarrassed by the printing costs of these ventures, Griggs grew discouraged and turned his attentions to a study of such Darwinian anthropologists as Herbert Spencer, Julian Sorell Huxley, and Benjamin Kidd.[25] He became convinced that the black communities had failed to follow his lead because they were indeed inferior—not innately, but in development of Christian civilization. In *Wisdom's Call* (1911), Griggs now set out to reason with the opposition on its own terms instead of blaming the whites for flagrantly abusing the rights of blacks. He sought to convince whites that their ill treatment and neglect of blacks were dooming the Anglo-Saxon civilization, a civilization he praised for being superior to any in previous history. The significant shift from black rights to white self-interest set the mood of Griggs's new approach to the role of blacks in Tennessee's social structure.

After becoming minister of the Tabernacle Baptist Church in Memphis in 1912, Griggs spent his next twenty years organizing black "welfare" leagues and "social reconstruction" associations.

---

[23] Sutton E. Griggs, *The Hindered Hand: or, The Reign of the Repressionist* (Nashville: Orion, 1905), 260.

[24] Fullinwider, *Mind and Mood of Black America*, 47; Cleveland *Gazette*, Aug. 25, 1906; August Meier, *Negro Thought in America, 1880–1915: Racial Ideologies in the Age of Booker T. Washington* (Ann Arbor: Univ. of Michigan Press, 1963), 180.

[25] Fullinwider, *Mind and Mood of Black America*, 74; Sutton E. Griggs, *The Story of My Struggles* (Memphis, 1914), 1–11, cited in David M. Tucker, *Lieutenant Lee of Beale Street* (Nashville: Vanderbilt Univ. Press, 1971), 60.

He worked diligently, particularly among the black clergy, in an effort to popularize his racial views of self-uplift.[26] He urged the black communities to recognize their own deficiencies, to seek white advice, and to abandon attempts to participate in the system that controlled their freedom and their lives. Black poverty and white prejudice were traceable directly to the failure and degeneration of the Negro, Griggs contended. His writings during the 1920s encouraged cooperation with whites rather than protest; black troubles sprang from "adverse mental attitudes," a weakness that "all the more advanced races" had overcome by acquiring a "new psychology." "Moral weaklings" were the responsibility of the race itself, and Griggs refused to ask any more than paternalistic encouragement from whites.[27]

The critical decade, 1900 to 1910, had convinced Griggs that white society had the answer in its segregation policies and that discrimination within this system was the natural lot of the black communities; under existing standards they deserved no better. Full citizenship could be expected only after years of evolutionary growth.[28]

The expansion of Jim Crow had a sharply different impact on a group of young black Nashvillians. The ill-fated streetcar boycott and founding of the black-owned Union Transportation Company stirred these men to action. In December 1905 they established the Globe Publishing Company and in January 1906 began pub-

[26]Memphis *Commercial Appeal*, Dec. 18, 1927, Jan. 29, 1928.

[27]*Ibid.*, April 17, 1927; Sutton E. Griggs, *Guide to Racial Greatness: The Science of Collective Efficiency* (Memphis: National Welfare League, 1923), 11. Other books by Griggs which carried out the theme of ultra-accommodation included *Kingdom Builder's Manual* (1924) and *The Winning Policy* (1927).

[28]This attitude incurred the anger and epithets of less accommodating black Memphians. In a letter to Walter F. White of the NAACP, on March 22, 1921, Bert M. Roddy, local banker and NAACP official, referred to Griggs as a writer of "bunk" for "local white dailies." George Washington Lee, prominent insurance official and politician, labeled Griggs an "apostle of peace at any price." In 1931 Griggs took self-exile in his native Texas. NAACP Papers, container G-122; Baltimore *Afro-American*, June 8, 1929, cited in Tucker, *Lieutenant Lee*, 66; Memphis *Press-Scimitar*, Jan. 5, 1933; interviews with Memphians Blair T. Hunt, June 14, 1972, Samuel Augustus Owens, June 27, 1972, Fred L. Hutchins, June 15, 1972, and George W. Lee, June 29, 1972.

lishing the Nashville *Globe*.[29] As Nashville's only secular black newspaper, the *Globe* emphasized a combined program of Booker T. Washington's economic self-help and an uncompromising sense of black pride. Encouraged financially by Richard H. Boyd, the newspaper's growth was directed by Joseph Oliver Battle, Henry Allen Boyd, and Dock A. Hart. The paper's crusades progressed steadily from the support of the boycott which had given it a *raison d'être* to a broad range of racially independent stands.

The *Globe* recognized the inferior socioeconomic status of black Americans but rejected the ideas of racial inferiority and dependence upon white paternalism. While accepting the reality of isolation within the white social and economic system, the young Nashvillians were nevertheless optimists, not pessimists. Their tone was aggressive, and they stressed the potential strength of the black population rather than the moral and economic weaknesses which obsessed Sutton E. Griggs. The *Globe* enthusiastically supported the efforts of Georgia Edwards and the ICC to end discrimination, but it seldom openly opposed segregation laws *per se*.[30] The newspaper placed its emphasis on economic growth and black business development. If blacks pooled their economic resources and fostered trust among themselves, they would gain white respect and thus end discrimination. On a more immediate level, the editors urged blacks to use their remaining political voting power and economic importance as consumers and laborers to demand respect and protection from the white hierarchy.

Circulation of the *Globe* was large, considering the poverty of its audience. By 1929, 20.5 percent of the black families in Nashville subscribed, and the paper reached nearly every black community in the state.[31] The outspoken policies of this news-

[29] Nashville *Globe*, Sept. 4, 1908.
[30] *Ibid.*, July 12, 1907.
[31] Paul K. Edwards, *The Southern Urban Negro as a Consumer* (New York: Prentice-Hall, 1932), 172–73.

paper were of obvious concern to the whites of Nashville and the state, as well as to black leaders throughout the country; between 1906 and 1930 it was regularly quoted and attacked in black and white newspapers alike. The Atlanta *Independent*, for example, often took issue with the *Globe* and its brand of selective militancy, but the editors stood firm.[32] The *Globe* was the voice of black men who were resigned to being unwanted in the white system—and who, accepting the dictates of caste, became advocates of a parallel black "system," with its own board of trade, its self-sufficient business community, its "equal" schools, its segregated parks, and pride in its own race. By racial pride, the young Nashvillians of the *Globe* meant studying Negro history, exclusively patronizing black business (especially banks), supporting the manufacture of Negro dolls, openly opposing mistreatment by whites, and demanding racial purity.[33]

The *Globe* constantly attacked white law enforcement for being obsessed with the thought of black men assaulting white women, and at the same time refusing to deal with the much more frequent assaults of white men on black women. But black prostitutes were excoriated as much as white "brutes," and the *Globe* continually urged black men to stand up for the protection of their wives and families. Editorials castigated black men who did not fight for their jobs as shirking their "responsibilities to the wife they [had] taken" and deplored continual mistreatment of black women on Nashville's streetcars. "Negro men," one editorial began, "in the name of high heaven, be men; be courageous men. Our women will never be respected until we conclude to lay down our lives in their defense whether they are right or whether they are wrong."[34]

No black hero was immune from censure in this journal if he

[32] Nashville *Globe*, March 14, 1913.

[33] *Ibid.*, Jan. 11, Feb. 1, May 31, June 21, 1907, June 12, Sept. 25, 1908, March 12, Dec. 3, 1909, Feb. 18, 1910, Feb. 16, March 1, 15, May 31, Nov. 8, Dec. 6, 1912.

[34] *Ibid.*, Jan. 25, April 26, June 7, 21, 1907, Jan. 3, Nov. 20, 1908, Dec. 3, 1909, May 26, 1911, Oct. 10, 1913.

violated the proud honor of black purity. The boxer Jack Johnson received the adulation of the *Globe* on July 8, 1910, for his victory over Jim Jeffries but was admonished for being a "fool-ass" in the February 12, 1912, issue. The change of opinion was the result of Johnson's attraction to white women. The *Globe* hotly commented that Johnson now represented a "Black Man's Burden," and should "be greatly pitied. . . . The leading Negroes of this country should set about to reach this man and show him the folly of his ways."[35]

While not specifically advocating black officeholding, the *Globe* paid keen attention to political affairs. "Lily-whitism" in Tennessee Republican circles led the editors to advocate independent voting, a policy unique among black newspapers in the South. Supported in this stand by a growing number of black leaders in Middle and West Tennessee, the paper usually endorsed the Democratic party on state and local levels. The reasoning was that such candidates as Governor Malcolm R. Patterson (1906–1910) and Mayor Hilary E. Howse of Nashville took more interest in upgrading the black communities than the Republicans, who seldom were in power anyway.[36] It seemed that constant support of the party of Lincoln served only to antagonize those who made the decisions affecting the black people of the state. The new idea was to use the political power of the black electorate (mostly in the cities) to forestall further restrictions and also to bargain for tangible gains locally instead of relying on vague promises from an impersonal administration in Washington. The *Globe* continued to support the Republican ticket in national elections, but it had determined that national and local politics were two different "ball games," played under different rules for different stakes.[37]

[35]*Ibid.*, July 8, 1910, Feb. 16, Dec. 6, 1912.

[36]*Ibid.*, Dec. 6, 1907, Aug. 7, Oct. 9, Nov. 6, 1908, Aug. 27, Sept. 17, 1909, July 29, 1910, Oct. 6, 1911, Aug. 29, 1913, Sept. 14, 1917.

[37]In the presidential election of 1912, however, the *Globe* joined a rather sizable segment of the black voters of Tennessee who ignored the scandal involving the dismissal

Neither the *Globe*'s systematic program of self-interest nor Sutton Griggs's patient search for a "new psychology" typified the response of blacks to the expansion of the caste system in Tennessee. Most black Tennesseans remained silent, either taking the line of least resistance or implicitly adopting the American faith in hard work and individual effort. W. H. Harrison's earlier admonition that "God is not dead" continued to carry great weight, as it had since the days of slavery. The Memphis *Times*, for example, voiced a similar view during the Ku Klux Klan campaigns of the 1920s: ". . . do good for evil. Give justice for injustice, love for hatred, remembering that these are the real tests of manly men." [38]

Events of the years 1915–1919, however, did add measurably to black dissatisfaction. Loss of traditional leadership, racial violence, and increased mobility strained the credulity of "separate but equal" assumptions and challenged the maintenance of strict caste criteria. Booker T. Washington died in 1915, the same year in which the National Baptist Convention, a body to which over 30 percent of black Tennesseans belonged and traditionally looked for guidance, suffered a bitter internal split. The church conflict erupted in a battle for control of the Nashville-based National Baptist Publishing Board, and the resulting litigation led to R. H. Boyd's legal control of the physical plant and to an especially wide division of loyalties among the Baptist leadership in Tennessee. [39] The combined impact of the loss of Washington's

---

of black soldiers at Brownsville, Texas, and supported Theodore Roosevelt in his Progressive party bid for the presidency. *Ibid.*, July 19, 26, Aug. 2, 9, Nov. 22, 1912.

[38] Memphis *Times*, n.d., quoted in *Christian Advocate* (Nashville), Jan. 18, 1924.

[39] Dr. Richard H. Boyd had exercised total authority over the National Baptist Publishing Board since its founding in 1896. In 1905 the National Baptist Convention initiated a campaign to limit his control, and in 1915 he took the internal conflict into the courts of Tennessee. The church split into two factions, the National Baptist Convention, Unincorporated (Boyd), and the National Baptist Convention, Incorporated. Numerous lawsuits followed in the wake of the split, and efforts to reconcile the two factions accomplished little. Owen D. Pelt and Ralph Lee Smith, *The Story of the National Baptists* (New York: Vantage, 1960), 101–13; Thomas Oscar Fuller, *History of the Negro Baptists of Tennessee* (Memphis: privately printed, 1936), 191–97; *Crisis* 9 (Dec. 1914), 63; 13 (Nov. 1916), 33; (Dec. 1916), 92.

symbolic guidance and the confusing competition of two church conventions (each with its publishing house in Nashville) left black Tennesseans with a heightened sense of uncertainty as they faced the tense and violent years of World War I.

The firm dedication to accommodation that had characterized Tennessee's various black communities in 1900 deteriorated noticeably during the next fifteen years. Racial attitudes and self-concepts did not change abruptly, but they were not static. Individuals became more aggressive and racial pride and self-help became accepted means of protest and struggle. The Reverend J. G. Robinson of Chattanooga felt free, for instance, to deliver a scathing denunciation of Southern "justice" in an open letter to President Wilson, and branches of the NAACP were formed rapidly across the state. Still, black Tennesseans were slow to shake off the traditional adherence to white paternalism.[40] The vacuum left by Washington's death and the popular indignation aroused by the blatant lynching and mob violence of the war years gave ample opportunity for a charismatic leader to mobilize blacks toward greater assertion and pride. No such figure appeared, the NAACP chapters lapsed into inactivity, and the white-oriented Commission on Interracial Cooperation (CIC) became the accepted vehicle of change. Black Tennesseans showed greater resentment of caste and made more requests of white leaders in the 1920s than they had earlier, but they rarely demanded equal rights or full citizenship.

[40] J. G. Robinson, open letter to President Woodrow Wilson, printed in Chattanooga *Daily Times*, July 28, 1919. The traditional barriers to change are the same ones noted by Robert Coles in the mid-1960s, when he explained that "It is their [blacks] inertia and resignation which are so formidable." Robert Coles, *Farewell to the South* (Boston: Little, Brown, 1972), 190.

CHAPTER II.

Jim Crow Streetcars and Black Protest

"We only want our rights as law-abiding citizens," protested Mrs. A. Watkins in 1900. "We do not want social equality."[1] She thus joined Richard Henry Boyd and many other blacks in making public an increasing concern for Negro freedom in Tennessee. In the case of Mrs. Watkins, talk of extending segregation to the streetcar systems in the state had raised to the surface a persistent sense of personal and racial pride. More than any other new limitation of caste, Jim Crow streetcars aroused black opposition; they represented a public, almost unavoidable, personal affront to dignity. Most importantly, black Tennesseans not only protested as individuals, but they also mounted significant organized resistance, even to the point of boycotting the streetcars.

As early as 1899 the Tennessee General Assembly came under pressure to broaden the scope of existing segregation in public transportation. A proposal in that year "to make the separate coach law apply to street cars" died in the House Judiciary Committee, but agitation among white groups continued. In letter-writing campaigns in Nashville and Memphis whites complained of "the odor of sweaty negroes" and the disrespectful conduct of black women on the cities' street railways. The 1899 proposal was presented again in 1901, this time being rejected only by a 48-to-30 vote of the lower house.[2]

[1] Nashville *American*, March 5, 1900.
[2] *House Journal of the Fifty-first General Assembly of the State of Tennessee* (1899), 225; Nashville *American*, March 5, 7, 8, 1900; *House Journal* (1901), 403.

Public pressure continued to build, and as the legislature convened for its biennial session in 1903, sentiment overwhelmingly
favored the adoption of a segregation statute. Debate raged for
weeks, however, over the etiquette and scope of such a law.
Would separate seats suffice, or should blacks be confined to
completely separate cars? Should all street railway systems in the
state be restricted, or should initial action be limited to Memphis,
where whites complained most vigorously? Successful lobbying
by the traction companies blocked the proposals for separate cars,
and strong newspaper objection in Nashville and Chattanooga
helped limit the Jim Crow streetcar law of 1903 to "counties
having 150,000 inhabitants." Only Shelby County (Memphis)
met this population requirement. Tennesseans, however, clearly
reflected many of the same racist pressures manifest in the more
extensive segregation laws of other Southern states; the Senate
vote in 1903 was 30 to 0 and in the House it was 77 to 8.[3]

The campaign had not ended. Despite public sentiment and
popular legislation, the Memphis Street Railway Company refused to implement the new law. Resenting the extra costs
involved, the company challenged the constitutionality of the
statute. Ironically, the appeal included the complaint that the
measure was "class legislation," since it applied "only to Shelby
county, and in its results only to the defendant road." Such
legislation, the company maintained, violated the Fourteenth
Amendment to the Constitution of the United States in that it did
not provide equal protection of the laws. The Tennessee Supreme
Court upheld the company's appeal in June 1903, but it did so on
technical grounds having to do with the wording of the streetcar
act. The way was still open for further action.[4]

Although the Nashville *American* continued to maintain that

[3] Nashville *American*, Jan. 20, 24, 1903; Memphis *Commercial Appeal*, Jan. 27, 30,
Feb. 3, 4, 6, 8, March 9, 1903; *Acts of Tennessee* (1903), ch. 43; *Senate Journal of the
Fifty-third General Assembly of the State of Tennessee* (1905), 63; *House Journal* (1905),
246.

[4] Nashville *American*, March 27, May 29, 1903; Memphis *Commercial Appeal*, April
26, 1903; *Memphis Street Railway Company* v. *State*, 110 Tenn. 602.

21

there was no "demand" for Jim Crow streetcars in its city, public pressure indicated otherwise. In an effort to quiet growing agitation, Nashville's streetcar company put "an extra car on the West Nashville line" to transport the blacks who worked in the evil-smelling fertilizer plant in that section of the city. The question of racial separation had gone beyond specific grievances, however, and had become firmly entrenched in the codes of the caste society. In the fall of 1904, the Nashville city council began consideration of a local streetcar ordinance, and in January the General Assembly opened debate on a new Jim Crow measure covering all cities in the state.[5] Passage of a state bill was certain; as the reluctant Chattanooga *Daily Times* explained, "most of the people of the State are in favor of some kind of separation of the races on street cars." Although some "hotheads" insisted upon separate cars, the law passed on March 30, 1905 left the method of separation up to the streetcar corporations, insisting only that the new program be in effect by July 5.[6]

During the six years of public debate, many blacks, particularly in Nashville and Memphis, had spoken out openly in their opposition to the proposed new restrictions. When a white woman wrote the Nashville *American* in 1900 stating her opinion that the Negro was hurt by suggested legislation "not because he wants to ride with us, but because, just as we would feel, he resents being set apart . . . ," two black women of the city immediately penned public letters of gratitude. One admitted that her "sensibilities" and "feelings" had been crushed so often that she actually hated to get on the cars any more, while the other pointedly observed that "you as white citizens demand respect from the negro. How can you expect it when you cast him aside and look upon him as an insignificant being?"[7]

Other black reactions varied. In 1903 a group of black business

[5] Nashville *American*, Jan. 24, June 15, 1903, March 2, 8, Nov. 4, 8, 1904; *Senate Journal* (1905), 59.

[6] Chattanooga *Daily Times*, quoted in Nashville *American*, Jan. 16, 1905.

[7] Nashville *American*, March 2, 5, 1900.

and professional men worked "in a determined but conservative manner" to arouse opposition to Jim Crow legislation for Memphis. This "conservative" campaign generated only a futile petition to the General Assembly, but black Nashvillians, meanwhile, exercised less restraint. Irritated by the deprecating claims made by whites in support of the streetcar law, George T. Robinson struck back in a letter to the *American:* "The Southern press . . . is very persistent in keeping before the public the fact of our inferiority. Why, then, are we not let alone? Why fear us? . . . There is a studied effort," he continued, "to curb our ambition and aspirations . . . simply because some white men will it. Our citizenship rights are left out of the calculation. . . ." Concluding with startling defiance, Robinson maintained: "We have our request to make of white people of the South and that is to 'get out of our sunshine.' "[8]

Public protest mounted in Nashville as the city council deliberated on special streetcar ordinances. On some occasions this protest was heavily tinged with racial pride; on others, it carried the thinly veiled threat of organized opposition. Pride burst forth "in a storm of applause . . . that lasted several moments" when the Meharry Medical School commencement speaker proclaimed on March 1, 1904: "I have come to the conclusion . . . that the race with which I am identified is like any other race and inferior to none other. It makes me proud and glad that I am a Negro and doubly proud that I have never yearned or tried to pass for a white man." Meanwhile, in a letter that foreshadowed events to come, the Reverend James A. Jones, outspoken pastor of St. Paul A. M. E. Church and later president of Turner Normal College, warned: "the day that the separate street car law goes into effect . . . that day the company will lose nine-tenths of its negro patronage and there will be practically only one class of colored passengers to contend with. . . . The self-respecting, intelligent colored citizens of Nashville will not stand for Jim-crowism on the

[8] Memphis *Commercial Appeal,* Jan. 24, 1903; Nashville *American,* Feb. 2, 1903.

street car line in this city. The shoe stores and livery stables will very likely profit by this move on the part of the City Council."[9]

Talk of a black boycott in Nashville grew louder and more explicit as it became evident that sweeping Jim Crow legislation was forthcoming from the 1905 General Assembly. The Nashville *Clarion*, published under the auspices of R. H. Boyd's National Baptist Publishing Board, advised "those of the race who are able to buy buggies and others to trim their corns, darn their socks, wear solid shoes and walk." While the bill was pending final approval, a mass meeting, estimated by one source to have been attended by some two thousand black Nashvillians, passed resolutions calling on blacks to walk except "in cases of urgent necessity." Several "red hot speeches" discussed the feasibility of "transporting our people about the city other than by street cars."[10]

The boycott idea also stirred support in Memphis. Some blacks even threatened "to pelt and stone every Afro-American found traveling on the cars."[11] As the date of implementation drew close, the more conservative black leaders of Memphis became somewhat alarmed at the loud talk and continued threats of some of the "lower-class" members of their race. Thomas Oscar Fuller, Baptist minister, principal of Howe Institute, and later a close associate of Sutton E. Griggs, wrote a concerned letter to the *Commercial Appeal* on July 3, voicing his hope "that those who have to ride the cars [would] display courtesy and a lack of arrogance." Fuller acknowledged that "a large number . . . will either walk or seek other means of conveyance," but he urged that, above all, "harmony and co-operation between the races" be maintained.[12]

Black Nashvillians offered the most consistent opposition to

[9] Nashville *American*, March 2, 5, 1904.

[10] Nashville *Clarion*, n.d., quoted in the Kansas City *American Citizen*, March 3, 1905; Cleveland *Gazette*, April 1, 1905.

[11] Cleveland *Gazette*, Feb. 25, 1905.

[12] Memphis *News Scimitar*, July 3, 1905; Memphis *Commercial Appeal*, July 3, 1905.

new restrictions, and in the late summer of 1905 they readily translated protest talk into protest action. Unity was particularly important in any attempt to oppose the dictates of the white system, and so was leadership. A large number and a diversity of leaders meant a large number and a diversity of supporters. For a variety of reasons, some perhaps selfish, prominent figures in Nashville's black community supported the idea of a peaceful boycott: a sizable number of ministers and educators gave both monetary and verbal support to the idea; business leaders, recently inspired by the ideas of a self-supporting black economic community as endorsed by Booker T. Washington's National Negro Business League, furnished most of the financing for a black transportation system to replace the Jim Crow streetcars; and the emerging group of young blacks formed the *Globe* in order to publicize the boycott efforts.

The boycott began on July 5, and some whites accused black leaders of being "agitators . . . who, for purposes of their own, are willing to play upon the fears and excite the prejudices of their more ignorant people." The rhetoric heated up, and a prominent black minister retaliated, charging that the real agitators were the legislators who "substitute race prejudice for brain."[13]

The original intent of the Nashville boycott was to force the white traction companies to demand repeal of the objectionable law in the next legislature. At a meeting of the local branch of the Negro Business League on July 30, such leaders of the boycott as Preston Taylor, Sutton Griggs, and Edward W. D. Isaac expressed their determination to launch a statewide movement among blacks to bring repeal. They noted that Memphis had already raised $5,000 for this purpose, and they took steps to help sustain the local effort. All black Nashvillians who had "express wagons" were urged to make them available for "carrying colored folks to the different parts of the city."[14] The initial actions met

[13] Nashville *American*, July 30, Aug. 1, 1905.
[14] Nashville *Banner*, Aug. 1, 1905.

success; many blacks who commuted long distances quit their jobs immediately after the law went into effect, and both of the city's daily newspapers noted a "falling off in the number of Negroes riding" the streetcars.[15]

Hopes of forcing repeal of the Jim Crow law dimmed quickly. Recent practices in nearly all Southern states indicated that the prevailing feeling among white Southerners favored continued discrimination within the framework of segregation. Few whites showed a willingness to assess objectively the economic impact of their actions. White intransigence and difficulty in uniting Tennessee's scattered black urban population caused several leaders of the Nashville boycott to seek an alternative to the dwindling expectations of repeal. Black entrepreneurship was a warm topic among these men. R. H. Boyd was president of the recently founded One-Cent Savings Bank and Trust Company and a former vice-president of the National Negro Business League. J. C. Napier, cashier of the One-Cent Bank and a good friend of Booker T. Washington, had at one time been offered the presidency of the National Negro Business League. Preston Taylor, a highly popular minister and former railroad contractor, was also the owner of an amusement park and Nashville's leading black undertaker.[16]

Facing almost certain defeat in their efforts to gain repeal, the business-oriented leaders of the boycott, not surprisingly,

---

[15]*Ibid.*, July 6, 7, 1905; Nashville *American*, July 6, 1905.

[16]Taylor, a former slave and drummer in the Union Army, came to Nashville from Kentucky in 1885 as an ordained minister in the Christian Church. He opened an undertaking establishment in 1888 and his business skills, dedication, and personal appeal soon made him a wealthy landowner, cemetery operator, and investment entrepreneur. On at least one previous occasion Taylor had chosen to meet racial exclusion head on. When local contractors refused to hire blacks while building a railroad between Mt. Sterling, Ky., and Richmond, Va., he responded by landing the contract for a $75,000 section of the route. Taylor and his black laborers received personal commendations from Collis P. Huntington for their work. See Nashville *Globe*, April 17, 1931; William Newton Hartshorn, ed., *An Era of Progress and Promise, 1863–1910* (Boston: Priscilla, 1910), 445; James T. Haley, comp. *Afro-American Encyclopaedia* (Nashville: Haley and Florida, 1895), 215–23.

brought forth the idea of a black-owned transportation company that would serve the Negro community as the streetcar company served the white community. Obtaining a charter for the Union Transportation Company on August 29, 1905, sixteen of Nashville's most prominent black leaders authorized the issuing of $25,000 in capital stock. The wording of the charter permitted the operation of street railway facilities in other Tennessee cities, but Nashville was clearly the target for immediate action.[17] Word of the new enterprise and the appearance of a temporary system of carriages for carrying black passengers about the city gave new impetus to the two-month-old boycott. On Labor Day, Sutton Griggs addressed several audiences and urged each of them to maintain its opposition to the Jim Crow law. The white street railway system suffered financially in the face of this black determination, and rumors started that job cutbacks on the traction lines were imminent.[18]

Black enthusiasm increased as the Union Transportation Company announced its plans. Enough stock was sold among the incorporators to send R. H. Boyd, acting as purchasing agent, to Tarrytown, New York, where he ordered five large (fifteen-passenger) steam-propelled automobiles and took an option on twenty more of the large machines. While awaiting the arrival of these "auto-buses," Preston Taylor, president of the new corporation, held stock-selling rallies in both East and West Nashville. He announced on September 21 that ten men would be hired to carry out the operations of the concern and that $7,000 of the stock had already been paid up. Blacks began wearing lapel buttons with pictures of the five automobiles on them. A two-story brick garage, containing a restaurant and connected to the Colored Odd Fellows Hall, was begun, and the Nashville *Clarion* admonished black domestics "to stay off the cars by all means . . .

---

[17] Nashville *American*, Aug. 29, 1905; Nashville *Banner*, Aug. 28, 1905; Indianapolis *Freeman*, Sept. 16, 1905.

[18] Nashville *American*, Sept. 5, 1905; Indianapolis *Freeman*, Sept. 16, 1905.

the motor cars will arrive in a few days . . . we can afford to walk a little longer."[19]

By mid-September, the boycott and general Jim Crow protest had reached their peak in Nashville. Not only was the Nashville Transit Company losing a reported five hundred dollars per week, but the rebellion against Jim Crow had also extended to the operations and practices of the Nashville postal authorities. On September 9, the *Clarion* printed a letter to Postmaster General George B. Cortelyou deploring the increased segregation of black postal employees at the local office. The protest was signed "by the Baptist Ministers' Conference in a body," and it emphasized "the debasing character of 'Jim Crowism' " rather than the principle of racial separation.[20] Voluntary separatism was no problem to black leaders, but the forced nature of legislation and the degrading rationale for the laws aroused keen racial sensibilities.

October appeared to be the dawning of a new era in Nashville. The first five cars of the Union Transportation Company arrived on September 29, and Postmaster General Cortelyou announced his intentions to investigate conditions in the city's post office. Hope seemed well founded as the new cars began to operate on four heavily traveled routes in the city, and local postal authorities took down their Jim Crow signs and denied any intention to "Jim Crow the government service."[21]

Other black communities responded favorably to Nashville's boycott and expressed their own protests in a variety of ways. From Jackson, the *Christian Index* reported that few blacks were riding the streetcars because "they prefer to walk and avoid being ordered around like boys." The *Index* noted actions in other cities and gave special praise to black Nashvillians: "They propose to

[19] Nashville *Banner*, Sept. 22, 26, 29, 1905; Chattanooga *Daily Times*, Sept. 18, 1905; Indianapolis *Freeman*, Oct. 7, 1905; Nashville *Clarion*, n.d., quoted in Cleveland *Gazette*, Oct. 14, 1905.

[20] Chattanooga *Daily Times*, Sept. 18, 1905; Nashville *Clarion*, Sept. 9, 1905, quoted in Cleveland *Gazette*, Sept. 23, 1905.

[21] Nashville *Banner*, Sept. 22, 29, 1905; Indianapolis *Freeman*, Oct. 14, 1905.

maintain their self-respect by avoiding the Jim Crow cars. The Negro is not as well contented with the humiliation that his manhood has been subjected to as some people suppose."[22] Despite such promise and indignation, protest activities did not progress so well outside Nashville.

On July 5, 1905, black Chattanoogans began a boycott which slowly increased in intensity, but they were hampered from the beginning by a lack of open support from the city's black political, educational, and clerical leaders. Belatedly admitting the presence of black opposition to the Jim Crow streetcar practices, the Chattanooga *Daily Times* indicated that "generally speaking . . . negroes [have] accepted the matter good naturedly, the more sensible ones . . . discrediting the boycott for the reason that the railway companies are not responsible for the law and are therefore not to be punished for its conservative enforcement."[23] The leading source of protest came from the diminutive but persistent and sharp-tongued Chattanooga *Blade*. Edited, published, printed, and circulated by top-hatted Randolph M. Miller, this black newspaper irritated the paternalistic *Daily Times*. An editorial in the white daily singled out the *Blade* for "advising against acquiescence in the law and in encouraging the spirit of resentment and race prejudice."[24]

Miller was one of the originators of a system of hack lines that traveled between the city and the outlying black communities of Churchville, St. Elmo, Fort Cheatham, and Tannery Flats. Beginning on July 16 with "three vehicles of sorry appearance," the hack operators found "race separation on street cars so obnoxious"

---

[22] *Christian Index*, July 29, Sept. 23, 1905.

[23] Nashville *American*, Aug, 30, 1905; Chattanooga *Daily Times*, July 6, 17, 1905.

[24] Chattanooga *Daily Times*, July 25, 1905. Miller was a former slave who came to Chattanooga in 1864 with Gen. William T. Sherman's army. He worked as a pressman for Adolph Ochs and the *Daily Times* until 1898, when he started the *Blade*. His one-man operation survived, it was felt by many, largely due to continued backing from Ochs. His picturesque style often irritated whites, but the *Blade*'s longevity far surpassed any previous black newspaper in Chattanooga. See Charles D. McGuffey, ed., *Standard History of Chattanooga, Tennessee* (Knoxville: Crew and Derey, 1911), 257–58; *Hamilton County Herald*, Feb. 2, 1945.

to the black workers that patronage kept the vehicles running almost to capacity. On August 29 nine small but enterprising black businessmen (including Miller) applied for a charter under the name of the Transfer Omnibus Motor Car Company. With an initial capitalization of $10,000, these men hoped to replace the hack lines with several forty-passenger motor cars.[25]

Inspired at first by resentment against "an insult to the negro race," the Chattanooga boycott, as in Nashville, evolved into an attempt to support an independent transportation system. Chattanooga blacks supported an early chapter of the National Negro Business League that was second in size and activism only to the branch in Nashville, and Booker T. Washington's precepts of economic self-sufficiency seemed relevant to the situation in 1905. Chattanooga, however, lacked one advantage that Nashville enjoyed: a sizable class of moderately wealthy black businessmen. Incorporators of the Transfer Omnibus Motor Car Company, therefore, had to rely on small investments from a large number of black stockholders.[26] When many of Chattanooga's black leaders refused to give their public support to the venture (in noticeable contrast with Nashville), they greatly hindered the achievement of essential popular economic support.

One source of income for the new corporation was the steady flow of five-cent fares collected by the four existing hack lines. Chattanooga white officials moved to close off these meager sums; however, W. J. Eddings, county humane officer, declared on September 6 that he intended to prosecute the hack operators for "working old worn-out animals from early morning until late at night and . . . only half feeding them."[27] Such harassment, coupled with the limited economic base available to the enterprising boycott leaders, prevented the Transfer Omnibus Motor Car

[25] Chattanooga *Daily Times*, July 26, Aug. 30, 1905.

[26] J. Bliss White, comp., *Biography and Achievements of the Colored Citizens of Chattanooga* (privately printed, 1904), 2; Hartshorn, ed., *Era of Progress and Promise*, 475; Chattanooga *Daily Times*, Aug. 30, 1905.

[27] Nashville *American*, Sept. 7, 1905.

Company from realizing its high aspirations. It did not silence, however, the critics of Jim Crow laws and other discriminations made against the black citizens of Chattanooga. Randolph Miller continued to complain, lamenting the fact, in an October 1905 issue of the *Blade*, that "They have taken our part of the library; they have moved our school to the frog pond; they have passed the Jim Crow law; they have knocked us out of the jury box; they have played the devil generally, and what in thunder more will they do no one knows."[28]

Memphis Negroes, many of whom had indicated an early disposition to enforce a black boycott, never achieved enough unity to carry this out, much less support a black transportation system. After the law went into effect on July 5, several sources observed that few blacks were riding on the streetcars, but the reasons for the obvious absence of black passengers were not clear. The Cleveland *Gazette*, which regularly carried news of Memphis blacks, described a condition of general confusion rather than an organized boycott: "Only a few days ago the street cars were over crowded . . . . But at present the capacity for travel is easy, and many of our people through fear of maltreatment are walking while not a few prefer to walk rather than comply with the 'Jim Crow' requirement."[29]

The problems facing would-be boycott leaders in Memphis centered in the conservative accommodationism of the city's black ministers. The emphasis upon "Harmony and co-operation between the races," expressed earlier by the Reverend Thomas O. Fuller, led to a meeting on August 6 "for the purpose of fighting [against] any attempt to repeal the Jim Crow law." The Memphis black community was relatively young and exhibited many rural characteristics; among these was the habit of looking

---

[28] Chattanooga *Blade*, n.d., quoted in Chattanooga *Daily Times*, Oct. 12, 1905. Hack line service on a few heavily traveled routes appeared again in the 1920s and continued until mid-century. This venture, however, served more as a cheaper means of transportation than as a protest against segregation. Interview with De Witt Clinton Alfred, June 7, 1972.

[29] Cleveland *Gazette*, July 29, 1905; Nashville *American*, July 31, 1905.

to black clergymen for social, economic, and political guidance. This tendency changed as the twentieth century progressed, but in 1905 black opponents of a boycott claimed the support of the majority of the laboring class.[30]

Despite the sizable opposition, several prominent blacks pressed their efforts to gain repeal of the "insulting measure." In spite of reports in the Cleveland *Gazette* that "a few wealthy men of Memphis are holding meetings preparatory to running automobiles as a general transfer of travelers," the major challenge offered to the Jim Crow streetcar law in Memphis took the form of a case testing its constitutionality. Mary Morrison, a member of "the society element of the city," provided the test when she refused to accept a seat in the segregated section of a streetcar. At a meeting in Church's Park on July 30, $5,000 was raised and two well-known black lawyers, Benjamin F. Booth and Josiah T. Settle, agreed to argue her case before the state supreme court.[31] Booth and Settle appealed Mrs. Morrison's conviction by the criminal court on the grounds that the Jim Crow car law violated her right to equal protection of the laws under the Fourteenth Amendment to the Constitution of the United States. In August 1906, Justice John K. Shields (later a senator from Tennessee) upheld Mrs. Morrison's conviction on the grounds that the law "applied equally to both races" and that it was "merely an extension to street railways of one [law] that has long been in force in this state, regulating the transporting of passengers upon commercial railroads, which, upon full consideration, was sustained

---

[30] Nashville *American*, Aug. 3, 1905; Memphis *Commercial Appeal*, July 3, 1905; William Durell Miller, "Rural Ideals in Memphis Life at the Turn of the Century," West Tennessee Historical Society *Papers* 4 (1950), 41–49. In 1910 there were forty-three Negro Baptist churches in Memphis, not to mention the numerous Churches of God in Christ, Colored Methodist Episcopal (C. M. E.), African Methodist Episcopal (A. M. E.), Congregationalist, Catholic, and even Seventh Day Adventist congregations. See Thomas Oscar Fuller, *Twenty Years in Public Life, 1890–1910* (Nashville: National Baptist Publishing Board, 1910), 278; and Fuller, *The Story of the Church Life Among Negroes in Memphis, Tennessee* (Memphis: privately printed, 1938), 49–50.
[31] Nashville *American*, July 31, Sept. 13, 1905; Cleveland *Gazette*, Sept. 23, 1905; *Morrison v. State*, 116 Tenn. 534, 95 S.W. 494.

by this court."[32] No formal boycott ever took place in Memphis; the only explicit challenge to Jim Crow was made in the courts, and it failed.

Knoxville had the smallest black population and, evidently, the most stable racial climate among Tennessee cities. A boycott was launched in this city on the day the despised law went into effect, but it apparently amounted to no more than a symbolic gesture of opposition. By July 8, a few ardent boycotters were resorting to physical violence in a futile attempt to keep blacks who worked in the Lonsdale railroad yards from patronizing the white traction company. Law enforcement officials arrested the "ringleaders" of the resistance and no more was heard of public opposition to the Jim Crow law.[33] Black leaders in Knoxville gave little support to those who would challenge the paternalistic white officials of the city.

While the resistance of Negroes in other Tennessee cities seemed to be broken by October 1905, the Union Transportation Company drew black Nashvillians to the threshold of significant economic and racial achievement. As soon as the five new automobiles began operating in early October, however, problems started appearing. The steam-propelled machines purchased by Dr. Boyd lacked sufficient power to travel the hills of Nashville and still meet a satisfactory schedule. This blunder was overcome when the unsuitable cars were traded later for "fourteen twenty-passenger electric autos." Unfortunately, the momentum needed to sustain the large financial undertaking had been halted. The company boasted of its monetary support from "the cooks, the hod-carriers, the man with the pick and shovel and the wash women," but payment on subscribed stock slowed down; only $9,000 had been paid in by December.[34] Black confidence in black businesses (especially financial ventures) was a fragile

---

[32] *Morrison* v. *State*, 95 S.W. 496–97.

[33] Knoxville *Journal and Tribune*, July 6, 9, 1905.

[34] "Nashville's Revolt Against Jimcrowism," *Voice of the Negro* 2 (Dec. 1905), 828–30; *Christian Index*, Jan. 3, 1906.

commodity. It was much easier to rally the uneducated masses in support of a boycott of white streetcars than to convince them that they should invest small, hard-won savings in dimly understood black enterprises. The failure of the steam-powered cars had raised fatal doubts as to the safety of money invested in the Union Transportation Company.

Encouraged by the support of the newly founded Nashville *Globe*, the company put its fourteen electric cars into operation in January 1906. Despite continued state and even national publicity, however, local problems seemed to multiply. Batteries had to be recharged and this meant buying power from a white competitor, the Nashville Railway and Light Company. After repeatedly having its equipment damaged by overcharging, the Union Transportation Company had to invest in "a dynamo and complete generating apparatus . . . installed at the National Baptist Publishing House."[35] Less surreptitious white opposition also appeared. As early as late November, one city councilman advocated revocation of the corporation's charter. And, just as the black company announced a new issue of stock, with intentions to expand its routes, the city of Nashville indicated its plan to levy taxes on the electric cars. On April 27, 1906 the law department declared that an annual privilege tax of $42 per car would be charged. These increased costs and persistent battery trouble led the company to cease operations by mid-summer.[36]

After a "six or seven month" period of inactivity, the Union Transportation Company called a stockholders' meeting for March 21, 1907. Preston Taylor spoke hopefully of rejuvenating the concern, saying: "Spring is coming and this summer the

[35] "Nashville's Revolt Against Jimcrowism," 829; Nashville *American*, Jan. 6, 1906; Nashville *Banner*, March 16, 1906; interview with James T. Chandler, June 28, 1972. In founding the *Globe*, the editors felt black Nashvillians "were greatly handicapped" in their "struggle to successfully maintain the opposition to the 'Jim Crow' laws . . . in that they possessed no public-spirited secular news medium through which they could reach the masses of people." Nashville *Globe*, Sept. 4, 1908.

[36] "Nashville's Revolt Against Jimcrowism," 830; Nashville *Banner*, March 16, 1906; Nashville *American*, April 28, 1906; Nashville *Globe*, March 29, 1907.

people must have some place to go. Our cars are and ought to be used. We want to see what the people think about it." The meeting was poorly attended, however, and Taylor explained that he "and another friend" had been meeting the notes of the company for several months, since many of the stock subscribers had failed to pay their obligations. Lack of interest on the part of Nashville's once enthusiastic black population led to the sale of eight of the electric cars in early April to a St. Louis, Missouri, firm which planned to use them to carry passengers between Norfolk and the Jamestown Exposition. The sale left only $734.26 to be paid on the original $20,000 debt incurred at the time the fourteen cars were purchased.[37]

The collapse of the black-owned transportation company left the heaviest investors, especially Preston Taylor, with sizable financial losses.[38] The mass boycott had ended long before the demise of the Union Transportation Company, but resentment lingered on—especially in the hearts of the young founders of the Nashville *Globe*, which proudly proclaimed in 1907 that "there are hundreds of Negroes in Nashville who have never 'bowed their knees to Baal' [the Jim Crow law]." Although maintaining that the "boycott is [still] a powerful weapon," the *Globe* realized that, without an effective alternative, blacks in a city the size of Nashville "would be lost . . . without a method of transportation in keeping with the rapid march of progress." More affluent blacks throughout the state avoided using the Jim Crow streetcars and railways whenever possible. Mary E. Spence, a white faculty member at Fisk University, reminisced in later years that "in Nashville about every colored person that can afford it buys an automobile. Then he is free from either local travel . . . or long distance by train." And a student of the black community in Memphis noted that "with the enforced segregation of races on

[37] Nashville *Globe*, March 15, 29, April 12, May 3, 1907.
[38] *Ibid.*, Sept. 4, 1908; William Edward Burghardt Du Bois, ed., *Economic Co-Operation Among Negro Americans*, Atlanta University Publications No. 12 (1907), 164.

streetcars . . . many of the upper-class Negroes, unwilling to play a lower-caste role, migrated to the North." Most, like Robert R. Church, Jr., stayed but carried lasting and "bitter memories" of the affair.[39]

The streetcar boycotts, like other less extensive protests, failed, but the resentment inspired by the growing restrictiveness of Tennessee's caste society smoldered among the young and the better-educated blacks. Later events would bring this bitterness to the surface again.

[39] Nashville *Globe*, Feb. 1, March 15, Oct. 18, 1907, Oct. 14, 1910; Mary E. Spence to W. Dickerson Donnelly, secretary of the Fisk General Alumni Association, n.d., Mary E. Spence Papers, Fisk University; Robert W. O'Brien, "Beale Street, A Study in Ecological Succession," *Sociology and Social Research* 26 (May–June 1942), 443; Robert R. Church, Jr., to Clarence L. Kelly, Jan. 29 and Feb. 19, 1952, cited in Clarence L. Kelly, "Robert R. Church, A Negro Tennessean in Republican State and National Politics from 1912–1932" (M.A. thesis, Tennessee State Univ., 1954), 7–8.

CHAPTER III.

To Fight, To Switch, or "To Hell With It"

The sentiment expressed in the public rantings of Senator Edward W. Carmack and the contagious success of racial demagoguery in neighboring states forced black Tennesseans to reassess their political loyalties and aspirations. Within the existing party framework, they faced the prospects of fighting an increasingly vocal "lily white" Republican movement or switching their support to the traditionally and blatantly unsympathetic Democrats. For many Negroes, the obvious answer was to follow the line of least resistance and stay at home. Black political participation in Tennessee, therefore, varied according to geographical region and the degree of urbanization, but the forces of Jim Crow and disfranchisement never totally succeeded. The black role diminished in both electoral and party politics, but it did not disappear.

The size of Tennessee's black population was never large enough to threaten white control of state politics or justify a period of "black Reconstruction," but blacks voted freely during the late nineteenth century and produced a small, steady supply of legislators and local officials. On occasion, the black voters even formed a decisive bloc in determining who held high state offices. This heritage of political participation carried over into the early twentieth century and is perhaps best illustrated by the continued presence of black local officeholders. Although blacks had no representatives in the General Assembly after 1889, they often utilized de facto segregation in urban housing patterns to elect aldermen, justices of the peace, and school directors.[1] Elected black officials came from all regions, but the Chattanooga area seemed to provide the most favorable political climate. There, a significantly large black population (approximately 40 percent from 1870 until 1910) combined with aggressive leadership and white tolerance to achieve regular representation in city government.

Chattanooga's undisputed black political leader at the turn of the century was Hiram Tyree. A large one-armed man who was reported to have close ties to certain high-ranking Democrats, Tyree virtually ruled over the heavily black fourth ward. Occasionally serving with a second black man (Eugene L. Reid, 1900–1902, and Charles Griggsby, 1904–1911), Tyree spent fourteen years on the Chattanooga board of aldermen and seven years on the city council. As an alderman, Tyree was more than a token representative. He brought some improvements to his ward, dispensed minor patronage posts, and served on special committees of the board. One noteworthy committee assignment was to a five-member group investigating favoritism in the conduct of the police department.[2]

Hiram Tyree worked hard to get out the vote of his black constituency, and black voters represented a large proportion of a diminishing Republican allegiance in the city. In 1901, however, the state legislature reorganized Chattanooga's city government along bicameral lines. Although race was never mentioned in discussions of the new system, Tyree's fourth ward was now

---

[1] A good general discussion and analysis of black political participation (especially in the legislature and in the Republican party) during the late 19th century is found in Joseph Howard Cartwright, *The Triumph of Jim Crow: Tennessee Race Relations in the 1880s* (Knoxville: Univ. of Tennessee Press, 1976). In 1896 another black man, Jesse Graham of Montgomery County, was elected to the General Assembly, but he was denied his seat and the position declared vacant when he was ruled not to have met state residency requirements.

[2] Chattanooga *Daily Times*, Feb. 21, Aug. 3, Oct. 10, 12, 1900, Oct. 15, 1902, Oct. 11, 1905; Chattanooga *Sunday Times*, July 11, 1937.

combined with two white wards in aldermanic elections. As a result of reorganization, Tyree lost his bid for reelection in 1902 and was forced, in 1904, to drop down to the larger and newly created city council. He served at this post with Charles Griggsby until the inauguration of the commission system of city government in 1911. All commissioners faced an at-large election and no blacks stood a chance of success.[3]

Even the limited and heavily personal role of black Chattanoogans constituted an exception in Tennessee politics. Knoxville produced a few black officeholders during the late nineteenth century, but this city lacked two of the key ingredients found in Chattanooga's political environment. First, the black population rarely exceeded 15 percent of the city's total and, second, no ambitious leadership like Tyree's existed. Joseph M. Trigg served as fifth ward alderman from 1898 until he resigned to become a federal clerk in Washington in 1901, and Dr. Henry M. Green filled the same position from 1908 to 1912. Green, like Tyree, lost his post to the "progressive" reform of commission government.[4]

Blacks had even less political success in Middle and West Tennessee. Fraud, whitecapping (Klan-style intimidation), and the threat of violence almost completely disfranchised rural blacks. Urban residents, meanwhile, occasionally sought office but rarely achieved the unity and organization needed to overcome white pressure and resistance. Nace Dixon served as alderman from Clarksville's predominantly black ninth ward during the years 1906–1910, and Solomon Parker Harris represented Nashville's third ward as city councilman from 1911 to 1913. Dixon and Harris eventually joined Tyree and Green, however, as victims of at-large commissioner elections.[5]

[3] Nashville *American*, Oct. 10, 1900; Chattanooga *Daily Times*, Oct. 15, 1902, Aug. 31, 1905, Aug. 23, 1907; McGuffey, ed., *Standard History of Chattanooga*, 320.
[4] Knoxville *Journal and Tribune*, March 8, 1901, Jan. 19, 1908, Jan. 13, 1910; Cansler, *Three Generations*, 153.
[5] Clarksville *Leaf Chronicle*, Dec. 3, 19, 21, 1908; Nashville *Banner*, Oct. 13, 1905; Nashville *Globe*, Sept. 22, Oct. 13, 1911; Nashville *Tennessean*, Oct. 13, 1911. A brief discussion of whitecapping is found in fn. 8, chap. 6.

The flexibility of Tennessee's caste system lessened as one moved westward across the state and forward into the twentieth century. Most of the state's black legislators during the 1880s represented the western region, but whites increasingly viewed blacks who sought political office with suspicion and hostility. Professional politicians such as Hiram Tyree could not survive in the less favorable environment, and those Negroes whose economic success had inspired wide black respect seldom wanted to risk white wrath by seeking election. In rare instances, and these usually occurred shortly after 1900, a black man might be elected to a minor post as a justice of the peace (J. L. Edwards and E. S. Earthman in Shelby County) or a school director (Green Allen in Carroll County), but such breaches in the white man's government were seldom if ever repeated in Middle or West Tennessee after 1905.[6] Extralegal pressures were important in the declining political role, but state and local governments also threw statutory roadblocks in the paths of potential black voters. Although Tennessee never resorted to explicit disfranchisement, by 1913 poll taxes, white primaries, and commission governments had effectively sealed off the ballot box from black politicians as well as a large number of Negro voters.

Tennessee established a one-dollar poll tax in 1890, an equivalent of from one to two days' wages for the average black citizen in the years 1890–1930. While the tax applied to all Tennesseans, regardless of color, it especially discouraged black voters who also had to risk white disapproval and economic pressure in order to vote. The poll tax, in effect, encouraged black apathy. In 1906, the state legislature added a white primary option to its list of electoral hurdles. Although most Negroes voted in Republican primaries and fewer than half the counties adopted the exclusive interpretation, the white Democratic primary significantly restricted potential black participation. The western counties having the heaviest black populations were the counties approving

[6] Memphis *Commercial Appeal*, Dec. 4, 1901, Jan. 8, 17, 1903; Nashville *American*, Oct. 28, 1904.

"whites only" primaries. With Democratic nomination tantamount to victory, racial restrictions made it impossible for blacks to have a meaningful vote, even though some began to show Democratic leanings as early as 1900.[7] The rapidly spreading commission system of government did not restrict opportunities for Negroes to vote, but as the careers of Nace Dixon, S. P. Harris, Dr. H. M. Green, and Hiram Tyree attest, it effectively closed the last remaining door to black officeholders.

Evidence of the cumulative impact of restrictive legislation and the apathy it encouraged among black voters in Tennessee can be seen by comparing voter participation in Fayette County (73 percent black) during the 1894 and 1906 gubernatorial elections. The Republican candidate on both occasions was Henry Clay Evans of Chattanooga, congressman from the Third District during the years 1889–1891. While in Congress he drew the wrath of whites and the praise of blacks for his support of the Lodge Force bill.[8] In his campaign for governor in 1894, Evans polled a sizable black vote in Fayette and other rural counties but lost the election on a court-directed recount. Evans ran for governor again in 1906 and was soundly defeated in a race-baiting campaign which featured great stress on his Force bill stand and limited black voting. The Republican vote (practically synonymous with the black vote) declined in Fayette County during this twelve-year period from 339 votes in 1894 to 3 votes in 1906.[9]

[7] Hardeman *Free Press*, July 29, 1904; Nashville *American*, Sept. 23, Oct. 12, 1900, Aug. 21, 1905, June 29, 1907; Nashville *Tennessean*, Dec. 1, 1909; Memphis *Commercial Appeal*, Aug. 3, 1926; Carroll County *Democrat*, Oct. 12, 1900. The Carnegie-commissioned Myrdal study in the late 1930s and early 1940s extensively documented the persistent racial disfranchisement resulting from Tennessee's application of the poll tax and white primary laws. See Ralph J. Bunche, *The Political Status of the Negro in the Age of FDR* (Chicago: Univ. of Chicago Press, 1973), xix–xxx, 457.

[8] The Force bill, introduced by Congressman Henry Cabot Lodge in 1890, would have given a federal supervisor final judgment on voter registration, voter challenges, and final ballot counts. The bill was reminiscent of Reconstruction and infuriated Southern Democrats.

[9] Nashville *American*, Feb. 24 (quoting the Chattanooga *News*), June 9 (quoting the Rockwood *Times*), June 28 (quoting the New Bern *Chronicle*), Oct. 26, 31, Nov. 14, 1906; Nashville *Tennessean*, Jan. 19, 1908; Robert H. White, ed., *Messages of the Governors of*

Black political participation declined most sharply in the rural counties, while in the cities interest and activity correlated closely with the presence of organized leadership and with periods of racial crisis. Of the four major urban centers, Knoxville and Nashville showed the least inclination toward black political unity. Knoxville blacks were loyal Republicans, but with their right to the ballot generally uncontested, they were as free as whites to factionalize and play politics on a personal rather than a racial basis. Mayoral elections usually stimulated the most interest, although voter participation was never high.[10] In Nashville, on the other hand, old-line political leaders seemed more interested in Republican party politics than getting out the vote. The Nashville *Globe* sought to lead black voters into a more independent political stance, but, for the most part, the electorate was ineffective and apathetic.

The two most noteworthy examples of black electoral assertion came from Chattanooga and Memphis during the Ku Klux Klan campaign of 1923. As the birthplace of the original Klan, Tennessee had clung rather nostalgically to this bit of its history. In 1907, the Middle Tennessee survivors of the old order held a reunion and went as a body to see Thomas Dixon's play *The Clansman*.[11] Such displays kept the fraternal and vigilante ideals of the old Klan alive. When post-World War I tensions arose, it was therefore no surprise that the revived Klan should reappear in Tennessee. It created little stir initially, and even took such an unlikely action as giving five hundred dollars to the black victims of an

---

Tennessee (Nashville: Tennessee Historical Commission, 1967), VII, 555; State of Tennessee, *Tennessee Pocket Manual, 1906–1908* (Office of the Secretary of State, 1909), 7.

[10] Interview with Mr. and Mrs. J. Herman Daves, July 2, 1970; interview with George W. McDade, May 29, 1972; Knoxville *Journal and Tribune*, Jan. 16, 1910, Aug. 26, 31, Sept. 3, 5, 1915; Nashville *Tennessean*, Jan. 18, 1910. East Tennessee's more tolerant atmosphere did, however, make possible sporadic flurries of political activity such as that which elected Dr. T. E. Stevens, a black physician, to the Cleveland board of aldermen in 1920. Stevens's election was an exception not repeated elsewhere in the state. *Crisis* 20 (Dec. 1920), 79; Knoxville *Journal and Tribune*, Oct. 4, 1922.

[11] Nashville *American*, Jan. 19, 1907.

explosion near Memphis.[12] By 1922, however, the Klan had ventured into the world of local city politics, and the 1923 municipal elections in Chattanooga and Memphis centered upon the presence of a complete slate of Klan nominees. In both cities, blacks played a crucial role in the outcome.

In Chattanooga campaign rhetoric centered upon religious minorities and rarely mentioned the race issue, but blacks obviously realized the perilous position they would occupy if the city government fell under hostile control. Black organizations joined with such white fraternal and civic groups as the Elks, the Rotarians, and the Civitans in denouncing the Klan and urging their members to oppose its candidates. By virtue of an almost "unprecedented" turnout in the solidly black fourth ward, the Klan city commission candidates went down to a very narrow defeat. The results showed that the four incumbent (anti-Klan) commissioners were elected by majorities of 402, 81, 60, and 58 votes over the nearest Klan opponent. In light of the average 705-vote majority given to each of the victors from the fourth ward, the black vote had been indispensable in stopping the hooded order from taking control of the city government. The Klan candidate for city judge won despite the heavy black opposition. The importance of the black vote in this election drew national attention, bringing A. Philip Randolph to exclaim in the *Messenger:* "The spirit of the New Negro is flaming high!"[13] With the passing of the Klan threat, however, this spirit declined and apathy returned.

At the other end of the state Memphis blacks played an almost equally important role in the 1923 elections. Since its arrival in the Bluff City in 1921, the Ku Klux Klan had grown rapidly, voiced strong opposition to non-Protestants, incurred the wrath of C. P. J. Mooney, the Catholic editor of the *Commercial Ap-*

---

[12] Kenneth T. Jackson, *The Ku Klux Klan in the City, 1915–1930* (New York: Oxford Univ. Press, 1967), 46.

[13] Chattanooga *Daily Times*, March 29, 30, 31, April 1, 12, 1923; "The Ku Klux Klan in Politics," *Outlook* 133 (April 25, 1923), 742; "Negroes Defeat Klan Candidates in Chattanooga," *Messenger* 5 (June 1923), 733.

peal, and generally left blacks alone. By 1923, however, support for the secret organization was so strong that several men, including the county coroner, publicly vied for its leadership. A full slate of candidates filed for the November municipal ballot. The incumbent mayor, Rowlett Paine, headed a Citizen's League ticket in opposition.[14]

Both sides, surprisingly, campaigned for the black vote. The Klan went so far as to hold a rally in Church's Park for the purpose of asking black support. Speakers at the meeting stressed the fact that "negroes and klansmen should be allies as both were native born Americans and both Protestant." It was even suggested that Negroes form a Klan of their own, but the estimated two hundred blacks in the audience reportedly listened with little conviction. Most black Memphians preferred the advice of a committee of sixteen black business and professional leaders who, after receiving written promises of civic improvements in the Negro neighborhoods, endorsed Paine.[15] The election was close, with Rowlett Paine receiving a majority of less than four thousand. Of the Klan candidates, only Clifford Davis, in a race for city judge, managed a victory. Black leaders, with much reason, claimed that the support of their race meant the difference between a total victory for the Klan and the spirit-smashing defeat that was realized. Black voters had turned out in force, and the most populous Negro precincts gave Paine large majorities.[16]

Unlike those in Chattanooga, however, Memphis blacks sustained their political activity throughout the 1920s. Leadership accounted for this continued political interest, and Robert R. Church, Jr., deserved most of the credit. Church had become a powerful figure in the Tennessee Republican party and during the Harding and Coolidge administrations was the undenied patronage boss for West Tennessee. On the Democratic side of

[14] Jackson, *The Ku Klux Klan in the City*, 45–58; Virginia M. Phillips, "Rowlett Paine's First Term as Mayor of Memphis, 1920–1924" (M.A. thesis, Memphis State Univ., 1958).

[15] Memphis *Commercial Appeal*, Oct. 28, Nov. 2, 1923; George Washington Lee, *Beale Street: Where the Blues Began* (New York: Ballou, 1934), 243–44.

[16] Lee, *Beale Street*, 244; Memphis *Commercial Appeal*, Nov. 2, 3, 9, 1923.

politics, Edward Hull "Boss" Crump controlled Memphis and much of the state. There was no "arrangement" or alliance between Crump and Church, but each respected the political power and domain of the other. By avoiding open challenges to one another, these two politicians co-existed during the late teens and twenties. Crump-controlled local government, on the one hand, rarely engaged in race-baiting and harassment of black political activities, while on the other hand, Church-influenced federal officials seldom interfered with Crump. Not until the decline in Republican power in Washington did "Boss" Crump feel free to openly attack Robert Church.[17]

During the 1920s, Crump's opponents often charged that he benefited from the black vote in Memphis. The most serious complaint came in 1926 when Crump was criticized for allegedly calling upon Robert Church to influence black voters to "crash" the previously de facto white Democratic state primary. In this election, Crump sought to oust Governor Austin Peay in favor of his little-known opponent, Hill McAlister, and, despite the screams of Crump's opponents, several thousand blacks were allowed to vote in the primary. There is no evidence that Church personally came to Crump's aid, but presumably the black voters contributed heavily to the twelve thousand vote margin which McAlister polled in Shelby County.[18]

On a more critical level as far as black Memphians were concerned, their candidate in 1923, Rowlett Paine, had proved a disappointment. Paine attempted to steer clear of Crump and plot his own course. Despite his campaign promises, he rejected any special consideration for the wishes of blacks. Paine publicly reneged on a pledge to hire black firemen and policemen (there

[17] Interviews with Roberta Church, Nov. 13, 1975, George W. Lee, June 15, 1972, Blair T. Hunt, June 14, 1972, Fred L. Hutchins, June 15, 1972. Crump's harassment of the Church family in the 1930s and 1940s involved both economic and political pressures, and led Church to move to Chicago in November, 1940.

[18] Memphis Commercial Appeal, Aug. 3, 6, 1926. Although Robert Church voiced his opposition to "cross over" voting in party primaries, his mobilization of black political awareness in Memphis indirectly increased the possibilities of just such events as occurred in 1926.

45

were none), and he further incurred the wrath of his former Negro supporters when he had a city incinerator built less than two hundred yards from the new Booker T. Washington High School. In 1927, as a result of Paine's lack of sympathy and unfulfilled promises, Robert Church, Wayman Wilkerson, Dr. J. B. Martin, Merah Steven Stuart, and George Washington Lee formally founded a black political organization known as the West Tennessee Civic and Political League. Lee, a bright young insurance executive and political assistant to Church, explained what he hoped would be the new role for blacks in city elections: "We are preparing the law-abiding Negro to vote . . . for self-interest."[19]

Self-interest included the ouster of Paine in favor of Crump's candidate, Watkins Overton. Aided by the black newspaper, the Memphis *Triangle*, the West Tennessee Civic and Political League launched a campaign that touched the life of every Negro in the city. Sutton Griggs opposed the campaign, saying it was "laying the foundation of a race riot." Labeled an "Uncle Tom" by Lee, Griggs eventually became so unpopular that he moved back to his boyhood home in Texas. Paine, meanwhile, in the face of a heavy turnout in the black wards which voted 80 percent against him, lost his bid for reelection.[20]

The West Tennessee Civic and Political League did not accomplish all its goals with the ouster of Paine. Nevertheless, Robert Church and his lieutenants had carried black political participation to a peak of effectiveness and had shown that electoral exclusion in Tennessee was not ironclad. The activities in

[19] Lee, *Beale Street*, 242–49; George Washington Lee, "The Political Upheaval in Memphis," *Messenger* 10 (Feb. 1928), 30–31; Memphis *Commercial Appeal*, Oct. 7, 30, Nov. 4, 6, 10, 1927. It was Ralph Bunche's observation in the early 1940s that still ". . . the only connection Negroes have had with the Memphis police force has been Negro heads colliding with nightsticks in the hands of white policemen." See Bunche, *Political Status of the Negro*, 495.

[20] Lee, *Beale Street*, 242–49; Lee, "The Political Upheaval in Memphis," 30–31; Memphis *Commercial Appeal*, Nov. 1, 6, 7, 8, 1927; Anna Church, wife of Robert Church, to Mary Church Terrell, Aug. 16, 1927, Terrell Papers, container 5.

Memphis may have constituted an aberration in Tennessee politics, but they also indicated that blacks could still be galvanized to action when pertinent issues arose and when effective leaders of their own choosing appeared.

The experience of black Tennesseans in Republican party politics roughly paralleled their exclusion from electoral affairs. As elsewhere in the South, black politicians during the late nineteenth century exercised greater importance in party circles than they did in governmental politics. Even as the twentieth century began, Negroes dominated many county and district Republican executive committees, served on state committees, and received numerous low-level federal patronage appointments. Patronage was particularly important in Memphis, for example, where at one time there were fifty-two full-time and twelve substitute employees in the postal service alone.[21] Party influence, however reflected the importance of blacks as Republican voters. It was hardly coincidental, therefore, that electoral restrictions were accompanied by the rise of a "lily white" wing in Tennessee's Republican party.[22]

Dr. R. H. Boyd, writing in 1900, was not alone in his concern that black Tennesseans would have "to carefully guard the political interest of the Negro race." In an interview with the Washington *Colored American* in 1901, J. C. Napier expressed similar concern. He denied that the black man had any desire for social equality, but he stood firmly for the race's right to political participation. Napier was a loyal Republican, however, and he assured a Murfreesboro audience in 1902 that "President Roose-

[21] Green Polonius Hamilton, *The Bright Side of Memphis* (Memphis: privately printed, 1908), 197 204.
[22] John W. Farley, Memphis attorney and Republican faction leader, to John C. Houk, Nov. 17, 1919, Houk Papers, container 95. The term "lily white," as applied to Republican politics, apparently originated in the intraparty struggles in Texas during the 1880s. Norris Wright Cuney, a black man, was the party leader, and he dubbed white members who sought to "eliminate Negro leadership" as "lily whites." The term caught on and came to apply to all efforts to remove blacks from the Republican party in the South. See Henry Lee Moon, *Balance of Power: The Negro Vote* (Garden City, N.Y.: Doubleday, 1949), 79.

velt was with them and the attempt of the so-called lily-white element to kick the negro out of the Republican party would prove a dismal failure."[23]

Napier, a Republican official and frequent holder of patronage, was responding in 1902 to the exclusionist proposals of a Republican gubernatorial candidate, Judge H. T. Campbell. Endorsing "lily whitism," Campbell had received support and publicity for his frank statement that "I think we ought to make it [Republican party] a white man's party in Tennessee." Campbell had spoken before a group of white Republicans in Memphis who had just dominated that district's congressional and legislative nominating convention. Black patronage bosses like Josiah T. Settle and William Porter joined Napier in professing faith in support from President Theodore Roosevelt, but other black Memphians (and a few whites) refused to be patient. Led by W. H. Melton, editor of the *Colored Citizen*, these "black and tan" Republicans denounced the "Federal building gang" as a bunch of "spittoon wipers" and nominated a slate of independent candidates to oppose the Democrats and "lily whites." Melton's faction campaigned hard, and similar groups sprang up in Jackson and Madison counties as well, but their independent ticket attracted few voters.[24] Such "rebellions" were mostly protests rather than serious attempts at political victory, but they also indicated that some black Tennesseans were considering alternatives to the continued allegiance to an unfriendly Republican party.

Roosevelt's first-term appointment policies and cordial treatment of Booker T. Washington temporarily discouraged Tennessee's "lily whites," although some observers noticed a marked decline in the number of blacks participating in the 1904 state

---

[23] Dr. R. H. Boyd to his fellow Baptist ministers in Tennessee, March 10, 1900, Citizens Savings Bank and Trust Company Scrapbook, private collection of the Citizens Savings Bank and Trust Company, Nashville; Washington *Colored American*, Nov. 2, 1901; Nashville *American*, Oct. 26, 1902.

[24] Nashville *American*, Oct. 14, 21, 26, 1902; Memphis *Commercial Appeal*, Oct. 18, 19, 21, 24, Nov. 5, 1902; State of Tennessee, *Tennessee Election Manual*, 1900–1902, 43.

convention.[25] The clear pro-white stance of Roosevelt's second administration, however, and William Howard Taft's public promises not to appoint black officeholders if elected in 1908 gave new life to "lily whites" in Tennessee. At first, black political opinion continued solidly in favor of staying in the Republican ranks and fighting to block the adverse trend. Therefore, when a series of white-dominated district and state conventions excluded blacks from being delegates to the 1908 Republican National Convention in Chicago, groups of Negroes in Nashville and Memphis openly challenged the "lily whites." Complaining that proper public notice had not been given when Nashville's representatives to the party conventions were chosen a large number of local black Republicans called for another convention. Although "it was open to whites as well," the second convention was attended only by blacks. The Nashville *Globe* praised the choosing of new delegates, saying: "This is a time when a death blow may be struck at the hydra-headed lily-whitism which has dominated political affairs in this county and district." Richard Hill, a black businessman and former chairman of the Negro Department of Tennessee's Centennial Exposition, led the fight. Hill and his supporters immediately began to collect evidence and to prepare a brief for the credentials committee at the national convention. Black efforts were greatly handicapped, however, by a lack of funds to aid in getting their case and their delegates to Chicago.[26]

Memphis blacks also held a second convention and chose a slate of challengers for the Tenth District's convention seats. Black "politicos" had the most at stake and interest soon waned among the rank and file. Even those chosen to go to Chicago showed little hope of successfully challenging white control. J. T. Settle, leader of the dissident blacks, lamented the fact that he found it

[25] Memphis *Commercial Appeal*, Jan. 25, 1903; Nashville *American*, Jan. 14, 1903, April 8, 1904.

[26] Nashville *Globe*, April 17, May 22, 1908; Richard Hill to John C. Houk, April 18, May 8, 9, 16, 18, 22, 23, 28, June 6, 1908, Houk Papers, containers 75 and 76.

"almost as hard to get the delegates and alternates to render me any assistance as to make a horse drink after leading him to water." Money, again, was a problem, but West Tennessee blacks had already begun to show the apathy which Robert Church fought to overcome later. Settle gathered affidavits and filed a brief, but he apparently was the only challenger to make the trip to the national convention.[27]

The credentials committee rejected the appeals of Tennessee's black delegations, allowing them only "the briefest presentation of [their] claims." The Nashville *Globe* praised the fight "for decency, justice and the square deal in politics," and predicted: "We shall yet see the day . . . when no one or two men holding federal offices can name a whole county convention and dictate every action of a congressional district. That day is coming!" Without specifically calling names, the *Globe* also took J. C. Napier and other traditional black party leaders to task for not fighting on the side of the challengers. "The most detestable lily-white republican under the high heavens," said the *Globe*, "is the Negro lily-white. If anyone could believe such a person to be sincere in his affiliations with such a faction . . . doubts might be entertained as to his sanity."[28]

Evidence of bitter resentment appeared among blacks throughout the state, but the majority maintained their allegiance to the Republican party. Blacks in Knoxville and Chattanooga had never lost the few nominal positions which the party hierarchy had allowed them since late in the nineteenth century. And, by 1912, splits within the party on both the national and state level had enabled persistent black politicians to work their way back into an active role in partisan affairs in both Nashville and Memphis.[29] "Lily-whitism" persisted, however, and blacks were

---

[27] Josiah T. Settle to John C. Houk, May 13, 16, July 7, 1908, Houk Papers, containers 75 and 76.

[28] Knoxville *Journal and Tribune*, June 7, 1908; Nashville *Globe*, May 22, June 19, 1908.

[29] Nashville *Globe*, March 15, 1912; Republican Executive Committee letterheads for Knox and Hamilton counties, Houk Papers, container 92.

rarely given recognition without constant intraparty feuding.

One faction of the black electorate, especially in Middle Tennessee, refused to swallow its growing sense of political frustration. In the face of insult and rejection, the Nashville *Globe*, commenting on the 1908 convention, urged the state's blacks to exercise a "spirit of independence" in their voting. While admitting that "some may forget their self-respect and take the draught," the young blacks of the *Globe* endorsed the Democratic nominee for governor in 1908. Other black Middle Tennesseans, including the aging but vocal R. H. Boyd, joined the plea for greater political independence. Robert L. Mayfield, in a well-publicized debate, urged members of his race to support the entire Democratic ticket. Blacks from other parts of the state also spoke out in favor of a rejection of blind party loyalty. As early as June 1906, the *Christian Index* (from Jackson) had made this observation: "He [the Negro] has the balance of power when the two great parties divide; and he should vote for those who will give him the best consideration. He ought to be independent in politics."[30] The 1908 election returns and numerous political observations indicated that many blacks on the state and local level did, indeed, refuse to support the state Republican nominees. Malcolm R. Patterson, the Democratic nominee for governor, carried the six wards in Nashville that contained the heaviest black registration. The third ward, in which potential black voters outnumbered white voters by a margin of over two to one, gave Patterson 178 votes and only 115 for his Republican opponent. Meanwhile, William Howard Taft carried this ward in presidential balloting by a vote of 207 to 100 over William Jennings Bryan.[31]

---

[30] Nashville *Globe*, June 12, July 24, Sept. 4, Oct. 9, 30, 1908; Nashville *Tennessean*, Oct. 28, Nov. 3, 1908; Hamilton, *The Bright Side of Memphis*, 25; Sutton E. Griggs, *The One Great Question: A Study of Southern Conditions at Close Range* (Nashville: Orion, 1907), 57; *Christian Index*, June 2, 1906.

[31] E. C. Linney, Nashville chemical manufacturer and Republican worker, to John C. Houk, Oct. 10, 1908, Houk Papers, container 76; Nashville *Globe*, Nov. 6, 1908; Nashville

While still considering the party of Lincoln as "the ship and all else the sea" in national elections, many black voters in Tennessee began supporting the straight Democratic ticket on a state and local level. In Nashville R. H. Boyd stated in 1910 that he believed that "the Republican party, with whom he [the Negro] has voted for the last thirty-five or forty years, has traded him off," and he lent his considerable support to the *Globe's* campaign for "independent" and "local" voting. Ira T. Bryant, manager of the A. M. E. Sunday-School Union Publishing House, echoed Boyd's advice, observing that he would "ever love and cherish the memory" of "departed [Republican] saints," but that the Republicans of his section resembled the party's founders "about as much as a Kentucky thoroughbred does the proverbial jackass." Robert L. Mayfield, meanwhile, spoke at gatherings throughout Middle Tennessee in favor of "the principles of Democracy."[32]

J. C. Napier remained loyal to the Republican banner. Even though he was ousted from the State Executive Committee in 1910, his reward for loyalty came from Washington. Since 1905 Napier had sought the top black patronage post as register of the treasury. Working through Booker T. Washington, Napier was finally rewarded in 1911. Even in victory, however, the "lily-white" influence intruded. Taft's appointment of Napier coincided with a significant loss of power in the office of the register and a move of the facilities from large, spacious quarters to a dark, dimly lit, and out-of-the-way location.[33] The *Globe* supported

---

Tennessean, Nov. 4, 1908. Based on voting-age males, the heaviest black wards in Nashville in 1910 were:

	3rd	4th	8th	12th	14th	16th
white	486	300	549	379	499	750
black	1,158	826	597	501	893	796

See United States, Bureau of Census, *Thirteenth Census of the United States: 1910. Population*, III, 766.

[32] Nashville *Globe*, Oct. 23, 1908, Aug. 27, Sept. 17, Oct. 8, 1909, July 29, Nov. 4, 1910, July 7, Sept. 22, Oct. 13, 1911, Oct. 18, 25, Nov. 1, 1912, July 22, 1910, Nov. 1, 1912.

[33] Nashville *Globe*, July 15, 1910; J. C. Napier to Washington, Dec. 6, 1905, Washington Papers, container 879; James E. Haney, "Black Politicians During the Pro-

Napier's work within the party, but aired its differences in a forthright manner: "The older men of the Negro race who have voted for years for every man who proclaimed himself a republican, are for the most part clinging to the 'Grand Old Party'. . . . but the younger men, the men who are close students of conditions, are not falling over themselves to vote the republican ticket. . . ."[34]

Race pride, protest, and self-interest contributed to these first open and concerted breaks with Tennessee's Republican party. Horace Slatter, a feature writer for the Nashville *Globe*, emphasized the importance of self-interest. He felt that the ending of blind opposition to local Democrats brought increased white willingness to improve conditions in black communities. "Not the least of these [changes]," he pointed out, "is making provisions for site and maintenance of a Carnegie library for Negroes, and the establishment of a city park for colored people at a cost of more than $20,000, and a Tuberculosis Hospital." In 1911, a Colored Citizens Association in Memphis set a precedent by pursuing this line of reasoning and attempting to use black votes as a means of extracting promises of civic improvements from both mayoral candidates.[35]

A sizable number of black voters supported Theodore Roosevelt's Bull Moose party in 1912 and a few were attracted to the Socialist party, but the great majority who remained interested either stayed with the Republicans and fought the "lily whites" or drifted into greater political independence.[36]

---

gressive Era, 1901–1912" (paper delivered at the meeting of the Organization of American Historians, Chicago, April 12, 1973). In 1906 Napier had been offered a post as consul at Bahía, Brazil, and in 1910 he was given an opportunity to be named consul-general for Liberia. He turned down both of these offers.

[34] Nashville *Globe*, Oct. 21, 1910.

[35] *Ibid.*, July 5, 1912; *Crisis* 2 (Aug. 1911), 139; 2 (Oct. 1911), 227–28; 3 (Dec. 1911), 53. The support given by a black electorate to local candidates is best observed in the election totals for Nashville's mayoralty campaigns of 1911 and 1913. The heavy black wards gave increasingly strong majorities to the Democrat, Hilary E. Howse.

[36] Nashville *Globe*, Aug. 2, 9, 16, 1912. T. Clay Moore (Nashville) to G. Tom Taylor, Oct. 1, 1912; T. P. Turner (Pulaski) To G. Tom Taylor (2), Oct. 2, 1912; E. M. Argyle

"Lily white" harassment gathered new voice in Tennessee during the emotion-laden woman suffrage campaigns of 1919–1920. As a result even some of the more conservative Negro leaders from East Tennessee began to offer their services to those Democrats who were sympathetic to black grievances. The Chattanooga *Defender* (black) endorsed Democratic Governor Albert H. Roberts in his unsuccessful bid for reelection in 1920 on the grounds that he had taken a courageous stand for "the enforcement of Law and Order." "Let us learn as a race to work and vote for men and measures," concluded the endorsement. J. J. J. Oldfield, editor of the *Defender*, worked in both the eastern and middle counties of the state on Roberts's behalf.[37] Oldfield clearly was not alone. Ticket-splitting continued in Nashville as the heavily black third ward gave large majorities to Warren G. Harding and Calvin Coolidge, respectively, in 1920 and 1924, and yet in 1922 gave overwhelming support to the Democrat Austin Peay over incumbent Republican Governor Alfred Taylor. In the Chattanooga and Hamilton County elections of 1926 and 1928, black voters and leaders showed similar inclinations to split tickets on all levels.[38]

By 1928, Tennessee politics had taken an ironic twist; for the first time Republicans were using the race issue against the Democrats. The Democratic candidate for president, Alfred E. Smith, was accused of being "a friend of the Negro" and of hiring black officials to supervise white secretaries. Whether or not such tactics had any bearing on white voting patterns is not clear, but many black Tennesseans spurned even their national loyalty to

---

(Maryville) to G. Tom Taylor, Oct. 3, 1912; A. W. Cammack (Columbia) to James J. Losier, Oct. 15, 1912; all in Houk Papers, container 83. Sally M. Miller, "The Socialist Party and the Negro, 1901–20," *Journal of Negro History* 56 (July 1971), 225.

[37] John W. Farley to John C. Houk on Nov. 17, 1919, Houk Papers, container 95; Chattanooga *Defender*, Sept. 11, 1920, clipping in Gov. Albert H. Roberts Papers, Tennessee State Library and Archives, container 23; J. J. J. Oldfield to Gov. Roberts, Sept. 13, 1920, in *ibid*. Oldfield claimed that the *Defender* reached "15,000 readers weekly."

[38] Nashville *Tennessean*, Nov. 4, 1920; Nashville *Banner*, Nov. 8, 1922, Nov. 5, 1924; Chattanooga *Daily Times*, Aug. 4, 1926, Nov. 4, 8, 1928.

the Republican party and supported Smith. Although still a small minority, these blacks publicly displayed their bowler hats and founded several Smith for President Colored Leagues.[39] Black political loyalties had loosened to the point that in 1932 even the conservative Webster L. Porter from reliably Republican Knox-ville voiced his concern. In an editorial in his *East Tennessee News,* he touched the key black political dilemma in Tennessee with the question: "just who does want his vote?" Porter noted that "thousands of Negro votes in Tennessee are drifting about" and that black voters were "not inclined to cast [their] votes for any candidate who is not . . . inclined to appreciate the same."[40]

While a growing number of black Tennesseans were either effectively denied passage or were deserting the "Republican ship," Memphis proved to be an exception. There blacks retained their party identity and joined Robert Church in his open and aggressive fight with West Tennessee's "lily white" Republicans. With this support, Church began a contest in Tennessee's Tenth District in 1912 which eventually brought him both state and national recognition. Church rose to power by recognizing that a vast majority of the Republican voters in West Tennessee were black. Realizing the limited electoral power of the "lily whites," he set about organizing his racial constituency and, with a poten-tial voting bloc of tens of thousands of blacks, forced his way into party councils. White Tennesseans resented Church's aggressive methods as flagrant violations of the state's caste structure. Forced to go along with the wealthy black Memphian at times, white Republicans never accepted Church, and though he regu-larly sat on the executive committee after 1916, his power was frequently challenged, sometimes successfully.

Robert Church sought to enhance his demands for greater

---

[39]"White Supremacy as Practiced by Tammany," flier in Thomas Henderson Papers, Tennessee State Library and Archives, uncatalogued. W. H. Henry to Henderson, Oct. 31, 1928; H. E. Cole to Henderson, Oct. 27, 1928; both in *ibid.* Interview with George W. McDade, May 29, 1972; with Owen Whital r and Rosa McGhee, July 13, 1972.

[40]*East Tennessee News,* Sept. 1, 1932, clipping in Napier Papers, container 2.

black representation on state and national party committees by dramatically challenging the white exclusionists at the polls. He presided over the formation of the Lincoln League on August 21, 1916 when an estimated sixteen hundred blacks from Shelby, Fayette, Tipton, and Hardeman counties nominated a full slate of congressional and legislative candidates. This was not simply a protest action as had been the case with W. H. Melton and his supporters in 1902. "Regular" (white) Republicans had previously named a ticket, and Church was inviting them to a show of voter strength. Mobilizing the diverse, uneducated, and largely apathetic black voters of Memphis was difficult, but the Lincoln League held voter schools, sponsored lemonade and motion pictures rallies, and by election time succeeded in placing the names of 10,612 Negroes on the registration rolls of Shelby County. The election results were below the league's expectations and the Democrats won every contest, but the black ticket outpolled the regular Republican ticket by almost four to one. Of particular satisfaction to Church was the fact that Wayman Wilkerson, a local black undertaker and banker, ran well ahead of the arch "lily whitist" John W. Farley in the congressional race.[41]

Because it furnished most of the Republican voters in the 1916 election, the Lincoln League laid claim to being the "regular" party organization in the Tenth District. Church won seats on the Tennessee delegation to the Republican national convention and on the National Republican Advisory Committee for Negroes. The Memphis *Commercial Appeal* branded the league a "hideous plot" to return blacks to office in Tennessee, but Church and the league drew favorable attention from blacks across the nation. The black New York *Age* praised the league lavishly, and black leaders from such distant states as Ohio and Colorado wrote to

[41] Memphis *Commercial Appeal*, Aug. 22, Sept. 17, Oct. 14, 21, 24, Nov. 2, 8, 1916; *Crisis* 13 (Dec. 1916), 93–94; 13 (March 1917), 244; Shirley Hassler, comp., *Fifty Years of Tennessee Elections, 1916–1966* (Nashville: Office of the Secretary of State, 1966), 129. The importance of dynamic political leadership in black communities is clearly seen in Church's personal supervision and financing of the Lincoln League. Clarence L. Kelly, "Robert R. Church," 20.

Church about his organization. They established similar leagues in many other cities. In Tennessee, the Lincoln League stayed active during off-election years, established a chapter in Chattanooga, and renominated Wilkerson for Congress as the "regular" Republican in 1920. Although Wilkerson lost, he polled more votes than any previous candidate had done in the Tenth District.[42]

The "lily white" Republicans of Memphis fought back, forcing blacks to fight for every committee post or patronage job they received. The white forces successfully challenged Church's seat at the 1920 national convention, but, ironically, Church perhaps reached the peak of his power as a result of that convention and the subsequent Harding victory. The national party organization had taken full notice of Church's activities as a result of a Lincoln League convention held in Chicago in February 1920. Over four hundred black representatives from thirty-three states attended this meeting and heard an encouraging address from Will Hays, the Republican national chairman. Hays began corresponding frequently with Church and appointed him to the Advisory Committee on Policies and Platform. Church's committee assignments were not critical ones racially, but they marked him as a man of importance.[43]

In spite of being unseated at the convention, Church traveled extensively and campaigned hard for the Republican ticket. His loyalty and political influence in Memphis earned Church the control of West Tennessee's Republican patronage throughout the 1920s and also enabled him to retain his seat on the state executive committee. Church complained publicly of Hoover's coolness to black Republicans in 1928, but he eventually en-

[42] New York *Age*, Nov. 30, 1916; Kelly, "Robert R. Church," 39; Chattanooga *Daily Times*, July 14, 1920; Hassler, comp., *Tennessee Elections, 1916–1966*, 102, 107, 111, 115, 119.

[43] John C. Houk to Robert R. Church, Feb. 25, 1920; Robert R. Church to John C. Houk, Feb. 26, 1920; Harry O. True to John C. Houk, March 5, 1920; Houk Papers, container 96. *Christian Index*, Feb. 19, 1920; Will Hays Scrapbook, Vol. I, 24–29, Vol. II, 260, press release Jan. 29, 1920, Hays Papers, Indiana State Library.

dorsed the national ticket. He still could wield considerable influence at national conventions as late as 1932.[44]

Robert Church's Memphis organization, of course, was not limited to Republican party politics. It had provided the nucleus for aggressive local political activities in 1923 and 1927, it made possible the foray into the 1926 Democratic primary, and it avoided open conflict with the Crump machine. Whether seeking local goals or party influence, black Memphians had shown that racial solidarity could be sustained in spite of caste restrictions and white hostility. Their will to continue the fight against political ostracism depended almost completely on the presence of a dominant, resourceful, and wealthy leader. Negroes in Middle and East Tennessee had no comparable leaders, and therefore most often drifted toward political independence or apathetically accepted the growing exclusiveness of the Republican party.[45]

[44] Kelly, "Robert R. Church," 59–62; Lee, *Beale Street*, 260–78; Memphis *Commercial Appeal*, June 13, Nov. 6, 1928; Chicago *Defender*, Oct. 27, 1928; Charles Willis Thompson, "The Two Hoovers at Chicago," *Commonweal* 16 (June 29, 1932), 231–32.

[45] Black Chattanoogans did gain some renewed political importance and limited influence around 1930 with the emergence of Walter Robinson, a black political "boss" like Robert Church. Nominally a Republican, Robinson wheeled and dealed with black votes on local issues and managed to keep over 2,000 black voters registered in Chattanooga throughout the 1930s. See Bunche, *Political Status of the Negro*, 201–2, 327.

CHAPTER IV.

A Respectful Distance Behind

Public education carried a low priority in post-Reconstruction Tennessee. Although in 1873 it had been the first Southern state to establish a permanent school fund, depressed agricultural prices, payment of the state debt, and racial prejudice inhibited progress in Tennessee.[1] State law required strict segregation in the schools, meaning that, in theory, economically hard-pressed taxpayers would have to provide separate and equal schools for white and Negro children, each teaching the same subjects, each poorly equipped, and each staffed by poorly paid, overworked teachers. In fact, equal schools for the two races did not exist. Inequality was encouraged in some counties by population distribution, in other counties by racial exploitation, and throughout the state by racial prejudice. Maintaining adequate schools for blacks in mountainous counties such as Claiborne and Fentress, which had less than one Negro child of school age per square mile, was financially impossible.[2] On the other hand, in Fayette County, where black children outnumbered whites by a ratio of three to one, but where white schools and expenditures exceeded

[1] Stanley John Folmsbee, Robert Ewing Corlew, and Enoch Lockwood Mitchell, *History of Tennessee*, 4 vols. (New York: Lewis Historical Publishing, 1960), II, 244. Statistics available for the study of early 20th-century public education in Tennessee are not always complete, and frequently are unreliable. The major statistical source is the *Biennial Report of the Superintendent of Public Instruction*. A detailed breakdown of black participation in the school system, however, was not made by the state superintendent until the 1922 report.

[2] *Southern Education Notes* (Jan. 10, 1903), 12.

those for blacks, state funds were obviously used to enrich white schools at the expense of Negroes.[3]

Even Tennessee's attitude toward public education for white students had been less than enthusiastic: after thirty years, the state required but did not enforce a five-month school term, school attendance ran below 50 percent of the scholastic population, teachers got an average monthly salary of $28.86, and no valid rural public high school existed. Under such handicaps, the average pupil in the state received very inadequate training. But at the bottom of this poor system was the black child. Except where the Negro's share of state funds was used to build up white schools, few white Tennesseans before 1900 approved of appropriations for black education. An educated Negro, they said, was a good plow-hand spoiled. By the beginning of the twentieth century, therefore, even by liberal estimates, only 36.1 percent of the school-age black children attended school regularly in Tennessee. This was a decrease from the 38.6 percent attending in 1877, and it was significantly below the 48.4 percent attendance record of white children in 1900.[4]

In effect, public education was a marginal institution in Tennessee before 1900. Debts, taxes, and a subsistence economy reinforced the long-standing aversion to public schools. Blacks of the state paid proportionally less taxes, and white political leaders were seldom inclined to apportion white tax funds to educate black children. Any money that could be spared for the luxury of education certainly should go where it would do the most good—white youth.[5]

[3] Andrew David Holt, *The Struggle for a State System of Public Schools in Tennessee, 1903–1936* (New York: Bureau of Publications, Teachers College, Columbia Univ., 1938, 101. Horace Mann Bond has shown how black school-age children in Southern states were actually used to gain funds for white schools. See Horace Mann Bond, "The Cash Value of a Negro Child," *School and Society* 37 (May 13, 1933), 627–30.

[4] *Annual Report of the State Superintendent of Public Instruction for the Scholastic Year ending June 30, 1906*, 119; Alrutheus Ambush Taylor, *The Negro in Tennessee, 1865–1880* (Washington, D.C.: Associated Publishers, 1941), 184.

[5] Nashville *American*, Feb. 1, 1900.

Since the days of the Freedmen's Bureau, northern philanthropy had invested substantially in the education of Tennessee's black children. Late in the nineteenth century private, generally church-related, schools for Negroes were established in Memphis, Jackson, Nashville, Chattanooga, and Knoxville, and also in many of the East Tennessee counties whose black population was too small to be of concern to white school officials. By one turn-of-the-century estimate, these counties contained 16,793 school-age blacks who depended solely on private beneficence for any education they might receive. The impact of these private schools was limited however, and they too were forced to conform to the pressures of Tennessee's caste system.[6] Black leaders praised private philanthropy and campaigned for greater state aid, but usually they chose to encourage white paternalism rather than seek equality. Implicitly they accepted the fact that black education should progress at a respectful distance behind that of whites.

Shortly after the turn of the century, however, two developments promised new educational growth in Tennessee. First, farm prices began to rise around 1900 and continued, with some fluctuation, until after World War I. Farmers might have expressed their gradual increase in wealth by spending more for public education, but a formidable hurdle remained; the state's citizenry and legislature first had to be converted to the belief that education was actually an investment, not an expenditure. The second development was that the annual Conference for Education in the South undertook this task of conversion. The impact of

[6] George Sherwood Dickerman, "Ten Years' Changes in East Tennessee," *Southern Workman* 34 (May 1905), 267. Private schools posed a very minor challenge to the constitutional requirements of segregation; the Presbyterian-supported Maryville College, for example, had long admitted a few blacks to its classes. The numbers were minimal and the treatment was discriminatory, but even this tiny infraction of the rules of Tennessee's dualistic society led to specific legislative action. In 1901, by votes of 85 to 2 and 28 to 1, the General Assembly made it unlawful for "any school, academy, college or other place of learning" to allow whites and blacks to be educated in the same institution. *Acts of the State of Tennessee* (Nashville, 1901), ch. 7; Ralph Waldo Lloyd, *Maryville College: A History of 150 Years, 1819–1969* (Maryville: Maryville College Press, 1969), 210–15.

this organization, often known as the "Ogden Movement," was particularly great in Tennessee because Knoxville was the base for the conference's propaganda agency, the Southern Education Board's Bureau of Information and Advice on Legislation and School Organization. Led by Charles William Dabney and Philander Priestley Claxton of the University of Tennessee, an evangelical crusade attacked the entrenched apathy of the state. Taxes rose; school terms, enrollment, and attendance increased; compulsory attendance came into being; and white secondary education was improved. Despite these gains, not all Tennesseans shared equally in the improvements.[7]

Although black Tennesseans could take early hope from the fact that Negro education, as well as white, had been considered at the first meeting of the conference at Capon Springs, West Virginia, in 1898, any real enthusiasm soon felt the smothering effects of the Southern caste system.[8] Northern philanthropists paid the bills for the Southern Education Board, but its administrators and publicists were local. Charles William Dabney, president of the University of Tennessee and director of the Knoxville Bureau of Information, quickly tempered black expectations and calmed fearful whites in his state when he said that "the place for the negro in the immediate future is upon the farms and in the simpler trades. He must work out his own destiny," Dabney continued, ". . . He must be treated very much like a child. The Southern people have learned how to handle him, and others who go down there are learning very rapidly." Dabney spoke clearly enough. The Nashville *American* informed its readers that the

[7] Charles William Dabney, *Universal Education in the South*, 2 vols. (Chapel Hill: Univ. of North Carolina Press, 1936), II, 74. In 1899, Robert Curtis Ogden, a successful New York and Philadelphia merchant, attended this conference and soon enlisted support for the educational crusade from other prominent Northern businessmen. He organized railroad excursions so that these men might see conditions in the South and talk with interested Southerners. These trips and the further work of Ogden were widely publicized, and to many people the activities of the Conference for Education in the South became known as the "Ogden Movement."

[8] *Proceedings of the First Conference for Education in the South* (Capon Springs, W. Va., 1898), 3; Nashville *Globe*, April 16, 1909.

educational program did intend to "educate the negro," making "him also an independent, self-respecting citizen," but that plans were to "educate the white man first."[9]

Nevertheless, when philanthropist Robert Curtis Ogden led one of his traveling conferences through Chattanooga and Knoxville on April 29 and 30, 1902, Tennesseans were openly skeptical. In the late nineteenth century, integration at Maryville College, the activities of the American Missionary Association, and the work of other Northern agencies had been distasteful to Southern tradition. White teachers in Negro schools administered by outsiders gave blacks an inflated image of their capabilities.[10] The Knoxville *Sentinel* expressed this feeling best when editorializing on the Ogden visit: "The *Sentinel* will confess that at first it felt some hesitancy as to the movement. We feared it was being entered on in the 'missionary' spirit. . . . The *Sentinel* objects to the missionary spirit. . . ."[11] Realizing that such skepticism could easily be turned into opposition, educational campaigners in Tennessee emphasized white schools. Those who needed a salve for their consciences could draw strength from the fact that, theoretically, any school legislation they achieved would be applicable to both races. Others could lean on a resolution of the second Capon Springs conference in 1899 that "the education of the white race is the pressing and imperative need."[12]

Fears of an educational thrust from "outsiders" who might meddle with racial traditions increased from east to west in Tennessee. The numerous Northern church schools of the Appalachian region had conditioned the white citizens of East Tennessee

[9] United States, *Reports of the Industrial Commission on Immigration and Education*, 19 vols. (Washington, D.C.: Government Printing Office, 1900–1902), XV, LIII; Nashville *American*, Jan. 10, 1903.

[10] Claude J. Bell, "Negro Teachers for Negro Schools," *Southwestern School Journal* 7 (March 1901), 17.

[11] Clipping from Knoxville *Sentinel*, May 1902, in Southern Education Board Papers, Southern Historical Collection, Univ. of North Carolina, scrapbook G-680F.

[12] Holt, *Struggle for Public Schools*, 102; *Proceedings of the Second Conference for Education in the South*, (Capon Springs, W. Va., 1899), 7.

to seeing philanthropic work among blacks. These institutions only rarely challenged the dictates of Southern tradition and, though given little local support, were tolerated. The assurances of Dabney and other Southern leaders, therefore, convinced such skeptics as the Knoxville *Sentinel* that the customs of the region would not be offended.[13]

The race-conscious editors and "concerned" citizens of Middle Tennessee proved more difficult to overcome. A letter to one newspaper adamantly stated that "it would be best for the negro and best for the poor white man . . . if they were left to work out their destinies without interference from over-zealous and so-licitous philanthropists." Meanwhile, as late as 1905, an editorial in the Nashville *American* blasted the education movement in a personal way: "As to Mr. Ogden and his fanciful theories concern-ing the colored race, they do not interest us. . . . He knows more about merchandising than he can ever possibly know about ethnological questions. . . ."[14] For many years West Tennes-seans tended to ignore the whole issue as best they could. The thought of equal education for blacks was a blasphemous absur-dity for whites in the heavily Negro and agricultural counties, and Memphis leaders had long practiced a policy of consciously neg-lecting the needs of the city's large black population. Eventually this region would come to accept the idea of industrial education and manual training, but strong doubts prevailed even among the educated whites as late as 1909.[15]

Despite the Southern Education Board's efforts to avoid the issue, race constantly intruded upon its campaigns. Some of the educators and several black spokesmen talked openly of the need for black advancements, but they chose very subtle and unassert-ive arguments; the suppression of crime, paternalistic duty, and

---

[13] *Minutes of the Presbytery of Union*, April 14, 1909; Nashville *Tennessean*, Dec. 14, 1907.

[14] Nashville *American*, May 5, 1901, June 10, 1905.

[15] Carl Holliday, "The Young Southerners and the Negro," *South Atlantic Quarterly* 8 (1909), 125–27.

economic gain dominated the positive white approach, while appeals to white self-interest characterized most public black reasoning. "It is not the educated Negro," explained one white writer, "that makes up our idle and vagrant class, that commits our murders, and despoils our women. . . . The trained Negro .ᵉ. . in times of friction is always to be found on the side of law and order."[16] This play upon the traditional Southern fear of Negro rape and murder appeared throughout the state, but in Middle Tennessee the most common rationale for a black school program was the paternalism conceived in the slave-master relationship. "The negroes are here with us . . . we have to take care of them . . . [and] the Southern people have long since recognized this," said the conservative editor of the *American*. "We had best enlighten them all we can if we wish to make our task of lifting them to a higher place of civilization easier."[17] Such white conversions emerged predominantly from the middle and upper classes in the cities, among whites who were accustomed to dealing with servants.

West Tennessee, on the other hand, was heavily agricultural, and even the cities, only recently created by migration from surrounding counties, reflected rural values. The western counties in 1900 were 38.8 percent black and by 1910 outmigration had reduced the figure only to 36 percent.[18] It was a region where night riding and whitecapping kept many black sharecropping communities in a state of fear and instability. Nevertheless, the cautious appeal for some improvement in black education made a few important converts. In a surprisingly patient appraisal of black education, the Memphis *Commercial Appeal*, while striking the fearful chord of Negro crime, went significantly further and raised the economic question: "The wisdom of the ages has

[16] Thomas Jesse Jones, *Negro Education: A Study of the Private and Higher Schools for Colored People in the United States*, United States, Bureau of Education Bulletin 38, 2 vols. (Washington, D.C.: Government Printing Office, 1917), I, 25–26.

[17] Nashville *American*, Jan. 10, 1900.

[18] Compiled from United States, *Twelfth Census, 1900, Population*, II, pt. 2, 484, and United States, *Thirteenth Census, 1910, Population*, III, 744–61.

taught us that while education may at times bring with it poignant mental agony . . . solely as an economic measure it wins out in the long, long run . . . for this same education, tending now to Negro discontent, bringing to him dissatisfaction and humiliation and often inciting to actual crime, will be recognized as a tax saver, a labor settler, and a crime preventive."[19]

Economic benefits became one of the most effective arguments in favor of increased black school appropriations—a better-trained Negro was an investment. It was a marginal investment, to be sure, but still it was a venture yielding significant returns, and many of the better-educated Tennesseans accepted this. In 1905, the superintendent of Chattanooga schools estimated that eight years of education would increase a black man's capital value to the community from $5,000 to $10,000.[20]

Education dispensed in such a grudging and paternalistic fashion was suspect in the eyes of some black leaders. Booker T. Washington once said that the Southern educational campaign meant "almost nothing as far as the Negro schools were concerned."[21] Nevertheless, "almost nothing," was better than "nothing at all," and Washington allowed his name to be used in the crusade. Black leadership, thoroughly schooled in the doctrines of accommodation, "walked softly," especially in the early years of the campaign for better schools. Once the upward direction seemed assured, however, the more assertive leaders agitated for more improvement. By 1907, for example, the young editor of the Nashville *Globe* could complain that "the inequality of the provisions made for the white and black children is too great at present . . . . In most of the affairs of the South, 'for the colored race' is synonymous with inferior accommodations. We hope

[19] Nashville *American*, Nov. 22, 1901, March 7, May 10, 1902; Memphis *Commercial Appeal*, Jan. 2, 1906.

[20] William Taylor Burwell Williams, "Colored Public Schools in Southern Cities," *Southern Workman* 34 (Nov. 1905), 615-24.

[21] Louis R. Harlan, *Separate and Unequal: Public School Campaigns and Racism in the Southern Seaboard States, 1901–1915* (Chapel Hill: Univ. of North Carolina Press, 1958), 94.

that such will not be the case with the Nashville schools."[22]

But most black leaders relied upon appealing to white self-interest: "The 'insolent' negro is really the uneducated negro. . . . If the white man would safeguard his own children, he must safeguard the children of his black neighbors also. . . . If our white brethren should lose every noble, generous impulse and forget the duty which the strong owe the weak, they would be compelled to lift up the negro and that as a means of their own advancement."[23] This accommodationist stand, taken by James Bond, a black Congregationalist minister in Nashville, fairly represented the dominant approach to race relations for the middle-aged Negro at the turn of the century. (Perhaps no family better illustrates the evolution of black thinking in the twentieth century than the generations from the Reverend James Bond to Dr. Horace Mann Bond, author and student of Negro higher education, to Julian Bond, civil rights leader and Georgia legislator.)

As late as 1908, Charles Victor Roman, a black Nashville physician and president of the National Medical Association, still avoided assertion of equal rights in his appeal for better Negro education. Instead he argued that "republican governments . . . provide for the education of their citizens not as a charity but as an act of self-defense—on the same principle that we look after a case of small-pox or yellow fever."[24] Expanding upon the health analogy, Sutton E. Griggs, having abandoned his earlier militancy, noted in 1911 that "the white man's great need of having an educated Negro race could hardly be more forcibly demonstrated than by referring to the anti-tuberculosis crusade. The chief reliance of the civilized world for stamping out the great white scourge is upon the dissemination of knowledge through the printed page."[25]

Investments, long-range returns, and theories of public health,

---

[22] Nashville *Globe*, Feb. 15, 1907.
[23] Nashville *American*, Jan. 4, 1903.
[24] Nashville *Globe*, Aug. 7, 1908.
[25] Sutton E. Griggs, *Wisdom's Call* (Nashville: Orion, 1911), 175.

however, were of little interest or consolation to most rural tax-payers accustomed to hard work, slight formal education, and subordinate blacks. In spite of the low-key arguments for reform, they (like many urban property owners) agreed with the small-town, Middle Tennessee newspaper editor who advocated leaving "the negroes to get education any way they can." Instead of accepting the economic arguments for educating black Tennesseans, the editor suggested that some "young Legislator" might make a name for himself by "introducing a bill to have the white and black school fund separated" on the basis of taxes paid instead of according to population.[26] At least one East Tennessee county (McMinn) adopted such a technique in dispersing county funds.[27]

Reduced to society's lowest denominator of race, neither the arguments of the white paternalists nor those of the black accommodationists could reach many caste-conscious whites. The ill-fated prohibitionist and race-baiting Senator Edward W. Carmack pinpointed the crucial problem faced by all black uplift programs in Tennessee. Carmack rejected the attacks of the educators with the observation: "It seems to me that most of what has been said on this line is a mere darkening of counsel by words without knowledge. I sometimes think we have tried not to see this question as it is, for when we strip it stark naked we must admit that it is not a question of literacy or illiteracy, but of white and black—it is a race question pure and simple." The fears underlying any caste system thus came to the surface in Senator Carmack's analysis. "They [education advocates] must say," observed Carmack, "that the negro, however well educated, will be happy in the position assigned to him as an inferior creature . . . or they must say that the effect of education will be to fill him with dreams of a perfect equality, the very thought of which fills the white man with loathing and disgust."[28]

[26] The Adams *Enterprise* (Robertson County), n.d., quoted in Nashville *American*, Dec. 25, 1904.
[27] Nashville *American*, Feb. 5, 1903.
[28] Edward Ward Carmack, "The Race Problem," *Olympian* 2 (Oct. 1903), 313–14.

Leaders of the Southern Education Board's campaign for better public schools continued to avoid the issue of black participation as much as possible. And yet, as legislative reform came near, the matter persistently arose. In an effort to assure the rural-dominated legislature that the Negro would still remain "in the position assigned to him," most proposals in Tennessee, as in the South, relied upon an industrial and agricultural training that was informal enough to avoid conflict with the caste system. A Negro, better trained in farming, would be a better tenant or more productive sharecropper. A well-trained cook or laundress would be a more dependable domestic servant. In 1909, Superintendent of Public Instruction Robert L. Jones summed up this viewpoint when he explained how he envisioned the end product of educational reform in Tennessee: "I believe that the negro should be educated along industrial lines so that he will be in a position to help himself and thereby the state. I would have his academic education limited, for I am inclined to think that the negro can best be *utilized* on the farms, in the shops, and, in fact, in all lines of trade."[29]

In their desire to avoid controversy, white campaigners made no real effort to marshal black support. Charles W. Dabney, Philander P. Claxton, and their supporters took their appeal for better schools directly to the white people of Tennessee. State Superintendent Seymour A. Mynders reported in 1906 that the popular campaign had been carried to "the pulpit, the bar, the stump . . . county fairs, race tracks, and at a wedding cere-

---

[29] Nashville *Tennessean*, Nov. 6, 1909. Author's italics. This approach also reflected an increasingly important tenet in the program of Northern philanthropy. Samuel Chapman Armstrong had preached the self-help and practical training values since his founding days at Hampton Institute and had instilled his ideas in his most famous student, Booker T. Washington. Washington, in turn, illustrated how self-help could be converted into self-maintenance and self-support, thus cutting down on black educational costs and making the program more palatable to whites. See Samuel Chapman Armstrong, *Ideas on Education Expressed by Samuel Chapman Armstrong* (Hampton, Va.: Hampton Institute Press, 1908), 20, 35, and Booker T. Washington, *Working With the Hands* (New York: Doubleday, Page, 1904), 38–39, 72–73.

mony."[30] He made no mention of school efforts among black communities. The legislature was the ultimate target, and black political influence, while never great, was declining. Nevertheless, the movement did not go unnoticed by the alert Nashville *Globe*. Whether solicited or not, this voice of many young black Tennesseans supported the educational campaign editorially during the fall elections of 1908, but added: "The state has been dealing liberally with its appropriations for the benefit of the whites, then why be parsimonious with the blacks?"[31]

Early legislative measures applied—on paper—to whites and blacks alike. In 1903 the legislature voted to add the annual budgetary surplus to the school fund. By 1905, $500,000 per year was being added to the fund.[32] Financial aid dispensed in this fashion was a further boon to those counties with large Negro populations; Haywood County, for example, drew money for three times as many black children as white. Yet in 1907 this county provided forty-four schools, seven of them high schools, for white children and forty-three, including only one high school, for black children.[33] Attempts were made in the 1905 legislature to bring county property taxes into the state treasury, for allocation on the basis of scholastic population across the state. The bill was defeated by the wealthier counties, but if passed, it undoubtedly would have increased racially disproportionate expenditures in poor black counties like Haywood.[34]

Educational evangelism intensified during the fall of 1908. When the General Assembly met the following January, public school proponents secured passage of a general education bill. Instead of relying upon a budgetary surplus for educational resources, the state now set aside 25 percent of its gross revenue in a

[30]*Proceedings of the Ninth Conference for Education in the South* (Lexington, Ky., 1906), 68.

[31] Nashville *Globe*, Sept. 11, 1908.

[32] Holt, *Struggle for Public Schools*, 239.

[33] *Biennial Report of the State Superintendent of Public Instruction for Tennessee for the Scholastic Years ending June 30, 1907–08*, 66, 94.

[34] Holt, *Struggle for Public Schools*, 241.

General Education Fund. Despite the continued discrimination arising from per capita apportionment in "black belt" counties, black Tennesseans gained significantly from the 1909 legislature. More money found its way to black schools, and most specifically, one of the four state-supported normal schools established by the general education act provided for "the industrial education of negroes and for preparing negro teachers for common schools."[35] But the black normal school received only one-half the appropriations given to each of the three white normal schools, and *Globe* editorials reacted indignantly: "Is the old saying true that half of a loaf is better than no loaf at all? Will it be proper to call upon the Negro people of Tennessee and exhort them to rejoice and be exceeding glad for this generous half of a loaf?" Blacks were urged not to accept discrimination passively: "How are the members of the Upper House to know the Negroes are not satisfied unless the Negroes themselves tell them so? The time to break the silence is now . . . the arrangement is an unjust one as it now stands, and if the Negroes of today fail to contend for justice in this matter their posterity will condemn them in their graves." And yet, finally, there was the old resort to accommodation: "On Tuesday, April 17, the general educational bill became a law . . . every Negro in our Commonwealth will receive this information with joyful heart."[36]

By 1909, it appeared that a significant number of Tennesseans had come to admit that education for the black population meant both social and economic gain for the state, but the nature of that education was deliberately limited. Originally, the general education bill of 1909 had made no distinction between the types of normal schools to be provided for white and black teachers. When West Tennessee legislators objected, the original provision was changed. Instead of providing for "one Normal School for the education and professional training of negro teachers," the

[35] *Biennial Report* (1909–1910), 45.
[36] Nashville *Globe*, March 12, 26, April 30, 1909.

bill was redrawn to read: "One Agricultural and Industrial Normal for the industrial education of negroes. . . ."[37] Likewise, some years later black secondary institutions were designated "training schools," and their white counterparts were called "high schools."

Neither the semantics nor the educational implications of the 1909 law especially concerned many black Tennesseans. With the exception of some close associates of the black liberal arts colleges in Nashville and East Tennessee, black leaders supported the Tuskegee idea of industrial training for their youth. While white spokesmen accepted this kind of education because it was less costly or it trained blacks for special "Negro jobs" or made them more readily utilized in the white economy, black advocates had similarly pointed reasons of their own.[38] The Nashville *Globe* supported manual and industrial training as a means of teaching regular work habits: "True, we learned it [laziness] from the white people of the antebellum days, but it is essential to our own welfare to lay that trait of the white man aside."[39] Black school principals, meanwhile, repeatedly complained of the sterility of "rote" learning and supported industrial training as "something more tangible than dry facts."[40] Therefore, instead of resenting the special legislative insistence upon agricultural and industrial training in their new "normal" school, the black press and the majority of the black educational leadership throughout the state welcomed the change. Discriminatory appropriations aroused some complaints, but not the curricular focus.

After the successes in 1909, much of the evangelical spirit of the educational crusade passed to the prohibition movement in Ten-

---

[37] Holt, *Struggle for Public Schools*, 103. Philander P. Claxton to Allison Norman Horton, March 27, 1953, in Allison Norman Horton, "Origins and Development of the State College Movement in Tennessee" (Ed.D. diss., George Peabody College for Teachers, 1953), 41.

[38] *Crisis* 4 (July 1912), 135; Nashville *Tennessean*, Nov. 6, 1909.

[39] Nashville *Globe*, June 4, 1909.

[40] James L. Murray, principal of Bransford High School, Springfield, Tenn., to Booker T. Washington, Jan. 17, 1913, Washington Papers, container 70.

nessee. Education reformers did summon enough strength in 1913 to pass two more significant bills—one act raising public school appropriations to one-third of the gross revenue of the state, and a second, more important, act making compulsory the "school attendance of all children between the ages of eight and fourteen for eighty consecutive days."[41] The compulsory attendance act had key racial implications; the average rural school term by 1913 had been expanded to 110 days per year, but the average term for the Negro rural school was only 60 to 65 days per year.[42] If every black child between eight and fourteen was to be provided with schooling for "eighty consecutive days," compulsory education in Tennessee meant more new expenditures on blacks than whites.

The new legislation generated varied opposition. Complaints arose from "farmers who needed their children in the fields, workmen who needed their children in the shops, and industrialists who had been profiting by the employment of cheap child labor."[43] But the racial implications of the law posed especially serious difficulties. In the five counties which, in 1913, had the highest proportional Negro population, 40 percent of the black children were in attendance as compared to 50 percent of the white children. Full compliance with compulsory education would require social and financial adjustments. On the other hand, serious problems also faced the white mountain counties of Sequatchie and Unicoi because they provided no schools at all for their small black populations.[44]

Better black schools would require heavy expenditures. Hesitant appropriations in the past meant that, throughout the state,

[41] Holt, *Struggle for Public Schools*, 255.
[42] *Biennial Report* (1913–14), 44; Samuel Leonard Smith, *Builders of Goodwill: The Story of the State Agents of Negro Education in the South, 1910 to 1950* (Nashville: Tennessee Book, 1950), 61.
[43] Holt, *Struggle for Public Schools*, 102.
[44] These five counties were Fayette, Haywood, Madison, Shelby, and Tipton. "Annual Statistical Report of the State Superintendent of Public Instruction of Tennessee for the Scholastic Year ending June 30, 1913," *Biennial Report* (1913–1914), 38, 40, 50, 52, 70, 71.

73

teaching loads in black schools were unmanageable and buildings were overcrowded. A teacher in one of West Tennessee's rural schools, describing her "typical experience," said that she had "an enrollment of forty children. There are six grades and these keep me more than busy . . . the building is owned by the colored church or the county would fit it with better furniture. There is no water on the grounds and this has to be hauled from long distances."[45] City systems, while superior to county schools, had not kept up with the migration of blacks from rural areas. William Taylor B. Williams reported in 1905 that Chattanooga was the only city in the state approaching adequate school accommodations for Negroes. Even so, only 46.7 percent of the black children were enrolled, and student-teacher ratios were much higher in black schools than in white schools. Many black parents in Knoxville, ambitious for their children, made sacrifices in order to pay the small tuition of the Presbyterian-run preparatory school conducted at Knoxville College because it had "better facilities, less pupil crowding, and better trained teachers." In Nashville, black teachers taught two half-day sessions in the primary grades, and yet Sutton Griggs wrote that he remembered "quite well the look of keen disappointment" on his seven-year-old daughter's face when the principal told her there was no room. Meanwhile, in Memphis only 23 percent of the eligible black children could even enroll. "Others desiring to attend school find no place in the public schools."[46]

To provide facilities for all the black school children would have required a considerable tax increase on white property holders.

[45] Myrtle L. Alexander, teacher in Covington (Tipton County), Tenn. to Dr. George Edmund Haynes, Urban League director and professor at Fisk University, Aug. 9, 1914, Haynes Papers, container 1914–1915.

[46] Charles Caswell Brown, "The History of Negro Education in Tennessee" (M.A. thesis, Washington Univ., St. Louis, 1929), 51; Williams, "Colored Public Schools in Southern Cities," 617; City of Chattanooga, *Mayor's Message and Reports of Departments of the City of Chattanooga for the Year 1905–1906* (Chattanooga: McGowan-Cooke, 1906), 37–38; interview with Carl A. Cowan, June 29, 1970. Cowan, a prominent East Tennessee Negro attorney and civic leader, was speaking of his own childhood experience in Knoxville. See also Griggs, *One Great Question*, 14.

Charles W. Cansler reported some improvements at the black high school in Knoxville in 1915, but in cities with more populous black communities, social custom, racial prejudice, and plain stinginess made enforcement of the Compulsory Attendance Law of 1913 impossible.[47] Failure to provide satisfactory physical facilities was the common urban problem in Tennessee, but attitudes and traditional practices (among whites and blacks) also had to be changed. The Nashville *Globe* stated that "Tennessee [had] never had a better law" than the compulsory attendance act, but warned that "it will require more truant officers than the city is able to furnish to keep all of the children in the school who have been in the habit of not attending. . . ." Knox County had adopted a required attendance program in 1911, but enforcement in black neighborhoods was erratic despite efforts by local Negro women's clubs to create interest and build up attendance.[48] In 1919, less than one-half of the black scholastic population of Memphis was in school and one-third of those who did attend were without seats. One school, originally built to accommodate eight classes, contained twenty-seven, with as many as eighty-eight students in one class.[49]

Public education was part of the "white system," and blacks did not gain significantly from new general legislation for many years. Few counties equalized their school terms or enforced compulsory attendance. In an outspoken moment, Booker T. Washington blamed the officials of the Southern Education Board for similar conditions throughout the South, charging that they did not put "themselves on record in a straight and frank manner as

---

[47] Cansler, *Three Generations*, 135. Improvements in Knoxville involved moving out of the worst "red light" district in the city to an enlarged elementary school. Helen Elizabeth Work, "An Historical Study of Colored Public Schools of Nashville, Tennessee" (M.A. thesis, Fisk Univ., 1933), 41.

[48] Nashville *Globe*, Aug. 15, 1913. Mrs. J. J. Johnson, president of the Knoxville Homemakers' Club, to George Edmund Haynes, Dec. 26, 1913; Haynes to Mrs. Johnson, Jan. 22, 1914, both in Haynes Papers, containers 1909–1913 and 1914–1915.

[49] United States, Bureau of Education, *The Public School System of Memphis, Tennessee*, Bulletins, 1919, No. 50, (Washington, D.C.: Government Printing Office, 1920), 112, 130.

they should."[50] Truth, however, lay within Tennessee's pattern of race relations; black development had to proceed, if at all, at a respectful distance behind white progress. Informal organizations such as the West Tennessee branch of the CIC might urge "colored ministers and other leaders . . . to impress upon their people the great importance of sending their children to school as soon as school opens, and every day until it closes . . . ," but formal enforcement lagged considerably.[51]

Black attitudes also had an important bearing upon the slow advance of Negro education in Tennessee. Many blacks were skeptical of formal schooling. Lack of opportunity had taken its toll, both economically and intellectually. The tenant farmer needed the help of every child to pay his expenses, and black parents felt compelled "to keep their children out of school or to withdraw them after the third or fourth grade to help support the family."[52] All farmers viewed their children as precious economic assets, but discrimination and racial suppression increased the hurdles for black children. The ambition of most blacks seemed to be fulfilled when they achieved literacy—which meant only the ability to read and write one's name. The caste system dulled enthusiasm for more education: academic training opened a world most blacks could not expect to join; inadequate facilities made learning difficult and unpleasant; and, in the view of one contemporary, "the negro without an education does not feel the same helplessness that an uneducated white man would feel, for most of the negroes are uneducated."[53]

The lack of white interest and the overriding sense of futility in Tennessee's black communities combined to perpetrate a sig-

[50] Harlan, *Separate and Unequal*, 94.

[51] Nashville *Banner*, June 10, 1922; *Biennial Report* (1917–1918), 15.

[52] Harvey Wish, "Negro Education and the Progressive Movement," *Journal of Negro Education* 49 (July 1964), 184–200. This tendency was observed by the Nashville *Tennessean* on Feb. 9, 1925.

[53] James L. Murray to Booker T. Washington, Jan. 17, 1913, Washington Papers, container 70; letter to the editor from Maria C. Kenney, Nashville *Globe*, Sept. 9, 1910; Charles Spurgeon Johnson, *Patterns of Negro Segregation* (New York: Harper, 1943), 12–13; Brown, "The History of Negro Education in Tennessee," 75.

nificant racial difference in school attendance. Black school attendance improved, but it remained below that of whites, and the black dropout rate in all grades was much greater. By 1920, black attendance had reached only 48.6 percent of those children eligible. (This was above the figure of 41.1 percent in 1913 but considerably below the 57.8 percent participation rate of white children in 1920.)[54] The 1920s closed the racial lag considerably, and the quality of black education also began to improve. Teachers were better prepared, especially through the program at the newly established Tennessee Agricultural and Industrial State Normal School (Tennessee A & I). By 1929, approximately 7 percent of the black teachers in the state were college graduates and over 50 percent had at least one year of college training. Average black attendance in 1930 was 70.5 percent of the total scholastic population as compared with 73.5 percent for whites.[55]

Not all aspects of black education improved noticeably. Despite expanding school terms and a growing legislative emphasis on the development of the state's secondary institutions, these two areas continued to show considerable racial inequality. Of the ten counties having the largest black populations in 1920, for example, only two had racially equal school terms as late as 1928 (see Table 1). Fayette County, having the highest black population percentage, provided 154 days of education to white children and only 58 to blacks. Eight mountain counties containing 1,422 blacks, meanwhile, furnished no black schools. As for high school education, only 7 percent of the blacks who enrolled in the first grade in 1922 had continued their schooling to the point of even enrolling in secondary school by 1930. This compared with a similar figure of 17 percent for the white children.[56]

[54] *Biennial Report* (1913–1914), 44–45; (1919–1920), 26–27. Comparative grade level dropout statistics for black and white students in Tennessee are found in Lester Crawford Lamon, "Negroes in Tennessee, 1900–1930" (Ph.D. diss., Univ. of North Carolina, 1971), 383–84.

[55] George W. Gore, Jr., "A Brief Survey of Public Education in Tennessee," *Broadcaster* 3 (Jan. 1931), 53; Tennessee, *Annual Report of the Department of Education for the Scholastic Year ending June 30, 1930*, 26, 31.

[56] Counties having no black schools in 1928 were Campbell, Cumberland, Fentress,

TABLE 1

Length of Terms of Black and White Schools
in the Counties Having the Largest Black Populations, 1928

| | | School Terms, 1928 | |
County	Black Population 1920	White Schools (in days)	Black Schools (in days)
Shelby	98,962	180	155
Davidson	44,528	174	174
Hamilton	27,120	175	174
Fayette	23,526	154	58
Madison	17,234	156	99
Haywood	16,959	156	101
Knox	13,310	156	154
Tipton	13,139	160	114
Maury	11,950	161	158
Montgomery	11,928	157	157

SOURCE: Charles E. Allred, S. W. Watkins, and G. H. Hatfield, *Tennessee, Economic and Social.* Part II: *The Counties,* in *University of Tennessee Record, Extension Series,* vol. 6, no. 3 (Knoxville, Sept. 1929), 30, 169.

The higher blacks sought to move up the education ladder, the less encouragement and support they received from the white system. Negro high schools, therefore, had a very low priority for school boards and state officials. In all three geographical divisions, blacks were forced to occupy outgrown white facilities or old elementary buildings, before being granted adequate schools of their own. In the late 1920s Memphis (1926) and Knoxville (1927) finally completed the new school buildings which had been promised, at least in Knoxville's case, since 1915.[57] Black Tennes-

---

Pickett, Scott, Van Buren, Unicoi, and Union. For secondary school figures see Lamon, "Negroes in Tennessee, 1900–1930," 383–84.

[57]Thomas Jackson Woofter, Jr., *Negro Problems in Cities* (Garden City, N. Y.: Doubleday, Doran, 1928), 209; William Durell Miller, *Memphis During the Progressive Era* (Memphis: Memphis State Univ. Press, 1957), 120; Mary U. Rothrock, ed., *The French Broad-Holston Country: A History of Knox County, Tennessee* (Knoxville: East Tennessee Historical Society, 1946), 317; Nashville *Globe,* Sept. 20, 1912; *Crisis* 9 (March 1915), 216–17.

seans thus found that keeping a respectful distance behind required patience. Fortunately, they did not have to rely on public resources and initiative alone.

Lagging educational opportunities became a target for renewed philanthropic activity midway into the second decade of the century. With the accomplishment of basic legislation, the General Education Board, the John F. Slater Fund, the Julius Rosenwald Fund, and the Anna T. Jeanes Foundation sought to spur greater state participation in Negro education and to inspire greater black support. The effort purposefully concentrated on rural schools. As early as 1910, the Nashville *Globe* observed the widening disparity in the quality of rural education, as compared with most city systems, and linked the conditions to increased black migration. Noting cries "from every section of our country that the young people are leaving the farms and flocking to the cities," the *Globe* turned to improved education as a "remedy" for "this influx." "We do not believe too much can be invested in education," the editorial explained, "for every dollar spent in that direction is a dollar well spent, but we do believe that it is essential that the schools in the rural districts be kept up. . . . the very best teachers that can be had ought to be secured in the primary schools in the rural districts. . . ."[58] Southerners, as well as Northern city-dwellers, grew increasingly disturbed by the moving black tides. This concern combined with a lessening fear of Yankee philanthropy to make the second decade of the century more productive with respect to black education than the first.

The limited racial goals of the Southern Education Board had diminished Southern defensiveness, and the new foundations (the Slater Fund was not really new) tried to avoid old antagonisms by working with and within the system. In 1913 the General Education Board offered to pay the salary and travel expenses of a state agent for Negro schools in Tennessee, and Samuel Leonard Smith, personable white superintendent of Montgom-

[58] Nashville *Globe*, Feb. 11, 1910.

ery County schools, took office as the first state agent in 1914. The newly created position was attached to the state education department, in accordance with the new approach of twentieth-century philanthropy. There was no evidence of what the Knoxville *Sentinel* had earlier termed "the missionary spirit." A former classics teacher, Smith had won statewide recognition for his work in the public and private schools of Tennessee. Extremely energetic and blessed with a folksy kind of charm, he was careful to work through existing authorities, applying funds only when public cooperation was assured. Smith had such success in Tennessee that in 1920 he was appointed Rosenwald Fund director for the entire South.[59]

In offering aid to black education, the General Education Board, the Slater Fund, and the Jeanes Foundation predictably emphasized industrial training. All three began large-scale activities in Tennessee in 1915. The Slater Fund and General Education Board directed their efforts toward building, equipping, and paying teachers' salaries for county "training schools" located in areas of heavy black concentration. The Jeanes Foundation, on the other hand, contributed money for the salaries of industrial supervisors, popularly known as "Jeanes teachers," for black schools.

Combined aid from the Slater Fund and General Education Board launched Tennessee's training school program by making possible the building of three schools during the academic year 1915–16.[60] Local authorities handled the construction and, along with the money donated by the black community, provided a large portion of the funds. To obtain philanthropic aid, however, local school systems had to agree to five conditions:

[59] Nashville *Tennessean*, Sept. 10, 1956; Nashville *Banner*, Sept. 10, 1956.
[60] Some earlier aid from the much older Slater Fund had supported a teacher in Knoxville's Austin Industrial School in the 1880s but this had been halted when the city system took over the school. Louis D. Rubin, Jr., ed., *Teach the Freeman: The Correspondence of Rutherford B. Hayes and the Slater Fund for Negro Education* (Baton Rouge: Louisiana State Univ. Press, 1959), 111–12.

1) That the building be modern, with equipment for industrial work, including practical manual training, home economics, agriculture and some elementary pedagogy in the last year.
2) That the school be under county and State control.
3) That the county board pay at least $750.00 a year for salaries in the school.
4) That the length of the term be eight months.
5) That the school have at least eight grades, with possibly one or two grades extra added as soon as conditions warrant it, and with the course of study thoroughly vitalized and socialized.[61]

Under these requirements, by 1922 thirteen counties had received financial help in the construction of Negro training schools. By 1932, twenty-six counties had been aided, and 1,495 students, or 17.3 percent of the state black secondary enrollment, attended these institutions. Eighty-two teachers, many given special training by General Education Board grants to Hampton and Tuskegee, composed the facilities of the twenty-six schools.[62] Contributions from the Slater Fund between 1915 and 1930 amounted to $74,845, but the participation inspired from local blacks and the state and county governments was of primary importance.[63] Such private grants often provided impetus that Tennessee counties themselves could never have generated.

Nevertheless, many white Tennesseans still questioned the wisdom of black education, even when it stressed vocational training, and even when someone else helped pay the bills. The status quo in race relations was important to the state's social structure. In 1916, Wilson County made arrangements through state agent S. L. Smith to obtain training school funds from the General Education Board and the Slater Fund. While construction was under way, a black man, arrested for bootlegging, killed the Lebanon police chief and consequently was lynched in the

---

[61]*Biennial Report* (1915–1916), 288.
[62]*Biennial Report* (1921–1922), 273; Edward Edgeworth Redcay, *County Training Schools and Public Secondary Education for Negroes in the South* (Washington, D.C.: John F. Slater Fund, 1935), 75.
[63]Redcay, *County Training Schools*, 168.

city square. Rumors circulated freely after the episode, and the frequently heard explanation was: "You see what too much education will do for a nigger!" Pressure mounted and school officials ordered construction on the new building halted. Smith stepped into the controversy and succeeded in lifting the training school question out of the affair by publicly establishing that the lynching victim had actually dropped out of school after the first grade, as was common among black children. Anti-school talk declined, construction resumed, and the school board professed that more education, not less, was needed to cut down on black criminality and violence.[64]

The Jeanes Foundation, meanwhile, sought to create a more productive and responsible black community. Revenue from Miss Jeanes's original million-dollar endowment was limited, however, and despite James C. Napier's presence on the board of trustees, for many years Tennessee received less than any of the twelve participating states. The agency, for example, donated only $2,750 to black education in the state between 1915 and 1917. Supplemented by state funds and occasional white donations, however, this money supported the employment of fourteen industrial supervising teachers in the black schools. "These supervisors made 1,510 visits to 400 rural Negro schools, introducing industrial work and sanitation, organizing community centers and helping to increase the teaching efficiency of the schools."[65] One student of Jeanes activities in Tennessee noted that the rural black communities were so neglected that immediate needs "like food, shelter, health, and improved sense of values" had to be met before "education might become meaning-

[64] Smith, *Builders of Goodwill*, 153–54.

[65] A treasurer's report to the board of trustees showed Tennessee receiving only $962 in the school year 1909–10, placing it last on the list and far behind Mississippi, the leading beneficiary, which received $8,883. Napier Papers, container 2; *Biennial Report* (1915–1916), 29. One example of white support came from Franklin in Williamson County, where "certain prominent businessmen" supplemented the salary of Jeanes supervisor J. K. Hughes. Nashville *Tennessean*, March 29, 1914.

ful to them." Therefore, most Jeanes teachers found their first job to be that of improving health conditions and providing a liaison function to the white community.[66] Jeanes teachers also sought financial support among blacks. In 1922, the twenty-four supervisors raised $55,470.23 in combined black and white donations.[67]

To the average Tennessean, the Rosenwald Fund became the most familiar member of the philanthropic quartet. Although the fund itself was not established until 1917, Julius Rosenwald had begun contributing money toward the building of rural black schools in Tennessee two years earlier.[68] The painful sight of black children trudging to and from drafty cabins, leaky pine-slab shacks, dilapidated churches, and converted corncribs in order to learn their numbers and scrawl their names had impressed Rosenwald. Grants distributed by his agency were limited in size ($300 per school at first) and emphasized the necessity for public support and black interest. And yet by 1922, despite wartime shortages, the Rosenwald Fund had helped to build 131 rural Negro school buildings in Tennessee with "a pupil capacity of 13,680, teacher capacity of 304, and a total cost of $512,581.00." The Rosenwald Fund contributed 18 percent of this cost, blacks gave 25 percent, interested whites provided 3 percent, and the balance was paid by state and county taxes.[69] By the time the fund's school-building program ended in 1932, its "seed" grants

---

[66] Darlene L. Hutson, "The Jeanes Supervisory Program in Tennessee" (Ed.D. diss., Univ. of Tennessee, 1964), iv; a similar, but less pointed, observation came from one of the Jeanes teachers, Mrs. W. P. Ware, in a letter to Julius Rosenwald, Oct. 24, 1929. The letter appeared in *Broadcaster* 2 (Jan. 1930), 30.

[67] *Biennial Report* (1921–1922), 272.

[68] Julius Rosenwald, president of Sears, Roebuck, became interested in Negro education after meeting Booker T. Washington in 1911. Upon becoming a trustee of Tuskegee Institute in 1912, he exhibited a "crusading zeal" for improvement of rural education for blacks.

[69] *Biennial Report* (1921–1922), 276, 282, 283; N. C. Newbold, "Money an Indisputable Argument," *Journal of Social Forces* 2 (Nov. 1923), 88–89; Isaac Fisher, "Multiplying Dollars for Negro Education," *ibid.* 1 (Jan. 1923), 149–53.

had generated total expenditures of almost two million dollars. The result was 373 schools with a capacity of 44,460 students.[70]

As philanthropic involvement increased in the state, the Rosenwald Fund expanded its function, furnishing books, buses, and even radios for some schools. In 1916, it announced it would pay half the salary of a black assistant to the state agent for Negro schools. State senator Parks Worley sponsored a bill to pay the other half of the salary, and he successfully overcame the opposition. Worley, an East Tennessean who was a consistent friend to blacks on all issues but voting rights, influenced the immediate appointment of Robert E. Clay of Bristol to fill the new education post.[71]

A large, affable man who could spin a yarn or give a speech to fit any occasion, Clay was an active participant in Booker T. Washington's National Negro Business League and had formerly traveled the lyceum circuit speaking on behalf of prohibition. His billing appealed to whites as well as to the vast majority of black Tennesseans—all supporters of Washingtonian accommodation. A broadside advertising a Clay appearance during the prohibition campaign described him thus: "By dint of hard labor and the seizing of every opportunity of self-development, he has risen from the humble though honest estate of shining shoes to that of a leader of his race, as an advocate of temperance reform and the industrial uplift of his people. . . . His message is dual in character—to the white people for sympathy and encouragement, to the Negro for self-restraint. . . ."[72]

Clay appeared innocuous enough to those whites with whom he would have to deal. And yet, on occasion, Clay and S. L. Smith ran into an unexpected problem with their building program.

[70] Edwin Rogers Embree and Julia Waxman, *Investment in People: The Story of the Julius Rosenwald Fund* (New York: Harper, 1949), 51.

[71] Mrs. W. P. Ware to Julius Rosenwald, Oct. 24, 1929, in *Broadcaster* 2 (Jan. 1930), 30; Smith, *Builders of Goodwill*, 43–45.

[72] Interviews with Mr. and Mrs. Aeolian E. Lockert, July 16, 1971, A. V. Boswell, June 20, 1972, James L. Jenkins, June 9, 1972, George W. Gore, June 21, 1972; broadside in Haynes Papers, container 1909–1913.

Ironically, the building of a "Rosenwald school" in some Tennessee counties meant that blacks would have the only modern rural school in the area. This awkward situation violated a cardinal principle of the existing caste system and sometimes generated insurmountable opposition. More often, however, in Smith's words "the program not only stimulated the building of rural Negro schools, but it created appetites among the whites for a modern school just as good as the Negro school—an appetite which was not satisfied until the whites had a school as good or better."[73] When such conflicts were encountered, the Rosenwald plans were made available, without cost, for the building of the white schools.

Without Northern money, rural education for black Tennesseans would have remained a world of underpaid teachers and one-room school houses. With one important exception, the causes that retarded the growth of education for the black child were also those that served to delay the development of education for the white child in the state. For the black youth of Tennessee, however, apathy and rural poverty were complicated by racial discrimination. At least one historian has blamed the educational campaigners of the early twentieth century with driving "the wedge of inequality" between the two school systems of the South.[74] Tennessee school officials needed no such wedge. State and county funds had always been used to build up white education at the expense of the black communities. One observer sarcastically concluded that "the provision for the dual system of education is the only legislation regarding Negro public schools that has been carried out in practice as well as in theory. . . ."[75]

In 1920, black schools in Tennessee were still noticeably inferior to white facilities. By 1930, the deviation had diminished but remained obvious. Teacher training, for example, had almost

---

[73] Smith, *Builders of Goodwill*, 120.
[74] Harlan, *Separate and Unequal*, 269.
[75] Mary Jackson Riley, "The Development of Secondary Education for Negroes in the State of Tennessee" (M.A. thesis, Howard Univ., 1935), 24.

caught up, but pay scales were clearly discriminatory (see Table 2). Not until 1942 did the courts force an end to the racial differential in teachers' salaries.[76] Nevertheless, Negro education had been improved since the passage of the school law of 1873. The quantity of public support had increased even though the racial distribution of funds had not significantly changed (and probably did not approach parity until several years after 1954). A study made by the CIC in 1927 showed Tennessee spending $21.02 on each white child, as compared to $11.88 on each black child. Illustrative of the quantity change, however, was the fact that in 1876 the value of all Tennessee's public schools, including furniture, was $1,011,854, whereas in 1930 the value of rural elementary schools for blacks alone was $1,666,671.[77] Philanthropic aid, therefore, particularly from the Rosenwald Fund, had an obvious impact.

TABLE 2

Average Monthly Salaries for Elementary
Teachers in Tennessee, 1930

County				City			
White		Black		White		Black	
Men	Women	Men	Women	Men	Women	Men	Women
$86.87	$77.01	$69.72	$63.27	$143.19	$104.47	$89.84	$85.22

SOURCE: State of Tennessee, *Annual Report of the Department of Education for the Scholastic Year ending June 30, 1930*, 116.

The work of the General Education Board, the Slater and Rosenwald funds, and the Jeanes Foundation was vital in Tennessee. In the eyes of most whites in the state, blacks had been and

[76]*Annual Report* (1930), 106–12; *Thomas* v. *Hibbits, et al.*, 202 District Ct. M.D. Tenn., 46 F. Supp. 368 (1942).

[77]Commission on Interracial Cooperation, *Race Relations in 1927* (Atlanta, 1927), cited in Scott Nearing, *Black America* (New York: Vanguard, 1929), 61; *Annual Report of the State Superintendent of Public Instruction for Tennessee for the Scholastic Year ending June 30, 1906*, 132; *Annual Report* (1930), 124.

continued to be marginal citizens; their improvement was justified only if it did not detract from white progress. Philanthropy served to make Negro education more advantageous by lowering its costs to Tennessee taxpayers. Moreover, the concern shown by these agencies had a profound effect on the black man's outlook. Black schools had been almost entirely dependent upon the local sentiment of white school boards and had to be satisfied with what these white administrators cared to give them. As a result of the state agents for Negro schools, the Jeanes teachers, and the various building programs, black Tennesseans could hope for and occasionally see better days. Not only could they hope, but they could participate in their own improvement.

CHAPTER V.

One Agricultural and Industrial State Normal School for Negroes

The founding and success of the Tennessee Agricultural and Industrial State Normal School (Tennessee A & I) was a significant milestone for black Tennesseans. Rarely had they labored so long and so persistently to extract a major concession from the white system. Nashville's leaders, again, played many of the early roles in the drama, but most of the state's black communities voiced their encouragement and support. J. C. Napier, testifying before a congressional investigating committee in 1912, expressed the underlying attitude of the black supporters of the school—an attitude repeatedly stressed by the campaigners of the Southern Education Board: "We aspire to be not ornaments, not puppets set up to look at, but useful, law-abiding, industrious and productive citizens. As such we are trying to grow into that usefulness that will be approved by the entire country, and we only ask that assistance that all others have."[1] When the first draft of the general education bill of 1909 was expanded to include provisions for "the industrial education of negroes and for preparing negro teachers for common schools," black Tennesseans deserved much credit.[2] The fight was not over, but their persistence had begun to pay dividends. The pride subsequently taken in Tennessee A & I

[1] *Hearings Before the Committee on Agriculture*, House Report, 62nd Cong., 2nd sess. on H.R. 23581, April 23, 24, 25, 26, 1912, p. 73. Located in Napier Papers, container 1.
[2] *Biennial Report of the State Superintendent of Public Instruction for Tennessee for the Scholastic Year Ending June 30, 1910*, 45.

by blacks throughout the state reflected the importance of their achievement, limited though it may have been by white political control.

The leading role played by Nashville's black community in keeping the higher education movement alive can perhaps be explained by a unique set of racial circumstances in the Nashville area. The descendants of house servants and free Negroes had a long-standing relationship with the progeny of the old Southern aristocracy of Middle Tennessee, a relationship based on the paternalism of the dominant group. A large, generally well-educated, black upper class articulated grievances that were at least listened to by white leaders. And the blatant prejudice exhibited by a large majority of whites in Middle Tennessee constantly pricked the sensibilities of the black leadership. This combination of paternalism, articulation, and chafing prejudice produced in these blacks the confidence to speak out boldly and the desire to sustain reform efforts (as expressed even more aggressively in the streetcar boycotts a few years earlier). Also, the issue-oriented and outspoken Nashville *Globe* gave blacks in that city a voice that Negroes in East and West Tennessee lacked.

The educational crusades at the turn of the century popularized the issue of agricultural and industrial training for black Tennesseans, but they did not initiate either the idea or the efforts at implementation. In theory, the issue goes back to the Morrill Act of 1862. All citizens came under this allocation of land-grant college funds, although the endowment was dispensed "in such manner as the legislatures of the several states . . . respectively prescribe[d]."[3] With no specific provision made for the racial distribution of funds, only four states (Virginia, Kentucky, Mississippi, and South Carolina) directed any of this "agricultural and mechanical" aid to black students. Sporadic black protests occurred in Tennessee, but the protesters gained little hearing.[4]

[3] R. Grann Lloyd, *Tennessee Agricultural and Industrial State University, 1912–1962* (Nashville: privately printed, 1962), 4.
[4] Roy V. Scott notes Mississippi's use of federal funds at Alcorn College in his "Land

Congress passed a second Morrill Act in 1890, which increased the original appropriations but withheld funds from any state not including Negroes in its benefits. The new provisions did not require integration; the requirements could be fulfilled by maintaining separate colleges, so long as the funds were equitably distributed. By 1896, all the former Confederate states except Tennessee had established separate land-grant colleges for Negroes.[5]

In a move that bordered on the fraudulent and certainly violated the state constitution, the Tennessee General Assembly, in order to qualify under the 1890 act, declared that the Negro department of its agriculture school was operated by the Presbyterian-controlled Knoxville College. The federal land-grant funds went directly to the University of Tennessee and then purportedly were distributed to the black school. Since state laws prohibited both aid to denominational schools and co-education of the races in public institutions, the arrangement was unconvincing.[6] In reality, the nefarious procedure got no farther than paper, and by 1901, some black citizens began to take public notice of the illegal discrimination. Several prominent Negroes petitioned the legislature in that year to provide a separate "mechanical college for the colored race." Representative John

Grants For Higher Education in Mississippi: A Survey," *Agricultural History* 43 (July 1969), 365. Dwight Oliver Wendell Holmes points out a very complicated arrangement which channeled some funds to Chaflin University in South Carolina in his book *The Evolution of the Negro College* (New York: Teachers College, Columbia Univ., 1934), 150–51. Napier notes the use of funds in Virginia and Kentucky in his testimony included in *Hearings Before the Committee on Agriculture*, 74. Protests against Tennessee's neglect are included in Joseph Howard Cartwright, "Black Legislators in Tennessee in the 1880's: A Case Study in Black Political Leadership," *Tennessee Historical Quarterly* 32 (Fall 1973), 273–74.

[5]Rayford W. Logan, *The Negro in American Life and Thought: The Nadir, 1877–1901* (New York: Dial, 1954), 367. The reasons for Tennessee's singular lag in black land-grant education await additional scholarly attention. Contributing factors would undoubtedly include the relative political impotence of the Negro population, the absence of a clear-cut period of black Reconstruction, and the control of Republican party and federal patronage influence by white East Tennessee.

[6]*Hearings Before the Committee on Agriculture*, 74–76.

Paul Murphy of Knoxville introduced a bill to this effect, but it was routinely tabled.[7]

The issue of equitable sharing of federal funds remained alive, and on February 16, 1903 Nashville's John Houston Burrus, a wealthy black businessman and educator, wrote a very pointed public letter to the Nashville *American*. Carefully itemizing the financial benefits owed the black youth of Tennessee, Burrus maintained that the Negroes of the state should have received approximately one-fourth (based on population percentage) of all federal monies given Tennessee under the Morrill acts; of the $1,136,000 received, he said, "the colored youth of the state were entitled to the benefits of $288,000." In pleading for action, Burrus conventionally reminded the white lawmakers that "increasing the agricultural and mechanical knowledge of those who labor . . . tends to increase the prosperity of the State."[8]

Less blatant, but more extensive, discrimination occurred in the allocation of funds for normal training of black teachers. The General Assembly of 1875 had taken over the facilities of the independent and financially hard-pressed University of Nashville and, with the aid of the Peabody Educational Fund, had established a state normal school for white teachers.[9] This school expanded its program under increased Peabody funding and after a large endowment bequest in 1908 became the privately controlled George Peabody College for Teachers. But proposed ap-

[7]*House Journal of the Fifty-Second General Assembly of the State of Tennessee*, 1901, pp. 153, 471.

[8]Nashville *American*, Feb. 16, 1903. John Houston Burrus was one of three brothers who migrated to Nashville after the Civil War. He and his brothers, James Dallas and Preston R. Burrus, attended Fisk University from the school's beginning. They accumulated considerable real-estate wealth in their various professions of teacher-lawyer, teacher-pharmacist, and teacher-physician, respectively. John Houston Burrus knew well the workings of Morrill funds at state black colleges, for he served as president of Alcorn A & M College in Mississippi from 1883 to 1893. Failing health led him to retire to Nashville, where he maintained his close interest in Negro higher education until his death in 1917. Nashville *American*, Feb. 24, 1903; Nashville *Globe*, Sept. 4, 1908, March 30, 1917; *Crisis* 36 (March 1929), 90.

[9]*Annual Report of the State Superintendent of Public Instruction for Tennessee for the Scholastic Year ending June 30, 1906*, 83–84.

propriations for a state-supported black normal school, as with black public education in general, aroused little interest. In 1881 Isaac F. Norris, a black legislator from Shelby County, had presented a petition from a group of black educators asking for a normal school for Negroes, but the General Assembly took no action.[10] The state provided funds for a few summer training institutes, but their irregularity caused resentment among black teachers, who wanted more training and felt it should be offered at public expense. The Colored State Teachers Association, meeting at Chattanooga in 1896, publicly condemned existing conditions and adopted a resolution "urging the claims of the colored people . . . toward receiving recognition in the state appropriations for normal work."[11]

Only scant improvement occurred before 1909. The 1901 legislature made available a total of $55,600 for teacher training in Tennessee, designating $6,600 of this appropriation for blacks in the form of scholarships. Following a precedent set by a much smaller allotment in 1881, "the appropriation . . . was distributed to approved colored normal colleges toward the payment of expenses for two colored students from each of the state's thirty-three senatorial districts."[12] This expenditure for black training amounted to less than one-half the fair proportion (one-fourth) of the total funds provided, and since all approved normal colleges were outside Tennessee, the individual one-hundred-dollar grant did not permit very extensive study. For a brief period, the state paid the way of "four or five students" to the private colleges of Fisk and Roger Williams, but this token appropriation was halted by the 1905 legislature.[13] Several prominent black citizens of Middle Tennessee, including Dr. Robert Fulton Boyd of Nashville and Dr. J. S. Bass of Murfreesboro, proposed the incorpora-

[10] Cartwright, "Black Legislators in Tennessee in the 1880's," 273.
[11] James Hathaway Robinson, "A Social History of the Negro in Memphis and Shelby County" (Ph.D. diss., Yale Univ., 1934), 172–73.
[12] Holt, *Struggle for Public Schools*, 81–82.
[13] Nashville *Globe*, Jan. 25, 1907.

tion of a summer normal institute and industrial college near Tullahoma to be owned by blacks,[14] but the plan failed for lack of financial support.

Still the legislature ignored the situation. An ill-fated bill, introduced in 1905 to create "a State Normal School in each of the three Grand Divisions," had shown that there was increased interest in supporting teacher training for whites, but it had made no mention of Negro normal training.[15] Until the black population began to organize and direct its criticism and appeals toward white educational paternalists and reluctant, caste-conscious legislators, the only Negro normal training in Tennessee was provided by church schools, most of which were supported by Northern philanthropy.

In order to be successful in Tennessee, proponents of black normal schools had to accept the philosophy of industrial education for Negroes, which implied social limitations upon the Negro race. The campaigns of the Southern Education Board endorsed the "trades" idea, and black leaders throughout the state enthusiastically added their support. The Nashville community, however, first translated the industrial training approach into the field of higher education, and, in effect, opened the door to both Morrill funds and a normal program for industrial education teachers.

When the *Globe* complained in 1908 that black taxpayers were "compelled to send their children to other states for industrial training," it studiously avoided putting open blame upon whites, professing that "the Negroes feel that they are largely to blame." Instead, the *Globe* editor took an indirect slap at the much-publicized "talented tenth" program of W. E. B. Du Bois, which

---

[14] Nashville *American*, Feb. 3, 1901. Another indication of black teacher concern was the determination of Davidson County's Negro educators to hold a summer normal institute even though the state superintendent refused them funds. "The teachers voted a tax upon themselves for . . . incidental expenses, and the instructors agreed to give their services free. . . ." *Ibid.*, June 2, 1903.

[15] *Ibid.*, Jan. 1, 1905.

was oriented toward academic education. The editor implied that black Tennesseans had put too much stress upon academics in higher education, "and as a result the Negro youth of other Southern states are out-stripping the black sons of the Volunteer State in the commercial world, and as scientific laborers."[16] The *Globe* campaigned hard for more industrial education in Tennessee, and on numerous occasions went out of its way to reject Du Bois and other blacks who insisted that Negroes needed the same kind of education as whites. On July 4, 1911 the editor assured whites that "the rank and file of the Negroes in Tennessee have buried their desires for office holding and instead are centering their efforts upon material progress. . . . They have learned that a trained mind without a trained hand is like a ship without a rudder or steam raised in a boiler without a valve."[17]

After making this practical concession to caste, the *Globe* and many black spokesmen in Nashville refused to be content with continued discrimination in state and federal funds. Taking direct action, they appealed to the General Assembly for approval of normal school appropriations, and they investigated the existing use of federal monies. In 1907 a committee of Negroes visited the education committee of the legislature and urged an appropriation for "a State institution where Negro children could get the benefit of an education, aided by the State as the other Southern states are doing." And during a summer meeting in Nashville in 1908, a state convention of black Baptist churches called for an "institution of learning for people of color, maintained by the state."[18] Realizing, however, that such appeals to state officials

[16] Nashville *Globe*, Nov. 13, 1908. For evidence that black students from Tennessee were going to other states to receive normal and industrial training, see the Indianapolis *Freeman*, Sept. 30, 1905. W. E. B. Du Bois was the foremost black spokesman for the view that the most essential group in any race was its "talented tenth." He feared that the new emphasis upon industrial education would mean the neglect of liberal arts and professional training for this elite.

[17] Nashville *Globe*, June 19, 1908, April 29, 1910, July 14, 1911.

[18] *Ibid.*, Oct. 9, 1908; Nashville *Tennessean*, July 26, 1908. The weight of *Globe* opinion is very roughly gathered from a white estimate of its readership at approximately 20,000 blacks. This estimate is found in the *Commercial Daily* (Nashville), March 5, 1918,

had made little progress in the past, black leaders simultaneously raised the question of Morrill funds. In 1907, the *Globe* reported a movement "to make a thorough investigation of these funds . . . that appear to be misappropriated so far as the Negro youth is concerned"; in 1908, a grudging trickle of money began to find its way to Knoxville College for the "agricultural training" of a few black students, but this amounted to only $3,000 in four years.[19]

J. C. Napier took a special interest in the distribution of federal funds. His contacts in Washington and in the Republican party went back to his days at the Howard University Law School and as a patronage holder in the 1870s. He and his wife still visited Washington regularly (she was the daughter of former black congressman John Mercer Langston), and he was perhaps more comfortable dealing with federal than with state officials. As an active member of the board of trustees of the Anna T. Jeanes Fund, Napier realized the need for more and better-trained black teachers in his state. Futhermore, he had become fully aware of the importance of federal aid to agricultural and mechanical schools in other Southern states.[20] Napier's first step in February 1908 was to set up a "special conference" with Brown Ayres, president of the University of Tennessee. Accompanied by James Hardy Dillard of the Jeanes Fund, Napier sought to determine exactly how the university dispensed its Morrill money. After this discussion, he went to a "national meeting of state superintendents" in Washington, where he repeated his appeal for equitable distribution of funds. The *Globe* followed Napier's travels closely. "It is to be hoped," exclaimed the optimistic editor, ". . . that the question of erecting a school where black children can profit from

---

located in the Gov. Tom C. Rye Papers, Tennessee State Library and Archives, container 38.

[19] Nashville *Globe*, Jan. 25, 1907; *Hearings Before the Committee on Agriculture*, 76.

[20] Napier Papers, especially container 1, include much correspondence with educational leaders concerning the Morrill funds. Among the correspondents are: Booker T. Washington of Tuskegee Institute, Walter S. Buchanan, president of the Alabama State Agricultural and Mechanical College for Negroes, and George A. Gates, the white president of Fisk University.

the money appropriated by the state and federal governments, will be pushed to a speedy conclusion."[21]

State support, especially for normal training, took on special importance as the fall elections of 1908 approached. The crusades of the Southern Education Board seemed sure to win a sympathetic legislature, and blacks pointedly insisted that they should benefit from the success. On hearing in September 1908 that state superintendent of education R. L. Jones planned to recommend the establishment of three new normal schools in Tennessee, the *Globe* editorialized that "one of these new normal schools . . . the one in Middle Tennessee where the whites have the Peabody Normal School with its million dollar endowment . . . should be for the use of the Negroes in the state." Two months later, the newspaper complained that "this making of wards of the white child and outcasts of the colored is not fair and we believe that if the proper effort is put forth to impress the members of the legislature of its unfairness, that body, with the support of the Governor Malcolm R. Patterson, who had recently received much black political support against a "lily white" Republican will be brought to change it."[22]

The *Globe*, under the direction of Dock A. Hart and Henry Allen Boyd, pursued the issue beyond its own editorial pages. Fearing "promises but no action" from the legislature, Hart and Boyd proposed the formation of an organization that could mobilize the black people of the state in a coordinated effort to make their needs and wishes known. After sending out letters to leading black citizens, the two men convened a meeting in Nashville on January 16, 1909, which was attended by representatives from nine of the ten congressional districts, excepting only the mountainous Third. The Tennessee Normal, Agricultural and Mechanical Association materialized, with Henry A. Boyd as chairman.[23] Most support and action came from Nashville, but

[21]Nashville *Globe*, Feb. 28, March 6, 1908.
[22]*Ibid.*, Sept. 11, Nov. 6, 1908.
[23]*Ibid.*, Aug. 7, Dec. 4, 1908, Jan. 22, 1909.

more importantly, legislative lobbying for a state normal school and the forces behind the Morrill fund appeal had now combined to make a single request for a teacher training school that would emphasize industrial education and that would benefit from the Morrill Act.

Even though blacks and whites constantly emphasized the wisdom of industrial education for Negroes, the general education bill of 1909 originally made no distinction between the type of normal schools to be provided for white and black teachers (four in total, one black and three white). There was immediate reaction from both sides. Fearing continued exclusion from Morrill funds, the *Globe* urged amendments providing that blacks "not only be prepared for teaching in the literary branches, but also other useful industrial arts." Later, some whites claimed that black students were already under the educational umbrella of the University of Tennessee; if this were true, the editor retorted, "no one has been able so far to find them."[24] Meanwhile, several West Tennessee legislators objected heatedly to the lack of distinctions between the normal schools for the two races. Ironically, this insistence upon caste distinctions eventually worked to the advantage of the black school. In order to specify "a distinctly definite, different and important purpose," the education bill was amended to create an "Agricultural and Industrial State Normal School for Negroes." Although the final act declared that "the courses of study [at Tennessee A & I] . . . shall be of such practical nature as to fit the conditions and needs of their race," and although the measure did not mention applying federal funds to the institution, the name and curriculum provisions meant that, in the words of the school's historian, "A. & I. *could serve* as Tennessee's normal school as well as its land-grant college for Negroes."[25]

[24]*Ibid.*, Feb. 5, April 9, 1909.
[25]*Acts of the State of Tennessee* (Nashville, 1909), ch. 264, section 7; Horton, "Origins and Development of the State College Movement," 41; Lloyd, *Tennessee Agricultural and Industrial State University*, 5; Holt, *Struggle for Public Schools*, 103. Author's italics.

The battle, however, had not ended for black Tennesseans. The original appropriation for their institution amounted to only $16,700, as opposed to $33,430 for each white normal school. It was at this point that the *Globe* reacted with such frustration: "Is the old saying true that half a loaf is better than no loaf at all?" Should blacks, indeed, now "be exceeding glad for this generous half of a loaf?"[26] In addition, there were still no specific provisions for equitable sharing in federal funds. Continued lobbying finally produced an act in July 1911 "which stipulated that the school should receive 'its just and equitable portion of funds appropriated under Acts of Congress.' "[27] Statutory victories were meaningless, however, unless white administrators accepted them. As late as April 1912, J. C. Napier still complained to the Committee on Agriculture of the United States House of Representatives that "We have never gotten our full proportion of it [Morrill money], and I wish I could get the ear of some authority that would see that we simply get what the law provides us." To a similar appeal Philander P. Claxton, now the United States Commissioner of Education, replied lamely, "Well we are doing the best we can."[28]

Blacks also discovered that the 1909 legislation did not provide for buildings nor faculty, nor did it even select a site for their school. Waiting began immediately. On the white side of the educational fence, however, events moved more rapidly. By the fall of 1909 an official committee had toured the state to determine locations for the three white normal schools; bids came quickly from competing communities; and construction work began in the summer of 1910. This enabled at least two of the white institutions (West Tennessee Normal was delayed by legislative

[26] Nashville *Globe*, March 12, 1909.

[27] Lloyd, *Tennessee Agricultural and Industrial State University*, 7. This bill passed only after much opposition in the lower house. See *Senate Journal of the Fifty-Seventh General Assembly of the State of Tennessee*, 1911, 944, 969; Nashville *Globe*, July 14, 1911.

[28] *Hearings Before the Committee on Agriculture*, 76.

technicalities) to open in 1911, the year that the state finally decided on a site for the black school.[29]

The slow evolution of Tennessee A & I was largely, though not entirely, the result of white control. The $16,700 legislative allocation hardly sufficed to buy property, build classrooms, and pay salaries. The General Assembly had intended that local communities raise the funds to create each of the four colleges. Cities and towns openly competed for the white schools, but they seemed to shy away from the black college. A certain distrust and fear of educated Negroes remained in the South. Partly as a result of this distrust no serious proposal for the black school ever came from West Tennesse, although having 50 percent of the state's black population made it the logical region for the school.[30] In Middle Tennessee, blacks in Columbia and Murfreesboro tried to generate enthusiasm in their communities, but only Nashville and the East Tennessee city of Chattanooga made serious attempts to get the agricultural and industrial school.[31] The problem was race, and the major obstacle was money.

Leadership was the key to overcoming these obstacles, as it was in stimulating any black assertiveness in Tennessee. Poverty and white control dulled the enthusiasm of the black masses. Henry Allen Boyd tried to stimulate statewide interest in the institution but became discouraged when blacks in the state did not show "the proper interest in this school."[32] Even the more vocal black citizens of Nashville were slow to respond to a call which affected their pocketbooks. By December 1909, however, the Negro leaders of the capital city had begun a drive for funds from both black and white sources. Wealthy minister-undertaker Preston Taylor led a "door-to-door canvass" of the black neighborhoods "in an effort to raise $10,000 for the purchase of a farm and

[29]*Biennial Report* (1911–1912), 295, 324; Nashville *Globe*, Nov. 12, 1909, Jan. 1, 1911.
[30]See ch. 4; Memphis *Commercial Appeal*, March 27, 1928; Bureau of the Census, *Thirteenth Census of the United States: 1910. Population*, III, 762–64.
[31]Nashville *Globe*, Oct. 8, Dec. 31, 1909.
[32]*Ibid.*, Nov. 26, 1909.

99

buildings to be offered as enducements," while Benjamin J. Carr spearheaded an appeal for a bond issue from the county court.[33] Carr, a successful black farmer from Trousdale County, had only recently moved permanently to Nashville. Often called the "Farmer-Citizen of Tennessee" by the *Globe*, this small, alert man was president of the state's Negro Farmers Alliance and also a strong supporter of Democratic Governor Patterson.[34] This political stand gave Carr influence with the heavily Democratic county court—influence which even the much-respected J. C. Napier could not have provided.

Carr, Napier, and Boyd went before the Davidson County Court, which passed a bond appropriation of $40,000.[35] The enthusiasm which the county's initial action stimulated was soon tempered by the citizens of Nashville. The all-white city council approved $25,000 in city bonds for the normal school but decided to put the measure before the electorate. White paternalism and political influence did not extend to the population at large, and the bond issue was defeated by nearly a two-to-one margin.[36] Black leaders had publicly stressed the industrial nature of the school and had constantly reminded the white community of past Negro support for raising taxes to finance a new white high school. Their persistence in campaigning for the black college seemed to make Nashville a natural location, but firm racial convictions and tight purse strings remained unmoved. Even the margins of support in the large black wards were disappointing, indicating that active black interest did not extend far beyond the community leaders.

Chattanooga, meanwhile, took definite steps to acquire the school. William Jasper Hale, an ambitious young black teacher, had used his position as an elementary school principal to raise some $11,500 from blacks in that city, and, supported by many

[33] *Ibid.*, Dec. 10, 1909, March 18, May 6, 1910.
[34] *Ibid.*, April 8, 1910; Nashville *Tennessean*, July 30, 1909.
[35] Nashville *Globe*, April 8, 1910, Feb. 17, 1911.
[36] Nashville *Banner*, Nov. 9, 1910; Nashville *Globe*, Nov. 11, 1910.

prominent white men, he had obtained a promise of $60,000 from the Hamilton County Court. In the face of this opposition and Nashville's bond-issue rejection, the *Globe* lamented that "Nashville demonstrated beyond any question that [it was] not favorable to the location of the Normal School for Negroes in this city."[37] Chattanooga's apparent victory was short-lived, however, when a second meeting of the Davidson County Court responded to new pleas from Ben Carr and Henry Allen Boyd by promising $40,000 in additional bonds. Nashville now became the choice of the State Board of Education. The *Globe* was quick to point out that the Democratic mayor of Nashville, Hilary Howse, and the much-praised Governor Patterson deserved large credit for bringing "victory out of defeat."[38] Both of these men counted on considerable black political support, and they apparently convinced the Board of Education to wait for Ben Carr's second appeal to the county court before making a decision.

All was not yet lost for the indomitable W. J. Hale. Allegedly related to R. L. Jones, the superintendent of Hamilton County schools who had recently become state superintendent, Hale had benefited greatly in his career from influential white friends. Outstanding ability often died in black America from want of opportunity. Hale lacked advanced formal education, but he lacked neither ability nor opportunity. Shortly after making Nashville the site for the new school, Superintendent Jones named Hale the "principal" of the institution. (The top administrators of the white schools were considered "presidents.") Hale served at this post (later as president) from 1911 until his retirement in 1943. In addition to the principal, the first faculty of Tennessee A & I included "three graduates of Atlanta University, three graduates of Fisk, one graduate of Hampton, one graduate of Howard and two graduates of Northern Universities."[39]

[37] Lloyd, *Tennessee Agricultural and Industrial State University*, iii–iv; Nashville *Globe*, Oct. 28, 1910.
[38] Nashville *Globe*, Jan. 13, 1911, April 19, 1935.
[39] *Crisis* 4 (June 1912), 62. The blood relationship between Hale and Jones was

Born in a time of political turmoil in the state and brought to maturity during a period of racial unrest, Tennessee A & I survived, and even thrived, largely through the efforts of William Jasper Hale.[40] The Board of Education knew the kind of school it wanted, and it sent Hale to Hampton and Tuskegee institutes in order to gain a proper perspective. Hale's subsequent educational conservatism won no accolades from radicals, but he was an accomplished politician and devoted to his school—a local Booker T. Washington, perhaps. Washington, not surprisingly, was lavish in his praise of Hale's work. When the thirty-seven-year-old Chattanoogan moved to Nashville, many predicted that his school "was doomed to failure." He faced the ever-present white suspicions, on the one hand, and an obvious rejection by some of Nashville's black "liberal arts types," on the other. Although sympathetic to the virtues of a more "liberal" curriculum, Hale reasoned that the best way to avoid defeat was to take active part in the black community and to praise even the "half-loaf" offering of the whites.[41] Such an approach enabled Hale to survive and prosper even after R. L. Jones departed. Ben Carr's political partisanship made him less adaptable. He was appointed superintendent of the new school's farm in 1911, but he had no special agricultural training (as the Morrill Act required) and was replaced when the Republican-Fusionist faction gained full control of the state's patronage in 1912.[42]

---

mentioned in interviews with Carl A. Cowan on June 29, 1970, Mr. and Mrs. J. Herman Daves on July 2, 1970, Mr. and Mrs. A. E. Lockert on July 16, 1970, and George W. Gore on June 21, 1972. Hale was a man of some wealth, even at this early stage in his career, and he had a close connection with the major financial institution in the area, the Hamilton National Bank. Interview with James L. Jenkins, June 9, 1972; letter from Mrs. W. J. Hale to the author, April 27, 1974.

[40] Political turmoil is chronicled in Paul E. Isaac, *Prohibition and Politics: Turbulent Decades in Tennessee, 1886–1920* (Knoxville: Univ. of Tennessee Press, 1965). Racial unrest is discussed in some detail in ch. 11.

[41] *Biennial Report* (1913–1914), 229, 230; letter from Mrs. W. J. Hale to the author, April 27, 1974.

[42] Nashville *Globe*, May 9, 1913. Carr did not leave Tennessee A & I willingly, and he blamed W. J. Hale for his dismissal. He persistently urged each new Democratic governor to investigate the school in an effort to have Hale removed. Samuel Leonard Smith,

In order to keep the goodwill of the all-important General Assembly, Hale regularly entertained the legislators at banquets, lining up as many as fifty-nine locally black-owned automobiles to transport the guests to the campus. On other occasions, the dubious practice of using the school's tailor shop "to make suits of clothing for certain members of the Board of Education" was reported.[43] Such methods apparently paid financial dividends for the struggling institution. In 1913, the legislature finally committed a proportionate share of Morrill funds to black education. A bill was passed, without dissent, "to relieve the University of Tennessee of the responsibility of the education of Negroes."[44] By 1916, Tennessee A & I was receiving $12,000 in federal money per year, a figure that amounted to approximately one-fourth of the Morrill funds available to Tennessee.[45]

Student and faculty life was rigorous during the early years at the new institution. The campus consisted of three buildings on a poorly developed farm overlooking the Cumberland River, more than a mile from the Nashville city limits. The land was exceptionally rugged and rocky, with no graded roads or sidewalks. Manual labor (at least one hour per day) was required of all students, and President Hale periodically declared a "Clean Up Day" in which the faculty and employees also joined in efforts to clear rocks, construct roadways, and generally improve the appearance of the campus. Using student help, the college farm consistently operated at a profit, and the money-conscious legislature was duly impressed. The spartan atmosphere at Tennessee A & I included very sparse furnishings in all the buildings. "In

---

Rosenwald general field agent for rural schools, to Dr. Francis W. Shepardson, secretary and acting director, the Julius Rosenwald Fund, Feb. 17, 1922, Julius Rosenwald Fund Archives, Fisk Univ., container 155.

[43] Nashville *Globe*, March 9, 1917; *Crisis* 14 (May 1917), 39; Nashville *Tennessean*, Feb. 12, 1922.

[44] John Allen Buggs, "Racial Legislation in Tennessee" (M.A. thesis, Fisk Univ., 1941), 114; *Senate Journal of the Fifty-Eighth General Assembly of the State of Tennessee*, 1913, 78, 87, 131, 449, 462, 471, 521.

[45] Jones, *Negro Education*, I, 312.

1912 each student had to carry his chair from one classroom to the the other, to Chapel, and/or to the dining hall; to get his own water from a spring . . . ; and sleep in crowded rooms, on stairway landings, and in dormitory halls. Often boards were placed across chairs to provide enough space for everyone to have a seat." Soon the school's workshop began to turn out a variety of tables, chairs, desks, and benches. In the early years, the institution's motto, "Think, Work, Serve," seemed to put special emphasis upon "Work." The legislature looked favorably upon the atmosphere created by W. J. Hale, and soon appealed to the city of Nashville to aid the school's struggle by extending streetcar lines and fire and police protection to the campus.[46]

Rising racial tensions in the state made Hale's job unusually challenging in the years 1917 to 1922. He become a leader in the interracial movement and worked diligently to use his school as a unifying force among the black population of Tennessee. He led war bond drives and stimulated wartime patriotism (if also postwar controversy) by administering a military training program at Tennessee A & I. Hale succeeded to an extent that more "radical" and racially "proud" leaders did not. Although he may have had private reservations, Hale publicly endorsed the Booker T. Washington "ideal" and catered to white paternalism. In this sense, he was a reflector rather than a molder of black thought. He won white support (as seen in a generally favorable local white press), but he also appealed successfully to the tradition-oriented blacks of Tennessee. By 1930, blacks and whites alike considered Hale the most prominent and powerful Negro in the state.[47]

The forging of some unifying bond among black Tennesseans required perseverance and devotion. The black population exhib-

[46] Lloyd, *Tennessee Agricultural and Industrial State University*, 11; *House Journal of the Sixtieth General Assembly of the State of Tennessee*, 1917, cited in Horton, "Origins and Development of the State College Movement," 95; letter from Mrs. W. J. Hale to the author, April 27, 1974.

[47] Personal interviews with James L. Jenkins, June 9, 1972; George W. Gore, June 21, 1972; Walter S. Davis, June 19, 1972; H. C. Hardy, June 20, 1972; and Alger V. Boswell, June 20, 1972.

ited every division found in the white citizenry—Middle versus East versus West, upper class versus lower class, and educated versus uneducated. In addition, Hale personally encountered resentment from some Fisk supporters and alumni in Nashville who deplored his limited education and also felt that "if we're going to have a school here, we ought to run it." Hale overcame most of the local animosity and slowly built his school into a binding force among the black communities in Tennessee. Faced with student travel and boarding expenses, the institution easily might have become parochial in its Middle Tennessee location, but Hale personally appeared at Negro meetings, sent exhibits from his school to Negro county fairs, and cultivated black newspapermen throughout the state. In the view of a former dean, the school became a popular, non-elitist, "grass roots" institution.[48]

In order to stimulate enrollment for the official opening in the fall, Hale held a special four-week summer session in June and July 1912. The course drew 247 teachers from several states, but the most impressive support came from eighty of his former colleagues in Hamilton County. They chartered a "special train" to go to Nashville that summer, and until 1927 this county continued to furnish more students for the school than any area but Davidson County. The appeal to Memphis, Jackson, and Knoxville met competition from long-established church-supported colleges, but by 1916 Hale was complaining to the legislature that applications were so numerous that dormitory space needed to be doubled. The growing statewide popularity of the school doomed some of the marginal black "colleges," especially Roger Williams University in Nashville, but this negative impact also served Hale's goal of unity by reducing educational fragmentation.[49]

By 1919 blacks were petitioning their legislative representa-

[48] Memphis *Commercial Appeal*, Oct. 14, 1916; Knoxville *Journal and Tribune*, Oct. 12, 1913; personal interviews with Carl A. Cowan, June 29, 1970, Walter S. Davis, June 19, 1972, H. C. Hardy, June 20, 1972, and George W. Gore, June 21, 1972.

[49] *Biennial Report* (1915–1916), 222; Fuller, *History of the Negro Baptists of Tennessee*, 129; Lloyd, *Tennessee Agricultural and Industrial State University*, 9; letter from Mrs. W. J. Hale to the author, April 27, 1974; Nashville *Globe*, Nov. 22, 1935.

tives to appropriate more money for "dormitory space at State Normal . . . that more girls and boys of this State may be helped by the excellent training given there."[50] A building bond issue of $75,000 in 1921 only temporarily eased crowded conditions. Not until 1925 was sufficient money available to meet demands placed on the institution by its growing popularity. At this time, yielding to a campaign directed by the CIC which had netted $67,000 in private black and white contributions and a $100,000 matching grant from the General Education Board, the Tennessee General Assembly appropriated $160,000 "for the erection of more buildings at A. & I. State Normal College." Still, of the $773,583 in federal money received by Tennessee for higher education in 1927, only the Morrill funds specified racial distribution. In practice, this meant black students (approximately one thousand entered Tennessee A & I in the fall of 1929) continued to receive only $12,000, or 6.5 percent of the amount justified by their proportion of the total population.[51] Among blacks conditioned to token gestures, discrimination in federal funds hardly dimmed enthusiasm for the 1925 legislature's "gift." Appreciative letters came to Governor Austin Peay from blacks throughout the state. During the five-year period, 1922–1927, Knoxville tripled its student participation and enrollment from Memphis increased by four and a half times.[52]

W. J. Hale tried to stay out of partisan state politics and thus maintained his successful working relationship with the governor

[50] Lillian M. White, Negro home demonstration agent in Knox County, to state senator John C. Houk, March 17, 1919, Houk Papers, container 95. Other similar letters are found in the boxes of uncatalogued papers in this collection.

[51] "Comparative Distribution of Federal and State Funds for Collegiate Education of Whites and Negroes in Seventeen States," a statistical compilation made in 1928 for Howard University, Haynes Papers, container "Misc."; *Broadcaster* 2 (Sept. 1929), 16.

[52] *Biennial Report* (1921–1922), 355–57; *Annual Report of the Department of Education for the Scholastic Year Ending June 30, 1927*, 238, 239, 242; Cleveland (Ohio) *Gazette*, May 9, 1925; *Crisis* 30 (June 1925), 75; M. E. Prowell, secretary of the City Federation of Colored Women's Clubs of Chattanooga, to Gov. Austin Peay, Sept. 16, 1925, and Robert E. Clay, Rosenwald agent and executive secretary of the Inter-Racial League of Tennessee, to Gov. Peay, Oct. 12, 1925, Gov. Peay Papers, Tennessee State Library and Archives, container 86.

and legislature. He once remarked to another A & I administrator that "you stay with the man that's in." Hale also utilized a broadening range of political and philanthropic contacts to his school's advantage. In addition to the General Education Board, the Rosenwald Fund was especially generous, providing several buildings, matching funds to improve library holdings, and faculty fellowships for advanced training. Nevertheless, Hale was forced to pinch pennies as he sought to build his institution. He ruled over the school almost by decree, but he benefited greatly from the liaison work of Robert E. Clay. Clay traveled the state during the 1920s using his "barber shop" philosophy to full advantage, whether before potential students, wary legislators, or disgruntled blacks. Clay freed Hale from many time-consuming demands (even cutting his hair), but Tennessee A & I was still Hale's domain, and he was responsible for much of the school's growth.[53]

Other important factors also contributed to A & I's success. Public education for Tennessee Negroes expanded significantly during the years 1912–1930, and, while elementary and secondary schools were of prime importance, these institutions needed increasing numbers of trained personnel. Nearly all the state's Jeanes teachers were graduates of A & I, and these supervisors carried Hale's message to even the most rural counties.[54] Of further, if somewhat less tangible, significance was the psychological impact of *public* higher education. Obtained only after significant black efforts and administered by a black "principal-president," Tennessee A & I offered not only financial aid but also hope to the entire black community in the state—discouraged parents as well as ambitious but frustrated children.

Although Hale had overcome most early opposition, a few

[53] Horton, "Origins and Development of the State College Movement in Tennessee," 97; Lloyd, *Tennessee Agricultural and Industrial State University*, 38; letter from Mrs. W. J. Hale to the author, April 27, 1974; interviews with Alger V. Boswell, June 20, 1972, and James L. Jenkins, June 9, 1972.
[54] *Biennial Report* (1921–1922), 272.

black Tennesseans remained discontented with the school's narrow curriculum. J. W. Manning, the Yale-educated supervisor of colored schools in Knoxville, explained to state senator John C. Houk that he felt "there [was] urgent need of an institution for Negroes in the State of Tennessee, which will stand somewhat in the same relation to them that U. of T. and Vanderbilt do the white citizens. It need not be a university, still it should be something more than a Normal and Industrial School at Nashville."[55] Manning also resented the continued large role played by church schools, but he spoke for only a small segment of the state's black population.[56] The *Broadcaster*, the official journal of the Tennessee State Association of Teachers in Colored Schools, undoubtedly spoke for the majority in a reflective editorial in 1930: "In establishing the program of industrial education, Booker T. Washington proved himself to be greater than his day and generation. He was the forerunner of a system of education which is coming into its own and demanding respectability from civilized peoples. In an economic age, the producer is king. The theorizer, the pedant and even the philosopher must rank below him." Though a steady flow of students left the state in the late teens and 1920s because of the limited curriculum at A & I, the vast majority of Tennessee's citizenry, black and white, was pleased with the program conducted by Hale's staff.[57] The importance of agricultural and industrial training declined during the 1920s, and the emphasis clearly fell upon normal training with the designation of the institution as a teachers' college in 1922. The legislature in that year increased the training program from two years to four years, required a high school diploma for admission,

[55] J. W. Manning to John C. Houk, Jan. 20, 1917, Houk Papers, container 89.

[56] Nashville *Globe*, Oct. 9, 1908. Four years after Manning's letter, the Knoxville chapter of the NAACP issued a similar complaint against the quality of black teacher training in Tennessee. These protests had some impact in that they encouraged the 1922 expansion of the existing program. Knoxville *Sentinel*, March 12, 1921.

[57] *Broadcaster* 2 (Jan. 1930), 31; interviews with Mr. and Mrs. J. Herman Daves, July 2, 1970, Carl A. Cowan, June 29, 1970, Walter S. Davis, June 19, 1972, and James L. Jenkins, June 9, 1972.

and authorized the offering of a Bachelor of Science degree.[58]

Tennessee Agricultural and Industrial State Normal School remained the stepchild of the state's higher education system. Its program was more restricted and its funding more inadequate than those of white colleges. Yet the question posed by the frustrated Nashville *Globe* in 1909 had apparently been answered by the uniting voices of its black constituency—"Shall we be satisfied with a half loaf?" Twenty years later, the answer came back, "Yes!" Most black Tennesseans accepted limited educational facilities as a matter of course: decades of inferior standards of living and laboring had taken their toll. Negroes were marginal workers in Tennessee's economy, serving as the least prosperous sharecroppers, the smallest farm owners, the lowest-paid and least secure industrial and transportation workers, and the most vulnerable and restricted businessmen. Conditioned to second-class occupations and earnings, most black Tennesseans viewed Tennessee A & I as an institution commensurate with their economic and educational expectations.

[58] Lloyd, *Tennessee Agricultural and Industrial State University,* 25, 40; Horton, "Origins and Development of the State College Movement in Tennessee," 97.

CHAPTER VI.

On the Agricultural Margin

Most Negroes in 1900 earned their livelihood from the soil. In Tennessee over 70 percent of the black population was rural, and, except for a few domestics and sawmill laborers, and scattered schoolteachers and physicians, these men and women were farmers. Either former slaves or the children of former slaves, most of these black Tennesseans lived on the margin of America's social and economic system. They never advanced far beyond subsistence in the best of times and were the first and hardest hit during the worst of times.

Life was difficult. As head of his household, the typical black farmer had to provide food, shelter, and clothing for a wife, four children, and an occasional aged relative. As in agrarian cultures everywhere, however, the man hardly bore these responsibilities alone. His wife, too, and any children more than ten years old worked in the fields from dawn to sunset, taking perhaps an hour at noon for lunch. Smaller children had a minimum of adult supervision. Housing varied, but for the majority it consisted of a two- or three-room cabin, constructed rather loosely of logs or slab boards. Having windows that were shuttered and rarely screened and only a fireplace or secondhand wood stove for heating and cooking, the cabins contained one or two crowded bedrooms and another room which served as a kitchen and living room. Sanitary facilities rarely existed. Household furnishings were sparse, consisting of beds (with straw, shuck, or cotton mattresses), oil lamps, a table and odd chairs, and a variety of cooking and eating utensils. Diet depended upon the nature of land tenure and the kind of farming involved. If the black farmer owned his own land or grew a variety of crops, his family tended to have balanced meals. But if he was engaged in one-crop tenancy or sharecropping (as most were), his family often subsisted upon fat pork (fried in two- or three-inch slices), corn meal, and collard greens. Deficient in vitamins and other nutrients, this diet aggravated health problems and undoubtedly accounted for the prevalence of "stomach trouble."[1]

Although a sizable minority (22.4 percent) of black farmers in Tennessee owned their land in 1900, the average holding was only forty-five acres. Meanwhile, 72 percent of the black farmers were either sharecroppers or cash or share tenants. By comparison, well over one-half of the white farmers in Tennessee owned their own land, averaging almost one hundred acres per farm. Conditions had changed little by 1910; the total number of black farmers had increased slightly and the size of the average farm had fallen to forty-two acres, but the owner-tenant ratio remained unchanged. The percentage of tenancy among Tennessee's farm operators (black and white) continued well above the national average during the years 1900–1930, but was always significantly below the figures for the entire South.[2]

Black farmers living in West Tennessee (65 percent of the state's total) experienced the most difficult conditions. Some owned ample land and prospered, but the great majority simply survived. Whether landowners, sharecroppers, or cash tenants,

[1] Details of living conditions among rural Negroes can be gathered from Carl Kelsey, *The Negro Farmer* (Chicago: Jennings and Pye, 1903), 45–56; Hortense Powdermaker, *After Freedom: A Cultural Study in the Deep South* (New York: Atheneum, 1968), 75–86; and the reminiscences compiled in the Federal Writers' Project, *These Are Our Lives* (Chapel Hill: Univ. of North Carolina Press, 1939), 17–30, 45–54, 61–69, 70–77.
[2] Bureau of the Census, *Twelfth Census of the United States: 1900. Agriculture*, 5 vols. (Washington, D.C.: Government Printing Office, 1901), V, pt. 1, 2, 14, 52; *Thirteenth Census: 1910, Agriculture*, VII, 582, 591; Charles E. Allred and Elmer E. Briner, *Tenure By Type of Farming Areas and Color in Tennessee*, University of Tennessee Agricultural Experiment Station, Rural Research Series Monograph, No. 85, (1938), 3.

ten- to twelve-cent cotton, from "sun up to sun down," was almost certainly their livelihood. Although the cash value of the crop averaged $270 for black farmers, white-owned gins and supply stores took their "cut," leaving scarcely enough income to sustain a large family through the winter. After 1907, the boll weevil demanded a share. If the black farm worker was a sharecropper, as most were, he had a particularly perilous existence. One Negro once explained the situation very succinctly: "Dat's all dey is to expect—work hard and go hungry part time—long as we live on de other man's land." Rarely able to live on his "share," the "cropper" was forced to borrow from the white farm owner or merchant. Prices of goods bought on time by sharecroppers and tenants averaged about 65 percent higher in Tennessee than prices of goods bought with cash. Therefore, it was not unknown for the black Tennessean to find himself in a state of peonage— regularly falling deeper into debt and subject to violence if he attempted to break the downward spiral by moving away.[3] A survey, for example, taken from a similar cotton-belt region in 1898 showed 60 percent of the farmers going in debt for the year, 20 percent breaking even, and 20 percent making a profit. Although some profits would later go as high as $1,000, the typical return would be only $50 or $60. Most cabins treasured copies of Montgomery Ward and Sears and Roebuck catalogs, and a few special pages were preserved for ordering "a string of clothes" should money be available.[4]

From spring through fall, black tenants and sharecroppers had little trouble finding farm work. In fact, white landowners pre-

[3] Rupert Bayless Vance, *Human Factors in Cotton Culture: A Study in the Social Geography of the American South* (Chapel Hill: Univ. of North Carolina Press, 1929), 95, 116–17, 176–77; interview with Grady E. Walker, June 19, 1973; Federal Writers' Project, *These Are Our Lives*, 20; P. O. Davis, "The Negro Exodus and Southern Agriculture," *Review of Reviews and World's Work* 68 (Oct. 1923), 407; Nashville *American*, March 30, 1905; letter in Memphis *Commercial Appeal*, n.d., quoted in Herbert Jacob Seligmann, *The Negro Faces America* (New York: Harper, 1920), 222. The best general study of peonage is Pete Daniel, *The Shadow of Slavery: Peonage in the South, 1901–1969* (New York: Oxford Univ. Press, 1972).
[4] Kelsey, *The Negro Farmer*, 52, 56; Federal Writers' Project, *These Are Our Lives*, 22.

ferred Negro laborers because they had little recourse when cheated or browbeaten. As expected, black workers preferred to work for black landowners; there they usually sold their own crop, thus insuring fairer treatment and higher profits. Yet only a relatively few Tennessee Negroes owned enough land to need additional labor, and the vast majority of black sharecroppers worked for whites. Under these circumstances, the only recourse to injustice was to move elsewhere. Black farm families were, therefore, highly mobile. Assuming they could get out of debt, they moved annually, losing any vestiges of voting rights (due to residency requirements) and disrupting their children's limited access to formal education.[5]

Blacks who labored for wages fared well during the growing season; demand for their services was high, and average monthly wages steadily increased from $12.83 in 1898 to $23.13 by 1913. At cotton-picking time additional women and children joined the work force, contributing significantly to the economic struggle for existence. Wage labor, even more than sharecropping, however, was seasonal, and during the long winter months there were few sources of income. Some men found employment cutting and hauling wood, and women raised chickens, made quilts, and earned some cash by doing occasional washing and ironing. But for most, winter was a time of inactivity and an even poorer diet. One black man who grew up in Hardin County remembered, seventy years later, that the winter diet consisted of potatoes and corn meal which had been laid by during the last summer.[6]

Security was a scarce commodity among black farm workers in Tennessee. Land ownership had been a high goal for forty years,

[5] Some discussion of this process is found in Powdermaker, *After Freedom*, 81–88.

[6] Charles Harris Wesley, *Negro Labor in the United States, 1850–1925* (New York: Vanguard, 1927), 228; C. O. Brannen, *Relation of Land Tenure to Plantation Organization*, United States Department of Agriculture, Bulletin 1269 (1928), 27; Lorenzo J. Greene and Carter G. Woodson, *The Negro Wage Earner* (Washington, D.C.: Association for the Study of Negro Life and History, 1930), 51–52; Powdermaker, *After Freedom*, 83; Federal Writers' Project, *These Are Our Lives*, 69; interview with Grady E. Walker, June 19, 1973.

but success had not been easy. For a time after the Civil War, land had been relatively cheap, and Tennessee had attracted colony-type migrations from other states. Even sharecropping seemed a natural transition between landlessness and landowning; a few years of profitable "cropping" could provide money for the purchasing price. But as early as 1875, black Tennesseans had begun to complain of organized efforts to prevent land sales to Negroes. In addition, once land passed from black to white hands, it became almost impossible to retrieve. The cotton culture, involving over 50 percent of all black farm labor in Tennessee and stretching eastward almost to Nashville, produced the lowest level of black landowning and was thus especially insecure. Occasionally it held unexpected rewards, as for Roman Cole, a black man near Jackson who plowed up $1,500 in gold coins in his cotton patch. Such a bonanza, however, could hardly be anticipated by the thousands of other hard-pressed sharecroppers and tenants.[7]

Those black farmers and laborers, concentrated in Middle and East Tennessee, who depended upon income and livelihood from hay, grain, and livestock, experienced fewer anxieties over basic sustenance. Their work was not as seasonal, more of their food was home-grown, and they depended less upon distant markets and unscrupulous merchants. Still, particular racial difficulties faced all black farm operators, East and West.

Competition between economically depressed white and Negro agricultural workers often led to threats and violence against successful blacks. Whitecapping (Klan-style intimidation) was common in West and Middle Tennessee and crimes against blacks, although usually deplored in the press, went unpun-

[7] Powdermaker, *After Freedom*, 95; Taylor, *The Negro in Tennessee*, 136; interview with H. C. Hardy, June 20, 1972; Nashville *American*, June 19, 1902. Alex Haley notes that in 1872 his great, great grandfather "led a 29-wagon train of black families out of Alamance County, North Carolina, and through the Cumberland Gap to Henning, Tennessee [Lake County]." Alex Haley, *Roots*, condensed in *Readers' Digest* 53 (June 1974), 263.

ished.[8] While most agricultural hazards were color-blind, burdens other than those of economics complicated life for the black farmer. In the West, particularly in the old black-belt plantation counties of Dyer, Shelby, Fayette, Tipton, and Haywood, a combination of economic and racial vulnerability created apathy among rural blacks. Parents needed children as income producers, and blacks expressed little opposition when white officials neglected their schools. Voting was often dangerous and nearly always a futile gesture; black men in this area seldom sought the franchise. Discrimination in public funds and at the polls predominated in the rural areas of Middle and East Tennessee also, but the factor of fear was less apparent. Small encouragements from paternalistic whites and more diversified economic activity made the blacks more optimistic and self-confident in the counties where cotton was not raised. It was the Negroes of East and Middle Tennessee, for instance, who pushed for the agricultural and industrial normal school before 1912.

The second decade of the twentieth century was an economic and social turning point for black Tennesseans, as, indeed, it was for the entire Afro-American population of the United States. Except for a sharp, temporary decline in 1914, cotton and other farm prices rose steadily.[9] Heartened by the success of Tennessee A & I and some limited governmental assistance, blacks showed increasing interest in improving their farm practices. In addition, the demand for industrial labor drew blacks increasingly to the

[8] Dyer *Reporter*, n.d., quoted in Nashville *American*, Jan. 14, 1902; Knoxville *Journal and Tribune*, Feb. 25, 1915. The origin of the term "whitecapping" is unknown, but it undoubtedly goes back to the Reconstruction exploits of the Ku Klux Klan. In a study of the causes and course of whitecapping in a neighboring state, William F. Holmes defines the phenomenon in these terms: "Although newspapers sometimes used the term to describe all manner of crimes inflicted by whites upon Negroes, in Mississippi whitecapping specifically meant the attempt to force a person to abandon his home and property; it meant driving Negroes off land they owned or rented." Holmes, "Whitecapping: Agrarian Violence in Mississippi, 1902–1906," *Journal of Southern History* 35 (May 1969), 166.

[9] A bumper cotton crop in 1914 coincided with market disorganization "attendant upon the outbreak of the World War" and drove prices for this commodity to 6.8 cents. By 1919, however, prices had risen to a post-Civil War high of 35 cents. Vance, *Human Factors in Cotton Culture*, 117.

cities, and the resulting reduction in the number of black farm laborers, combined with the rising agricultural prices, led to higher wages and a stronger bargaining position for those who remained. The external conditions which brought economic betterment often created corresponding social difficulties. There were frequent and violent convulsions in Tennessee's caste system, especially during World War I, but the average standard of living for black families in 1920 noticeably surpassed that of 1910.

Rural societies foster individualism and shun collective action. Negro farmers demonstrated these traits throughout the early twentieth century and thus tended to face their complicated challenge as individuals, even though black leaders constantly preached racial solidarity and cooperation as means of self-improvement. The Colored Wheel and the Colored Farmers' Alliance had gained considerable support from black farmers in West and lower Middle Tennessee between 1888 and 1891, but the collapse of these movements discouraged later cooperative ventures.[10] Talk of black agricultural unity persisted, but rarely did serious action materialize. In 1904 a West Tennessee Negro Farmers' Institute was begun in connection with Lane College of Jackson. The purpose of this yearly conference of "farmers and laborers" was "to promote the economic, moral, educational and agricultural interest of [the] people." Until 1911, however, the institute amounted only to an annual get-together of blacks from the neighborhood of Jackson.[11]

[10] The Colored Farmers' National Alliance, preceded by the Colored Wheel, was organized in Tennessee in the spring of 1888 by C. D. Vaughan of Tipton County, and by July 1890, R. M. Humphrey, the white general superintendent of the alliance, reported from his Texas headquarters that the Tennessee Colored Alliance had enrolled 100,000 members. Such claims were doubtlessly exaggerated since initial memberships were for a six-month duration, and few black farmers could sustain dues payment for long. Black farmers held state conventions in Memphis in 1889 and Pulaski (Giles County) in 1890, but attendance was generally local. Debts incurred by the white alliance cut down on the aid given to the blacks in 1891 and the Tennessee Colored Alliance deteriorated, eventually disappearing during the winter of 1891–92. Gerald H. Gaither, "The Negro Alliance Movement in Tennessee, 1888–1891," West Tennessee Historical Society Papers 28 (1973), 50–62.
[11] James Franklin Lane, president of Lane College, to Gov. Ben W. Hooper, Dec. 23,

Black tobacco growers in Montgomery County made another attempt to organize collectively in 1905. An organizational meeting of blacks held on September 30 was part of an attempt by growers of both races along the Kentucky-Tennessee border to resist the low prices set by buyers for the American Tobacco Company monopoly. White producers had already decided to organize in order to force an increase in prices, and frequent destructive raids had been carried out on farms of those who did not join the struggle. A black observer in Clarksville urged his "brothers of the patch to make no mistake," but "if you see proper to organize, then stick together and let no man break the ranks. Together is the only method by which you may cause the enemy to retreat. . . ."[12] There was no further comment on cooperation among black tobacco growers, but night-rider violence and white resistance to the tobacco monopoly continued.

Efforts such as those at Jackson and Clarksville slowly multiplied. The state had supported and published the reports of four regional farm conventions since the early 1890s. These were white meetings, and in 1909 Governor Malcolm R. Patterson, perhaps motivated by black political support, but probably responding to new reports of Negro migration from farming areas, turned official attention on the black farmer. He called a conference of black Middle Tennessee farmers in Nashville, July 28–30, 1909. Commissioner of Agriculture John Thompson planned the program and explained the purpose as being "to encourage the negro to purchase land." Thompson went on to explain that he felt "the negro through his very nature is better off in the country than in the cities" and that ownership "of a small patch of ground" would make the black man a better citizen. The Nashville *Globe* commented favorably on Thompson's remarks but warned that the Negro also needed a "guarantee that when he show[ed]

1912, Feb. 5, 1913, Gov. Hooper Papers, Tennessee State Library and Archives, containers 5 and 6.

[12] Indianapolis *Freeman*, Sept. 16, 1905; Folmsbee, Corlew, and Mitchell, *History of Tennessee*, II, 218.

signs of prosperity that nightriders [would] not fall on him in the night and drive him from his home." The *Globe* might also have pointed out to Thompson that whites in many counties refused to sell land to black farmers.[13] The future of black farming, as with black voting and black education, was not fully within the power of the race to determine.

The Farmers' Institute, however, did meet at the state capitol and blacks heard addresses by George Washington Carver of Tuskegee on "diversified farming," by Preston Taylor on "The Value of State and County Fairs to Negro Farmers," and by Professor Thomas Washington Talley of Fisk on "The Importance of Education for the Negro Farmers." Unfortunately, most of those in attendance were residents of Nashville, but the *Globe* was enthusiastic that the state government had shown interest in black economic problems and prophesied "that after the news shall have reached the rural sections the Negro farmers will catch the inspiration and the second annual session will see Nashville crowded with men anxious to learn the art of tilling the soil in a way to make it profitable."[14]

A second annual session was never held, but in 1913 the new Republican agriculture commissioner, Thomas Peck, sought to rejuvenate the Farmers' Institute program. He corresponded with James Franklin Lane of Jackson and promised to attend or send a representative to the West Tennessee Negro Farmers' Institute in February. Peck also expressed a desire "that the Negro farmers have a state organization first of all, and that from this state organization there be organized in every county a Farmer's County Institute." The *Globe* endorsed Peck's idea and urged black farmers to take advantage of railroad excursion rates

[13] Nashville *Tennessean*, July 28, 1909; Nashville *Globe*, July 23, 1909; interview with H. C. Hardy, June 20, 1972.

[14] Nashville *Tennessean*, July 28, 30, Aug. 1, 1909; Nashville *Globe*, July 23, 30, 1909. As evidence that Nashville Negroes predominated, all the officers chosen at the institute were from the capital city and two—E. W. D. Isaac and Dock A. Hart—made no pretense of being farmers. Ben Carr, as president, maintained a 320-acre farm run by four tenants in Trousdale County, but he lived permanently in Nashville.

during the week of the Tennessee State Fair and meet with state authorities at the capitol for the perfection of a state organization. Faulting the first Nashville meeting for being dominated by "professional men residing in the cities," the *Globe* stressed the necessity for *farmer* cooperation "in this progressive age when every section of our country is reached by the agents of the great monopolies."[15] No permanent state organization materialized, but in 1916 the Colored Farmers Association of East Tennessee was formed to promote "more and better farming by colored people," and it met annually throughout the 1920s. The West Tennessee Negro Farmers' Institute, meanwhile, remained active and by 1918 involved blacks from eighteen counties.[16]

Governmental concern for agricultural conditions among blacks had been prompted by a noticeable Negro exodus from rural areas and a growing number of jobless blacks in the cities. The boll weevil, whitecapping, and city lights made for a scarcity of farm labor and an abundance of crimes related to idleness.[17] Blacks as well as whites expressed concern. In 1910, a group of Negroes from Dickson County in Middle Tennessee promoted the formation of an all-black farming community which, by example, might encourage economic self-sufficiency. Called Hortense, and regularly described in idyllic phrases by the *Globe*, this community sponsored excursions of as many as sixty potential residents from nearby towns, particularly Nashville. There was little evidence that this utopian plan actually converted many urban blacks to an agrarian way of life, but by 1913, two thousand acres of land in the vicinity of Hortense was owned by blacks.[18]

The industrial cities of East Tennessee experienced an increase of almost 54 percent in their black populations between 1900 and 1920. Black migrants came principally from the surrounding east-

[15]James Franklin Lane to Gov. Ben W. Hooper, Feb. 5, 1913, Hooper Papers, container 6; Nashville *Globe*, Sept. 5, 1913.

[16]Chattanooga *Daily Times*, Aug. 24, 1922; Nashville *Globe*, Feb. 22, 1918.

[17]Greene and Woodson, *The Negro Wage Earner*, 214–15; Nashville *American*, Feb. 27, 1905, Oct. 24, 1906; Nashville *Tennessean*, Dec. 1, 1907.

[18]Nashville *Globe*, Nov. 24, 1910, July 25, 1913.

ern counties, causing concern among both races and leading to several black-fostered "back-to-the-farm" movements. In 1913 G. W. McNair of Jefferson County explained the purpose of one of these: "We . . . have begun a movement whereby we can better the conditions of our people and keep them away from the cities. We have begun a farm life plan, that is, we believe we can do better on the farms than flocking to the cities in large numbers, as is now the condition."[19]

Black urban growth in Middle Tennessee was only 20 percent during the first two decades of the century, but a Back to the Farm Association and Negro Farmers Alliance met in Nashville in November 1915. George Edmund Haynes, Fisk University professor and executive secretary of the National League on Urban Conditions Among Negroes (Urban League), sent a message to the group, expressing his belief that "the great relief from the rush and the ware [sic] and tear of our modern city life is in the country." Haynes cautioned further that "the thousands who are flocking from the country to the city to-day do not realize that they are leaving their greatest opportunities and joining the struggling mass which is fighting for mere existence in the congested districts of our cities." The Nashville *Globe* joined in this plea for the black man to "turn his attention more to horticulture and agriculture," but the editors warned governmental authorities: "it is useless to tell these young men to turn their attention to farming unless they can be convinced that it would be profitable to do so."[20]

Slowly state and federal agencies in Tennessee realized the wisdom in the *Globe*'s advice and began to give some attention to improving black farm practices. As with all other programs, how-

---

[19]*Twelfth Census: 1900, Population*, I, pt. 1, 680–81; II, pt. 2, 484; *Fourteenth Census: 1920, Population*, III, 970–72, 961–69; letter from McNair to Attorney-General R. A. Mynatt of Knoxville, printed in the Knoxville *Journal and Tribune*, Oct. 4, 1913.

[20]George Edmund Haynes to The Back to the Farm Association and the Negro Farmers' Alliance, Nov. 6, 1915, Haynes Papers, container 1914–15; Nashville *Globe*, March 26, 1909, Sept. 5, 1913.

ever, efforts on behalf of blacks came at a respectful distance behind whites. Money, for example, had been provided by Congress under the Hatch Act of 1887 for the creation of state agricultural experiment stations, but of the $1,248,000 spent by 1909, "not one penny of this amount was expended for the establishment of a . . . station, in any of the States for . . . colored youth."[21] In conjunction with the experimental program, the United States Department of Agriculture (USDA) in 1904 adopted the farm demonstration method of Seaman Asahel Knapp, and with initial financing from the General Education Board, Knapp employed two Negro agents in 1906 for demonstration work in Alabama and Virginia.[22] Both twentieth-century philanthropy and federal aid, however, had become very conscious of Southern racial sensibilities. One federal official noted that "It is very important that Negro agents not only have a knowledge of the work to be done but also have an understanding of the relationship of the races in their respective communities. The employment of Negro agents," he said, "cannot be pushed more rapidly than public sentiment can be educated to appreciate and receive them."[23]

By 1912, thirty-three demonstration agents were at work among the black farmers in the South, but there were none in Tennessee. As in higher education, public aid evolved slowly and discriminatorily in Tennessee. There was some indication of "special attention being given to agricultural experiments" by Jeanes teachers in 1910, but it was a noteworthy first when "Mr. H. D. Tate, one of the agents on the staff of Dr. S. A. Knapp,"

[21] J. E. Johnson, a member of the staff of the U.S. House of Representatives, to J. C. Napier, Sept. 7, 1911, Napier Papers, container 1.
[22] J. A. Evans, *Extension Work Among Negroes, Conducted by Negro Agents*, 1923, United States Department of Agriculture, Circular 355 (Washington, D.C., 1925), 1; Dabney, *Universal Education in the South*, II, 179–87.
[23] W. B. Mercier, *Extension Work Among Negroes, 1920*, United States Department of Agriculture, Circular 190 (Washington, D.C., 1921), 4; O. B. Martin, *A Decade of Negro Extension Work, 1914–1924*, United States Department of Agriculture, Miscellaneous Circular 72 (Washington, D.C., 1926), 3–5.

attended the eighth annual meeting of the West Tennessee Negro Farmers' Institute in 1911. Two hundred Negro representatives from twelve western counties enthusiastically received Tate's discussions on "Seed Selection," "Cultivation of Corn and Cotton," and "How the Soil May Be Improved," but they "deplore[d] the discrimination so often made on account of race in this work." The following year, Harcourt A. Morgan, dean of the School of Agriculture at the University of Tennessee, and H. S. Nichols, a USDA extension worker in Tennessee, spoke to the gathering.[24]

In 1914 Congress passed the Smith-Lever Act, providing, on a matching basis with the states, federal grants for agricultural extension work. The bill passed over the vehement objection of the NAACP, which had unsuccessfully fought for explicit reference to proportional black participation in the program. Aware of past discrimination in state-administered Morrill funds, black leaders accurately assumed that agricultural extension appropriations would be spent similarly.[25] In Tennessee, for example, regular funds were channeled through the University at Knoxville, and money passed on to the agriculture department at Tennessee A & I was negligible. Also, with the passage of the Smith-Lever Act, Tennessee immediately appointed several white home demonstration and farm agents. The first black home agent, however, did not receive placement until July 1916, and the first black farm agent not until October 1917. Funds for all agents were derived from the USDA, the Smith-Lever Act, county appropriations, and personal donations. Not a single county or individual made money available for black agents in Tennessee. Only Florida and South Carolina showed similar disinterest.[26]

[24]Nashville *Globe*, March 4, 1910, March 3, 1911: *Christian Index*, March 7, 1912.
[25]NAACP activities are discussed in Charles Flint Kellogg, *NAACP*: (Baltimore: Johns Hopkins Univ. Press, 1967), 190–91. Evidence of racial discrimination in Smith-Lever funds is recorded in James Hardy Dillard, *Twenty Year Report of the Phelps-Stokes Fund, 1911–1931* (New York: Phelps-Stokes Fund, 1932), 41–43.
[26]G. C. Wright, *Negro Farm Families Move Ahead in Tennessee*, University of Tennessee Agricultural Extension Service Bulletin 298 (1946), 1–2; Evans, *Extension Work*

The concerted effort to increase food production during World War I and the sharp increase in Negro migration to the cities during the war finally directed significant attention to Tennessee's black farmers. Eleven agents, at a cost of $5,638, and thirty-one agents at a cost of $15,249, operated among black Tennessee farmers during 1918 and 1919, respectively. Federal emergency funds helped finance most of the new workers.[27] In addition to emphasizing methods of increasing crop yields, these agents also demonstrated gardening and canning techniques that would improve traditional rural diets. Their reports repeatedly stated that black farmers appreciated having Negro officials, and the Lane College conference of the West Tennessee Negro Farmers' Institute in 1917 invited both black and white speakers. In addition to white representatives of the USDA, instructors included Thomas M. Campbell, a demonstrator for Tuskegee Institute before being named the first USDA Negro agent in 1906, Scott Bond, a successful black cotton farmer from Madison, Arkansas, and R. H. Boyd, who delivered an urgent plea for cooperative and collective efforts among black farmers.[28] When the war ended, the rapidly expanded federal programs faced severe cutbacks, both for whites and blacks. By 1921 Tennessee had only 63 white agents (down from a 1918 peak of 173) and 9 black agents (5 farm agents and 4 home demonstration agents).[29]

Among Negroes, 6. Distribution of Smith-Lever funds in Tennessee is generally discussed in Samuel Henry Shannon, "Agricultural and Industrial Education at Tennessee State University During the Normal School Phase, 1912–1922: A Case Study" (Ph.D. diss., George Peabody College for Teachers, 1974), ch. 5.

[27] Martin, A Decade of Negro Extension Work, 1914–1924, 29; Almon J. Sims, A History of Extension Work in Tennessee; Twenty-five Years of Service to Rural Life, 1914–1939 (Knoxville: Agricultural Extension Service, Univ. of Tennessee, 1939), 33.

[28] Annual Reports, 1922, 1923, Agricultural Extension Service, College of Agriculture, University of Tennessee (Knoxville, 1922, 1923): Nashville Globe, Feb. 16, 23, Mar. 9, 1917. A sketch of Thomas M. Campbell is found in David Manber, The Wizard of Tuskegee: The Life of George Washington Carver (New York: Crowell-Collier, 1967), 108. Grady E. Walker, in an interview with the author, June 19, 1973, described Scott Bond as the owner of 3,900 acres of cotton land, a two-stand cotton gin, a mercantile store, and most of the community of Madison.

[29] Sims, History of Extension Work in Tennessee, 33.

In the face of the overwhelming number of farmers and counties served by each black official, state extension officials had repeatedly tried to coordinate the Negro program with the efforts of private philanthropy, notably the Jeanes Fund and the General Education Board. However, USDA officials, especially Bradford Knapp who was responsible for state relations in the South, consistently urged a limited role for black agents and denied the use of any Smith-Lever money to aid private programs, either "directly or indirectly."[30]

Tennessee's black farmers received some additional governmental aid from the Smith-Hughes Act of 1917. Again, no provisions for equitable distribution of funds were included in this program of vocational instruction, and great discrimination took place in the South. Tennessee, however, along with Oklahoma, Texas, and Arkansas, did provide instruction in vocational agriculture for almost as large a percentage of rural blacks as rural whites. This was accomplished primarily by action of the State Board of Vocational Education, which voted in 1918 to spend at least one-fifth of the Smith-Hughes funds in Negro training schools.[31]

Some ambitious blacks sought to avail themselves of federal aid on their own initiative. When Congress established the Federal Farm Loan Board in 1916, the Nashville *Globe* urged a meeting of the Davidson County Negro Farmers Alliance. A group of more than twenty black farmers reportedly met at the People's Savings Bank and Trust Company to hear of the new, long-term (five to forty years), low-interest (5 to 6 percent) loans being made available. While these Nashville-area blacks were organizing as the National Farm Loan Association, Bert M. Roddy, a black entre-

[30] Shannon, "Agricultural and Industrial Education at Tennessee State University," ch. 5.

[31] Dillard, *Twenty Year Report of the Phelps-Stokes Fund*, 43–44; H. O. Sargent, "Progress in Training Negro Farmers," *Southern Workman* 57 (Jan. 1928), 8–9; *Biennial Report of the Superintendent of Public Instruction of Tennessee For the Scholastic Years ending June 30, 1917–1918*, 14–15; Monroe Nathan Work, ed., *Negro Yearbook, 1918–1919* (Tuskegee Institute: Negro Yearbook Publishing, 1920), 27–28.

preneur, banker, and NAACP official from Memphis, helped found a similar organization—the Three States Better Farming Association.[32] The significance of these actions lay more in the awareness of black Tennessee farmers that they could now obtain economic aid from the federal government than in the actual practices (apparently none) of their associations.

Perhaps encouraged by state and federal interest, blacks overcame some of their hesitancy and formed increasing numbers of cooperatives, associations, and agricultural fairs after 1910. Earlier examples of black economic initiative, such as cooperative cotton gins, had regularly run into white opposition. One gin, operated near Jackson in 1903, under the name of the Colored Joint Stock Company, had its boiler blown up in its first year and its buildings burned down a few months later. By 1910, however, the *Globe* reported that in the same area blacks had begun to organize a few cooperative supply stores, sawmills, grist mills, and cotton gins. In 1917 R. H. Boyd urged them to extend the practice to new capital-intensive machinery such as tractors as well.[33]

Evidence of concern in agricultural improvements was also demonstrated by the formation of the Tennessee Colored State Poultry Association in July 1912, regular Tennessee representation at meetings of the National Negro Farmers and Rural Teachers Congress, the formation of numerous black county fairs, and publicly expressed interest in importing African animals for stock raising.[34] Fairs played a very important role in stimulating

[32] Nashville *Globe*, March 9, Oct. 26, 1917; *Crisis* 13 (April 1917), 298; 14 (May 1917), 35. For a very general discussion of the nature of Negro participation in the Federal Farm Loan program, see Greene and Woodson, *The Negro Wage Earner*, 222.

[33] Nashville *American*, Oct. 1, 1903; Nashville *Globe*, Dec. 9, 1910, March 9, 1917.

[34] Nashville *Globe*, July 7, 1911, Aug. 2, 9, 1912; Edward R. Kone, Texas Commissioner of Agriculture, to Gov. Ben W. Hooper, April 22, 1913, Gov. Hooper Papers, container 6; and numerous letters from leading black agriculturists such as E. L. Blackshear, principal of the Prairie View Normal and Industrial College of Texas, to Gov. Thomas C. Rye in 1915–1916, Gov. Rye Papers, Tennessee State Library and Archives, container 28; E. W. Irving, president of the Colored Tri-State Fair Association of Memphis, to Booker T. Washington, Sept. 4, 1912, Washington Papers, container 832.

the black farmer to take pride in his produce and to practice scientific farming. Black farm agents sought to arouse competition by soliciting prizes or premiums from local merchants and offering them to champion producers. Meanwhile, W. P. Ware, an early Tennessee A & I graduate and black vocational instructor at the Fayette County Training School, spoke before numerous Negro audiences throughout the state on "How the County Fair Can Be Made to Help the Farmer." The state made a special effort to encourage county and regional fairs during the 1920s, but, as expected, put its emphasis on attracting whites. During the fiscal year 1929–30, for example, approximately $80,700 in state funds went to pay premiums for white fairs and only $2,332 for black fairs. With the coming of depression, the disparity widened.[35]

Despite state and federal efforts during the late teens and early 1920s, blacks continued to leave the farms. Out-migration was not a new phenomenon; a colony of early Tennesseans had migrated to Kansas with Benjamin "Pap" Singleton between 1871 and 1880, and another group moved to the cane fields of Hawaii in 1901.[36] But except for several groups of blacks recruited from East Tennessee's industries during World War I, most post-1910 migration was spontaneous and unorganized. This independent movement, especially among rural Negroes, had a noticeable impact upon Tennessee; there was an absolute decline in the number of black farmers between 1910 and 1920, a decrease of over 4.5 percent in the total black population of the state, and a

---

[35] Interview with H. C. Hardy, June 20, 1972; Chattanooga *Daily Times*, Aug. 17, 1917; State of Tennessee, *Biennial Report of the Department of Agriculture, 1929–1930*, 20–22.

[36] Singleton, former slave from Nashville, led several parties of Tennessee Negroes onto the public lands of southeast Kansas between 1871 and 1880. The motivation for the migration was economic—land-owning—in nearly every case. Most educated blacks opposed the programs of the illiterate Singleton, however, and white planters sought to discourage their laborers from joining the exodus. Walter Lynwood Fleming, " 'Pap' Singleton, The Moses of the Colored Exodus," *American Journal of Sociology* 15 (July 1909), 61–82. In 1901, the Hawaiian Commercial and Sugar Co. of Honolulu recruited parties of Negroes from Nashville, Columbia, Clarksville, and Knoxville. Passage was paid to the islands and housing was provided on arrival. Blacks who made the trek spoke

rise of more than 13 percent in the number of black urban residents for the period.[37]

The most highly mobile black farmers were the wage laborers or "standing renters." Unlike the debt-shackled sharecropper, they were free to migrate to the city in search of service and industrial jobs. The 1920 census showed a decline in the number of standing renters of over 33 percent. The collapse of cotton prices in 1920 sped up the exodus of farm laborers and also led to the loss or sale of many black-owned farms. After having remained practically stationary in percentage since 1900, tenancy in Tennessee jumped from 41 percent of all farm operators in 1925 to over 46 percent in 1930. By 1930, the number of black farmers who owned their own land had decreased by 26 percent, leaving behind mostly black sharecroppers. It was "a painful experience," in the words of H. C. Hardy, a former black farm agent who grew up in West Tennessee, to see so much land, previously owned by Negroes, pass irretrievably into the hands of whites.[38]

Seasonal laborers had been forsaking the farms in a small but steady flow even before the outbreak of European hostilities. "Mines, lumber camps, sawmills, and other industrial employments" had previously attracted numbers of these floating workers, but the mass exodus after 1914 created a real scarcity in the cotton belt of West Tennessee. One explanation for the reduction in available farm labor was the high incidence of urban migration by younger blacks. The wages of most young men and women were pooled by the parents to support the family; those who left the farm, therefore, sought independence and their own spending money. In the face of this shift, monthly wages for remaining black laborers more than doubled, but white plantation owners

expectantly of good salaries and greater "political and racial privileges." See *Nashville American*, Dec. 20, 1900, Feb. 7, 1901; Knoxville *Journal and Tribune*, March 19, 1901.

[37]*Thirteenth Census: 1910, Population*, III, 762–64, 744–61; *Fourteenth Census: 1920, Population*, III, 970–72, 961–69.

[38]*Fourteenth Census: 1920, Agriculture*, VI, 438; *Fifteenth Census: 1930, Agriculture*, II, pt. 2, 878; Allred and Briner, *Tenure By Type of Farming Areas and Color*, 1, 3; interview with H. C. Hardy, June 20, 1972.

still complained loudly of a shortage.[39] G. Tom Taylor, former Progressive party leader, ex-treasurer of Tennessee, and a wealthy cotton planter, unhappily noted that many alert, if unscrupulous, blacks were taking advantage of the favorable labor market:

> Down in this Cotton Country all bus. is done on a credit and when a negro wants to move from your place to my place it is the custom that I pay you what the negro owes you and often pay other bills for the negro or white man . . . .
> Last week a negro came to my plantation & said he lived in Memphis & wanted to move to my place. I furnished him transportation & paid 3.00 for a pawn shop & 12.00 for coal for him. He went down on the place that day but left the next day & came back to Memphis & all I can do is to sue the negro. . . .[40]

White reaction to persistent black restlessness appeared mixed. Occasional observers viewed the black exodus as a blessing: "the Southern whites should encourage Negro migration to the North . . . to relieve the South of the entire burden and all of the brunt of the race problems, and make room for and to create greater inducements for white immigration that the South very much needs." But most leaders feared the economic consequences of the movement, particularly the loss of cheap labor. The Memphis *Commercial Appeal* credited the Negro with being "a tremendous factor in the development of agriculture and all the commerce of the South" and admitted that "if we are to keep him here . . . and have the best use of his business capacity, there is a certain duty that the white man himself must discharge in his relation to the Negro." Former governor Malcolm R. Patterson advocated arming "the Negro with the weapons of knowledge and scientific education" so that he could "solve our problem of untilled lands in the South." And Knoxville Republican politician

[39]Greene and Woodson, *The Negro Wage Earner*, 51–52; Brannen, *Relation of Land Tenure to Plantation Organization*, 27; Nashville *Banner*, Feb. 28, 1918; Earnest J. Eberling, "A Social Interpretation: Tennessee," *Journal of Social Forces* 5 (Sept. 1926), 27–28; interview with H. C. Hardy, June 20, 1972.
[40]G. Tom Taylor to John C. Houk, March 12, 1917, Houk Papers, container 90.

John Childs Houk supported federal control of the Muscle Shoals nitrate plants because they could be used to provide fertilizer which would enable "the negro in the cotton fields of the South [to] raise more cotton per acre with the same labor."[41]

As the exodus continued into the 1920s, efforts to stop the outflow of human resources increased. Most attention was directed toward improving the racial and, especially, the economic environment. One of the main programs of the white-dominated Tennessee Interracial Commission, for example, was to encourage black farmers to adopt modern methods of agriculture and to give assistance in the marketing of their products. As a result, bankers in Jackson gave aid "to Negro boy farmers" in the form of cotton seed, fertilizer, and "minute instructions as how best to plant, etc." Many "boys" reportedly took advantage of the offer and were expected to pay back their "benefactors" when the cotton was sold.[42]

More important than such private efforts were the activities of governmental agencies. Black farm and demonstration agents, even though there were only ten agents, with less than $20,000 annually, to serve almost 300,000 rural Negroes, had the explicit responsibility of stemming the tides of migration as well as bringing agricultural instruction to Negro farmers. One of the great agricultural panaceas of the 1920s was the cooperative movement, and Tennessee officials became infected with "co-op fever." The gospel of cooperative agriculture thus became a major part of the plan to upgrade black farming and stop the outmigration from Tennessee.[43]

[41] Nashville *Banner*, n.d., quoted in Selma Warlick, "Negro News in the Southern Press" (M.A. thesis, Columbia Univ. School of Journalism, 1931), 64; Memphis *Commercial Appeal*, Oct. 5, 1916, and n.d., quoted in *Crisis* 29 (Feb. 1925), 83; John C. Houk to Republican national chairman Will H. Hays, Jan. 26, 1920, in *Speeches by Political Leaders of Tennessee*, compiled by the Univ. of Tennessee Library.

[42] 1922 *Minutes of the State Inter-Racial Commission of Tennessee*, 16; *Bulletin of the Commission on Inter-Racial Cooperation*, 1923, found in Peay Papers, container 100.

[43] Evans, *Extension Work Among Negroes*, 7, 8, 23; interview with Mrs. Henry R. Duncan, June 10, 1970; Sims, *A History of Extension Work in Tennessee*, 34; "Cooperative Creameries," *Tennessee Agriculture* 5 (Jan. 1922), 12–13.

The cooperative movement was by no means aimed at black farms alone. Between 1918 and 1927 over 550 co-ops were organized in Tennessee, and only a very small number were made up of black farmers. Nevertheless, black officials worked hard to encourage such efforts. W. P. Ware, for example, helped form a cooperative program among black truck and dairy products in Fayette County. At least forty farmers participated, jointly using some thirty cream separators and shipping as many as three carloads of strawberries at one time. On occasion, white growers participated in the collective effort.[44] Still, very few white co-ops, and even fewer black organizations, lasted more than one season. Farmers of the 1920s, despite the efforts of vocational agriculture specialists like Ware, simply lacked the business expertise to manage the programs.[45]

Rural black Tennesseans had been relatively prosperous during the second decade of the twentieth century. Migration, rising prices, government aid, and cooperative programs improved farm methods and, at least temporarily, gave farmers greater bargaining power. Some observers noted a change in the traditional relationship "from that of lord and serf to one of employer and employee."[46] The 1920s, however, had stabilized agricultural conditions—again, on a low-price, sharecropper basis. Thousands of younger Negroes had fled to the city, and a higher percentage of those blacks who remained on Tennessee farms were sharecroppers and tenants in 1930 than in 1900 (77 percent as opposed to 72 percent). Migrants to the cities found that many of the unskilled jobs so plentiful in wartime disappeared after

[44] Benjamin D. Raskopf and P. W. Voltz, *Farmers' Marketing and Purchasing Associations in Tennessee*, University of Tennessee Agricultural Experiment Station Bulletin 177 (1941), 4; Memphis *Commercial Appeal*, Oct. 28, 1927; *1922 Minutes of the State Inter-Racial Commission of Tennessee*, 10.

[45] Charles E. Allred, S. W. Watkins, and G. H. Hatfield, *Tennessee, Economic and Social. Part II: The Counties*, in *University of Tennessee Record, Extension Series*, Vol. VI, no. 3 (Knoxville, Sept. 1929), 30, 82, 103–4; interview with H. C. Hardy, June 20, 1972.

[46] Elbert Lee Tatum, *The Changed Political Thought of the Negro, 1915–1940* (New York: Exposition, 1951), 60.

1920, but fewer than 15 percent were estimated to have returned.[47] Numbers of blacks who remained on the farm from 1900 to 1930 had achieved a significantly higher standard of living, but the majority still floundered on the margins of the state's economic system.

[47] Davis, "Negro Exodus and Southern Agriculture," 404.

CHAPTER VII.

"He Will Go Where He Can Live Best"

Movement seemed to dominate the lives of black Tennesseans after 1900. Sometimes unwillingly, but mostly by choice, Negro men and women changed jobs, moved residences, and steadily expanded the state's urban population. Many whites became uneasy, criticizing blacks for threatening to disrupt traditional race relationships. In 1903, J. W. Grant, a black Nashville lawyer and Republican politician, minced few words in answering these critics: "It is not a question of freedom alone," he said, "it is a question of meat and bread. . . . The negro is just like other men—he will go where he can live best."[1] This search for a better life meant leaving farms for wages paid at sawmills, phosphate mines, and coal fields; it meant vacating the countryside for the brighter lights and economic diversity of the city; and it meant changing jobs because of white competition and union exclusion.

For many it was an easy step from the tenant farm to one of the extractive industries located in rural Tennessee. Employment in the logging camps and sawmills of the West, the phosphate mines of the lower middle portion of the state, or the coal mines of Southern Appalachia in the East did not always bring significant improvement. Surroundings were still primitive and harsh, living standards rose slightly, if at all, and blacks still experienced the violence and prejudice ingrained in rural Southern society.

[1] Letter to the editor from J. W. Grant, Nashville *American*, Feb. 15, 1903.

132

Timber-cutting, lumber-milling, and stave-turning expanded rapidly in West Tennessee around 1900. By 1902, Negro labor gangs and camps were in use in several counties, and their efforts contributed toward Memphis's development as one of the South's leading lumber markets. Blacks, usually called "flatheads," found employment in this industry because they would perform jobs for wages that few white men would accept. But in the western counties and throughout the heavily Negro-populated Mississippi Delta, blacks who moved from their traditional agricultural pursuits ran into resistance. Whitecapping regularly disrupted operations of those timber, milling, and stave companies that employed black labor. Tents were shot into at night, workers were harassed, and written threats were made to the effect that "if the owners . . . did not discharge the negroes . . . the mill[s] would be burned." Often no reason other than general resentment at black employment was evident, but, on occasion, whitecappers specifically indicated that white men, at higher wages, should be given many of those jobs held by Negroes. For economic reasons, employers generally rejected racial demands, but fearful black workers often quit their jobs rather than risk harm.[2]

In Middle Tennessee a "great phosphate boom" took place in Maury County at the turn of the century. "Several thousand miners . . . nearly all of them negroes" hired on to perform the back-breaking tasks associated with both the strip (brown phosphate) and shaft (blue phosphate) mining operations. These blacks, most of whom were former farm tenants, labored willingly, at first, for regular pay of $1.20 per day. White resentment at this low-wage competition flared openly, however, causing many blacks to flee from their homes and jobs. Implying conditions of peonage, one black newspaper reported in 1907 that

[2] Nashville *American*, April 20, May 10, 1902, June 2, Oct. 6, 1903; Fuller, *Story of the Church Life Among Negroes in Memphis*, 1. A racially prejudiced general account of the timber industry near Memphis is found in Shields McIlwaine, *Memphis Down in Dixie* (New York: Dutton, 1948), 248–59.

armed guards were used to keep black workers on the job.[3]

The racial pattern in the East Tennessee coal-mining industry was similar. Between 1890 and 1908, the yearly output of the bituminous coal fields of the state increased fivefold. Such a tremendous expansion increased the demand for labor, especially between 1890 and 1900, and the number of blacks employed in the industry jumped from 769 to 3,092 during this period. Black laborers were desirable both for their availability and their willingness to work for daily wages that ranged between $1.50 and $2.00. White workers commanded wages from $.50 to $.75 per day higher, and consequently, the percentage of blacks among coal miners in Tennessee increased from 15.7 in 1890 to 28.4 in 1900.[4]

As early as 1902 reports of white opposition to black miners reached the press, but shortly after the bloody race riot in Springfield, Illinois, in August 1908, racial violence flared openly in the Tennessee coal fields along the Kentucky border. White mountaineers lacked the paternalism found in the region's urban centers and often insisted that no blacks even be allowed into their communities. When mining companies imported black laborers, tensions mounted. In late July 1908, mine operators in the Jellico–La Follette area attempted to integrate their work gangs. White miners ordered the blacks to leave, using violence and threats of violence to enforce their demands. Most black miners fled, but on August 17, 1908, "a band of some seventy negro miners collected at Antras [where they] were given arms by the white authorities with which to protect themselves. . . ." After considerable shooting, sheriff's authorities dispelled the white

[3] Nashville *American*, Aug. 3, 1900; Richard W. Smith, "Mining and Washing Phosphate Rock in Tennessee," *Engineering and Mining Journal-Press* 115 (Feb. 3, 1923), 221–26; Nashville *Globe*, Nov. 20, 1908; *Christian Index*, Aug. 17, 1907.

[4] Sterling D. Spero and Abram L. Harris, *The Black Worker: The Negro and the Labor Movement* (New York: Columbia Univ. Press, 1931), 214; Herbert R. Northrup, *Organized Labor and the Negro* (New York: Harper, 1944), 156–57; George T. Surface, "The Negro Mine Laborer: General Appalachian Coal Field," *Annals of the American Academy of Political and Social Sciences* 33 (March 1909), 123.

attackers.[5] An editorial in a Knoxville paper evaluated this mining dispute in these terms: "the underlying cause is prejudice against the negroes and a disposition to deny them the privilege of working for a living. . . . There are many men who object to working side by side with the colored laborers; but the objection lies more in the fact that it is thought that white men should have their places than to their race or color." In a seemingly prophetic statement, the paper observed that "if the negro miners are withdrawn from the mines where the disturbances have arisen, then the white miners will have gained their point and it . . . would surely cause the white miners at other camps to make the same demands and the upshot would be a situation such that not a negro miner could be employed in the locality." The editor concluded: "No man, no matter what his race or color should be deprived of the privilege of working to earn a living."[6]

Occasionally interracial cooperation did take place in the coal fields, but usually in times of tragedy, and the general trend after 1908 was to replace black laborers with whites. Census statistics indicated a drop of black miners to 14.5 percent of the total number of workers in 1910, 7.5 percent in 1920, and 6.6 percent in 1930. Unemployed Negroes either drifted into Knoxville and other urban areas or were imported by West Virginia companies to serve as deterrents to unionization.[7]

In addition to those blacks seeking industry-related jobs in rural Tennessee, a steadily broadening stream of Negro migrants left their poverty-encircled tenant cabins and moved expectantly to the cities. Although many found less work and more misery than they anticipated, it seemed that blacks as well as whites were committed to that belief in Progress so characteristic of the

[5] Nashville *American*, July 19, 1902, Feb. 26, 1907; Knoxville *Journal and Tribune*, Aug. 18, 1908.

[6] Knoxville *Journal and Tribune*, Aug. 19, 1908.

[7] "Program for Memorial Services in Memory of Those Who Lost Their Lives in Fraterville Mine Explosion, Coal Creek, Tennessee on Monday, May 19th, 1902," located in Houk Papers, container 69; Northrup, *Organized Labor and the Negro*, 155–59; Spero and Harris, *The Black Worker*, 220–21.

evangelistic New South and described so well by Wilbur J. Cash in *The Mind of the South*—and the city represented Progress. There had always been blacks in the cities of Tennessee. Whites had long been dependent upon Negro domestics; and black barbers, tile and brick layers, and riverboat stevedores had dominated their occupations since the days of slavery. In Memphis, Chattanooga, and several smaller towns, blacks also maintained a virtual monopoly of the hack and dray business until squeezed out by the automobile.[8] Yet these black men and women moved in a very limited world of their own and infringed only slightly upon the dominant white society. Interspaced among the boulevards of Memphis and Nashville or the narrow streets of Knoxville and Chattanooga "were alleys lined with one-and-two-room shanties of colored domestics. In the 'worst sections' of every city sprawled the jungle of darktown with its own business streets and uproarious, crime-infested 'amusement' streets."[9] As thousands of new migrants entered this world, they overcrowded traditional facilities, frequently fell victim to their own naiveté, and frightened whites by their numbers.

Newly arriving blacks experienced a greater sense of personal freedom and a life filled with many new options, and yet, for most, the physical standard of living improved only slightly. Wages for steadily employed breadwinners ranged from $1.00 to $2.50 per day, but almost all food now had to be purchased, and rent on those one- and two-room shanties varied from $6 to $12 per month. Life remained very basic. One observer found, for example, that after rent and food were purchased "absolutely nothing [was] left for clothing, education, medicine or life insurance." A contemporary later reminisced that clothing usually consisted of castoffs from "the boss"; as on the farm, ten-year-old boys and mothers of young children sought work in order to supplement

---

[8] Lee, *Beale Street*, 165–66; Nashville *Globe*, Sept. 2, 1910; Chattanooga *News*, Dec. 14, 1915; interview with Blair T. Hunt, June 14, 1972.
[9] C. Vann Woodward, *Origins of the New South, 1877–1913* (Baton Rouge: Louisiana State Univ. Press, 1951), 227.

TABLE 3

Urban and Rural Death and Birth Rates
for Tennessee, 1927

	Average Deaths per 1,000		Average Births per 1,000	
	White	Black	White	Black
State as a whole	10.2	19.3	22.7	19.0
Urban areas	15.3	28.8	25.0	22.8
Rural areas	9.0	14.6	22.2	17.1

SOURCE: Charles E. Allred, S. W. Watkins, and G. H. Hatfield, *Tennessee, Economic and Social*. Part III: *The Counties*, in *University of Tennessee Record, Extension Series*, vol. 6, no. 3 (Knoxville, Sept. 1929), 194.

meager incomes. Housing shortages and high rents produced the lodger. After several years of urban expansion, a Knoxville survey indicated that of 3,151 black homes visited, 1,624 contained lodgers.[10]

Owning a home hardly ended the struggle. Although residential segregation ordinances made little headway in Tennessee, blacks lived only in scattered pockets in the cities, and their neighborhoods consistently lacked adequate sewer, water, and electrical facilities. A prospective black homeowner found it almost impossible to obtain a loan for a purchase outside the zones approved by white society. Living in such confines was unpleasant, but more importantly, it was hazardous to health (see Table 3). A Chattanooga health report in 1916 observed: "Insanitary living, poor housing conditions, and certain habits, resulting in tuberculosis, organic heart disease, pneumonia and pellagra are shown by the statistics to be rapidly decreasing the negro race in

[10] Daves, *Social Study of the Colored Population of Knoxville*, 3–4; Chattanooga *Daily Times*, June 19, 1916; Fred L. Hutchins, *What Happened in Memphis* (Kingsport: privately printed, 1965), 50.

this city." Particularly during the winter months, reported deaths often exceeded reported births by a ratio of two to one.[11]

Articulate black leaders regularly protested the urban conditions of their race. "The white man is constantly sounding the alarm about us weaklings," said Nashville's George T. Robinson in 1903, but "there is a studied effort to curb our ambitions and aspirations. . . ." The Nashville *Globe* pointed out how discrimination against Negroes differed from that against the Jews and Irish: "The Negro's case is far different: as he increases in intelligence and as he accumulates wealth the louder the cry that he must be segregated." J. A. Crump, a black minister in Chattanooga, lambasted landlords and city authorities alike for allowing unsanitary housing conditions to exist. Crump described rental housing as having "poor ventilation, small rooms and hundreds of unsanitary water arrangements." Wash water and waste that should have found "ready passage to the city sewerage" was, instead, disposed of "out on the yard, or in some corner."[12] Continued migration compounded the hazards.

Health and housing deficiencies were complicated by the ignorance of the residents. In ageless fashion, ignorance, vulnerability, and unfamiliar dependence upon a money wage led to the exploitation of blacks by loan companies and also to their being fined constantly by overanxious police authorities and justices of

---

[11] Daves, *Social Study of the Colored Populaton of Knoxville*, 2–3; Nashville *Globe*, June 24, 1910; Nashville *Banner*, March 18, 1934; Arch M. Trawick, "The Social Gospel and Racial Relationship," *Fisk University News*, 7 (Dec. 1916), 4; Woofter, *Negro Problems in Cities*, 54–61, 109–10; Chattanooga *Daily Times*, June 14, 15, 19, 1916; R. G. Sanford, "The Economic Conditions of the Negroes of Knoxville," *Minutes of the University Commission on Southern Race Questions*, May 24, 1912 to Aug. 31, 1917, p. 70; interview with Meredith G. Ferguson, president of Citizens Savings Bank and Trust Company, Nashville, Tennessee, Nov. 10, 1970. Ferguson explained how potential black buyers were able, on occasion, to buy into a white borderline neighborhood by getting a loan from one of Nashville's Negro banks and purchasing the property through one of the white "liberals" in the community.

[12] Letter to the editor from George T. Robinson, Nashville *American*, Feb. 2, 1903; Nashville *Globe*, Nov. 7, 1913; letter to the editor from the Rev. J. A. Crump, Chattanooga *Daily Times*, June 19, 1916.

the peace, black and white. Loans advertised at fantastically low interest rates often included "balloon" contracts whose fine print reduced the black man and "his family to sleeping on the bare floor in a bare room after the loan shark had 'foreclosed' on all possessions" when the huge balloon or final payment could not be met on time. In 1915 Memphis Negroes organized a program to teach thrift to the growing numbers of West Tennessee blacks migrating to the Bluff City, and the organizers were especially concerned that the new (and old) residents be able to "protect themselves against loan sharks." Nevertheless, high living costs and irregular employment frequently put Negroes in a position of depending upon credit. Knoxville blacks, for example, were reported in 1914 to be patronizing local pawnshops six times as often as whites.[13]

As more Negroes, particularly young men and women, entered the cities, the traditional trades could not absorb them all. Frightened by the prospects of "large numbers of negroes constantly . . . on the streets of the cities of this state [and] the increasing crime committed by this class," city councils in Nashville and Memphis (as elsewhere in the South) passed stern vagrancy laws. Nashville officials regularly arrested and tried unemployed blacks, giving them a choice of jail sentences or working for whatever wages and conditions a white employer might offer. For a domestic servant this often meant a sixteen-hour day, at "beggarly wages," with insufficient food, and under abusive and nagging supervision. For a Cumberland River roustabout, unwilling employment carried "brutal and inhuman treatment" as well as unsatisfactory compensation.[14]

Educated and outspoken blacks acknowledged that it was

[13] Col. Arthur S. Colyar, publisher of the Nashville *American* and industrial kingpin in the state, in the Nashville *American*, Aug. 2, 1903; Nashville *Globe*, Jan. 12, 1912; Memphis *Commercial Appeal*, Jan. 8, 30, 1903, June 21, 1915; Sanford, "The Economic Conditions of the Negroes of Knoxville," 70.

[14] Nashville *American*, April 16, 18, 20, Dec. 12, 1903, Jan. 3, 1904; Nashville *Globe*, June 21, 1907, Aug. 27, 1909; Nashville *Tennessean*, April 1, 1909; Griggs, *The One Great Question*, 15–16.

"difficult to get a majority of colored youth to settle down to steady work," but they opposed the misuse of vagrancy legislation. The Reverend James Bond, a member of the Berea College board of trustees and pastor of the Howard Congregational Church (Negro) in Nashville, criticized local vagrancy laws for being used to force blacks to work against their will at the waterfront and on riverboats. "The campaign against negro loafers," he said, lost "its moral and corrective influence" when it was designed only to keep down wages. He pointed out that "it is not claimed that these negroes will not work. The charge is they will not work for a certain wage. . . ." Some "forty or fifty" local churches sought to influence better treatment for roustabouts by forgoing their traditional summer excursions and boycotting the riverboats. No improvement occurred, and Bishop Evans Tyree of the African Methodist Episcopal Church was moved to a strong indictment of conditions in Tennessee's cities: "In many ways [the town] is a veritable trap . . . they will be allowed to do menial labor, but when they begin to show efficiency as mechanics, they do not get a fair chance. . . ."[15]

Other black Tennesseans, viewing successful employment as the main problem, took a more practical approach toward urban confusion. The principal of the "colored school" in Lebanon, for example, organized the Lebanon Bureau of Domestic Labor in 1905 for the purpose of providing prospective employers with information leading to a better understanding of the background, character, and training "of the labor hired." Meanwhile, W. E. B. Du Bois's outspoken *Moon Weekly Illustrated*, published in Memphis, ran advertisements in 1906 for black agencies that wanted to "furnish nice positions for reliable girls who are good domestics."[16] Neither vagrancy laws, ministerial appeals, nor black-run employment agencies, however, could find suit-

[15] Letter to the editor from the Rev. James Bond, Nashville *American*, April 20, 1903; Griggs, *The One Great Question*, 15-16; Bishop Evans Tyree, "Greatest Needs of the Negro Race," in Hartshorn, ed., *An Era of Progress and Promise, 1863-1910*, 390.
[16] Nashville *American*, Sept. 23, 1905; *Moon Weekly Illustrated*, June 23, 1906.

able occupations for the growing numbers of black breadwinners in Tennessee's urban areas.

Steady white encroachment upon traditional "Negro" jobs complicated the black economic pattern in Tennessee cities and also contributed to racial mobility. Negro artisans and mechanics such as bricklayers, carpenters, and blacksmiths held their own, maintaining regular employment and often accumulating property. Other skilled blacks, particularly barbers and firemen, lost out to whites. Although affiliated with the American Federation of Labor in cities like Nashville and Chattanooga, black barbers faced increased white competition throughout the state. They were shunted aside into Jim Crow locals, denied leadership in mixed unions, and threatened with state licensing requirements. Experience in other states had shown licensing laws to be forerunners of exclusion since whites invariably controlled official commissions.[17] A bill sponsored by white barbers failed to pass in 1903, and again in 1905, but the economic squeeze continued, and the traditional black barbering monopoly collapsed rapidly.

In 1907, the Nashville *Globe* struck hard at what it termed the "leech treatment" of that city's black firemen. Pointing out that at one time there had been "two complete fire companies composed of colored men," the *Globe* traced the step-by-step replacement of the personnel of these companies with whites. As blacks retired or were released, white firemen took their places, so that by 1907 one of the formerly all-black groups contained only a single Negro. In addition to complaints of job discrimination in this case, the *Globe* also implied that Negro property did not receive adequate fire protection from white fire-fighting companies. A few black firemen were still on the job as late as 1913, but only in minor and subordinate roles.[18]

As traditional jobs disappeared, the rise of heavy industry in

[17] Nashville *American*, May 13, July 24, 1900, Sept. 2, 1902, Feb. 6, July 27, 1903, March 22, 1905; Chattanooga *Daily Times*, March 20, 1900; interview with Carl A. Cowan, June 16, 1970; Spero and Harris, *The Black Worker*, 59.
[18] Nashville *Globe*, July 12, 1907; Nashville *Banner*, Sept. 11, 1913.

southeastern Tennessee offered new opportunities for many black workers. The proximity of coal and iron and the industrial credo of a New South prompted the development of a series of furnaces and foundries from Knoxville, west to Harriman, and south to Dayton, Chattanooga, and South Pittsburg. From the beginning, these industries hired a large number of black workers for the unpleasant and physically dangerous positions near the blast furnaces. Of the principal iron producers, the Tennessee Coal and Iron Company (TCI), the Roane Iron Company, and the Cahill Iron Works employed the most Negroes, TCI employing over one thousand in 1910.[19] At the furnaces, black laborers regularly filled all positions except those of foremen and engineers. They frequently held the skilled jobs as scaleman and ore grader, and instructed newly hired managers in "the fundamentals of the grading of Southern iron."[20]

Iron production in lower East Tennessee led to a proliferation of secondary and fabricating industries. Several foundries, including three stove companies, the United States Cast Iron Pipe Works, and the Chattanooga Plow Company, also employed much black labor. Skilled and semiskilled puddlers, straighteners, and especially molders were numerous. Some concerns hired black workers exclusively for all but the supervisory jobs, claiming that their work was satisfactory and that their lower wages made competition with larger firms possible. Not unionized in any way until after 1911, black foundry workers either labored on a piece-work basis or received daily wages of between $1.50 and $2.00. This was, in the words of a contemporary, "fairly good money," even though white laborers could command at least $2.75 per day. Other related industries, including several brick kilns and the Dixie Portland Cement Company near South

[19] Greene and Woodson, *The Negro Wage Earner*, 129, 136; Wesley, *Negro Labor in the United States*, 243; Nashville *Globe*, Sept. 2, 1910; "Knoxville Negroes," *Crisis* 9 (Feb. 1915), 186; W. M. Bowron, *The Iron Ores of the Chattanooga District* (Chattanooga Chamber of Commerce, n.d.), 1–2.

[20] Benjamin Franklin Wilson, III, *The Negro As I Have Known Him, 1867–1943* (Nashville: Parthenon, 1946), 77–81.

Pittsburg, provided a steady demand for black industrial labor in this part of Tennessee.[21]

Not content to labor for the white man's benefit, a few ambitious blacks sought a share of the New South's industrial expansion. As might have been expected, several Chattanooga Negroes went into the foundry business. Two concerns started operation around 1900. One burned in 1905, but the other, the Rising Sun Manufacturing Company, sporadically produced "stoves, grate baskets, fenders and fronts . . . and hollow-ware" for several years. Small, black-owned industries sprang up in other localities—a shirt factory owned by Taylor G. Ewing and a shoemaking operation run by H. H. Keller in Nashville, a mattress factory owned and operated by several Knoxville Negroes.[22] But the life expectancy for such ventures was short, and the number of jobs they created was insignificant.

World War I had a tremendous, if temporary, economic impact upon nearly all black Tennesseans, and it speeded up the process of movement. Migration from the rural districts to the cities and from Tennessee to the North was primarily a response to economic opportunity. Therefore, when the war created thousands of new industrial jobs, poverty-stricken farm tenants, displaced miners, underpaid domestics, and low-wage industrial workers looked optimistically to the Du Pont powder plant at Jacksonville, the Alcoa aluminum operations near Maryville, and the numerous war industries in Chicago, Cincinnati, Pittsburgh, and Wheeling, West Virginia.

The huge Du Pont powder plant and its accompanying "village" of 34,000 inhabitants created by far the largest single war-

[21] Chattanooga *Daily Times*, Feb. 19, 21, 24, March 20, 1900; Nashville *American*, Feb. 20, 1900, March 22, 1906; *Proceedings, Hampton Negro Conference*, July 1900, quoted in Greene and Woodson, *The Negro Wage Earner*, 136; *Crisis* 2 (Aug. 1911), 141; Nashville *Globe*, Sept. 2, 1910; Chattanooga *News*, Dec. 14, 1915; interview with De Witt C. Alfred, June 7, 1972.

[22] Chattanooga *Times*, March 2, 1970; White, comp., *Colored Citizens of Chattanooga*, 14; Nashville *American*, Aug. 21, 1903; Nashville *Globe*, Sept. 2, 1910; *Crisis*, 7 (March 1914), 220.

time demand for Negro labor in Tennessee. By November 1918, ten thousand blacks were employed at the plant, 5,375 of whom lived in the company's Negro "reservation," while the remainder commuted by train (often on flatcars) from the Nashville area. Most black workers were construction laborers, porters, and janitors, but some held skilled jobs which paid as much as ten dollars per day, including overtime. Blacks from as far away as New Orleans also flocked to the Du Pont plant, at first "living in tents which dotted the hillside," and later moving into houses "first occupied by white labor." The Du Pont management consistently provided white housing, entertainment, and YMCA programs before turning to the needs of other workers. In order to comply faithfully with segregation practices, a special Mexican compound was also constructed. Influenza and fire frequently ravaged black quarters, but the pull of "fantastic" wages could not be denied and continued to bring hopeful workers into the area until operations slowed down in the spring of 1919.[23]

Special wartime employment and black migration noticeably affected local economic patterns and white attitudes. Nashville, for example, had a short supply of "cooks, maids, nurses, and especially general house workers." In this instance, the Du Pont plant was largely to blame, and observers noted "that Negroes who have been receiving $5, 6, and 7 per week are now being paid $3.30 and $6.00 per day [and] common laborers receive from $2 to $3.30 per day." Also short of laborers and domestics, Memphians warned black migrants that "boom" conditions would not last and urged them to "stay down here because when things get a little tight every one of you knows the road to the back door of some white man's kitchen." So many blacks traveled north to

[23] Lou Cretia Owen Diary, Oct. 1, 1918 to Jan. 25, 1919, Tennessee State Library and Archives; *Old Hickory News*, Aug. 3, 1918 to Dec. 14, 1918; letter to the editor from Albert Hall, head janitor at Du Pont, *ibid.*, Oct. 5, 1918; *Crisis* 16 (Oct. 1918), 293; George E. Haynes to L. A. Turner, Nov. 16, 1918, Haynes Papers, container 1918–1922; Nashville *Globe*, Feb. 15, 1918; interview with Mr. and Mrs. A. E. Lockert, July 16, 1970. Mr. Lockert dropped out of school at Tennessee A & I briefly and rode the commuter train to work as a laborer at Du Pont.

Henry Allen Boyd, founder of the Nashville *Globe*, president of the Citizens Savings Bank and Trust Company, and secretary of the National Baptist Publishing Board, was a driving force for change among black Tennesseans. *(Courtesy of National Baptist Publishing Board)*

145

Robert R. Church, Jr., became a powerful black political leader after forsaking a banking career. He is shown here in his Beale Street office, flanked by photographs of prominent national Republican leaders who aided his organization of black voters in Tennessee. (*Courtesy of Roberta Church*)

The Solvent Savings Bank and Trust Company in Memphis figured prominently in the black business expansions of the 1910s and 1920s. Founded by Robert R. Church, Sr., it was the second oldest black bank in Tennessee. *(Courtesy of Roberta Church)*

The Lincoln League dominated Republican politics in Memphis during
the late 1910s and 1920s. This photograph was taken at a 1916 meeting of
the league in Church's Park. *(Courtesy of Roberta Church)*

The first faculty of the Tennessee Agricultural and Industrial Normal School, 1912, included "three graduates of Atlanta University, three graduates of Fisk, one graduate of Hampton, one graduate of Howard and two graduates of Northern Universities." Principal William Jasper Hale is at front row, center. (*Courtesy of Bureau of Public Relations, Tennessee State University*)

The widely-traveled Fisk Jubilee Singers, pausing for a photograph about 1905, gaine national stature and instilled concern for the development of Fisk University. *(Cou tesy of Fisk University Library)*

ack men played a critical role as laborers in the Cumberland River freight traffic. This notograph of the men at work was taken shortly after 1900 in Nashville. *(Courtesy of nnessee State Library and Archives)*

Black "roustabouts" provided essential labor, loading and unloading cotton and oth
goods at Memphis, a major cotton terminal for the Mississippi Delta. *(Courtesy
Tennessee State Library and Archives)*

hown in this photograph are black workers in a marble quarry near Knoxville shortly ter 1900. *(Courtesy of Tennessee State Library and Archives)*

Black workers "won" the jobs at hard labor—with little compensation. This phosphate miner toils in Maury County, 1914. (*Courtesy of Tennessee State Library and Archives*)

ost black laborers in West Tennessee worked in agriculture, usually raising cotton on
meone else's land. Here a black sharecropper poses with his white landowner, just
tside Memphis circa 1905. *(Courtesy of Tennessee State Library and Archives)*

Cooperative groceries succumbed to the problems of inexperience and low capitalization. Shown above is the interior of one of Roddy's Citizens Co-operative Stores in Memphis, 1919 (*courtesy of* THE CRISIS). Below is a delivery truck for Roddy's Citizens Co-operative Stores. Bert M. Roddy founded the grocery chain, with great flair and borrowed capital. (*Courtesy of* THE CRISIS)

Cincinnati via Knoxville that Cincinnati officials began advertising in the Knoxville *Journal and Tribune*, warning of an oversupply of unskilled laborers in their city and the necessity to enact vagrancy laws. Tennessee blacks went to Chicago in such numbers that a "Tennessee Home League" was formed; it was also a common expression among East Tennessee Negroes that "any day you go to the corner of 35th and State Streets in Chicago, you will see someone from Knoxville if you wait long enough."[24]

While the majority of those black Tennesseans who migrated out of the state did so independently and ended up in the labor pools of Northern cities, labor agents also came south in quest of both skilled and unskilled black industrial workers. Wage offers were attractive by Southern standards, but still below the demand-inflated rates given to whites in the North. Tennessee passed legislation to prevent the "enticement of labor," but "this law never seriously affected the migration of laborers." An agent for the Wheeling Molding Foundry, for example, came to Chattanooga in June 1916 and, despite being arrested, recruited a party of black laborers to return with him. By February 1917, at least one hundred and fifty black foundry workers from Tennessee had migrated to Wheeling. Many remained only briefly, yet those with families usually stayed. Earnings ranged up to "$55 every 12 days," but new residents often had to endure union opposition and the prejudice of both whites and Northern blacks. Beyond a guarantee of return passage, recruited laborers had little advantage over independent migrants—jobs could be of short duration, housing was inadequate, and alcoholic diversions were many.[25]

[24] Memphis *Commercial Appeal*, Oct. 24, 1916; Knoxville *Journal and Tribune*, April 26, 1917, and letter to the editor from Charles W. Cansler, April 22, 1917; Arch M. Trawick to George E. Haynes, Aug. 31, 1917, and Haynes to Dr. R. R. Wright of Philadelphia, May 30, 1918, both in Haynes Papers, containers 1916–1917 and 1918–1922; Nashville *Globe*, Aug. 23, Dec. 6, 1918; interview with Carl A. Cowan, June 26, 1970.

[25] George E. Haynes to Dr. R. R. Wright, May 30, 1918, and "Negro Exodus Questionnaire" completed by H. H. Jones and E. L. Shields of the Wheeling, W. Va., Negro

Wartime industrial demand had diminished by 1920, and black workers faced the realization that their relative position in Tennessee's economic system had changed little—in industry as in agriculture, Negroes were still marginal. If they could be hired cheaply to do the lower status jobs, they were hired; if not, whites got first preference. Nevertheless, the cities and especially the North represented a kind of promised land for black Tennesseans. Much of the exodus of the 1920s continued to be from the farms because, in the view of one observer, "a southern farm family that moved to town improved its economic status if even one member could earn as much as $20 a week." Northern cities appeared to offer even more. One black man left his job at a Memphis stave mill in 1923 and followed a recruiter to the Studebaker operations in South Bend, Indiana. He told his "boss" to keep his $37.50 per month wages because he would "make that much in two days" in South Bend.[26]

One inhibiting and dislocating force in Tennessee throughout the early twentieth century was the attitude of organized labor. Although migrants found little improvement in the North, union practices clearly contributed to the economic insecurity of blacks in the South. Exclusionist practices not only closed newly opening doors in the Southern economy, but also forced blacks out of many previously established positions. Negro workers seldom had satisfactory relationships with either craft or industrial unions. Few labor organizations explicitly excluded them, but the autonomy of most locals gave rein to the prejudices of white members. White Tennesseans opposed the idea of working in comparable jobs with blacks because it tended to put them on a level of social equality. At times this caste consciousness not only

Playground Association, Haynes Papers, containers 1918–1922 and "Misc."; Chattanooga *Daily Times*, June 29, 1916.
[26]Thomas J. Woofter, *A Study of the Economic Status of the Negro*, quoted in Marion Hayes, "A Century of Change: Negroes in the U.S. Economy, 1860–1960," *Monthly Labor Review* 85 (Dec. 1962), 1365; interviews with Grady E. Walker, June 19, 1973, H. C. Hardy, June 20, 1972, and George McDade, May 29, 1972.

hurt blacks but also aided management and hindered unionization; as CIC executive secretary Will Winton Alexander commented, white workers "fear Negroes more than they fear exploitation by factory employers." In Tennessee's craft unions, meanwhile, W. E. B. Du Bois had observed as early as 1902 that "they
do not receive Negroes as apprentices and when Negroes are
employed as helpers they prevent them from receiving promotion according to merit."[27]

Where craft unions were especially weak or where blacks constituted a large percentage of a region's skilled craftsmen, labor
organizers had to accept all qualified workers. This meant, except
in Nashville, that black brickmasons, stonemasons, tile setters,
and cement finishers, for example, generally operated from
mixed unions. The trend in Tennessee, and elsewhere in the
South, however, was to become more exclusive as the percentage
of white membership increased and as the union's bargaining
position improved.[28]

Samuel Gompers, president of the American Federation of
Labor (AFL), at first resisted admission of craft unions that excluded blacks, but he soon surrendered to the realities of racial
discrimination. By 1900, practically all of Nashville's black artisans had been forced to operate independently or from segregated unions. After the first decade of the century AFL locals
became increasingly segregated in Memphis, Chattanooga, and
Knoxville. The result was second-rate union membership. Social
custom dictated preeminence for the white union, and white
leaders took little interest in their black "brothers." White unions

[27] Will W. Alexander, "Negroes and Organized Labor in the South," *Opportunity* 8
(April 1930), 109; William Edward Burghardt Du Bois, ed., *The Negro Artisan*, Atlanta
University Publications No. 7 (1902), 143.

[28] Greene and Woodson, *The Negro Wage Earner*, 192–93; W. E. B. Du Bois and
Augustus Granville Dills, eds., *The Negro American Artisan*, Atlanta University Publica-
tions No. 17 (1912), 76–77; interview with Carl A. Cowan, June 26, 1970; George Brown
Tindall, *The Emergence of the New South, 1913–1945* (Baton Rouge: Louisiana State
Univ. Press, 1967), 163; Nashville *American*, Jan. 29, 1905; "The President's Annual
Address to the Eighteenth Annual Convention of the National Negro Business League
Held at Chattanooga, Tennessee, August 15–17, 1917" Napier Papers, container 1.

supported the licensing of barbers and frequently opposed industrial education for Negroes because it trained potential black competition. Although given representation on trades and labor councils, black unions were forced to endure insults, to march in the rear of Labor Day parades, and to remain quiet. During the construction boom of the 1920s, white building trades unions pushed through licensing laws that discriminated against blacks and virtually excluded them from the new electrical trades.[29]

Black workers found industrial unions more sympathetic, but still subject to local prejudice and exclusion. The International Molders' Union of North America, for example, made numerous attempts to organize Chattanooga's black iron and steel workers, but national officials were met each time by white resistance and black suspicion. Similar campaigns to unionize furnace operations in South Pittsburg also failed from lack of either white or black enthusiasm.[30] In 1911, the International Molders "placed a southerner . . . in the southern field and he gave special attention to the matter of organizing the Negroes in Chattanooga with considerable success and also with much opposition from the foundry men." Owners, having used unorganized blacks to keep wages low, threatened to discharge any Negro who joined the union and used their influence to have "Negro moulders out on strike arrested for loitering, etc." Although having shown previous hostility to increases in the black work force, white union members now made an uncharacteristic switch in priorities, subordinating race to unionism and striking in order "to protect the

[29] Greene and Woodson, The Negro Wage Earner, 189–90, 192–93, 322; Nashville American, Sept. 3, 1901, Sept. 2, Aug. 5, 1903, March 22, 27, 1905; Du Bois and Dills, eds., The Negro American Artisan, 77, 93; Crisis 19 (March 1919), 276; Knoxville Journal and Tribune, Aug. 31, 1913; letter from George Edmund Haynes to H. H. Thomas, president of the Brick Layers Union No. 1 (black), May 20, 1918, Haynes Papers, container 1918–1922; W. S. Turner, "The Negro and the Changing South," Journal of Social Forces 7 (Sept. 1928–June 1929), 117; Tindall, Emergence of the New South, 163; Northrup, Organized Labor and the Negro, 18–19, 38.

[30] Chattanooga Daily Times, Feb. 19, 21, 24, March 20, 1900; Nashville American, Feb. 20, 1900; Wilson, The Negro As I Have Known Him, 102–4; Booker T. Washington, "The Negro and the Labor Unions," Atlantic Monthly 111 (June 1913), 764.

Negro membership." The national union also paid "strike benefits" to blacks and went "to considerable expense in keeping
Negro members, who [were] on strike, out of jail." Union leaders
credited their success to convincing white members that "the
question was one of economics . . . not one of social equality." By
1920, many of Tennessee's four thousand black iron and steel
workers were union cardholders.[31] Otherwise, industrial unionism was weak, and most white Tennesseans accepted blacks into
membership only after racial exclusion became a detriment to all
workers.

The strongest Southern unions were those connected with the
railroads, and these unions were staunchly anti-Negro and racially exclusive in their demands. Their antagonism undeniably
eliminated Negro jobs in Tennessee. Black railroad work was of
three different types: laborers such as roadbed repairers, track
layers, section hands and freight handlers; janitorial and service
workers such as porters, waiters, and sweepers; and skilled or
semiskilled switchmen, enginemen, and even security guards.
The first group had taken over from the Irish as the principal
railroad builders of the South. Their jobs, and even lives, were
much too insecure to attract or seek union involvement. The
black track laborer in Tennessee earned little more than a dollar a
day, was subject to attack from fearful white communities, and
lived often in a state of peonage which rivaled that found in the
Congo Free State. Federal authorities attempted on one occasion
to put a stop to the whippings, starving, forced labors, and killings
which reportedly went on in a railroad camp operated by Robert
B. Oliver and Brothers in Blount County. The contractors were
charged with holding black workers in debt servitude, and two
trials were held in Knoxville between November 1906, and
March 1907. Both juries (one of which included a black man),

---

[31] Editor of the *International Molders' Journal*, quoted in Du Bois and Dills, eds., *The Negro American Artisan*, 86–87; Washington, "The Negro and the Labor Unions," 764; Wesley, *Negro Labor in the United States*, 293–94; Charles Spurgeon Johnson, *The Negro in American Civilization* (New York: Henry Holt, 1930), 47.

however, refused to convict any of the whites involved, and the inhuman conditions persisted as late as 1913.[32]

At the other end of the black railroad employment scale were the porters and waiters. Blacks dominated these fields as they did other occupations of the "domestic servant" type. Jobs were competitive, pay was good, and opportunities for travel and glamor were attractive. Ignored by white unions, these workers established a local of A. Phillip Randolph's Brotherhood of Sleeping Car Porters in Chattanooga in 1926. They immediately called for a basic wage increase of from $67.50 per month to $100 per month, but a long-time porter and former Randolph organizer recalled later that only through gradual improvement did blacks become "more than a piece of equipment."[33]

Skilled railroad workers such as firemen and switchmen encountered very different employment conditions. Unlike track laborers, their main concern was for their jobs rather than their lives; they competed directly with whites for jobs (unlike porters and waiters) and therefore were of great concern to white unions. "By 1921 nearly all Southern railroads had granted recognition to the operating unions," and these unions had a persistent record in Tennessee of attempting to remove skilled black workers and to replace them with unionized whites. In 1906 white switchmen in the South Memphis yards of the Illinois Central threatened a wildcat strike unless thirty-five black switchmen were replaced with whites. Railroad authorities complied with the demands but rehired the black workers when the "lily white" Brotherhood of Railroad Trainmen reminded its members that their contract required at least 50 percent of the Memphis switchmen to be

[32] Federal Writers' Project, *These Are Our Lives*, 337-40. John C. Houk to Robert R. Church, Feb. 20, 1920; Houk to Gen. James S. Clarkson, Feb. 8, 1907, Houk Papers (Clarkson letter in container 74, but Church letter uncatalogued as of June 1970); W. M. Bowron, *Iron Ores of the Chattanooga*, 1; Nashville *American*, Feb. 26, 1907; Knoxville *Journal and Tribune*, Sept. 15, 19, Nov. 21, 24, 1906; March 6, 1907. Indications that cruel treatment and "peonage" conditions persisted come from recollections of the author's grandfather, who worked briefly as a guard for Oliver Construction Co. in 1913.
[33] Interviews with De Witt C. Alfred, June 7, 1972, Luther J. Fearn, June 8, 1972, and Owen Whitaker, July 13, 1972.

Negroes. The contract had been negotiated as a compromise after a previous white demand for exclusion of lower-wage blacks.[34] A similar agreement was reached when the Brotherhood of Locomotive Firemen and Enginemen struck the Cincinnati, New Orleans and Texas Pacific (C.N.O. & T.P.) Railroad in 1911. White firemen claimed first preference on "work runs and promotion" on the line between Chattanooga and Cincinnati, and the C.N.O. & T.P. initially responded by hiring full crews of Negroes, but when angry violence broke out almost immediately along the route between Oakdale, Tennessee, and Somerset, Kentucky, a new contract was accepted. The brotherhood failed to dislodge all black workers as it intended, but as always the employment opportunities for black Tennesseans again diminished: striking whites were rehired; black firemen were banished from the route north of Oakdale and restricted to no more than one-half of the company's passenger and preferred freight runs; and, "in the district between Oakdale and Chattanooga, the percentage of colored firemen hereafter employed [was] not to exceed the percentage in service on Jan. 1, 1911."[35]

Unpleasant working conditions and lack of employment security led many black railroad employees in Tennessee to leave their jobs in 1917 and 1918 and take advantage of the more remunerative jobs in war industry. Companies hired white replacements, and the union program of Negro exclusion appeared to have been given an unexpected boost. When the federal government took control of the railroad system, however, Acting Director-General William Gibbs McAdoo issued an order equalizing pay of black and white workers, effective June 1, 1918, and the exodus of skilled black labor halted.[36] This order, made by a Southerner "as an act of simple justice," infuriated white

---

[34] Tindall, *Emergence of the New South*, 163; Memphis *Commercial Appeal*, Aug. 13, 14, 1906; Nashville *American*, Aug. 14, 15, 1906.

[35] Chattanooga *Daily Times*, March 7, 9, 11, 15, 24, 26, 1911; Knoxville *Journal and Tribune*, March 24, 1911.

[36] Spero and Harris, *The Black Worker*, 294–95.

railroad employees, particularly in Memphis. On January 13, 1919, the white switchmen in the yards of the Illinois Central, the Yazoo and Mississippi Valley, the Frisco System, and the Union Railway went on strike. They maintained that equal pay was degrading and that all black switchmen should be discharged. The strike quickly fizzled, but white determination hardly lessened. In 1920 and 1921, "anonymous notices were posted, warning colored trainmen that unless they quit their jobs they would be killed." After several blacks were killed and both Memphis and national NAACP officials protested, a reluctant investigation by federal and Illinois Central agents turned up the existence of a $300 bounty on the head of each Negro who did not comply with the orders of a terrorist group called the Zulus.[37] There were a few arrests and most black workers stood firm, but discriminatory contracts, accepted by federal authorities, had permanently reduced Negro job opportunities on the railroads. Remaining workers continued under constant union pressure and were often demoted to lesser-paying jobs. In 1924, 115,937 of the 136,065 black railroad workers in the South were in the laborer and porter categories. Of the 8,100 black workers in Tennessee at that date, an increasingly large percentage undoubtedly were common laborers.[38]

Whether coerced or inspired, the great population and occupational movement of black Tennesseans during the first twenty years of the century wrought some significant change for the 1920s. Outmigration and urbanization continued, and nonagricultural employment rose another 20 percent between 1920 and

[37] Memphis *Commercial Appeal*, Jan. 14, 15, 16, 1919; Memphis *News-Scimitar*, Jan. 14, 1919; Nashville *Banner*, Jan. 14, 1919; Spero and Harris, *The Black Worker*, 296–303; F. Ray Marshall, *Labor in the South* (Cambridge: Harvard Univ. Press, 1967), 53–55; Northrup *Organized Labor and the Negro*, 51; "Colored Trainmen," *Crisis* 22 (Sept. 1921), 212–13; Minutes of the Board of Directors of the NAACP, Feb. 10, 1919, p. 27, NAACP Papers, container A-9.

[38] "Negro Employment in the Railroads," *Monthly Labor Review* 19 (Nov. 1924), 161; Walter F. White to James Weldon Johnson, Jan. 22, 1919, NAACP Papers, container G-199; interviews with De Witt C. Alfred, June 7, 1972, and Owen Whitaker, July 13, 1972; Marshall, *Labor in the South*, 57.

1930. The increase was mostly in the domestic, unskilled, and semiskilled areas and reflected an expanded role for black women as wage earners. Wages for black women, even in menial jobs, could not support a family, but they were essential in meeting higher urban living costs and, all too often, were the most stable source of family income.[39]

White encroachment and union exclusive practices continued to eat away at black job opportunities. A survey of the economic conditions of all Negroes in Nashville in 1929 showed a decrease of almost 50 percent in the number of distinct job occupations held by blacks in the nine years since 1920. Evidence indicated that, while some unskilled industrial jobs were opening up, others, particularly in the craft areas, were closing at a much faster rate. In 1929, 71.5 percent of the men and 84.5 percent of the women were classified as common and semiskilled laborers; average per capita income for this, the state's most prosperous black community, was only $347.[40] A National Planning Association study of Chattanooga in 1955 documented the continuation of this trend. Referring to the railroads, among the more serious discriminators, an investigator reported that "the number of firemen and shop-helpers is probably declining. No new Negro locomotive firemen are being hired. Apparently the only shop classifications for which Negroes are being hired are those requiring no skill."[41]

---

[39] Clarence Heer, *Income and Wages in the South* (Chapel Hill: Univ. of North Carolina Press, 1930), 6; Bureau of the Census, *Fifteenth Census of the United States, 1930. Population*, 3 vols. (Washington, D.C., 1931), III, 1512ff., Daves, *A Social Study of the Colored Population of Knoxville*, 6; United States Department of Labor (USDL), *Women in Tennessee Industries*, Bulletin of the Women's Bureau, No. 56 (Washington, D.C.; Government Printing Office, 1927), 1, 3–5, 39; USDL, *Negro Women in Industry in 15 States*, Bulletin of the Women's Bureau, No. 70 (Washington, D.C.: Government Printing Office, 1929), 33, 39; Willis D. Weatherford and Charles Spurgeon Johnson, *Race Relations: Adjustment of Whites and Negroes in the United States* (Boston: Heath, 1934), 381; Greene and Woodson, *The Negro Wage Earner*, 286.

[40] Edwards, *Southern Urban Negro as a Consumer*, 13–14, 32–36, 45; *Nashville Globe*, March 4, 1932.

[41] National Planning Association Committee of the South, *Selected Studies of Negro Employment in the South* (Washington, D.C.: National Planning Association, 1955), 438.

Facing the physical and spiritual onslaught of the Great Depression, black Tennesseans were 50.3 percent urban, almost double the figure for 1900, but they still stood on the bottom rung of the economic ladder.[42] Overcrowding, disease, debt, and job insecurity offered few tangible advantages over the fear, hard work, lien entanglements, and economic backwardness of the tenant farm. The black worker was easily dislodged by those forced down the scale from above, and his position remained the most precarious one in the state's economy. The decades from 1900 to 1930 seemed to solidify a permanently restrictive economic environment for black Tennesseans.

[42]*Fifteenth Census: 1930, Population*, III, 873.

CHAPTER VIII.

Operating in the Black

The late nineteenth century was the age of big business and the mythical domain of Horatio Alger. But it was a white world; the poor black farm boy never made it to the top, and black entrepreneurs had little impact upon the national market. In Tennessee, the typical black businessman in 1900 operated a small retail concern which grossed well under $5,000 per year. The prospects for significant growth were meager, and the likelihood of failure was high. During the first three decades of the new century, Negroes made several efforts to determine the inhibiting factors and to encourage black business growth in Tennessee. Finding limitations of race and caste to be the major obstacles, the more aggressive black entrepreneurs used the rhetoric of racial solidarity to cultivate a black clientele. Although one black contemporary later called "the 'opportunity' to operate a separate business" one of the most "cruel mockeries to which . . . the American Negro has been subjected," many black businessmen felt that their profit lay in catering to an exclusively black patronage.[1]

The basic restriction placed upon Negro businesses was their "blackness." They were forced by the unwritten laws of caste to locate within informally designated Negro areas. Location and social consciousness, in turn, limited the clientele to blacks. A

---

[1] Merah Steven Stuart, *An Economic Detour: A History of Insurance in the Lives of American Negroes* (New York: Malliet, 1940), xix. Stuart's own business career, beginning in the second decade of the century, centered in Memphis.

business which thus relied solely on the patronage of an economically marginal neighborhood had a future as precarious and vulnerable as its patrons. In contrast, the white merchant or saloon keeper had the choice of serving the more affluent white community or competing with the disadvantaged black businessman for Negro customers.

There were other handicaps. A white person who "patronize[d] a Negro in a certain business" was considered to have "sunk to the lowest dregs." On the other hand, as one black businessman said later, "[B]lacks then, and some now, they think the white man's ice is colder than the black man's ice, his sugar is sweeter, and whatever he's doing is just a little better." For instance, in March 1912, Andrew N. Johnson, a successful Nashville undertaker, opened the Majestic Theater in the middle of the capital city's black business district. Described by the Nashville *Globe* as a "magnificent playhouse erected at an enormous expense," the Majestic failed to draw the expected number of customers, despite the appearance of two consecutive first-class black theater companies. Blacks in the community complained that prices were too high but continued to patronize white houses, paying "as high as $1.00 and sometimes $1.50 to stroll through some side door and make their way to the last story in the house, and their [*sic*] strain their eyes and ears to see and hear a performance."[2]

Still, if the glowing description of the *Globe* was accurate, the Majestic Theater was not a typical black enterprise. Most black businessmen lacked the capital to compete directly with the attractions offered by white concerns. In 1900 Booker T. Washington estimated that in the nation there were only 9,838 black-run businesses which had required an initial capital investment. Nashville and Memphis, especially, contained many of these, and the number continued to grow in Tennessee throughout the first

---

[2]Interview with James T. Chandler, June 28, 1972; Nashville *Globe*, March 15, 1907, March 1, May 31, 1912.

thirty years of the century. But seldom was much capital involved. Rarely could a black man receive a large loan from a white bank, and black corporate stock enterprises always had trouble raising their authorized capital.[3]

Without the necessary capital, the black businessman found it hard to give service equal to that of the white competitor and still maintain comparable prices. Moreover, his black customers were poor. The *Globe* observed that blacks were "great race lovers until it comes to business matters." When money was involved, the *Globe* continued, "then he brings his brother down to this cold, double proposition: 'Can you give me better service than the white man and can you make me a cheaper price?' " A black shoemaker, for example, working with hand tools, found it difficult to make repairs as cheaply and as satisfactorily as the white craftsman who operated with modern machinery.[4] He either continued on a small, subsistence scale or was driven from the field.

The same was true for black laundries and groceries. A. G. Price, former manager of Negro-owned steam laundries in Nashville and Memphis, blamed the stockholders in the small corporations: "They will not invest enough in the beginning. In order for the colored man to be successful in the laundry business, he must install the latest machinery and stop using what the white laundries have put aside. . . ." In February 1911, the People's Steam Laundry in Nashville failed precisely for the reasons cited by Price.[5] Grocery stores and restaurants, which were the most numerous black-operated enterprises in Tennessee's Negro communities, suffered similarly from a lack of capital. Limited investment led to inadequate stock and facilities; inadequate stock and facilities meant small patronage; small patronage lim-

[3]John Henry Harmon, Jr., "The Negro as a Local Business Man," *Journal of Negro History* 14 (April 1929), 143; Booker Taliaferro Washington, *The Negro in Business* (Boston: Hertel, Jenkins, 1907), 16; interview with George McDade, May 29, 1972.
[4]Nashville *Globe*, May 3, 1907, Jan. 21, 1910.
[5]*Ibid.*, June 5, 1908, Feb. 17, 1911.

ited profits and the optimism of the owner; low profits and a lack of optimism restricted the growth of the business. Although Nashville's college-educated I. E. Green turned a $200 investment in 1913 into a grocery concern grossing $25,000 per year by 1928, not many blacks had access to the $200, and in a 1929 Nashville survey, twenty of thirty-five black groceries "were either in a run-down and dilapidated condition, or were otherwise unattractive." The same study found that "of 52 housewives interviewed in Nashville from skilled labor families, 49 . . . were found to be buying groceries from white stores, and 26 . . . from Negro stores. Of the 49 housewives buying from white units, 26 . . . were doing all of their trading with them. Of the 26 housewives buying from Negro stores, only 3 . . . were going to these stores for all their groceries." In Knoxville, the black groceries were very small; the twenty-four in existence in 1925 gave work to only twenty-nine Negroes.[6]

Not only a lack of capital, but also the virtual absence of either formal business education or job training played a significant and frustrating role in the poor performance of black businesses. The curriculum in black schools focused upon manual labor, farming, and teacher training, but not business administration or even bookkeeping. Until 1916, when Fisk offered "a few general courses" and organized a two-year secretarial training program, no black college in the United States offered any business courses. As late as 1929, the subjects of accounting, business organization, finance, and marketing were just beginning to find their way into the average Negro college curriculum. The black youth with the desire and means to gain education in fields such as engineering or business usually had to go north, and, finding a more hospitable climate, he seldom returned.[7]

[6] Edwards, *The Southern Urban Negro as a Consumer*, 120, 131, 140, 147; *Crisis* 20 (July 1920), 149; Daves, *Social Study of the Colored Population of Knoxville*, 22–23.
[7] Vishnu V. Oak, *The Negro's Adventure in General Business* (Yellow Springs, Ohio: Antioch Press, 1949), 174; interviews with Mr. and Mrs. J. Herman Daves, July 2, 1970, Mr. and Mrs. A. E. Lockert, July 10, 1970, George McDade, May 29, 1972; Edwards, *The Southern Urban Negro as a Consumer*, 125, 139.

The other method of learning sound business practice—on-the-job training—was effectively closed to blacks by segregation. Rarely was a Negro employed in a white concern except as a janitor, cleaning woman, or errand boy. Most black enterprises, meanwhile, were either one-man operations or provided work for only one or two other people, usually members of the owner's family. Black businesses in Knoxville, for instance, employed an average of slightly more than two persons each, including the proprietor, in 1925.[8] The result of this dearth of practical training was a high business mortality rate and a nagging distrust of black concerns among Negroes. Part of the distrust was also an internalized sense of racial inferiority and a reluctance by the more successful blacks to risk the level of economic security they had already achieved. The small black middle class, heavily professional, were afraid to invest their savings in black ventures, to patronize black stores, or to deposit money in black banks not only because Negro businesses had a high rate of failure or were less attractive physically, but also because, for some, it was a reminder of their blackness. Trading with white merchants gave a vicarious identification with the ruling class, of being "the white man's nigger," as some of the younger blacks said.

From the time of its founding in 1906 throughout the 1910s, the *Globe* preached race pride and devotion to black business. Sensitive to slurs on the business ability of blacks, the *Globe* was confident that "slowly but surely, the Negroes of this city and of the country at large [would reach] the conclusion that a black man [would] come nearer giving a square deal to a black man than [would] those of another race."[9] The concern with racial business solidarity was not original or peculiar to the Nashville *Globe*. A black Memphis educator reported in 1908 that ministers and other leaders in that city were "exhorting" members of their race

[8] Daves, *Social Study of the Colored Population of Knoxville*, 22–23; Edwards, *The Southern Urban Negro as a Consumer*, 125.
[9] Nashville *Globe*, March 15, 1907, Jan. 29, 1909, Jan. 21, 1910, March 29, 1912.

171

to "throw their strength in support of every worthy enterprise of the colored people." And as early as 1895, Robert Fulton Boyd, a Nashville Negro surgeon with a national reputation, had publicly posed the question: "Why should not our people spend their money with men of the race?" Slightly anticipating Booker T. Washington's famous Atlanta speech, Boyd envisioned the rise of rich black "merchants and capitalists" and an end to prejudice "and the iniquitous legislation against the race in the South." As a man of some means, Boyd practiced his convictions, investing heavily in black banking and real estate enterprises before his death in 1912. Nashville's Richard Hill was another early advocate of "buying black." A small contractor who had been in charge of the Negro Building and race exhibits at the Tennessee Centennial Exposition of 1897, Hill spoke before the National Negro Business League in 1903, declaring: "if the Negro was fit to make fortunes for others, he was fit to make fortunes for himself."[10]

The Nashville *Globe*, however, turned the idea of economic solidarity into a virtual crusade. Formed in an attempt to sustain black pride and enterprise during the streetcar boycotts of 1905–1906, the *Globe*, in its earliest extant edition, praised two local livery stables for buying their coaches from a black carriage-maker in Greenfield, Ohio. Although admitting that poor Negroes could not afford to buy services from a black concern when better or cheaper equivalents could be purchased from whites, the editors made a plea for loyalty and sacrifice if necessary. "We owe it to ourselves," they said, "to strive with all of the power within us to keep our little business enterprises alive." Yet the *Globe* also realized that basic attitudes and practices had to be changed. The benefits of cost accounting were discussed briefly in a 1912 editorial which ended with the warning that "education is a necessity in this age of big business, and no *race* can hope to permanently succeed in business . . . when it reaches the con-

[10] Hamilton, *The Bright Side of Memphis*, 15–16; Robert Fulton Boyd, "Business Men Among the Race," in James T. Haley, comp., *Afro-American Encyclopaedia*, 202–3; Nashville *American*, Aug. 20, 1903.

clusion that education is of no use." The *Globe* sought to educate black people both by informing them of successful Negro enterprises and also by urging potential investors to "plan well every undertaking" and avoid "the haphazard way [of] investing a few dollars here and a few yonder." The *Globe* usually recommended low-yield conservative business ventures rather than high-risk investments.[11]

Support for black banks played a particularly important role in the *Globe*'s "buy black" crusade, perhaps because one of the editors, Henry Allen Boyd, had a family financial interest in the One-Cent Savings Bank and Trust Company, the older of Nashville's two black banks. Maintaining that these concerns had the ability to create capital for business expansion, the *Globe* attacked race organizations such as fraternal orders that did not patronize them. Explaining that "a bank is one institution that you cannot run on moral [support] or sympathy," editorials blasted so-called leaders who "preach their sermons on the housetops of 'Race Loyalty,' but . . . do not practice their preachments."[12] Other blacks, both in Nashville and other parts of the state, offered support to the *Globe*, and several black newspapers endorsed the ideas and activities of Nashville's "race loyalists."[13]

The *Globe* sought to educate black Tennesseans in the use of banking facilities and also to inform them of the activities of a growing number of race institutions. In November 1907, this newspaper ran its first article on the role of black banks—extolling their stability during that year of financial panic. It announced a policy in January 1908 of publishing financial statements from all thirty-eight black concerns in the country. In

[11]Nashville *Globe*, Jan. 11, 1907, Feb. 7, 1908, Feb. 10, Sept. 15, 1911, May 31, Sept. 6, 1912. Author's italics.

[12]*Ibid.*, Jan. 13, 1911, Jan. 12, 1912, April 4, 1913. Nashville's two black banks were the One-Cent Savings Bank and Trust Company (1904) and the People's Savings Bank and Trust Company (1909).

[13]*Ibid.*, anonymous letter to the editor, June 25, 1909, letter to the editor from black Nashville lawyer James Bumpus, July 7, 1911, the Norfolk *Journal and Guide*, quoted March 11, 1910, and *East Tennessee News*, quoted Jan. 31, 1913.

addition, a standing bank directory was published, including individual capitalization, so that "Negroes having business from one town to another might send it directly through one of these banks." Part of the interest was selfish—an attempt to make Nashville "the clearing house of the South so far as Negro banks are concerned." But there was also a genuine desire to acquaint the public with the presence of black financial institutions and win its trust.[14]

The *Globe's* repeated emphasis on winning public trust from blacks was made necessary by past failures. The old Freedmen's Savings Bank and Trust Company, headquartered in Washington and chartered by Congress in 1865, operated branches in Nashville, Memphis, Chattanooga, and Columbia, Tennessee. Although the management of the Freedmen's system was almost completely dominated by white directors, black men were highly visible in the ranks of lower officials and employees, and many black Tennesseans had trusted the bank with their hard-earned savings. Therefore, when serious mismanagement caused the collapse of the entire banking structure in 1874, outraged depositors in Tennessee blamed men of their own race. The failure of a private black bank in Chattanooga in 1893 simply underscored racial distrust. The *Globe*, therefore, sought to deflate damaging rumors, to play down failures such as that of the True Reformers bank in Richmond, to remind blacks that "each individual ought to feel a personal responsibility for the success of these banks." Bankers, too, were admonished that their institutions could "do more to establish confidence than any other branch of business."[15]

The same handicaps worked against black lawyers as against black entrepreneurs. Many Tennessee Negroes felt that white

[14]Nashville *Globe*, March 15, Nov. 8, 1907, Jan. 17, Sept. 4, 1908, Jan. 22, 1909.
[15]Taylor, *The Negro in Tennessee*, 162–64; Walter Lynwood Fleming, *The Freedmen's Savings Bank: A Chapter in the Economic History of the Negro Race* (Chapel Hill: Univ. of North Carolina Press, 1927), 38–39, 50–51, 66, 98–99, 128, 159–62; Nashville *Globe*, Jan. 29, 1909, Jan. 21, 1910, Aug. 11, 1911, March 29, 1912.

lawyers had better training, but more importantly, a white lawyer would make a more favorable impression on a white judge or jury. Negroes who refused to retain men of their own race, however, began to draw fire from other blacks. The *Globe* lambasted the National Baptist Convention in 1910 because it had refused the legal services of Robert L. Mayfield, favoring white counsel instead. Responses from the three Negro Baptist publications in Nashville failed to mollify either the *Globe* or Mayfield, who charged breach of contract and won a fifty dollar court judgment. In East Tennessee, Randolph Miller of the Chattanooga *Blade* ran afoul of one of his subscribers, for "always preaching race solidarity" but employing a white lawyer when involved in a traffic accident.[16]

White businessmen in Nashville seem not to have become very alarmed at the "buy black" campaign, but some did take notice. White banks sent letters to black community leaders, extolling the size and safety of their institutions and seeking new accounts. And when R. H. Boyd announced that he intended to manufacture Negro dolls for families "which cared to instill race pride in their children," the *Globe* charged that white merchants tried to ward off the Christmas competition by asserting in the press that Boyd's Negro doll factory would never materialize. The dolls were produced for some twenty years, and efforts to encourage black business growth persisted, but it was doubtful that black competition damaged white business greatly.[17]

Black enterprises begun in the early twentieth century entered a national market characterized by monopolies and the emergence of chain stores. And yet, beyond the emphasis upon racial loyalty, black businessmen were rarely innovative and generally were closely attuned to the traditional economics of natural

[16] Nashville *Globe*, Feb. 18, March 3, 11, April 8, 1910; *Hamilton County Herald*, Feb. 2, 1945. [17] The American National Bank to George Edmund Haynes, Nov. 9, 1915, Haynes Papers, container 1914–1915; Nashville *Globe*, Dec. 3, 1909; interview with T. B. Boyd, Jr., July 2, 1972.

law and individual initiative. Booker T. Washington, a man for all seasons in the eyes of most black Americans, provided static, if not backward-looking, economic leadership. In establishing the National Negro Business League in 1900, Washington took what was essentially the idea of W. E. B. Du Bois and turned it into a conservative institution for separating business affairs from the "sociological and other such questions."[18] The Business League successfully corralled the support of most black entrepeneurs for Washington's multifaceted "Tuskegee Machine."

Tennessee Negroes accepted Washington's business philosophy as well as his approach to other racial matters and set about organizing local chapters of the National Negro Business League. J. C. Napier, a friend of Washington, organized the first Tennessee branch of the league in Nashville in 1902. In a gesture to Napier and in an attempt to gain support in Tennessee, Washington brought the annual national meeting to Nashville in 1903. Chapters soon sprang up throughout the state. By 1909, black businessmen in sixteen communities had organized, seven in East Tennessee, five in Middle Tennessee and four in the heavily Negro, but largely rural West Tennessee. Undertakers like George W. Franklin, Jr., of Chattanooga, Preston Taylor of Nashville, and J. Jay Scott and Wayman Wilkerson of Memphis played key roles.[19]

Meetings and talk, however, were not enough for the ambitious young newspapermen of the Nashville *Globe*, despite their acceptance of Washington's emphasis on business development. Basically agreeing with Du Bois's original intention to form a national business association through "the gradual federation" of

[18] Louis R. Harlan, "Booker T. Washington and the National Negro Business League," in William G. Shade and Roy C. Herrenkohl, eds., *Seven on Black: Reflections on the Negro Experience in America* (Philadelphia: Lippincott, 1969), 76-78; Booker T. Washington, "The National Negro Business League," *World's Work* 4 (Oct. 1902), 2673.

[19] Nashville *American*, Aug. 1, 1902, Aug. 20, 21, 22, 1903; Nashville *Globe*, July 23, 1909; Washington, *The Negro in Business*, 99; Indianapolis *Freeman*, Dec. 2, 1905.

local leagues into "state and national organizations,"[20] the *Globe* charged in 1907 that most black movements which were "national in scope" showed no tangible accomplishments. The Business League was its prime example. Accusing the organization of being "planned on democratic lines . . . but really aristocratic in [its] workings," the *Globe* maintained:

it is evident to the most casual observer that much of the good that the body attempts is neutralized by the fact that so little stress is placed upon the local organization. Here in Nashville the local organization . . . has been asleep so long that one is almost justified in saying that it is dead. Yet, when the time for the national meeting comes, Nashville is represented and that, too, by able business men.

The men who organize these various national movements have high ideals, but it seems to us they put the stress at the wrong place. Instead of starting with local organizations . . . they usually begin—and end—with a national meeting at which only the well-to-do can be present, and at which they represent only themselves.[21]

The *Globe* did not so much want to call "the attention of America to our conditions as . . . to awaken in the race itself a realization of our present standing." Without local organizations where the pronouncements of the national league could be carried out, "these national meetings will not be worth to the race as a whole, the amount of money paid out for transportation and for having a good time. . . ."[22]

While these criticisms did not reject the idea of the National Negro Business League, they led to the formation in 1908 of a new "progressive" Business and Professional League, headed by a forty-one-year-old newcomer to the city, Andrew N. Johnson. Interestingly, its young membership did not include J. C. Napier, Preston Taylor, or other elder statesmen. In 1909 this organization "agreed to cooperate" with the older Negro Business

[20]Nashville *Globe*, April 5, 1907; Harlan, "Booker T. Washington and the National Negro Business League," 77.

[21]Nashville *Globe*, Feb. 1, 1907.

[22]*Ibid.*, Nov. 1, 1907.

League of Nashville, but it chose to remain separate. Neither body established much momentum, however, bringing a critical evaluation from the *Globe* in 1912: "The Business Men's League of Nashville is out-distancing the ground hog. For the weather rodent only promises to stay in his hole six weeks at a time; but our business league makes it about eleven months out of twelve."[23]

At his national meetings, Booker T. Washington paraded testimonials of successful black businessmen in an attempt to inspire "a spirit that turns the impossible to the possible, from that which is artificial and unstable to that which is natural and enduring. . . ." The *Globe* accepted the need for a new spirit but was more concerned with practical results, stressing specific local needs: business education, financial institutions, and community solidarity. The National Negro Business League "never seriously grappled with the real problems of Negro Business"; the Nashville *Globe* did.[24]

Although other blacks, particularly those writing in the *Crisis*, came to hold similar complaints against the league, none were as specific and as penetrating as those of the *Globe*—at least not until after Washington's death in 1915. And, in spite of the practical criticisms of the younger men in Nashville, black businessmen in Tennessee continued to hold prominent national offices, organize local chapters, and pay their dues to the national organization. Over a dozen of the approximately one hundred "life members" of the league were from Tennessee in 1912 (ten from Nashville alone). J. C. Napier, meanwhile, succeeded Booker T. Washington as president in 1915, and Robert R. Church, Thomas H. Hayes, and Bert M. Roddy of Memphis and Richard Henry Boyd and W. D. Hawkins of Nashville all held high offices in the organization prior to 1917. Occasionally, evidence of concrete achievements came from the local chapters in Tennessee. The Bristol branch, headed by the versatile Robert E.

---

[23]*Ibid.*, March 19, 1909, March 1, 1912; Nashville *Tennessean*, Nov. 24, 1907.
[24]Nashville *Globe*, Aug. 18, 1911; Harlan, "Booker T. Washington and the National Negro Business League," 82.

Clay, for example, had furnished most of the momentum for building the town's Mercy Hospital. The mortgage on this hospital for Negroes was burned in Business League ceremonies on January 2, 1922. Normally, however, the league was ineffective. A great opportunity for Tennesseans to benefit from the "spiritual impact" of the national meeting came when the convention was held in Chattanooga in 1917. The program dealt exclusively with farming, however; it hardly figured to stimulate business enterprise, and probably was aimed more at slowing down the rural-to-urban migration.[25]

The Nashville *Globe* was not alone in its desire for concrete action to meet black business problems, and some black Tennesseans, recognizing the increasing handicaps of small, individual concerns, took a more forward-looking approach than that of the Negro Business League. These men stressed the necessity of cooperation among those black businessmen with similar interests. First the Nashville *Clarion* and then the *Globe* publicly endorsed the combining of efforts. The numerous black carpenters and small contractors in Nashville, for example, were being constantly underbid on jobs by white concerns which, as members of a Builder's Exchange, could obtain their materials at wholesale prices. In 1911, the *Globe* urged the black men to combine to form their own wholesale company so as to become more competitive. As if to rule out the ingrained individualism of older blacks, both the *Globe* and the *Clarion* appealed to "young" men. "Young Negroes must accept these conditions," said the *Globe*, "and prepare to meet them, or the opportunities to do business will fly over their heads higher than the clouds." In an action less indicative of combination than of vertical consolidation within the industry, two Nashville Negroes, Moses McKissack, an architect, and Searcy Scales, a contractor, bought the old,

[25] R. McCants Andrews, "Wanted—A Real Business League," *Crisis* 24 (Aug. 1922), 160–63; Nashville *Globe*, Aug. 9, 1912; correspondence between Emmett J. Scott and T. H. Hayes, April 17, 23, May 19, 1914, Washington Papers, container 841; Chattanooga *Daily Times*, Aug. 15, 16, 18, 1917; Bristol *Herald Courier*, Jan. 2, 1922.

179

white-owned Capital Planing Mill, intending to manufacture all the material used in their businesses. The venture was reasonably successful for a time, although McKissack soon focused almost exclusively upon architecture.[26]

The spirit of organization and cooperation found its most fervent disciple in Bert M. Roddy of Memphis, "a little brown man with a sardonic scowl on his face and a dream of corralling the grocery business among colored people and making Beale Street the greatest economic center of Negro America."[27] Roddy was a joiner, economically and socially. In addition to National Negro Business League activities, he annually held office in the Knights of Pythias, was the first Memphian to express interest in the NAACP, was an officer almost from the beginning in the Solvent Savings Bank and Trust Company, joined other black businessmen in the mid-teens to form the Ten-Men Investment Club (which among other ventures built the first Negro-owned movie theater in Memphis), formed the eight-city Negro Southern Baseball League, and in 1919 launched an operation known as Roddy's Citizens' Co-operative Stores.

In August 1918 Roddy attended a meeting, organized by W. E. B. Du Bois for those Negroes "interested in the idea of co-operation and its spread and adoption among colored people." Roddy returned to Memphis with the inspiration to spread the cooperative idea throughout the South. This ambitious black Memphian was riding a business tide that had both national and local importance. Grocery, drug, and variety chain stores were becoming firmly established as part of the American retail scene and, in Memphis, Clarence Saunders was launching the Piggly Wiggly stores, the first of the "super chains."[28]

To the chain store fad, Roddy added the popular concept of the

[26] Nashville *Clarion*, n.d., quoted in Nashville *Globe*, Oct. 18, 1907; Nashville *Globe*, Nov. 17, 1911, March 29, 1912; *Crisis* 9 (April 1915), 269. McKissack's became one of the best-known black architectural firms in the South, accounting for many of the religious and fraternal buildings in Tennessee.

[27] Lee, *Beale Street*, 174.

[28] *Crisis* 19 (Dec. 1919), 48; Ross M. Robertson, *History of the American Economy*

cooperative. In February 1919 the state of Tennessee issued a charter to Roddy's Citizens' Co-operative Stores, a proposed chain of neighborhood grocery cooperatives which would buy merchandise at wholesale prices and sell the goods at "reasonable" retail rates, thus cutting out the white middlemen. By August of that year the concern had sold $10,000 in stock (with $125 being a maximum single holding) and established five branches. Fifteen stores had opened "throughout the city and the towns surrounding Memphis" by the end of 1920, and 9,000 investors owned stock. Each neighborhood store was run by a "guild" of stockholder advisers, but Roddy was the moving force. Profits were to be divided according to shares owned, but debts far outstripped rewards. Roddy used his position as cashier of the Solvent Savings Bank to borrow almost $100,000 in an effort to sustain his cooperative venture. He claimed to have the active support of all 75,000 black Memphians, but white chain store competition, lack of business training, dishonest employees, and too rapid expansion led to the collapse of the grand design in 1922. The problem of inexperience in black enterprise was pointed out years later by a black contemporary to whom Roddy had offered a job: "I didn't know how to weigh a pound of sugar, yet I was to be the manager of that store."[29]

Black businessmen found no easy solutions to their difficulties in Tennessee. Businesses continued to remain small, capital and training remained limited, and while distrust declined, it never went away. The overriding problem was race; restricted to a generally impoverished clientele, black enterprise suffered the perils of economic malnutrition. If any indigenous solution

---

(Chicago: Harcourt, Brace, 1964), 364; James R. Chumney, "The Pink Palace: Clarence Saunders and the Memphis Museum," *Tennessee Historical Quarterly* 32 (Spring 1973), 5.

[29]Lee, *Beale Street*, 174–75; W. E. B. Du Bois to Bert M. Roddy, Aug. 20, 1919, Du Bois Papers, container 73; *Crisis* 19 (Dec. 1919), 48–50: Louisville *News* (Negro), Jan. 1, 1921, quoted in Frederick German Detweiler, *The Negro Press in the United States* (Chicago: Univ. of Chicago Press, 1922) 207–8; Memphis *Press-Scimitar*, May 31, 1928; Tucker, *Lieutenant Lee*, 43–44, 64; interview with Blair T. Hunt, June 14, 1972.

existed in Tennessee, it was the appearance and seeming prosperity of a number of financial institutions. These businesses, however, also labored under the traditional economic burdens of black Americans.

CHAPTER IX.

Bootstrap Capitalism

Tennessee's nineteenth-century experience with black financial institutions had severely damaged but not destroyed black initiative. As early as 1867, Negroes in the state had shown serious interest in starting their own banks, and even the devastating failure of the Freedmen's Bank had not destroyed the idea. In 1890, two ambitious black Chattanoogans founded the Penny Savings Bank, and they attracted investors from as far away as Nashville and Atlanta. Embezzlement weakened this concern, and it collapsed in the financial panic of 1893.[1] Nevertheless, when serious consideration of black business weaknesses arose after 1900, awareness of the special economic role of banks and insurance companies came alive again. Any attempt to achieve

---

[1] During 1867 and 1868, the General Assembly gave charters allowing limited banking operations to three black corporations in Tennessee, two in Memphis and one in Nashville. There firms apparently never became operational, probably because the branches of the Freedman's Bank obviated the need for them. See Taylor, *The Negro in Tennessee*, 158–59, 162–64. The Penny Savings Bank of Chattanooga was founded in 1890 by Squire J. W. White, a leading Negro figure in the city, and H. N. Willis, a fast-talking newcomer. As cashier, Willis apparently traded heavily upon the good name of Squire White and allegedly used the bank's deposits to build "for himself and family a mansion comparable to any in town." Almost immediately, however, the financial panic of 1893 exposed fraudulent weaknesses in the Penny Bank, closed its doors, revealed its empty vaults, and supposedly sent Willis scurrying to Mexico. The *Directory of Chattanooga, Tennessee, 1891* (Chattanooga, 1891), 14, 169; *Acts of the State of Tennessee, 1891* (Nashville: Tavel, 1891), 590; E. R. Carter, *The Black Side: A Partial History of the Business, Religious and Educational Side of the Negro in Atlanta, Georgia* (Atlanta, 1894), 63; Hamilton National Bank, *A History of Banking in Chattanooga* (Chattanooga, 1949), 19; interview with Owen Whitaker, July 13, 1972.

uplift and improvement through self-help would require capital-producing institutions. These concerns were also potential sources of personal profit. Success, however, had been complicated by distrust born of repeated failures.

Tennessee gave birth to four black banks and one black insurance company before 1930, but Nashville, as might have been expected, furnished the earliest impetus to overcome past difficulties. Race "confidence" was the central topic discussed when a small group of black business and professional leaders met in an upstairs room in Napier Court on the night of November 5, 1903. These black Nashvillians met to plan the launching of still another black banking institution in Tennessee. When the One-Cent Savings Bank and Trust Company opened its doors on the wintry morning of January 16, 1904, its announced purpose was "to encourage frugality and systematic saving among our people, to secure the safe keeping and proper investment of such savings and set in motion business enterprises. . . ." The paramount questions before the incorporators, one officer later recalled, were "first confidence, and second, financiering." Confidence in Negro institutions, so damaged by the collapse of the Freedmen's Bank, was therefore the primary target. Subsequent black financial concerns reversed the emphasis, but the problems of making a success of an all-black venture faced each one.

On the ninth anniversary of the bank's opening, Richard Henry Boyd, its first president, lingered on the continued existence of black distrust in Tennessee: "Some of the elder citizens still living remember and often refer to the lamented calamity of the so-called Freedmen's Savings Bank. They have transmitted this lamented tradition to their children. And for years throughout the length and breadth of the State of Tennessee, and many other parts of the South, whenever a Negro banking institution was referred to the cry was always raised by them . . . 'Remember the Freedmen's Bank.' "[2] Boyd went to great lengths to show how

[2] Minutes of the organizational meeting of One-Cent Savings Bank and Trust Co., Nov.

blacks, especially "that noble statesman, Frederick Douglass," had been made scapegoats for the Freedmen's collapse. The real blame, Boyd concluded, lay with white "promoters," and henceforth "Negro banking institutions all over the South have been very careful how they have allowed white officials to mingle in their affairs."[3]

The founding officers of the One-Cent Bank were bound by virtually no state restrictions when they received their charter in 1904. Like most Southern states, Tennessee had failed to recognize the public nature of banking institutions and, until the 1920s, did little to insure bank safety. Investment portfolios were uncontrolled, leaving the bank free, if it wished, to lend every dollar of its resources to officers, a single concern, or on speculative real estate.

Undirected by state regulations and subject to the temptations of an increasingly money-conscious society, few bankers "toed the line" of financial conservatism as closely as did those of the One-Cent Savings Bank and Trust Company. The bank grew slowly, but R. H. Boyd annually reminded stockholders that "the idea of 'getting rich quick' was never in the minds of the officers of this institution." As president, he refused to apologize for "not taking greater risks" and claimed, instead, a practice of "dealing only in gilt-edged securities." Opening-day deposits had totaled almost $6,500, a creditable beginning, but after six years of operations the deposit balance showed less than $36,000, only a small fraction of which was composed of the more desirable time accounts. An additional restriction on growth and investment was

---

5, 1903; minutes of the board of directors of the Citizens Savings Bank and Trust Co., Feb. 9, 1904; reports of the fourth and ninth annual stockholders' meetings of the One-Cent Savings Bank and Trust Co., published in the Nashville *Globe*, Jan. 17, 1908, Jan. 17, 1913.

[3]Report of the ninth annual stockholders' meeting of the One-Cent Savings Bank and Trust Co., published in the Nashville *Globe*, Jan. 17, 1913. Abiding by Boyd's warning against "mingling," stockholders of the Citizens (One-Cent) Savings Bank have been "99 per cent" black, and there has never been a white officer or employee of the bank throughout its first seventy years of operation.

the slow advance of paid-in capital stock. Despite a capitalization of $25,000, only $4,290 had been paid in by 1910.[4]

Growth, however, was not as important as stability. J. C. Napier, the bank's cashier from 1904 until his death in 1940, insisted upon the primary importance of teaching blacks that deposits not only earned interest, but also benefited the economic progress of the race. Napier had been a stockholder and director of the scandal-scarred Penny Savings Bank in Chattanooga, and his Nashville career stretched back to the collapse of the Freedmen's Bank. In order to prevent a recurrence of such defaults, Napier, "by special agreement with his wife," pledged his personal fortune as security for the operation of the One-Cent Bank during its first year. This institution prided itself on the claim that no deposit was too small, and the name was deliberately chosen to show that as little as "one cent" could open an account. Stock was also listed at a low figure of five dollars per share in the only partially fulfilled hope that it would be "within reach of the common people."[5]

Despite the slow growth and limited profits of Nashville's first black bank, but possibly because of the confidence generated by its conservative administration, a second Negro banking institution opened in Nashville on July 31, 1909. Several of the founders of the newly formed People's Savings Bank and Trust Company had previously been directors of the older One-Cent Bank. R. H. Boyd professed no ill will toward his new competitors and explained the defection of some of the younger black supporters on the grounds that they "thought the officers of the One-Cent

[4] Reports of the fourth, fifth, sixth, and ninth annual stockholders' meetings of the One-Cent Savings Bank and Trust Co., published in the Nashville *Globe*, Jan. 17, 1908, Jan. 22, 1909, Jan. 14, 1910, Jan. 17, 1913; Nashville *American*, Jan. 17, 1904.

[5] *Directory of Chattanooga, Tennessee, 1891*, p. 169; report of the fifth annual stockholders' meeting of the One-Cent Savings Bank and Trust Co., published in the Nashville *Globe*, Jan. 22, 1909; Sept. 4, 1908; Henry Allen Boyd, "The One Cent Savings Bank of Nashville, Tennessee—Its Organization and Progress," *Alexander's Magazine* (March–April 1909), 252–53; interview with George W. Gore, Citizens director and former president of Florida A & M University, June 21, 1972.

Savings Bank were too exacting in their . . . securities and made money a little too hard for borrowers to obtain." The Nashville *Globe* gave a blow-by-blow description of the opening-day activities at the new bank. Calling the appearance of a banking firm run by "younger Negroes" a "healthy sign," the *Globe* applauded what it sensed was "the spirit to do business and not to quibble over trivial things."[6] Whereas the One-Cent Bank had put race confidence above all else, the new bank indicated a desire for more active and direct promotion of black economic growth.

The People's Savings Bank and Trust Company proposed a capitalization of $50,000, but it experienced the same slow growth of paid-in capital and deposits that had characterized the One-Cent Bank. The officers had announced their goal to stimulate black Nashvillians "in purchasing homes and embarking in business" but found that limited investment funds made this difficult. The *Globe* blamed many of the bank's directors for the slow progress, especially citing their failure to become depositors in their own institution.[7]

Nashville was an old and traditional town, and its black community was heavily influenced by an educated and professional elite that had close ties with the black colleges and church publishing houses of the area.[8] Despite the "liberalizing" statements of the founders of the city's second black bank, the prevailing economic philosophy in the community was conservative. In establishing the banks, great care was taken in both cases to explain the service function of the institutions, and the sales pitch for both depositors and stockholders emphasized building confidence and improving standards of living among blacks. Relegated to the background, especially among the officers of the One-Cent Bank, was the importance of personal gain.

[6] Report of the ninth annual stockholders' meeting of the One-Cent Savings Bank and Trust Co., in the Nashville *Globe*, Jan. 17, 1913; March 26, May 28, Aug. 6, 1913.

[7] Report of the third annual stockholders' meeting of the People's Savings Bank and Trust Co., published in the Nashville *Globe*, Jan. 12, 1912; Aug. 6, 1909.

[8] When the One-Cent Savings Bank was founded, there were four black colleges in

Memphis, however, reveals another and probably more common background for the founding of black financial institutions. While the black banking ventures in Nashville had pursued a slow and racially self-conscious future, black entrepreneurs in the young, expansive, and often violent city on the banks of the Mississippi River also sought the potential benefits of banking enterprise. Practically depopulated during the yellow fever epidemics of 1878 and 1879, Memphis was rebuilt in the days of the New South. This city, therefore, had no entrenched aristocracy of either race and thus was open to the rise of men who could establish their place on the basis of money rather than tradition.

The most notable black man to emerge from this environment was undoubtedly Robert Reed Church, Sr. Church had been born a slave in Mississippi and raised by his white father on the Mississippi riverboats. He survived gunshot wounds and white threats during the violent years of Reconstruction in Memphis and derived a sizable income from the saloon business. In the years of the yellow fever threat, Church had speculated heavily in Memphis real estate and then parlayed these holdings into a fortune as the city experienced its late nineteenth-century rebirth. By the early 1900s Church's wealth, heavily tied up in rental properties, was estimated in excess of $500,000.[9]

"Bob" Church, as he was commonly called by both blacks and whites, was the moving force behind the establishment of the first black bank in Memphis. On June 18, 1906, the Solvent Savings Bank and Trust Company opened its doors at 392 Beale Street, the office building housing Church's various enterprises. Joining Church as officers of the new concern were a group of men whose

---

Nashville—Fisk, Roger Williams, Walden, and Meharry—and Tennessee A & I began operations in 1912. Denominational publishing houses in Nashville included those of the African Methodist Episcopal Church, the National Baptist Convention, and the National Baptist Convention, U.S.A. A majority of the founders of both Nashville banks had direct connections with one of the schools or one of the publishing houses, or both.

[9] Memphis *Commercial Appeal*, Aug. 3, 1912; Mary Church Terrell, *Colored Woman in a White World* (Washington, D. C.: National Association of Colored Women's Clubs, 1968), 1–12.

occupations and backgrounds indicated both entrepreneurial zeal and relatively short attachments to Memphis. The atmosphere surrounding the opening of the Solvent Bank bore little similarity to the "holy mission" ideals of the One-Cent Savings Bank. Money-making and business encouragement were the advertised benefits; and, if it was encouragement for the business projects of the founders, so much the better. Stock sold for ten dollars per share, with Church owning a large percentage of the initial subscription, and the organizers made no specific appeals for the little man's investment dollar. They also set a one-dollar minimum on deposit accounts. The report of the cashier, Harry Herbert Pace, to the fourth annual stockholders' meeting summed up the basic assumptions of the founders of the concern: "Every time you say a good word for this institution you are putting money into your pockets and are helping make yourselves and it bigger."[10] There was no mention of black pride or confidence in black institutions.

Despite an early scandal involving an embezzlement of $4,500 by the first cashier, the Solvent Savings Bank and Trust Company grew rapidly. By 1910 the institution had far surpassed Nashville's older One-Cent Bank in both deposits ($86,568 to $35,914) and paid-in capital ($10,821 to $4,290).[11] A large banking constituency, a dynamic economic environment, and the public charisma of "Bob" Church gave the Memphis venture added impetus.

The apparent success of the Solvent Bank did not go unnoticed by a group of even more aggressive and ambitious newcomers to Memphis's black business community. Seeking to take advantage of the city's economic opportunities, Wayman Wilkerson, Edward F. Scott, and J. Jay Scott joined several other black inves-

<hr />

[10] Nashville *American*, June 5, 1907; report of the fourth annual stockholders' meeting of the Solvent Savings Bank and Trust Co., published in the Nashville *Globe*, April 29, 1910; Nov. 4, 1910.

[11] Report of the sixth annual stockholders' meeting of the One-Cent Savings Bank and Trust Co., published in the Nashville *Globe*, Jan. 14, 1910; Nov. 4, 1910.

tors in launching Memphis's second black banking enterprise. J. Jay Scott served as the first president. The Fraternal Savings Bank and Trust Company, described later by W. E. B. Du Bois as a "more popular effort," opened its doors on February 10, 1910.[12] Competition reportedly stimulated deposits and investment activity for both the city's black banks. Despite the death of Robert Church, Sr., in 1912 and the resignation of the talented Harry Pace in 1913, the deposits in the Solvent Savings Bank passed one million dollars in 1920, making it the fourth-largest black bank in the nation.[13] The Fraternal Bank, meanwhile, had attracted over a half-million dollars in deposits and was becoming deeply involved in a series of real estate investments.

World War I had a remarkably stimulating effect upon the American economy in general and the nation's banking institutions in particular. Tennessee banks shared in this prosperity, and all four of the state's black banks increased their capital stock.[14] As soon as wartime restrictions were removed, officers of both Memphis banks initiated a variety of personal business ventures, using, in each case, the expanded resources of their respective institutions as investment capital. Memphis was growing rapidly, and its ambitious black entrepreneurs paid little heed to the need for inspiring public trust or the special handicaps facing black businesses. Solvent cashier Bert M. Roddy obtained almost $100,000 in unsecured loans for the launching of his chain of cooperative grocery stores, and the bank's president, Thomas H. Hayes, borrowed heavily for investments in two black insurance companies and the Tri-State Casket and Coffin Company. Wayman Wilkerson and Dr. J. B. Martin of the Fraternal Bank

[12] Nashville *Globe*, Nov. 4, 1910; William Edward Burghardt Du Bois, "Black Banks and White in Memphis," *Crisis* 35 (May 1928), 154.
[13] Memphis *Commercial Appeal*, Aug. 3, 1912; Nashville *Globe*, June 27, 1913; *Crisis* 21 (Feb. 1921), 176; Lee, *Beale Street*, 168–69. J. W. Sanford, a building contractor, and Bert M. Roddy replaced Church and Pace, respectively.
[14] Utilizing deposit statistics during the war as a rough guide to bank growth, one can obtain all-bank balances on both a national and state level (not for specific banks, however) from the Board of Governors of the Federal Reserve System, *All-Bank Statistics: United States, 1896–1955* (Washington, D.C., 1959), 36, 954.

joined Hayes in the casket and coffin company, a concern boasting "a main factory and outlet in Memphis and assembling plants in St. Louis, Indianapolis, Chicago, Dallas and New Orleans." Especially attractive to these black speculators was the potential housing market opened by the influx of rural blacks from the Mississippi Delta. Consequently, through the formation of the American Home Investment Company, a large percentage of the Fraternal Savings Bank and Trust Company's investment portfolio was channeled into cheap rental property and other real estate in the black neighborhoods of Memphis.[15]

It was to the detriment of black banking in Memphis that Robert R. Church, Jr., divorced himself from the operations of the Solvent Bank shortly after his father's death. Despite having been given five years of banking training on Wall Street by his father, the younger Church was more interested in politics and the managing of the 350 to 500 rental dwellings he and his brother and sisters had inherited. The presence of this very able and influential man might have headed off the growing, but shaky, financial empire of Alfred F. Ward. Ward, a former boilermaker and piano hauler, moved into the hierarchy of the Fraternal Bank as cashier during the war. By 1920 he was a bank director and secretary of the American Home Investment Company. Parlaying great audacity, an air of success, and a ready handshake into the presidency of both corporations by 1923, Ward became the jeweled prince of Beale Street. Among his prized possessions was a "straight-eight Packard," and he promised Memphis blacks that "he would bring more wealth to Beale Street than Alexander saw in India."[16]

Meanwhile, in Nashville, as in Memphis, new employment opportunities and higher wartime wages, especially at the mam-

[15] Lee, Beale Street, 168–69; Crisis 20 (Sept. 1920), 239; Wayman Wilkerson to Mary Church Terrell, Terrell Papers, container 3; Tucker, Lieutenant Lee, 44; Bureau of the Census, Fourteenth Census of the United States: 1920. Population, III, 977; Fifteenth Census: 1930. Population, III, pt. 2, 903.

[16] Memphis Press-Scimitar, April 18, 1952; interview with Roberta Church, Nov. 13, 1975; Lee, Beale Street, 175–76.

moth Du Pont powder plant, increased the prosperity of the black community. Both the One-Cent and People's banks shared in the boom times. Both saw their demand deposits and time savings accounts more than double between January 1917 and the Armistice in November 1918. Despite bad publicity resulting from a minor embezzlement during the previous spring, J. C. Napier was able to report to stockholders in the One-Cent Bank in January 1918: "We have had an unprecedented business year. The biggest months in the history of the institution were the fall months of last year."[17]

Both Nashville banks issued new capital stock after the war, and the One-Cent Bank was reorganized. Perhaps so that its name would appear more commensurate with its new status, the One-Cent Savings Bank and Trust Company became the Citizens Savings Bank and Trust Company in 1920. Having neither as large a black community to draw upon nor as aggressive and speculative a leadership, Nashville's black banks did not enter as fully into the business mania of the 1920s as had those in Memphis. Nevertheless, the newly available capital was invested, and the investment process illustrated the degree to which the philosophies of the two Nashville banks differed. While the Citizens (One-Cent) Bank invested its funds in blue chip railroad stock and a very few large real estate loans, the People's Bank sought to fulfill the promise of its name, making hundreds of small, short-term loans, mostly on real estate.[18] The People's Bank undoubtedly was a more significant economic force in Nashville, but it was leaving itself open to risk and possible

[17] Lou Cretia Owen Diary, Oct. 1, 1918 to Jan. 25, 1919, Tennessee State Library and Archives; George Edmund Haynes to L. A. Turner, Nov. 16, 1918, Haynes Papers, container 1918–1922; interview with Mr. and Mrs. Aeolian E. Lockert, July 16, 1970; Nashville *Globe*, Jan. 12, 19, 1917, Jan. 18, Nov. 15, 1918.

[18] Interview with Meredith G. Ferguson, president of Citizens Savings Bank and Trust Co., Nov. 10, 1970. Tennessee State Bank Examiner's reports for 1934 and 1935 indicate the nature of past banking policy for the Citizens Savings Bank and Trust Co.; evidence concerning the practices of the People's Bank is found in the Receivership Records of the People's Savings Bank and Trust Company, Tennessee State Library and Archives, Insurance and Banking Department, archive 174.

failure, something R. H. Boyd, J. C. Napier, and the nonsalaried officers of the Citizens Bank wanted to avoid at all cost. When R. H. Boyd died in 1922, his son, Henry Allen Boyd, became president of Citizens, and despite his earlier support of aggressive banking in the *Globe*, he continued the bank's cautious and conservative policies.

In Tennessee, as in most states, the public had little statutory protection from unsound banking practices; at the same time, small and inexperienced bankers had almost no professional guidance from state agencies. The absence of control and direction created what one prominent economist has called an "inherently weak" national banking structure. Generally unsound trends within the banking industry, therefore, led to some 4,925 bank failures in the United States during the years 1921–1929—59 of these being in Tennessee.[19] The onset of depression, of course, doubled these national figures, and with their artificially limited and impecunious market, Tennessee's black bankers were in an even more precarious position than their white counterparts. The result was that three of the state's four black banks went bankrupt during the years 1928 to 1930.

The Memphis banks were the first to go. Most of their grandiose business ventures of the early 1920s ended heavily in debt. Personal loans to officers increased in size and frequency and the collateral virtually disappeared. In October 1927, the two banks merged (becoming the Fraternal and Solvent Savings Bank and Trust Company) in an effort to stave off impending crisis. Ward, now the dominant black banking figure in Memphis, became president of the new concern. The collapse was only postponed. Two months after the merger, Christmas Fund withdrawals caught the bank short of cash reserves and created a disastrous

---

[19]For a discussion of early 20th-century banking laws and practices in Tennessee, see Claude A. Campbell, *The Development of Banking in Tennessee* (Nashville: privately printed, 1932), 174ff.; John Kenneth Galbraith, *The Great Crash, 1929* (Boston: Houghton, 1954), 184; Joseph Stagg Lawrence, *Banking Concentration in the United States: A Critical Analysis* (New York: Banker's Publishing, 1930), 62–63.

run on the weakened institution. On December 29, 1927 representatives of the same State Department of Banking which recently had approved the merger took over the offices of the bankrupt concern. They found evidence of incredible corruption and mismanagement. Auditors discovered shortages in excess of a half-million dollars, over $170,000 of which was tied directly to the president, A. F. Ward. Six bank officials, including Ward and vice-president T. H. Hayes, served prison terms for their parts in the affair.[20]

Nearly every Negro business concern or black leader in the city was embarrassed in some way by the publicity given to the bank failure. The 28,000 depositors who had trusted the bank officials received only 9.4 cents on the dollar in the liquidation of the bank's assets. Passbook holders included some 7,700 school children who absorbed a confidence-shattering shock not unlike that which their grandparents took from the Freedman's Bank in 1874. Black fraternal orders, meanwhile, having originally hesitated to place their funds with black banks, had their worst fears confirmed. Over fifty black-owned businesses and corporations sustained losses, both in financing and in customer confidence. In a run spawned by the turbulence in Memphis, the Delta Penny Savings Bank of Indianola, Mississippi, failed less than a week after the Fraternal-Solvent closing, and the $100,000 mortgage, loan, and deposit deficits encountered by the National Benefit Life Insurance Company of Washington, D. C., started it on a road that led to its demise in 1931.[21]

[20] Du Bois, "Black Banks and White in Memphis," 154; Memphis *Commercial Appeal*, Dec. 30, 1927, Jan. 5, Feb. 7, 1928; Memphis *Press-Scimitar*, Dec. 30, 31, 1927. In trials during May and June 1928, A. F. Ward was sentenced to ten years in prison, Thomas H. Hayes to one year, and four lesser officers to five years each.

[21] Memphis *World* (black), July 12, 1932; Receiver's Final Report in the Chancery Court of Shelby County, Tenn., and John Vorder Bruegge to superintendent of banking D. D. Robertson, May 28, 1936, Receivership Records of The Fraternal and Solvent Bank and Trust Co., Tennessee State Library and Archives, Insurance and Banking Department, Archive 159, container 7498F; Memphis *Press-Scimitar*, Dec. 30, 1927, Feb. 6, 16, 1928; Memphis *Commercial Appeal*, Dec. 31, 1927, Feb. 7, 1928; Du Bois, "Black Banks and White in Memphis," 174.

Memphis's black leaders, with the exception of the white-oriented faction led by Sutton Griggs, had been discredited in both the black and the white communities. Mrs. Wayman Wilkerson, president of the local chapter of the NAACP, wrote officials of the association: "We have had a hard time since the bank closed. Our leading men are being attacked on every hand, and everything possible is being done to intimidate the colored people. For that reason we are trying to be as quiet as possible to avoid trouble. I don't think it wise to work just now for the NAACP. . . ."[22] Conservative black newspapers like the Cleveland *Gazette* deplored the Memphis troubles and blamed them on the preference of "our so-called business men" for "starting at the top of the ladder . . . instead of starting at the bottom and climbing up." The *Gazette* was further incensed at the light sentences drawn by the bank officials.[23] The chairman of the bank's board of directors, Wayman Wilkerson, facing bank-related embezzlement charges from his fraternal order, the Knights and Daughters of Tabor, committed suicide in the mill room of the Tri-State Casket and Coffin Company on July 1, 1928. For this black Horatio Alger, defeat had been both total and devastating. Pinned to his lapel was a note reading in part: "I am now 56 years old, spirit crushed—nerves shattered—ambition gone—health failing. . . ."[24] But other blacks refused to give up. Robert Church, Jr., had deposited $50,000 in the bank just before it closed in a vain attempt to shore up its deficits and also had raised $150,000 from outside black sources in an effort to reorganize the bank, rather than have it liquidated. Neither gesture could cover the shortages found by the state examiners, and reorganization was refused. George W. Lee, race champion and fiery young black capitalist who had escaped the tentacles of the

[22] Mrs. Wayman Wilkerson to Robert W. Bagnall, director of branches, April 16, 1928, NAACP Papers, container G-199. The Memphis chapter, formerly the most active in Tennessee, ceased activities for two years following the bank collapse.
[23] Cleveland *Gazette*, Jan. 4, June 16, 1928.
[24] *Ibid.*, July 14, 1928; Memphis *Commercial Appeal*, July 2, 1928.

Fraternal-Solvent debacle, stood resolute: "We must step forward and build upon the ashes of the ruins," he urged. "To turn back means disintegration and economic slavery.' The only road to the 'Promised Land' ran 'across the Red Sea of disappointment and sorrow' to the building of a new bank." W. E. B. Du Bois echoed Lee's cry for the establishment of a new bank, and a group of depositors headed by Dr. A. N. Kitrelle soon formed the Wheatley National Bank Association. This organization aided blacks who "found [it] impossible to secure [loans] at some of the local banks," but the ultimate goal was "eventually [to] bring about rehabilitation of a Negro financial institution in Memphis." Until 1946 and the founding of the Tri-State Bank of Memphis, blacks were unable to marshal the reserves of spirit and resources necessary to achieve this goal.[25]

Reaction from white Memphians ranged from jocularity to hostility. W. Alonzo Locke, a bank director and widely known headwaiter at the Peabody Hotel, lost everything "except $3 in his pocket." While one patron reportedly left a $100 tip the next day, most "sympathetic" white customers thought the bank collapse a joke and "kidded" Locke unmercifully. Both Robert Church and the black Universal Life Insurance Company of the city were "tried" in the daily press because of the involvement of their associates and officers in the troubles. Church pulled through unscathed, although his disgrace would have been balm to those whites who had experienced the impact of his political muscle. The more vulnerable black insurance company, whose president was also a vice-president of the bank, eventually had to wage a four-year court struggle to avoid being drawn into the bank's entanglements.[26]

[25] Memphis *Commercial Appeal*, Jan. 1, 1928; George W. Lee, "The Negro's Next Step," Memphis *Triangle* (black), Jan. 28, 1928, quoted in Tucker, *Lieutenant Lee*, 64–65; Memphis *World*, July 12, 1932.

[26] Memphis *Press-Scimitar*, Aug. 4, 1947; Memphis *Commercial Appeal*, Dec. 31, 1946; Du Bois, "Black Banks and White in Memphis," 174; Memphis *Commercial Appeal*, Jan. 1, 3, 1928; Memphis *Press-Scimitar*, Dec. 31, 1927, Feb. 7, 1928; Lee, *Beale Street*, 173. During his days as headwaiter at the two most famous hotels in the city, the Gayoso

The full extent of black losses in Memphis had hardly been realized before financial tragedy visited black Nashvillians. On November 21, 1930, the People's Savings Bank and Trust Company closed its doors. This institution had pursued a very liberal loan policy throughout its twenty-year existence, purchasing numerous bonds and second mortgages from fraternal and religious institutions as well as making hundreds of loans to working-class blacks. Defaults had caused concern as early as 1924, but the bank hardly altered its investment policy. It was this very leniency, along with some incredible carelessness and the lack of business experience, that left the People's Bank so susceptible to the rigors of the Great Depression. Dishonesty was never seriously charged.[27]

When closing seemed imminent, officers of the ill-fated institution borrowed $10,000 from the Universal Life Insurance Company of Memphis and also appealed for aid from the large white American National Bank in Nashville. The white bank turned down the plea, and the doors had to be closed. Black bank officials, urged on by the National Negro Bankers Association, tried for over a year to reorganize, but the People's Savings Bank and Trust Company remained permanently defunct.[28]

The People's Bank had been far more conservative than the Fraternal-Solvent Bank, and depositors eventually received 35 percent dividends. Most of the approximately four thousand active accounts were small (less than fifty dollars); as one resident later recalled, "that maybe wasn't much, but it's all they had. . . . A lot of people were practically ruined. People lost homes; it was tragic for a while."[29] The impact was, of course, strongest in

---

and the Peabody, Alonzo Locke became one of the better-known personages of Memphis. One writer described him this way: "More white people know him and he knows more white people than any Negro in the tri-States, perhaps in the entire South." McIlwaine, *Memphis Down in Dixie*, 316.

[27]Receivership Records of the People's Savings Bank and Trust Co., archive 174, containers 7476D and 7476E.

[28]*Ibid.*, containers 7476E and 7675F.

[29]Interview with George W. Gore, June 21, 1972.

Nashville, but blacks in Chattanooga, Dyersburg, McKenzie, Memphis, and Clarksville, and even in other sections of the country—Louisiana, Ohio, Illinois, New York, and Pennsylvania—experienced losses. The heaviest loser, and also a contributor to the bank's weakened condition, was the Sunday School Publishing Board of the National Baptist Convention of the United States of America. Created to compete with the Boyd publishing house, this business had overextended itself in building extensive facilities in downtown Nashville. In 1928, the People's Bank made a series of very large loans to the Sunday School Publishing Board, despite the fact that the religious concern was later judged to be insolvent at the time of the loans. When the bank failed, only the leniency of the holders of the first and second mortgages, who were white, kept the Publishing Board from collapsing also.[30]

The crisis at the People's Bank almost dragged down the only remaining black banking institution in the state. Officials of the closed concern brought their portfolio to the Citizens Bank and asked for either financial support or a merger. Perhaps aware of the earlier difficulties in Memphis and, as one officer put it, "after careful examination and racial soul-searching," the Citizens Bank refused to extend aid. Shortly after this decision, rumors raced through the black community that the second bank was also on the verge of collapse.[31] The Citizens Savings Bank and Trust Company survived a two-day run on its reserves in October 1931 by placing stacks of currency in the windows and drawing on the financial and public support of the American National Bank.[32]

[30]C. K. White, liquidating agent, to H. E. Robinson (M.D.), of New Rochelle, N.Y., March 18, 1935, and other letters, records, and memoranda in the Receivership Records of the People's Savings Bank and Trust Co., archive 174, containers 7476D, 7476E, and 7475F.

[31]Interviews with Meredith G. Ferguson, Nov. 10, 1970, and George W. Gore, June 21, 1972; Nashville *Globe*, Oct. 2, 1931.

[32]Nashville *Globe*, Oct. 2, 1931; Lockert interview, July 10, 1970; interview with T. B. Boyd, Jr., secretary-treasurer of the National Baptist Publishing Board and vice-president and chairman of the executive committee of Citizens Savings Bank and Trust Co., July 2, 1972.

Conservative banking policies and personal friendships largely accounted for the Citizens Bank's receiving aid previously denied to the People's Bank. Also, as the Depression continued, there seemed to be a clear determination among Nashville banking officials to keep the last remaining (and now oldest in the nation) black institution in operation. This bank received a large Reconstruction Finance Corporation loan in 1934, and bank examiners regularly allowed a questionable loan condition to remain on the books.[33]

The cumulative impact of Tennessee's early experience in black banking, in addition to the narrow escape of the 1930s, was to leave the Citizens Bank of Nashville with a determination to maintain its financial conservatism. Many enterprising and more daring blacks resented these tight money policies, and their unmet demands encouraged the creation, in 1961, of the black-owned Community Federal Savings and Loan Association.[34] Most blacks, as in 1900, however, continued to depend upon white financial institutions.

Black banking in Tennessee illustrated most completely the difficulties facing black enterprise in the first three decades of the twentieth century. Only the One-Cent (Citizens) Savings Bank and Trust Company of Nashville, with its overriding concern for security, was able to overcome the handicaps of marginal clientele, limited capital, lack of business training, black distrust, and white prejudice. Conservative investments, careful cultivation of both black confidence and white approval, and the integrity of its officers pulled the Nashville bank through its perilous formative period. One, two, or a combination of these ingredients were missing from the portfolio of the other banking ventures.

The infectious wheeling and dealing of the 1920s brought

---

[33] Bank Examiners' Reports on Citizens Savings Bank and Trust Co., Tennessee State Library and Archives, Insurance and Banking Department, archive 59.

[34] Interviews with Alger V. Boswell, June 20, 1972, and George W. Gore, June 21, 1972.

Tennessee its only indigenous black life insurance company in 1923. The founding of the Universal Life Insurance Company in Memphis, however, did not initiate insurance for black Tennesseans. Fraternal assessment and mutual benefit plans had been popular in the state from the early years of freedom, and the number of such insurance organizations increased significantly from 1880 to the early 1900s. In the beginning, these fraternal and mutual societies simply provided a rural-oriented people with savings opportunities; later, as whites began to reap benefits from union membership, the black insurance societies performed similar functions for those workers excluded from the unions. Nashville's largest benefit organization in 1910, for example, was the Railway Employees Protective Association, founded by Preston Taylor in 1905 "to take care of the aged, and especially [to] look after the families of our deceased co-laborers."[35]

Perhaps the main factor spurring the growth of black benefit societies, however, was the reluctance of the large white insurance companies to issue policies or pay full benefits to blacks. Citing high mortality rates and a high percentage of lapsed policies, the Prudential Insurance Company, in 1881, was the first concern to cut back on policies issued to blacks. Metropolitan Life soon followed. In addition, there were constant complaints from blacks that agents of those companies that did accept black policyholders were often abusive and insulting.[36] Although insurance alternatives increased after 1910, the black fraternal and mutual plans continued to operate in Tennessee. A very successful organization, for example, the Union Protective Assurance Company, was launched in Memphis as late as September 1933. This company, closely associated with the funeral businesses of Thomas H. Hayes and two other local undertakers, specialized in

---

[35] Nashville *Globe*, Jan. 28, 1910.

[36] Stuart, *An Economic Detour*, 36; Winfred Octavus Bryson, Jr., "Negro Life Insurance Companies: A Comparative Analysis of the Operating and Financial Experience of Negro Legal Reserve Life Insurance Companies" (Ph.D. diss., Univ. of Pennsylvania, 1948), 7–8.

burial insurance and managed to show total assets of $133,990 when it received its charter.[37]

By 1910, a few white companies, particularly the young, Nashville-based Life and Casualty Insurance Company, began actively to seek black policyholders. In 1904, Life and Casualty created a special district for the black community in Nashville and operated it entirely with black personnel, including a black superintendent, Mark William Bonner. Bonner found Negroes impressed by these actions and he soon was able to employ twelve agents. Bonner's success in Nashville led to similar Life and Casualty efforts elsewhere. In 1908, eighteen of the nineteen black life insurance agents in Memphis worked for the company. Other white concerns, such as Provident Life, also stepped up their activities, but, more importantly from a black business point of view, so did Negro companies. The Standard Life Insurance Company, organized in Atlanta in 1911 with heavy investments from such black Tennesseans as Thomas H. Hayes and Harry H. Pace of Memphis and Henry Allen Boyd and Ira T. Bryant of Nashville, announced in November 1913 that "plans have been carefully laid to capture Nashville." The plans included an all-out program to convince blacks of the safety of the new concern and an instruction session for "hundreds of men and women to serve as agents." Other black companies followed similar procedures, and even the small West Tennessee town of Dyersburg could boast of "no less than twenty colored insurance agents" with headquarters in the area at one time. By 1926, a branch office of the Atlanta Life Insurance Company was writing $700,000 worth of business in Nashville in a single year.[38]

[37] Union Protective Assurance Company, *How Long Is 20 Years . . .* , Twentieth Anniversary Booklet (Memphis, 1953), 3–4.

[38] Nashville *Globe*, Oct. 1, 1909, July 22, 1910, July 14, 1911, Nov. 7, 1913; Stuart, *An Economic Detour*, 176–78; Harry Herbert Pace, "The Attitudes of Life Insurance Companies Toward Negroes," *Southern Workman* 57 (Jan. 1928), 6–7; "Business and Industry," *Messenger* 9 (March 1927), 81; Olney David, Nashville general agent for Provident Life Insurance Co., to George Edmund Haynes, Oct. 25, 1917, Haynes Papers, container 1916–1917; Hamilton, *The Bright Side of Memphis*, 228; interview with James T. Chandler, June 28, 1972.

The economic importance of fraternal associations diminished in the face of this onslaught, and a set of unusual circumstances led a group of Mississippi émigrés to launch Tennessee's own Universal Life Insurance Company. On at least three occasions before 1915, there had been talk of black Tennesseans establishing "an insurance company of their own." Robert R. Church, Sr., had made such a proposal to the stockholders of the Solvent Savings Bank in 1910, but no action was taken at that time. Nor did anything come of a *Globe* observation in 1912 that "Negro men of Tennessee who have money could organize an industrial insurance company if they would." A group of black Chattanoogans, meanwhile, tried to launch "the Southern Central Life Insurance Company" in late 1912, but it never got off the ground.[39]

The chain of events that led to the founding of the Universal Life Insurance Company in 1923 actually began with the chartering of the Mississippi Beneficial Insurance Company (Mississippi Life) in Indianola, Mississippi, in January 1909. Associated with the Delta Penny Savings Bank, this new concern was authorized to write only industrial (weekly premium) policies. The company grew steadily, almost tripling its annual premium income during World War I and reaching close to one million dollars by 1923. Outgrowing the facilities available in Indianola, and aware of increasing hostility to its success among local whites, Mississippi Life moved to Memphis in 1920. Dissension among the officers led to the resignation of the president, Dr. Joseph Edison Walker, in 1923. During the period of uncertainty that followed, Heman E. Perry, a black baron of high finance much like Alfred F. Ward, wangled control of Mississippi Life and absorbed it into his own Standard Life Insurance Company of Atlanta. In short order, Perry's concern experienced financial trouble and was taken over by the white-owned Southern Life Insurance Company of Nashville. The passage of this important Negro financial

---

[39] Nashville *Globe*, April 29, 1910, Aug. 23, 1913; *Crisis* 5 (Dec. 1912), 62.

institution into white hands infuriated many former officials of the defunct Memphis firm.[40]

Dr. Joseph E. Walker began laying plans for a new black insurance company shortly after Heman Perry became involved in Mississippi Life. The entrance of the white corporation into the picture increased interest in Walker's program and enabled him to sell a $100,000 stock authorization in only six months. In September 1923 the Universal Life Insurance Company received its charter from the state of Tennessee. Major shareholders included Dr. John Thomas Wilson, a famous black surgeon operating in Nashville, Memphis, and Chicago; Moses M. McKissack, Nashville architect and contractor; and Preston Taylor of Nashville. Mark W. Bonner left Life and Casualty and joined Walker as secretary of the new firm. By the end of 1925, Universal Life "had assets of $130,608, with a total income for the year of $104,499, and with insurance in force of $4,136,049. . . ."[41]

Such a small operation could hardly have steered a safe course through the difficult years ahead had it not been for the reinsurance in 1926 of some $837,000 in premium income from the receivers of the then-collapsed white company, Southern Life of Nashville. In essence, Universal retrieved the black business that had been lost when Mississippi Life disappeared in 1923. One black principal in the negotiations called the transfer "the largest and most important financial transaction in the history of the race" because "it was of [such] great importance in restoring confidence in the financial ability of Negro business leaders."[42]

Race consciousness played an important role for the Universal Life Insurance Company from its inception. While black insurance companies faced the same handicaps of economically marginal clientele that black banks did, the Memphis promoters

---

[40]Stuart, *An Economic Detour*, 274–310; Nashville *Globe*, Feb. 5, 1909; Universal Life Insurance Co., *Souvenir Booklet, Silver Anniversary* (Memphis, 1948), 8.

[41]Stuart, *An Economic Detour*, 168, 170; Harry H. Pace, "The Business of Insurance Among Negroes," *Crisis* 32 (Sept. 1926), 224; interview with James T. Chandler, June 28, 1972.

[42]Stuart, *An Economic Detour*, 168–69.

relied even more on racial solidarity. James T. Chandler, a former salesman and later executive with Universal, recalled that "the principal advantage [was] selling race. That was what we did. . . . We sold employment; we sold jobs; we sold economic progress; we sold fine homes, and financing churches. . . ."[43]

By 1930, with almost $11.5 million of insurance in force, Universal Life was one of the eight largest black insurance corporations in the United States. This position was not achieved, however, without several awkward months after the collapse of the Fraternal-Solvent Savings Bank in 1927–1928. Dr. Walker had accepted a "window dressing" vice-president's position with the unfortunate institution; although performing no duties, he had allowed A. F. Ward the use of his name. White prosecutors attempted to tie Walker to fraudulent operations and also sought to recover a sizable withdrawal of first-mortgages notes which Walker had made for Universal the day before the bank folded. After a four-year court fight, Universal recovered over $20,000 of approximately $40,000 it had deposited with the Fraternal-Solvent Bank. Even as the company recuperated from the bank jolt, the Great Depression began to take its toll in lapsed policies and uncollected premiums. In the words of company officials, "it was a struggle to keep afloat." Dividends were passed up for several consecutive years, beginning in 1929, and the assets of the company remained almost unchanged from 1930 to 1935.[44]

The early success, survival, and later prosperity of Universal Life, despite the stock deals and bank defaults in its history, helped Memphis retain some of its claim to being the center of black capitalism in Tennessee. It did not, however, go far in convincing the Negroes of the state that black financial institutions were preferable to those run by whites. Four black insurance companies operated full-time in Tennessee in 1929, and in a

[43]Interview with James T. Chandler, June 28, 1972.

[44]Universal Life Insurance Co. *Souvenir Booklet Silver Anniversary*, 8–9, 59; Lee, *Beale Street*, 173; Memphis *Commercial Appeal*, Jan. 4, 8, 1928; Memphis *Press-Scimitar*, Dec. 31, 1927; Memphis *World*, Feb. 23, April 1, 1932.

survey of 1,000 black families in Nashville during that year, 940 "had insurance policies of one sort or another." Nevertheless, of 264 common and semiskilled labor families surveyed, "77.7% reported insurance policies with white institutions, and 11.7% with Negro institutions"; of 57 skilled labor families visited, "96.5% reported insurance policies with white institutions, and 15.8% with Negro institutions"; for 79 business and professional families, the figures were 72.2 percent and 31.6 percent, respectively.[45] Black pride in the business realm clearly had not overcome the educational, financial, and racial handicaps that obtained at the turn of the century.

Both the caste system and black ideological convictions contributed to the continued economic weakness of Negroes in Tennessee. The racial self-sufficiency programs of Du Bois and Washington were hardly feasible. Reflecting on the first three decades of the twentieth century, Merah Steven Stuart, an official with the Universal Life Insurance Company, described the period quite caustically as an "economic detour." It was a mistake, he said, for blacks, "economically naked just three-quarters of a century ago, [to be] expected to establish a separate economy, within the general economy."[46] Nevertheless, an appeal for racial solidarity was the only option blacks consistently exercised as an alternative to their nineteenth-century role as the South's mudsill. Booker T. Washington was their ideological guide, and his philosophy of rugged individualism, tempered with a penchant for organization, called for "creating positions for *ourselves*—positions which no man can give or take from us."[47]

Washington's racial introspection and his willingness to accommodate, in public, to white restrictions increased black eco-

---

[45]Carter G. Woodson, "Insurance Business Among Negroes," *Journal of Negro History* 14 (April 1929), 216–17; Edwards, *The Southern Negro as a Consumer*, 42, 136–37.

[46]Stuart, *An Economic Detour*, xix–xx.

[47]Booker T. Washington before the National Negro Business League in Aug. 1913, quoted by the Nashville *Tennessean*, Aug. 26, 1913. Author's italics.

nomic marginality. Educational curriculums served to reinforce low job status, training black students for manual labor jobs and crafts which were becoming increasingly obsolete or closed to blacks. In pleading for the formation of Tennessee A & I, Ben Carr told whites: "We want to go out in Davidson county and build *you* a Tuskegee . . . we want to get this school started so that we can get men who know how to farm and women who know how to cook and launder."[48] This application of Washington's program of industrial education perpetuated the master-servant tradition—a tradition of black economic subordination.

[48] Nashville *Globe*, April 8, 1910. Author's italics.

CHAPTER X.

Progressivism – For Whites Only?

Intense and well-publicized social action shook the laissez-faire attitudes of white Americans and branded the early 1900s as years of progress and reform. Almost unnoticed in the ferment of this rather elusively described "Progressive Era," however, were black men and women who also felt compelled to take positive action. Not content simply to be acted upon by white society, they responded to national and social stimuli in their own right. In general, white progressivism in the South was "for whites only." But all Southerners were not white, and neither were all Southern progressives.[1]

Progressive reforms took many directions, depending upon the experience of those people responding to a pervasive call to action.[2] Blacks carried into the twentieth century a set of ideological and experiential luggage which differed markedly from that carried by whites; their response to the progressive impulse, therefore, had a narrower focus. Instead of clinging to a heritage of individualism, Negroes were still struggling to achieve initial recognition of their individual freedom. Only rarely allowed to participate significantly in politics, concerned more with imme-

[1] Woodward's *Origins of the New South*, ch. 14, is misleading when it discusses Southern progressivism under the sweeping heading "Progressivism—For Whites Only."
[2] George B. Tindall has conveniently categorized progressive reforms under five headings: (1) democracy, (2) efficiency, (3) corporate regulation, (4) social justice, and (5) the public service concept of government. See Tindall, "Business Progressivism: Southern Politics in the Twenties," *South Atlantic Quarterly* 62 (Winter 1963), 93.

diate and local economic problems than with the impersonal threat of monopoly, and conditioned to the indifference of governmental agencies, black Tennesseans concentrated upon an expanded concept of social justice, a more efficient pattern of living, and a greater emphasis upon local organizations.

Disease, illiteracy, inadequate housing, and crime were both real and personal. In addition, tightening Jim Crow restrictions and increased white violence haunted the lives of black Tennesseans in the early years of the new century. The large majority of Negroes in the state remained apathetic about their fate— numbed, it seemed, by years of poverty, fear, and repression. Such was not the case for the small, but growing, class of educated and moderately successful blacks in Nashville, and to varying degrees in other cities in Tennessee. Articulate, often well read, and with a stake in society, these middle-class blacks adopted a rhetoric and program of reform which were fully in keeping with the spirit of the age. Invariably calling themselves "progressive Negroes," black Tennessee urbanites gave birth to a full spectrum of Negro betterment leagues, progressive Negro fairs, and home improvement clubs, each supporting what it termed "progressive lines of thought."

Extensive and rapid change created new pressures upon white society and offered real threats to the black middle class. Almost entirely urban, black professional and business men had gained positions of importance and respect within their own communities. The increased tensions felt by white Southerners, translated so often into further restrictions and repression of blacks, threatened both the cultivated dignity and relative economic security of the black leaders. Booker T. Washington's accommodation was, itself, a "search for order," perhaps partly as a means of preserving his own personal position. He urged blacks to accept white values and mores in order to remove causes of racial conflict and in order to soothe the disruptions of an industrializing New South. His ideals were strong among black Tennesseans, and accommodation to white values was the essence of those black uplift movements so numerous in the state during the early years of the twentieth century. A cleaner, healthier, more efficient, and better-educated Negro meant a less anxious, more respecting white man and a more secure black middle class.

Young black leaders, and the Nashville *Globe* in particular, criticized their elders for starting a "fad" of national "leagues, councils, movements, brotherhoods . . . all dedicated to the purpose of improving our race mentally, morally or financially," but accomplishing little. The *Globe* maintained that Washington's goals of racial uplift and interracial peace could be "accomplished only by local organizations"; individual and community relationships were the foundations of order. [3] Some national black organizations functioned nominally in Tennessee prior to 1920, but as the *Globe* predicted, most change was accomplished by local groups.

Nashville, with its articulate and sensitive black middle class, experienced the most active progressive impulse. As on so many other occasions, the Nashville *Globe* played an important role. Although the *Globe* encouraged and publicized all black reform programs in the city, it gave most persistent attention to the need for greater moral direction of youth. Citing repeated examples of black children and adolescents wandering the streets and dance halls until late at night, the *Globe* warned: "It is the height of folly for parents to conceive the idea that they can turn their children out to run at large and expect them to grow to respectable manhood and womanhood." Particularly aggrieved at the presence of so many "immoral and dishonest men and women in the race," the newspaper attacked gambling and prostitution vigorously; a black woman who would "comingle" with a white man was "a harlot of the lowest and most debased character." Bawdy houses were specifically identified and exposed. [4] Not content to crusade only by exposure, the *Globe* avidly supported reform

[3] Nashville *Globe*, Nov. 1, 1907.
[4] *Ibid.*, July 30, Dec. 3, 1909, May 3, 10, 1912.

programs through improved educational and recreational facilities. When Henry Allen Boyd headed a building campaign in 1914 to raise $30,000 for a fledgling black YMCA program, the *Globe* published daily editions giving the front page over to progress reports.[5]

As early as 1905 a group of black church and professional leaders in Nashville launched a campaign to provide adequate correctional facilities for black juveniles. The *Globe* supported and publicized these efforts and called attention to the "inhuman" treatment given black prisoners "under the name of law."[6] Since the state provided no juvenile reformatories, young boys were thrown into cells with hardened adult criminals. Petitions to the legislature proved futile, even when Booker T. Washington added his presence to the campaign in 1907. Black reformers founded several private institutions, but donations were insufficient to sustain the efforts.[7] The *Globe* continued to hammer at the problem. It praised Governor Malcolm R. Patterson for releasing eleven black youths (average age of twelve years old) from the state prison in 1909, but deplored the continued presence of immoral and debasing treatment of prisoners, and even tackled the issue of capital punishment—questioning in 1913 the "right for man to take what man cannot give."[8] When blacks initiated reforms involving the white system, however, they generally gained scant recognition. Reformatory facilities were eventually established for black boys (1917) and girls (1923), but only after urban pressures and World War I violence had turned the attention of white reformers to racial problems. Black progressivism had the greatest opportunity for success when it concentrated upon its own separate community.

[5] Nashville *Tennessean*, March 15, 22, 24, April 1, 1914, April 16, 1916; *Crisis* 8 (May 1914), 8; 9 (Nov. 1914), 35; 12 (Oct. 1916), 296; Dr. S. S. Caruthers, chairman of Colored YMCA Committee, to George E. Haynes, April 4, 1914, Haynes Papers, container 1914–1915; Nashville *Globe*, May 17, 1912; Nashville *Banner*, Feb. 10, 1918.

[6] Nashville *American*, Nov. 22, 1905; Nashville *Globe*, Feb. 14, 1908.

[7] Nashville *American*, Nov. 22, 1905, Jan. 15, 1907; Nashville *Globe*, July 12, Dec. 6, 1907, April 23, Nov. 12, 1909; *Crisis* 2 (Sept. 1911), 184.

[8] Nashville *Globe*, Nov. 12, 26, 1909, Feb. 21, 1913.

In 1912 a Nashville Negro Board of Trade replaced the inactive Negro Business League as the accepted voice of the city's "business, professional and industrial colored men." Instead of holding "an annual meeting and an annual adjournment" as the older League had done, the Board of Trade immediately sought out community involvement. Intending to become "instrumental in the amicable adjustment of any and all differences which may arise . . . between white man and black man," the board urged black Nashvillians to realize that "a community is progressive" only when it "is a creature of design and of concerted intelligent effort." The "design" and "effort" of the board was expressed clearly by its secretary, D. Wellington Berry:

> . . . community organization is business and . . . it will pay in Nashville among the colored people the same as among the white citizens, and will pay best when every Negro will get into the development organization and do his share, for as the community morals are at a low ebb, so the morals of the citizens are destined to be. For if the community is sanitary, its people are healthy. Community organization is not a matter of sentiment, but . . . pays the largest dividends for the amount of time and energy invested.[9]

The Nashville Board of Trade claimed to be the first black organization of its kind in the nation, and it reflected the long-expressed feeling of the Nashville *Globe* that local impetus was the important factor in improvement and reform. Knoxville (1913) and Memphis (1914) later formed boards of trade, but they never had the zeal and reform leadership found in Nashville.[10] Serving frequently as an informal clearinghouse for the community programs of women's clubs, ward improvement associations, charities, and professional organizations, the Nashville board was especially active in the years before American entry into World War I. In 1912, representatives worked with the mayor, city park

[9]*Ibid.*, March 15, Nov. 22, 1913.

[10]Nashville *Tennessean*, Nov. 2, 1913; Nashville *Globe*, Oct. 18, 1907, Dec. 31, 1909, April 14, 1911; Daves, *A Social Study of the Colored Population of Knoxville*, 16; Knoxville *Journal and Tribune*, Oct. 23, 1913, April 18, 1924; Memphis *Commercial Appeal*, May 12, 1914.

commission, and other black groups to attain the first municipal park open to Negroes in the capital city. Also during its first year, the organization sponsored an "open air carnival" in the black business section to stimulate trade and encourage businessmen to clean up their facilities. This became an annual affair, expanding by 1916 to include vaudeville shows.[11] The board later agitated for better water sanitation at black schools, campaigned success-fully for the appointment of a black nurse in the city health department, raised money and purchased a lot for a Colored Carnegie Library, and sponsored a Negro Booster Club for younger black businessmen. The Booster Club was closely associ-ated with the *Globe* and made trips throughout Middle and East Tennessee "boosting" the board-of-trade idea and also proclaim-ing the efficiency and success of black businessmen in Nash-ville.[12] "Efficiency" and order were key tenets in the reform philosophy of Nashville's black middle class, and they served as a common rationale for the black-supported welfare and uplift pro-grams in Tennessee.

The most publicized single action of the Nashville Negro Board of Trade came in March–April 1916, after a disastrous fire, start-ing in one of the worst slums in the state, quickly destroyed the homes of 324 black and 301 white families who lived east of the Cumberland River. Led by its president, Andrew N. Johnson, the Board of Trade immediately formed a relief committee which obtained food, clothing, and temporary shelter for the black victims, collected money for relief work, and sponsored resettle-ment supervised by trained black social workers from the Social Sciences Department at Fisk University. The committee served as a central agency for collecting relief funds from churches, schools, benefit performances, and white charity.[13] This act of

[11] Nashville *Globe*, July 12, 1912, June 6, 1913; Nashville *Tennessean*, Oct. 24, 27, 1912.

[12] Nashville *Globe*, Jan. 17, 24, 1913; *Crisis* 12 (May 1916), 13; Nashville *Tennessean*, Oct. 26, 1913; Knoxville *Journal and Tribune*, Oct. 21, 22, 23, 1913.

[13] George Edmund Haynes to James Hardy Dillard, April 29, 1916, Haynes Papers,

charity, although it did not involve long-range reform, demonstrated a strong sense of community responsibility and indicated that reform-minded blacks were willing to put talk into action.

Black women, as well as men, demonstrated the progressive impulse. In 1895, a group of black women in Nashville, wives of prominent church, business, and professional leaders, organized the Phyllis Wheatley Club and affiliated with the National Federation of Colored Women's Clubs. The organization was especially active from 1900 to 1920, working among "the sick, the poor, the unfortunate, and the aged." It supported "a day-care home for neglected children and those of parents who [were] gone during the day." And, with money and provisions donated by both blacks and whites, the club sewed and cooked for hospital patients and needy children, furnished and maintained a room in Mercy Hospital, campaigned for needed equipment in the city's black high school, and joined the *Globe* in its drive for better treatment of black criminals.[14]

Blacks in other Tennessee cities formed chapters of the National Federation of Colored Women's Clubs and pursued the federation's objectives: "To enlist the hearty co-operation of all good women in the general education and uplift of the people; to work for the improvement of home, moral and civil life and to encourage all efforts toward worthy citizenship." In Knoxville, Mrs. J. J. Johnson, wife of a prominent black lawyer, helped found the Homemakers' Club in 1913. This organization, subdivided into smaller "ward clubs," carried out campaigns for the enforcement of compulsory school attendance laws, for kindergarten and evening classes, and for domestic science courses in black schools. Other women's organizations functioned in Memphis, Chattanooga, and Jackson. The Jackson club, whose presi-

---

container 1916–1917; Nashville *Tennessean*, March 22–25, 30, April 1, 2, 28, 1916; *Crisis* 12 (June 1916), 64.
[14]"Phyllis Wheatley Club's Call," a pamphlet located in Gov. Ben W. Hooper Papers, Tennessee State Library and Archives, container 3; Nashville *Globe*, Jan. 31, 1908, June 14, 1918; Nashville *Tennessean*, Nov. 24, 1907.

dent, Mrs. James Franklin Lane, served as president of the National Federation in 1916, declared "a great need of improvement in the race in general" as its motive for organization and sponsored a drive for the building of an old folks' home as its major undertaking.[15]

Smaller organizations supported an Old Folks' and Orphans' Home in Memphis, a Colored Chautauqua Association in Clarksville, and a Reformers' League in Mt. Pleasant. The latter two organizations were closely associated with the African Methodist Episcopal Church, and the Mt. Pleasant league directed its work particularly toward the moral uplift of black youth—petitioning the mayor and city council to enforce saloon laws and "also to break up the dens of vice in connection with the saloons."[16] Most black reformers, like white progressives, sought to formalize their efforts by establishing a club or league, with officers, committees, and specified projects. Some counted only a few members, others more, but in its own way each of these had a common spiritual bond of social concern and each contributed to order and stability in a time of migratory pressures and racial hostility.

The National League on Urban Conditions Among Negroes (National Urban League) was the only national reform organization that was active in Tennessee's black communities before World War I. A merger of three New York-based organizations which were financed and directed by wealthy white progressives, the Urban League was represented in Tennessee by George Edmund Haynes.[17] A thirty-year-old Fisk University graduate

[15] Mrs. J. J. Johnson to George Edmund Haynes, Dec. 26, 1913; Haynes to Mrs. Johnson, Jan. 22, 1914; undated memo of Haynes, all in Haynes Papers, containers 1909–1913, 1914–1915, "Misc." Nashville *Tennessean*, July 9, 1916; W. E. B. Du Bois, ed., *Efforts for Social Betterment Among Negro Americans*, Atlanta University Publications, No. 14 (1909), 60.

[16] Du Bois, *Efforts for Social Betterment*, 74; D. A. Graham, pastor of St. Peter A. M. E. Church in Clarksville, to Booker T. Washington, April 24, 1912, Washington Papers, container 832; Nashville *American*, April 6, 1906.

[17] The founding of the National Urban League and the process by which George Edmund Haynes became its Nashville representative is adequately documented in Guichard Parris and Lester Brooks, *Blacks in the City: A History of the National Urban*

and native of Pine Bluff, Arkansas, Haynes had studied at Yale and joined the Fisk faculty as associate professor of sociology and economics in 1910. With encouragement from such Northern progressives as Mrs. William H. Baldwin, William Jay Schieffelin, Eugene P. Roberts, and Frances A. Kellor, Haynes returned to Nashville with high ambitions. Formally designated as the Urban League's director of Southern field activities, he set out to found a training school for black social workers and to use the league as a coordinator of black social reform programs in Tennessee.

To his surprise and frustration, Haynes ran headlong into the subtle caste etiquette of Southern liberalism. Even the most sympathetic white Southerners rarely looked upon blacks as equals. They supported segregation, and also wanted to control any major racial reforms, even those that were largely self-contained in the black communities. When Haynes made known his plans to found a school of social work in Nashville, he met a sharp rebuff from these white "progressives." The white president of Fisk, George Augustus Gates, already under attack from the Nashville *Globe* for "Jim Crowing" the school's commencement exercises and replacing black teachers with whites, advised Haynes that whites already had plans for the training of social workers, including Negroes.[18]

The white institution, known as the American Interchurch College for Religious and Social Workers, was directed during its four-year (1912–1915) existence by James E. McCulloch. A native of Virginia with social work training in Europe and a Bachelor of Divinity degree from Nashville's Vanderbilt University, McCulloch had a low regard for Negro ability. He opposed Haynes's plans, pointedly explaining that the Urban League "was

---

League (Boston: Little, Brown, 1971), chs. 1–4. For a detailed biography of Haynes, see Daniel Perlman, "Stirring the White Conscience: The Life of George Edmund Haynes," (Ph.D. diss., New York Univ., 1972).

[18] Nashville *Globe*, June 23, July 7, 1911. C. C. Poindexter, Fisk teacher and friend of George E. Haynes, to Haynes, July 6, 1911; Haynes to Poindexter, July 17, 1911; George A. Gates to Haynes, June 20, 1911, all in Haynes Papers, container 1909–1913.

a Northern Institution out of sympathy with Southern life." Conservative Nashville Negroes, such as Charles Victor Roman and James C. Napier, joined Booker T. Washington in support of McCulloch and the white liberals.[19]

George E. Haynes reluctantly gave in to the whites, but he localized his goals and incorporated his training methods into the program of the Social Sciences Department at Fisk. He worked through Nashville's Bethlehem House, a black-operated training center financed by the Woman's Council of the Methodist Episcopal Church, South. Haynes's social workers helped develop domestic efficiency and good health and hygiene practices in the black slums, served in emergencies like the 1916 fire, and also sponsored wide-ranging recreational programs for black youth. Providing local services was far removed from those visions of a national training center for social workers held by Haynes and his Northern white supporters in 1910, but the efforts were lasting. Aided by student trainees from Fisk, Bethlehem House later became Bethlehem Center, providing kitchen, sewing, bathing, laundry, and gymnastic facilities and sponsoring the "first colored Girl Scouts of the South."[20]

Haynes's second objective in Tennessee had been to "develop cooperation among and encourage efficiency in social welfare agencies." In true progressive fashion, he wanted to establish a formal means of avoiding duplication and of bringing focus to reform efforts. Although ambitious attempts to achieve statewide

[19]"Memorandum of Conference with Dr. W. D. Weatherford Re: Nash. Institute," Jan. 18, 1915; George A. Gates to George E. Haynes, June 20, 1911; Haynes to James E. McCulloch, Aug. 14, 1911, all in Haynes Papers, containers 1909-1913, 1914-1915. Nashville *Banner*, Aug. 6, 1911; Charles Victor Roman, *American Civilization and the Negro: The Afro-American in Relation to National Progress* (Philadelphia: F. G. Davis, 1916), 238.

[20]"Memorandum of Conference with Dr. W. D. Weatherford Re: Nash. Institute"; George E. Haynes to L. Hollingsworth Wood, chairman of the executive board of the Urban League, Oct. 23, 1915; "Report of the Director From September 22 to October 20, 1913 to the National League on Urban Conditions Among Negroes," all in Haynes Papers, container 1914-1915. Martha Nutt, "Bethlehem Center, Nashville, Tennessee," *Southern Workman* 53 (Sept. 1924), 401-4; *Crisis* 18 (Sept. 1919), 252.

cooperation languished, Haynes had some success in Nashville where he could make regular personal contacts. By February 1912, he had succeeded in bringing together representatives from most black alliances, clubs, and associations in a Nashville League on Conditions Among Negroes. The organization listed goals which included improved housing in black neighborhoods, occupational training programs in night schools, and better cooperation with "such organizations among white citizens that aim for social betterment among Colored people." The *Globe* gave its hearty support to the new group and especially applauded its emphasis upon neighborhood action groups. "These meetings," the paper explained, "will develop courageous citizens and will enable the people to ferret out everything objectionable to the community and move it out." Prominent black men such as alderman Solomon P. Harris, school supervisor Hardy L. Keith, and lawyer-politician J. W. Grant took the lead, and within a year three neighborhood "unions" or "civic clubs" had been formed.[21]

Ironically, the new emphasis upon cooperation, especially cooperation with sympathetic whites, diminished the role of distinctly *black* progressivism. Interracial efforts during the East Nashville fire in 1916 stimulated interest in the "chronic problems of public welfare," and leaders of both races expressed a need for the formation of an interracial "public welfare league." By June 1916, the Public Welfare League had been founded and formally affiliated with the National Urban League.[22] The Phyllis Wheatley Club and the Negro Board of Trade continued their local charities and business efficiency efforts, but the interracial Public Welfare League siphoned off many of the community reform programs so characteristic of black progressivism and

[21] Form letter from George E. Haynes, May 20, 1911; "Minutes of Meeting of Representatives of Organizations, May 23, 1911"; report of meeting of North End Neighborhood Union, Nov. 4, 1912, all in Haynes Papers, container 1909–1913. Nashville *Globe*, Feb. 2, Nov. 8, 1912, Jan. 10, 24, Aug. 15, 1913.
[22] George E. Haynes to James Hardy Dillard, April 29, 1916, Haynes Papers, container 1916–1917; *Crisis* 12 (Aug. 1916), 197.

molded them to fit the paternalism of the league's white membership.

The chairman of the interracial league was not George Edmund Haynes, but Arch M. Trawick, a white Nashville manufacturer with impeccable "liberal" credentials, who led the Public Welfare League increasingly into the work of race relations rather than black social uplift.[23] This is not to say that no concrete accomplishments came from the Welfare League—it pressured the city into equipping the Negro park established four years earlier, conducted a variety of health education campaigns, and, with the encouragement of city judge Madison Wells and the field work of Haynes's trainees from Fisk at Bethlehem House, established a probation program for juvenile offenders.[24] But white leaders assumed most of the organization's responsibility and received virtually all of the publicity and credit for its achievements.

Blacks accepted this arrangement, although an occasional black man might be provoked into "setting the record straight." In 1917, the Reverend James A. Jones wrote a bitter letter to the *Globe*. "The Nashville Negroes," he said, "have become so accustomed to taking just what is thrown out to them so long, that they really have come to believe that they are receiving what is due them. They actually believe that the new Pearl High School building is a gift. They don't think they are entitled to it at all . . . I have lived in and around Nashville from childhood," Jones continued, and "the city of Nashville has not *given* the Negro race anything."[25]

[23] Trawick's "liberal" activities included financial support of Fisk University, membership in the Southern Sociological Congress, and, later, an active role in the work of the Commission on Interracial Cooperation.

[24] George E. Haynes to Board of Directors of National League on Urban Conditions Among Negroes, March 11, 1916; Haynes to Lee J. Loventhal, Feb. 4, 1917; Haynes to R. M. Dudley, March 17, 1917; "Report of George E. Haynes, Executive Secretary to the Executive Board, National League on Urban Conditions Among Negroes from March 11 to June 6, 1917"; Haynes to Rev. E. F. Goin of New Haven, Conn., Oct. 23, 1917; Paul F. Mowbray, field director for Nashville's Public Welfare League, to Haynes, Nov. 10, 1917; Haynes to W. A. Simpson, April 27, 1918, all in Haynes Papers, containers 1916-1917, 1918-1922. Nashville *Tennessean*, Feb. 9, 1918; *Crisis* 22 (Sept. 1921), 226.

[25] Nashville *Globe*, Sept. 21, 1917. Author's italics.

Nashville Negroes clearly offered the most fertile soil for the seeds of progressivism, but black reform movements also existed in other Tennessee cities. Yet when George Haynes attempted to interest blacks of Chattanooga and Knoxville in a coordinated program of social uplift supported by the Urban League, he ran into more difficulties than he had experienced in Nashville. Chattanooga lacked one necessary ingredient for reform—a sizable, educated middle class (partly due to the absence of a black college). And in Knoxville, where there was a black college and a significant black professional faction, there was also a tradition of white paternalism.[26]

After 1900, black Chattanoogans became increasingly aware of the health hazards associated with industrial communities. Smallpox, tuberculosis, and pneumonia haunted the unpaved alleys and slab-shack tenements of black neighborhoods such as St. Elmo, Churchville, and Tannery Flats. In 1912, black leaders asked for a city investigation of the high black death rate, but they received little satisfaction. Publication of statistics compiled by city health officials in 1916, however, showed "a larger number of deaths of colored folks than of whites, though we have in the city only half as many colored as we have of whites." White officials expressed concern, but they accepted no responsibility.[27] In the summer of 1916, George Haynes used contacts with Chattanooga's Negro Business League to form a Central Community Betterment League, associated with the Urban League and emphasizing the "improvement of living and working conditions." Haynes spoke enthusiastically of the potential of the Betterment League, but evidence indicates that activity amounted to little beyond health week programs, appeals for housing codes, and letters of protest against lynching in Tennessee.[28] Whereas

[26] "Knoxville Negroes," *Crisis* 9 (Feb. 1915), 186. This article reported the presence of "six colored lawyers, seventeen physicians, three pharmacists, three dentists, twenty-two graduate nurses, [and] eighty-five teachers in public and private schools."

[27] *Crisis* 4 (June 1912), Chattanooga *Daily Times*, June 14, 15, 1916; letter to the editor from the Rev. J. A. Crump, Chattanooga *Daily Times*, June 19, 1916.

[28] Chattanooga *Daily Times*, Aug. 27, 31, 1916, April 24, 1917. George E. Haynes to

Nashville blacks repeatedly formed and sustained their own organizations, Chattanoogans, reflecting a stronger East Tennessee tendency to rely upon white paternalism, did little more than publicly protest undesirable conditions.

Knoxville's black population, although smaller in number, was far more active in the area of social reform. Here, however, most of the city's black action groups preferred to work through the often sympathetic, but always caste-conscious, white leaders in the community. Some ideas for civic improvement were conceived and implemented by blacks (development of a park in 1908), but many more, while initiated in the spirit of racial progress, were realized only with the support of whites.

Matters of health and sanitation received considerable attention from Knoxville black leaders. Dr. Henry M. Green, prominent Republican politician and head of the Wallace Memorial Hospital at Knoxville College, played an important role in encouraging improvements in health practices among members of his race. In a book entitled *Pellagra in Monograph* (1927), he noted the dietary nature of pellagra, taking his conclusions from years of studying the disease among black Knoxvillians and from a fact-finding tour of the United States and Europe made as chairman of the Pellagra Commission of the National Medical Association. As an alderman (1908–1912), Green consistently fought for sewer and street extensions. In 1919 he joined Charles W. Cansler, principal of the black high school, in an unsuccessful effort to persuade the city to build "a tuberculosis hospital for the care and treatment of colored persons."[29]

the Rev. E. F. Goin, Oct. 23, 1917; Haynes to J. O. Blanton, principal of the Colored High School in Louisville, Ky., Oct. 24, 1917; W. H. Singleton, principal of Howard High School (Negro) and secretary of the Central Community Betterment League, to Haynes, Aug. 21, 1917, all in Haynes Papers, container 1916–1917. Central Community Betterment League to Gov. Thomas C. Rye, Feb. 21, 1918, Gov. Rye Papers, Tennessee State Library and Archives, container 33; interviews with Dr. J. Monroe Bynes and Ms. Rosa McGhee, July 13, 1972.

[29]Chattanooga *Daily Times*, Aug. 12, 1911; Knoxville *News-Sentinel*, March 20, 1939. Dr. Henry M. Green to John C. Houk, April 3, 1911; copy of a bill for a Colored Tuberculosis Hospital prepared by Charles W. Cansler for submission before the Tennes-

White assistance made possible the operation of a YMCA (in a building donated by Calvin F. Johnson, probably the wealthiest black person in the city) beginning in 1906 and the establishment of a YWCA in 1920. In addition, white city officials consented to the creation of two public parks in 1915 and supported Charles Cansler in his successful campaign to obtain a Carnegie Library in 1918.[30] The work of homemaker's clubs, ministerial alliances, and education associations reflected a general desire among the middle-class Negroes of Knoxville to improve living conditions among the people of their race. Because the black community was small, however, it generally appealed for support to the reform instincts and self-interest of the white middle class. Despite considerable effort, George E. Haynes was never able to generate much enthusiasm for affiliating with the Urban League.[31] The number and scope of the reform and uplift ideas emanating from black leaders in Knoxville, nevertheless, gave ample evidence of black response to the progressive impulse.

Memphis, meanwhile, offered a very different response to race relations and reform. A young town, populated by black and white immigrants from the rural areas of West Tennessee, Mississippi, and Arkansas, turn-of-the-century Memphis was characterized by violence, rapid economic growth, and black poverty. Black leaders were ministers and politicians; few of them were well educated; and a significant black middle class did not develop until after 1910. Health conditions in the residential alleys near

---

see General Assembly, 1919, both in Houk Papers, miscellaneous uncatalogued papers. Information relating to Dr. Green's study of pellagra was provided by his nephew, Wilbur E. Sims, in a letter to the author, Feb. 12, 1971.

[30] J. W. Manning, general secretary of Alice Johnson Memorial Young Men's Christian Association (Negro), to Gov. Ben W. Hooper, March 12, May 16, 1912, Gov. Hooper Papers, container 5; Daves, *A Social Study of the Colored Population of Knoxville*, 16, 20, 21; Rothrock, ed., *The French Broad-Holston Country*, 319–20; *Crisis* 18 (May 1919), 36.

[31] George E. Haynes to R. W. McGranahan, president of Knoxville College, Sept. 10, 1913; Haynes to Mrs. J. J. Johnson, Oct. 16, Nov. 20, 1913, Jan. 22, 1914; Webster L. Porter to Haynes, Sept. 15, 1913; the Rev. J. W. Mayes to Haynes, Oct. 21, 1913; Charles W. Cansler to Haynes, Oct. 29, 1913; Mrs. Johnson to Haynes, Nov. 3, Dec. 26, 1913, all in Haynes Papers, containers 1909–1913, 1914–1915.

Beale Street and the Mississippi River reflected municipal neglect and habits of the open country that had been brought
unsuitably to the city. Malaria, tuberculosis, and pellagra regularly ravaged residents. Blacks sought relief by turning to the
fleeting pleasures of cocaine, emotional religion, saloons, prostitution, and, on rare occasions, attempts at social reform.

Beyond the presence of arrest-happy and corrupt law enforcement officials, the black community of Memphis received almost
no stabilizing municipal or state services. Crime and disease ran
rampant. Steadily crowded by new immigrants, black Memphians lived in a world of chaos and uncertainty. Two stabilizing
forces appeared out of this fluid, undisciplined society; one, the
Solvent Savings Bank and Trust Company founded by Robert R.
Church, Sr. in 1906, and the other, the political acumen and
audacity of his son, Robert R. Church, Jr. Around the former
gathered an ambitious and able group of business and professional
men, winning the respect of the black community and providing
the nucleus for the potent, political bloc envisioned by the
younger Church.

Coinciding with the emergence of leaders among the growing
black population was the rise to power in Memphis of Edward H.
"Boss" Crump. Described by his biographer as being "fully in the
stream of the progressive current," Crump was, however, no
humanitarian. His progressivism was that of business efficiency
and corporate regulation, not social justice. He declared war on
monopoly control of the city's utilities, threatened public ownership, and demanded improvement of municipal services.[32] Having narrowly won election over a corporation–city hall alliance,
Crump found himself, however, in an insecure political position.

Aware of both Crump's tenuous power and his progressive
leanings, black leaders sought to include their race in the promised reforms. During the mayoralty campaign of 1911, the Col-

[32] William Durell Miller, *Mr. Crump of Memphis* (Baton Rouge: Louisiana State Univ.
Press, 1964), 61, 103.

ored Citizens Association of Memphis, Tennessee, appeared. Leaders of this group were Harry H. Pace, Bert M. Roddy, and Robert Church, Jr., all officers in the Solvent Bank, and they used a successful registration drive in the black community to gain an audience with both Crump and his opponent. They requested "assurance of park facilities, paved streets in the sections where Negroes reside, and an extension of the sprinkling service to such streets. . . ." At a heavily attended black meeting Pace recommended voting for Crump, "for the other candidate promises everything and I fear he will do nothing; but this redheaded fellow frankly declines to promise some of the things we want, but convinced me that he will fulfill the promises that he did make."[33] This was the beginning of a working relationship between Crump and black political leaders which surfaced intermittently throughout the "Boss's" reign of approximately forty years. As a result, Crump was never guilty of the race-baiting that characterized most Southern political progressives, and he allowed blacks, though generally with a time and quality lag, to share in many of the social advancements that reform accomplished in Memphis.

In organizing politically, black Memphians pursued the only realistic route to reform open to them in 1911; and it was a route frequently taken by various other ethnic groups in Northern cities. Lack of strong community ties, absence of an old-line black middle class, and constant mobility left Memphis without the black civic, business, and social clubs that had been the agencies for progressive uplift programs in Nashville. It was also discouraging to formation of social action groups that Memphis was almost totally lacking in white liberalism. Nashville had a large white academic population and an established "aristocracy"; Memphis had neither. The two advantages possessed by potential black progressives in the Bluff City were numbers and active political competition among the whites. The Colored Citizens Association

---

[33]*Crisis* 2 (Aug. 1911), 139; 3 (Dec. 1911), 53; Miller, *Mr. Crump of Memphis*, 104.

and, later, Robert Church's Lincoln League and West Tennessee Civic and Political League exploited these advantages, always with an eye, however, to staying within the limits of white tolerance. Blacks needed to provide the initiative, but whites had to be allowed to make the decisions.

The issue that gave birth to the Colored Citizens Association was the neglect of public park facilities for blacks. Through the efforts of the National Playground Association, money was raised in 1908 for the improvement and increase in number of Memphis's outdoor recreational facilities. Blacks were not specifically excluded from the new parks, but caste etiquette made official exclusion unnecessary. When it became evident that no provisions were to be made for black usage, various leaders protested. C. P. J. Mooney, editor of the Memphis *Commercial Appeal* and perhaps the nearest thing to a white liberal in the city, began a campaign in April 1910 for recognition of the recreational needs of the city's forgotten 40 percent. Before announcing for office, Crump had proposed the development of Negro park on a fifty-acre plot "several miles beyond the city's eastern limit," but nearby residents persuaded officials to reject his proposal.[34]

The park controversy and the formulation of the Colored Citizens Association not only drew the attention of many national progressives of both races, but also led to a period of significant gain in public services for Memphis's black community.[35] Crump won the 1911 election and also subsequent approval for his Negro park plan. Douglass Park opened in 1913, forcing blacks to wait two years but eventually meeting one of their modest requests. Although usually following similar white gains of greater magnitude, other improvements took place in the city's black communities. In late 1911, four white visiting nurses and one black nurse were added to the Health Department's staff in an effort to reach indigent families of the city. In connection with city welfare

[34] Miller, *Memphis During the Progressive Era*, 84–86, 105.
[35] *Crisis* 1 (March 1911), 8, 28; 2 (June 1911), 76–77; 2 (Aug. 1911), 139; 3 (Dec. 1911), 53; *La Follette's Weekly* 6 (Feb. 14, 1914), 6–7.

work, a special department for "family rehabilitation" among blacks was set up in 1912. And, in 1915, the city recreation commission appointed a "supervisor of recreation and social survey" for the black community.[36]

Reforms benefiting black Memphians sprang mainly from white self-interest and came with certain strings attached. Mooney explained his support in these terms: "The Negro is the great wealth producer in this territory, and an appreciation of this fact in the shape of improved living conditions for him would be responded to by more generous effort on his part to observe the law and to merit the trust that is put in him." White sensibilities needed protection, and while creating Douglass Park in 1913, the city commission also warned blacks that if they used the streetcar for transportation to the new facilities (thus inconveniencing nearby white residents), the park would be closed.[37]

Well aware of the limits of their own political importance and the patience of white society, members of the Colored Citizens Association followed up their political activities by implementing their own progressive reforms. Expressing a desire "to assist in as humble but in as intelligent a way as we can to better the condition of our people in our City and County," the officers appealed to Booker T. Washington in 1912 for support in their attempts to establish "a Farmers Institute, a YMCA. and a center of trade." When the Tuskegean finally got around to coming to Memphis in 1914, he urged blacks to "prove that we can be just as clean, just as progressive . . . as the people of any other race," but he put his stress on the necessity for appealing for white aid.[38] More encouragement and direction than this was needed if the general apathy and disorganization among black Memphians was to be

[36] Miller, *Mr. Crump of Memphis*, 85–87; Paul R. Coppock, "Parks of Memphis," *West Tennessee Historical Society Papers* 12 (1958), 122; Miller, *Memphis During the Progressive Era*, 116; Francis H. McLean, "Memphis Today," *Survey* 30 (July 19, 1913), 565; Memphis *Commercial Appeal*, Sept. 23, 1917.
[37] Memphis *Commercial Appeal*, n.d., quoted in *La Follette's Weekly* 6 (Feb. 14, 1914), 7; Miller, *Memphis During the Progressive Era*, 86.
[38] Colored Citizens Association to Booker T. Washington, Sept. 7, 1912; "Extracts from

overcome. Neither a successful YMCA, farmers' institute, nor board of trade came into existence. With the aid of "four or five young men just out of Tuskegee," a YMCA was opened in 1914. But after operating on a shoestring budget of black donations for two years, the program ceased. As one of the early founders later recalled, "I realize now that our wings were too weak. They had been soiled, broken or crippled by poverty, misdirection, ill-fortune."[39]

Black Memphians continued to respond to the progressive impulse, but their success in bringing significant change was minimal without white support. In 1915 a group of black businessmen chartered an organization known as the National Association for Thrift Among Colored People, but their ambitious efforts "to supply a definite and nationwide plan . . . to reduce expenses and to have regular and inspiring education in 'how to be thrifty' " made little impression, even in Memphis.[40] A somewhat less ambitious, but more successful, venture was the organization in September 1915 of the Industrial Settlement Home. Established to care for underprivileged black children, the home began with "a single borrowed cot and one worker." Blacks made up the board of directors of the home, and it was operated rather precariously for several years on the charity they raised. After 1917 it received aid from the city and county boards of education, and later, from the juvenile court, the Rosenwald Fund, and the Interracial Commission.[41]

George E. Haynes had hoped to expand his Urban League reform program into Memphis. A foothold existed in the form of a Working Girls' Home maintained under the auspices of the Memphis Association for the Protection of Colored Women,

address delivered by Booker T. Washington at Church's Park, Memphis, May 14, 1914," both in Washington Papers, containers 832, 841.

[39]Interview with Blair T. Hunt, June 14, 1972; Hunt quoted in the Memphis *Press-Scimitar*, March 26, 1947.

[40]Memphis *Commercial Appeal*, June 21, 1915.

[41]*Ibid.*, Sept. 1, 1916; Robinson, "A Social History of the Negroes of Memphis and Shelby County," 132–35.

which worked through matrons at the Union Railway Station to contribute "to the race's continued progress and improvement along all lines," especially by keeping migrant black women from falling into the trap of prostitution. Haynes used this nucleus and the financial support of the American Missionary Association to organize a branch of the Urban League in Memphis in 1911. The branch started ambitiously, employing one full-time staff member. The league appeared destined for some success when, in the spring of 1912, it prevailed upon white officials "to put up a camp and house more than two-thousand colored folk" during a tremendous flooding of the Mississippi River. Factionalism and lack of leadership, however, caused interest in the league's activities to diminish when the crisis passed. It was not until August 1916 that Haynes was able to revive the program.[42]

Working through black recreation supervisor William N. Jones and a newly organized Young Men's Business Club, Haynes held several conferences in 1916 and 1917 with black leaders and "public spirited white men" in an effort to stimulate social work among the city's Negroes.[43] These conferences gained impetus from increased racial tension. Memphis was a funneling point northward for migrants from the entire Mississippi Delta, and social friction was constant. Tensions had exploded on May 22, 1917, in the public burning of Ell Persons, a black man accused of rape and murder. Charred remains of the dead man were strewn about Beale Street, and Memphis received much adverse national publicity.

Unlike Nashville, Memphis did not accept interracial reform organizations. When on September 22, 1917, the Memphis Welfare League was organized and affiliated with the Urban League,

---

[42] Nashville *Globe*, Nov. 4, 1910. George E. Haynes to Mrs. A. E. Tackett of the Memphis Association for the Protection of Colored Women, Sept. 12, 1911; Haynes to Professor J. T. Larsen of Le Moyne Institute, Oct. 22, 1911; Haynes to Prof. D. Butler Pratt of Talladega College, Nov. 13, 1911; Clifton L. McAllister, president of Nelson Merry College in Jefferson City, Tenn., to Haynes, Nov. 11, 1912, all in Haynes Papers, container 1909–1913.

[43] Memphis *Commercial Appeal*, Aug. 25, 1916, Sept. 23, 1917.

it was headed by the unassertive Sutton E. Griggs and Thomas O. Fuller, and there were no white members.[44] Instead of leading the Welfare League as Nashville whites had done, Memphis Chamber of Commerce officials formed their own industrial Welfare Committee which, in turn, advised the pliant Griggs on how blacks could best "improve their general efficiency by the suppression of lawlessness and vice." White business leaders managed only a selfish concern for their mudsill class and generally agreed with the opinion of a local banker who concluded that "anything . . . that will make our colored people contented and happy, will necessarily be of great advantage to us in the future." Specifically black accomplishments were few, but included the launching of a short-lived newspaper, the Memphis *Times*, in March 1918, which promised to be "a factor for social uplift, mental, moral and spiritual development, as well as commercial and financial." Some tangible action, if not solutions, did take place. The Chamber of Commerce proposed a "survey of housing conditions and general sanitation of the negro districts," the city purchased Church's Park (privately constructed by Robert R. Church, Sr., in 1901) for $85,000 and turned it into an "uptown recreation park for the race," and both black and white objections to overcrowded school conditions led the Board of Education in 1919 to request a survey of its system by the United States Commissioner of Education.[45]

The pressures of migration and world war finally awakened urban leaders to the fact that white progressivism in Tennessee had paid little attention to that 25 percent of the state's population which was most in need of uplift and reform. Response to the deplorable conditions discovered in black urban communities

[44]*Ibid.*, Sept. 23, 1917; George E. Haynes to Sutton E. Griggs, Nov. 13, 1917, Haynes Papers, container 1916–1917; Bert M. Roddy to James Weldon Johnson of the NAACP, Jan. 26, 1918, NAACP Papers, container G-199.
[45]Memphis*News-Scimitar*, March 4, 1918; Memphis*Times*, March 9, 1918, quoted by Robert Thomas Kerlin, *The Voice of the Negro, 1919* (New York: Dutton, 1920), 11–12; Mary Church Terrell to her brother Thomas A. Church, March 21, 1922, Terrell Papers, container 4; U.S. Bureau of Education, *The Public School System of Memphis.*

during the war was usually shallow and selfishly inspired, and yet the widely publicized work of such white-dominated agencies as the Commission on Interracial Cooperation has blinded most historians to the earlier presence of real progressive spirit within Tennessee's black middle class.

Black progressivism in Tennessee was almost as diverse and even less coordinated than the abundance of white movements, crusades, reformers, and uplifters whose faith in progress and insistence upon change dominated the spirit of the age. George Edmund Haynes attempted to use the Urban League as a coordinating force for the charity and uplift efforts of the women's clubs, the business efficiency programs of Negro business groups, the morality crusades of colored ministerial alliances, and the housing and school improvement appeals of other black community organizations. Haynes sought to form a State Wide City Community Betterment Organization, but no one was interested. Even citywide cooperation was difficult to maintain among black reformers.[46]

An unfulfilled individualism, poverty, and insecurity undoubtedly worked to fragment and localize Southern black progressivism. While urging that blacks be given "the chance to earn an honest living," along with adequate protection from crime and disease, black leaders in Tennessee repeatedly voiced the individualist themes of Booker T. Washington: "do your part and you will succeed," and "the thing that the negro needs to-day is to go to work."[47] Generally rejecting the idea of combining to "force" recognition of grievances, black Tennesseans were accustomed to "taking care of their own" or appealing to white paternalism. Individual recognition by white society and white individuals was important to the black man who had never known such accep-

[46] William Jasper Hale, president of Tennessee A & I, to George E. Haynes, Aug. 18, 1917; W. H. Singleton, principal of Howard High School in Chattanooga, to Haynes, Aug. 21, 1917; Mrs. J. J. Johnson to Haynes, Dec. 26, 1913, all in Haynes Papers, container 1909–1913.

[47] Nashville *Globe*, Jan. 31, 1913; *East Tennessee News*, n.d., quoted in Nashville *Globe*, Jan. 13, 1911; Nashville *American*, June 21, 1901.

tance. Whites feared and opposed assertive black organizations, and black leaders, therefore, sought to gain or maintain status by accommodating to white opinion.

Black progressivism was the child of business and professional men who depended on the patronage of common laborers and domestic servants, and who thus attained economic security only by giving close attention to their affairs. They could not devote much time to committee meetings and travel. The distances separating Knoxville, Chattanooga, Nashville, and Memphis hindered the sharing of progressive ideas and programs, but there was also a great difference in racial climates. White paternalism and a general feeling of comparative well-being encouraged Knoxville blacks to concentrate on local self-improvement. Lack of community stability, established black leadership, and white sympathy discouraged black Memphians from undertaking individual efforts like those in Knoxville and made impossible the more sophisticated programs attempted in Nashville.

Black progressive programs in Tennessee were local in scope and varied in direction, but the leaders consistently operated from the same impulse: they knew and accepted the uplift and efficiency tenets of the "Progressive Era" on one hand, and they resented the increase in white racism on the other. The racial atmosphere of the South was growing worse—in Tennessee, the Jim Crow system was tightened, the Republican party leaned toward "lily-whitism," and racial violence became epidemic. The black middle class was stung by these blows to its carefully cultivated self-esteem, and the growing pressures of black migration indicated the very real possibility of further restrictions. In reaction, black leaders intensified their efforts to improve the Negro race in the eyes of white society.

CHAPTER XI.

Race Relations Under Pressure

Black Tennesseans lived under the shadow of fear and violence. They had little protection because legal discrimination and abuse occurred even more often than mob attacks and lynching. World War I presented new problems of race relations in Tennessee. Newspapers, federal officials, and local orators resorted to emotion-laden language and the cultivation of nativistic hostility in order to unite the nation in a campaign of patriotism and "100 percent Americanism." These injections unfortunately heightened racial tensions. New social and economic tendencies, although predating the war, now became even more disturbing. Unionization and black urbanization seemed particularly threatening to the "American" status quo in Tennessee and throughout the South. Understandably, the war years, including the tense months just preceding American entry, applied new pressures upon race relations.

Blacks had frequently complained that "people of color are made to suffer out of proportion to punishment meted out to others," and they had occasionally organized to improve conditions, without noticeable success. A common reaction among black leaders was to lay the blame for white violence on the crimes committed by members of their own race. In one of his early prohibition speeches, Robert E. Clay expressed the opinion that "where there is racial strife, in nine cases out of ten, worthless and shiftless negroes and liquor are the cause of it all."[1]

[1] Griggs, *The One Great Question*, 16–20; Nashville *Tennessean*, July 26, 1908, Dec. 24, 1909; Nashville *Banner*, May 18, 1905; Nashville *Globe*, March 3, 1911.

Rarely had Tennessee Negroes met or even threatened to meet violence with violence. There were, however, a few indications of a changing black attitude as the century progressed. "Four companies of militia" had been necessary in Chattanooga in 1906 in order to "control" an estimated "2,000 to 4,000" Negroes who gathered to protest the blatant and semiofficial lynching of Ed Johnson. In 1909, a letter to the Nashville *Globe* forecast greater black assertiveness in the future because "Discussions rendered by the white man do not please the young Negro . . . the law is not with him. The younger generation can not stand this. They will rise up and protect themselves."[2]

Between the years 1910 and 1916 white violence directed against blacks decreased significantly. Whitecapping, or night-riding, had largely died out, and reported lynchings had been reduced to less than one per year. But by 1916, black urban migration had begun to strain the traditional relationships of the caste society. Whites complained of farm labor shortages and streetcar congestion, and black leaders tried to discourage the disturbing urban trend by starting "back-to-the-farm" societies and warning potential migrants of city problems. George E. Haynes advised black workers to exploit increased demands for their labor by improving existing working conditions rather than by seeking a better life and a better job elsewhere. He suggested to white employers that higher wages and a healthier and safer working environment would "improve the efficiency of labor," make it more "valuable," and "make for better feeling between the races."[3]

When the United States formally entered World War I in the spring of 1917, blacks throughout the state rushed to show their

---

[2]"Memorandum of Statement of J. M. Bynes of Chattanooga, re: Lynching of Edward Johnson (1906) and trial of Sheriff at Washington," NAACP Papers, container C-367; unidentified Tennessee newspaper clipping, March 21, 1906, Du Bois Papers; Nashville *Globe*, June 25, 1909.

[3]George Edmund Haynes to Walter Buchanon, president of the Alabama State Agricultural and Mechanical College for Negroes, Dec. 14, 1916; Paul F. Mowbray to Haynes, Aug. 31, 1917, both in Haynes Papers, container 1916–1917.

loyalty to flag and country. Army recruiting stations in Knoxville and Chattanooga reported more black applicants than whites, and they filled their Negro quotas within two weeks, turning others away. Tennessee A & I alone furnished one hundred students and five faculty members to the armed services. While some young blacks undoubtedly used the army as an escape from Southern prejudice, black community leaders praised the enthusiasm as evidence that white fears of disloyalty were groundless.[4] War drives for Victory Gardens, Red Cross aid, Thrift Stamps, and Liberty Bonds met with wide popular response among black Tennesseans. One older black man in Knoxville was observed "digging up a splendid stand of grass and planting the space in potatoes." Columbia blacks established a prize for the best garden, while black Memphians "pledged $174,823 in Thrift Stamps." Led by Bert Roddy, Robert R. Church, Jr., Thomas Hayes, Thomas O. Fuller, and James W. Lane, West Tennessee Negroes announced their intentions to double their quota of $75,000 during the United War Work campaign in the fall of 1918.[5]

Many black Tennesseans, however, did not view their support as being entirely the result of blind patriotism and nationalistic loyalty. Their rallies and pronouncements spoke of the black domestic future as well. Addressing a meeting of the Nashville Colored Ministers' Alliance in February 1918, Dr. James A. Jones, a presiding elder in the A. M. E. Church, noted the emphasis placed on a "war for democracy" and commented on the significance of such a crusade. "It is our earnest hope," he said,

[4] Knoxville *Journal and Tribune*, April 22, 24, 1917; Chattanooga *Daily Times*, April 24, 1917; Nashville *Banner*, April 10, 1917; Nashville *Tennessean*, April 23, 1917; Memphis *Commercial Appeal*, May 5, 12, 1918; *Biennial Report of the State Superintendent of Public Instruction of Tennessee for the Scholastic Years ending June 30, 1918*, 104; "The President's Annual Address to the Eighteenth Annual Convention of the National Negro Business League held at Chattanooga, Tennessee, August 15–17, 1917," Napier Papers, container 1.
[5] Nashville *Banner*, April 23, 24, 1917, Feb. 26, Dec. 12, 1918; Memphis *Commercial Appeal*, Oct. 24, 1918; letter to the editor from Charles W. Cansler, Knoxville *Journal and Tribune*, April 22, 1917; *Crisis* 14 (May 1917), 37; 16 (July 1918), 141; 16 (Sept. 1918), 238.

"that should this country win, the democracy will be something more than a hollow sham. . . . We hope that this war may serve to lift the scales from the eyes of prejudice-ridden America, and that the part we take in this fight will accomplish the required result, making the democracy of which we so much boast be a reality and not a mockery." In a subsequent letter to Governor Tom C. Rye, Jones deplored the inability of Tennessee's "democracy" to protect black citizens at home, while there were Negro "boys at the front, fighting for this country." The *Christian Index* (Jackson) reminded Americans that the "high sense of honor and duty" should also be "practice[d] among her own citizens." "We are glad the time has come," the *Index* said, "when this country can unite in a fight for 'liberty and human rights.' These rights have been trampled under foot and outraged in a most uncivilized fashion, not only upon the high seas, but upon dry land right here in America. . . ."[6] Although some Negroes urged blacks to "debate *our* question after the war," the conservative J. C. Napier undoubtedly spoke for the majority when he remarked before a National Negro Business League convention in Chattanooga in 1917 that, if the participation of his race in the war effort did "not entitle us to a fair chance in the race of life, pray tell us what any set of people ever has done or can do to win that chance." His audience responded with "prolonged applause."[7]

Despite the obvious displays of black loyalty, World War I was a time of violence in Tennessee. Neither the black hopes of proving their worthiness nor admonitions that whites should practice what they preached were realized. Beginning in May 1917, Tennessee's apparent racial calm exploded into a spate of hangings, burnings, and rioting, and the "Negro problem" took on a new urgency. During a two-and-a-half-year period, six lynch-

[6] Nashville *Banner*, Feb. 10, 1918; Dr. James A. Jones to Gov. Thomas C. Rye, April 24, 1918, Gov. Rye Papers, Tennessee State Library and Archives, container 33; *Christian Index*, April 19, 1917, Sept. 5, 1918.

[7] Nashville *Banner*, April 23, 1917; "The President's Annual Address to the Eighteenth Annual Convention of the National Negro Business League held at Chattanooga, Tennessee, August 15–17, 1917," Napier Papers, container 1.

ings and a small riot took the lives of at least seven Negroes and threatened the safety of the entire black population of the state. White officials further complicated race relations by discriminatory enforcement of vagrancy laws and general harassment of black citizens in an effort to meet unskilled labor shortages. The Memphis Chamber of Commerce, for example, urged the city's police commissioner to close "Negro pressing and bootblack stands" as being "unnecessary from a business standpoint." The commissioner complied, and blacks were ordered "to get out and go to work at a legitimate calling"—that is, to work for low wages at "essential wartime" jobs in the cotton warehouses.[8]

The brutality of white violence and the blatancy of economic and legal coercion shocked black leaders who had rallied support for the war and infuriated many younger Negroes. A group of blacks from Chattanooga warned Governor Rye that "Tenn. is sewing [sic] the wind, beware lest she reap the whirlwind."[9] From Memphis, Bob Church reported to NAACP officials in the spring of 1919 that "antagonism between the races" was growing in West Tennessee, and he privately warned the mayor of Memphis that "the Negroes would not make trouble unless they were attacked, but in that event they were prepared to defend themselves."[10]

One group of white Tennesseans responded constructively to the increased racial tensions, although their primary motives were neither altruistic nor humanitarian. Aroused by the vicious outbreak of lynching and burning, a committee of "two lawyers, two business men, two college men, and one preacher" in Nashville met on February 24, 1918 and formed the Tennessee Law and Order League. Their manifesto, signed by three hundred

[8] Memphis *Commercial Appeal*, Oct. 17, 18, 23, 24, 1918.
[9] Central Community Betterment League of Chattanooga, Tennessee, to Gov. Rye, Feb. 21, 1918, Gov. Rye Papers, container 33.
[10] Charles Flint Kellogg, *NAACP*, 235; August Meier and Elliott Rudwick, "Black Violence in the Twentieth Century: A Study in Rhetoric and Retaliation," in Hugh Davis Graham and Ted Robert Gurr, eds., *The History of Violence in America* (New York: Bantam, 1969), 403.

235

white Nashvillians, sought to arouse public opinion "to the end that mob violence and at least the more serious crimes shall be condemned by public sentiment and certainly punished by the established processes of the law."[11] The Law and Order League gained a great deal of publicity throughout the state and received solid support from many religious and educational figures. Much of the support, however, came from individuals like Bishop Thomas F. Gailor of the Episcopal Diocese of Tennessee, who accepted the idea because "the time is coming, when men who recklessly lynch Negroes are going to lynch white men, and then we shall see trouble sure enough." The Nashville *Commercial Daily*, a short-lived, business-oriented newspaper, gave half-hearted support but denied the seriousness of "mob-violence" in the state. Instead, it noted "that the Negro race [had] an inherited tendency toward crime and viciousness" and called upon black leaders to quiet their protests and concentrate on stopping "those crimes and conditions" that caused lynching.[12]

The league issued an invitation to the black community to join in the campaign, but also appeased the predominant white fear of Negro crime by blaming black leaders for not controlling crime:

> In this constructive program of law enforcement, we earnestly invite the co-operation of the colored race. . . . Unfortunately the impression prevails with some that Negroes tend to expend their indignation against the crime of lynching and to lose sight of the crime which often leads to the lynching. . . . Our efforts will be futile unless the leaders of the colored race . . . condemn with all possible vigor and earnestness the crimes which most frequently lead to lawlessness and to mob law.[13]

Established black leaders, pressured by deteriorating race re-

---

[11]*Law and Order League of Nashville, Tenn.*, pamphlet in Gov. Rye Papers, container 38; *Crisis* 17 (March 1919), 231. In May 1917, Ell Persons was burned to death in Memphis; in December, Lathan [Lation?] Scott met a similar fate in Dyersburg; and in early February 1918, Jim McIlheron was burned to death in Estill Springs; interview with H. C. Hardy, June 20, 1972.

[12]Bishop Thomas F. Gailor to Gov. Thomas C. Rye, Feb. 21, 1918, Gov. Rye Papers, container 33; *Commercial Daily*, Feb. 26, March 5, 1918, located in *ibid.*, container 38.

[13]Nashville *Banner*, Feb. 25, 1918.

lations and personal feelings of betrayal, eventually joined a Jim Crow "auxiliary" of the Law and Order League. But black Tennesseans created their own protest as well. After the third "burning at the stake" within a year's time, some two thousand Negroes left their jobs in the middle of the day on February 19, 1918, and staged a silent parade through the capital square. J. C. Napier and the Reverend W. S. Ellington then presented a petition to Governor Rye, reminding the governor that they had "no voice in making, nor in enforcing the laws which [they were] called upon to obey" and urging him to use his office to prevent further violence.[14] The governor's office was also besieged with letters from individuals and groups across the state, both black and white. Charles W. Cansler, a conservative but concerned black Knoxville educator, warned that if "the reign of the hoodlum" was allowed to continue, "the sooner the law-abiding colored citizens get out [of Tennessee], the better off they will be." Citing Booker T. Washington's phrase, "cast your buckets down where you are," Cansler told the governor that blacks were now appealing to state and local officials because "the so-called war amendments to the federal constitution [had become] but high sounding verbiage which guarantee much and give but little."[15] The black leaders of Chattanooga's Central Community Betterment League wrote to Governor Rye in a similar vein, complaining that when they had appealed "for justice" to federal authorities in the past, they had received only "a theory of government" and a "question of jurisdiction."[16] To these appeals Rye curtly responded that he could do nothing to prevent or curb the lynching epidemic.[17] No arrests were made by either state or federal officials, and another

[14]Nashville *Banner*, Feb. 20, 1918; *Commercial Daily*, Feb. 26, 1918; Nashville *Globe*, Feb. 22, March 1, 1918 quoted in *Commercial Daily*, March 5, 1918). The copies of the *Commercial Daily* are located in the Gov. Rye Papers, container 38.

[15]Charles W. Cansler to Gov. Tom C. Rye, Feb. 28, 1918, Gov. Rye Papers, container 33.

[16]Chattanooga *Daily Times*, Feb. 22, 1918; Central Community Betterment League to Gov. Tom C. Rye, Feb. 21, 1918, Rye Papers, container 33.

[17]Nashville *Globe*, March 1, 1918 (quoted in *Commercial Daily*, March 5, 1918).

lynching took place at Lexington in April, and still another at Erwin in May.

As the General Assembly prepared to open its biennial session in January 1919, blacks urged their legislators to take positive steps toward controlling lawlessness, and the Law and Order League stepped up its publicity campaign in white communities. A national surge of antiradicalism and labor strikes intensified public pressure. Two bills introduced in the 1919 session offered encouragement. One, a measure proposing that the county in which a lynching occurred "be required to pay the next of kin of the victim the sum of $5,000 and the state should pay $5,000 and all the officials responsible for the crime should immediately forfeit their offices," never got out of committee. The other proposal, known as the "State Police" or "Constabulary" bill, was less punitive and thus stood a better chance of success. It eliminated one of Governor Rye's excuses by creating a six-hundred-member police force, responsible only to the governor and available "when acts of violence occur or are threatened . . . whereby rights of persons or property are violated or threatened with violation."[18]

Black citizens, as well as antilabor forces, gave strong support to the "Constabulary" bill. A new and aggressive governor, Albert H. Roberts, also promoted the idea. J. C. Napier, Robert L. Mayfield, and J. A. Jones delivered a petition in the name of the newly formed Nashville branch of the NAACP, supporting the bill "in the name of righteousness, justice and fair play . . . and in the name of the soldiers who bled and died to make the world a better place to live." References to wartime "gallantry" and "returning soldiers" were emphasized also in the petitions of mass meetings of black citizens in Knoxville and La Follette.[19] Although white

[18]Nashville *Banner*, March 12, 1919; *Acts of Tennessee*, 1919.

[19]Nashville *Banner*, March 23, 1919; Nashville *Tennessean*, March 22, 1919; Knoxville *Journal and Tribune*, March 22, 1919; telegram from "Loyal Colored Citizens of La Follette" to state senator E. E. Patton on March 17, 1919; Houk Papers, container 95; undated letter from "Colored Citizens of Knox County" to Houk, *ibid.*, uncatalogued miscellaneous papers.

fears and influence were crucial in the eventual passage of the measure, black Tennesseans had held more public meetings and spoken out more strongly on this police measure than they had at any time since the efforts for improved education ten years earlier.

Many Negroes, despite the past record of white law enforcement, took new hope. Robert Church continued to urge political muscle as a surer guarantee of protection than dependence upon whites, and the Nashville *Globe* advised economic sanctions upon cities which allowed violence to go unpunished—urging black fraternal and professional groups to take their annual meetings elsewhere. The *Globe* happily announced that the black National Medical Association had canceled a convention previously scheduled for Memphis in August 1917. But such resistance was not widespread. [20]

As the nation moved toward the fateful "Red Summer" of 1919, a sense of false security had returned to Tennessee. [21] The well-publicized, though middle-class-dominated, rallies of the Law and Order League, the passage of the State Police Law, and the assurances of Governor Roberts lulled Tennesseans of both races into the feeling that their racial situation was at last under control. On May 25, 1919, the Nashville *Tennessean* proudly reminded its readers "that during the entire period since reconstruction days no sharp clash has come between the white and colored races in or about Nashville. On the contrary, cordial relations and uniform cooperation have existed between the races here. . . ."[22]

When racial violence exploded in Washington (July 19) and Chicago (July 27), many white Tennesseans delighted in reprimanding the North and extolling the virtues of segregation of the races. The Chattanooga *Daily Times* expressed the opinion: "It

[20]Nashville *Globe*, June 1, July 6, 1917.
[21]Violence occurred in many places, including Charleston, S. C. (May 10), Longview, Tex. (July 10), Washington, D. C. (July 19), Chicago (July 27), Knoxville, Tenn. (Aug. 30), Omaha, Neb. (Sept. 28), and Elaine, Ark. (Oct. 1).
[22]Nashville *Tennessean*, May 25, 1919.

has served the purposes of our northern and western friends to discuss this matter academically while the issue was confined to the South, but when it gets up among them they argue it with pistols, guns and rope." Northerners who criticized Jim Crow laws were hypocrites. The Chicago riot was started when a black bather supposedly encroached upon the white portion of a divided beach; apparently Chicago, like the South, had "recognized segregation as essential not only to the peace of the country, but to the integrity of the two races."[23] On August 1, Chicago officials telegraphed Southern governors, asking about employment conditions if Negroes migrated back to the South. Governor Roberts, cognizant of complaints about a shortage of agricultural labor, confidently assured Chicago that "industrious negroes could find all the employment they wished" in his state. As a few black families began to arrive in Tennessee, Roberts issued a declaration welcoming them to a state whose "perfect understanding and efforts to maintain friendly relationships for the past century" stood it in "good stead in the present period of unrest. . . . We need the Negro here, and I do not fear that Tennessee will ever be the scene of such troubles as are now existing in Chicago."[24]

Tennessee's rallies, proclamations, and editorials, however, told only part of the story. A Memphis woman warned that "enlightened public sentiment may be" opposed to lynching, "but enlightened public sentiment is in the minority. . . . One of the most surprised people I ever saw was a dairyman whom I ceased patronizing because he had taken part in a lynching. He thought he had been doing a public duty!"[25] While newspaper editorials denounced violence, their effect was offset by front pages that told tale after tale of Negro crime and racial violence in

---

[23]Chattanooga *Daily Times*, July 30, 1919; *Christian Index*, Aug. 1919. Much of what follows in this chapter was previously published in my article, "Tennessee Race Relations and the Knoxville Riot of 1919," East Tennessee Historical Society *Publications*, No. 41 (1969), 67–85.
[24]Chattanooga *Daily Times*, July 31, Aug. 3, 1919.
[25]Letter to the editor from Irene Brown Jenkins, Houston (Texas)*Post*, Jan. 19, 1919, in Du Bois Papers.

the North where, frighteningly, the blacks fought back.[26] Even though blacks in Tennessee had shown a desire to accommodate to white dictates, and no evidence of black violence existed, whites began darkly to suspect Negro conspiracies.

The emotion-laden issue of woman suffrage and the nascent activity of the NAACP also stirred beneath the illusory calm in Tennessee. A divisive matter in itself, woman suffrage had been regularly compounded with the race issue. In 1915, for example, A. A. Lyon of Nashville circulated a pamphlet arguing that the voting of black women alongside white women would tarnish "the spotless white banner that symbolizes the purity and the chastity and the modesty that has hitherto ever been so luminously exemplified by the women of the South."[27] Race became a popular issue in suffrage debates during the 1917 and 1919 General Assemblies: Memphis legislators expressed concern that Robert Church would use black women voters to enhance his power; Senator Parks Worley of Bristol, previously a staunch supporter of black education, opposed additional black voters, saying he could "remember that the old confederate soldier, when he returned to this country from the war was not allowed to vote and that the black man was"; and Miss Josephine A. Pearson of Monteagle, president of the Tennessee division of the Southern Women's Rejection League, described the entire woman suffrage movement as "an outgrowth of abolition."[28] After the passage of a limited suffrage law in 1919, newspapers gave ample coverage to Negro meetings at which women were instructed in voting procedures.[29]

Outside agitation, especially with racial overtones, was an

[26]Chattanooga *Daily Times*, July 24, 1919.

[27]Quoted in A. Elizabeth Taylor, *The Woman's Suffrage Movement in Tennessee* (New York: Bookman, 1957), 79.

[28]Memphis *Commercial Appeal*, Jan. 21, 1917; Nashville *Tennessean*, Feb. 2, 1917; letter to the editor, Chattanooga *Daily Times*, n.d., clipping in Josephine A. Pearson Papers, Tennessee State Library and Archives (uncatalogued).

[29]Chattanooga *Daily Times*, Aug. 6, 1919; Memphis *Commercial Appeal*, Aug. 23, 1919.

anathema to white Tennesseans. While a few whites publicly deplored the revival of the Ku Klux Klan, they almost unanimously rejected efforts of the NAACP to organize in Tennessee. Blacks in Knoxville, Chattanooga, Nashville, and Memphis showed interest in the association during the summer of 1917, and, with the exception of Knoxville, all had chartered branches by late 1918. The Memphis chapter was the first and by far the most active in the early years, protesting mistreatment of blacks and holding several public meetings during the war. Conservative whites in all parts of the state voiced their opposition, denouncing those "pestiferous agitators who seem to be abroad in the land to stir up trouble between the races. . . ."[30] Public protests to Governor Rye from the national office of the NAACP coupled with local black activity led Bolton Smith, a self-styled Memphis "liberal," to attack the radicalism of the association in an article appearing in the *Public* in 1918. The Chattanooga *Daily Times*, meanwhile, became obsessed with the threat of agitation in Tennessee. On July 31, 1919, an editorial bemoaned the existence of fanatics on the race question and urged that if any such radical movement appeared in Chattanooga, blacks should report it to white leaders immediately. On August 14, the *Daily Times* blasted its black counterpart, the Chattanooga *Defender*, for publishing articles written by NAACP "agitators": "They are encouraging a state of mind, not alone among the men and women of their own race but among the heedless and violent whites, that will not be good for the peace and order of this city."[31]

Nevertheless, convinced by their own rhetoric and blind to the rising expectations of blacks and intensifying fears of whites, most of Tennessee's leaders felt by August 1919 that they had weath-

[30]Chattanooga *Daily Times*, Dec. 17, 1918, Aug. 3, 1919. James Weldon Johnson to W. L. Zimmerman of Knoxville, Aug. 13, 1917; W. H. Singleton of Chattanooga to Johnson, June 22, 1917; Charles Victor Roman of Nashville to Johnson, July 20, 1917; Johnson to Bert M. Roddy of Memphis, June 26, 1917; Robert R. Church, Jr., to Johnson, March 19, Oct. 25, 1918, NAACP Papers, containers G-198, 199, 200.

[31]Bolton Smith, "The Negro in War-Time," *Public* 21 (Aug. 31, 1918), 1110–13; Chattanooga *Daily Times*, July 31, Aug. 1, 3, 14, 1919.

ered the violent storms of racial antagonism. Admittedly, Memphis had narrowly averted a serious race riot on May 23 and 24 over the alleged killing of a streetcar conductor by a Negro. The Memphis *Commercial Appeal* described the situation fearfully: "There was a powder train all over Memphis Saturday. That there was no explosion was due to sheer luck. . . . Somehow we have drifted into a tense racial relation."[32] Governor Roberts ignored this tension when he extended his invitation for black migrants to enter the state's atmosphere of "perfect understanding."

Both blacks and whites in Knoxville were particularly confident. That city had the smallest Negro population of the four metropolitan centers in the state, five blacks served on the police force, and there was a general air of paternalism and accommodation in the area.[33] A brochure advertising the National Conservation Exposition in 1913 had described East Tennessee as the home of the "first abolition newspaper," a region which "no lynchings of Negroes and no race riots have ever disgraced," and where "the colored people . . . [are] law-abiding, orderly, industrious, and intelligent, and . . . the white citizenship [is] a unit in the effort to give our people a fair opportunity to succeed in the race of life." Charles W. Cansler had emphasized this favorable climate in his letter to Governor Rye in 1918. Praising the interest of Knoxville's white citizens in aiding black reform, Cansler closed his letter with the statement that "no race riots have ever disgraced our city and no mob has ever vented its fury here upon any Negro victim."[34]

White leaders in this East Tennessee city were no less confident. When Mayor John E. McMillan received a letter seeking

[32] Memphis *Commercial Appeal*, May 27, 1919.
[33] Bureau of the Census, *Fourteenth Census of the United States: 1920. Population*, III, 970. Knoxville had a Negro population of 11,302, which accounted for 14.5 percent of the total. Memphis census figures revealed a Negro population of 37.7 percent, Nashville 30.1 percent, and Chattanooga 32.6 percent. *Crisis* 14 (June 1917), 89; interviews with Carl A. Cowan, June 16, 1970, and George McDade, May 29, 1972.
[34] "The National Conservation Exposition," Washington Papers, container 835; Charles W. Cansler to Gov. Thomas C. Rye, Feb. 1918, Gov. Rye Papers, container 33.

support for a branch of the Klan in his city, he called together a group of leading black men in the community, denounced the Klan, and denied that there was a need for it in Knoxville. Earlier, when the Law and Order League held a meeting in March 1918 preparatory to establishing a branch in the city, a confident group of "about 20 gentlemen" met and "discussed this matter, but adjourned after practically deciding that the League could serve no good purpose."[35]

In August 1919, a few cracks began to appear in the façade of racial harmony. The chartering of a Knoxville branch of the NAACP on August 4 indicated that at least the eighty-five charter members were not completely satisfied with conditions as they stood. On August 22, the Knoxville *Sentinel* editorialized against the agitation of organizations like the NAACP and voiced sympathy for those Southern whites who physically abused the "agitators." Concern, therefore, existed beneath the calm surface. Mayor McMillan, in the midst of a bitter campaign for reelection, gave further evidence that Knoxville was not immune to racial pressures. He felt compelled, for example, to make a public statement on August 26 playing down the numbers of black women who were registering to vote in his city.[36]

Against what appeared to be a background of cooperation and toleration, the events of Saturday, August 30, 1919, were shocking. Sunday newspapers across the nation reported another racial outburst, this time in Knoxville, Tennessee—the state whose governor only a month before had predicted that no such occurrence was possible. The editor of the Chattanooga *Daily Times* immediately suspected outside agitation. If "staid old Knoxville" could be struck by such violence, "there is not the slightest doubt

[35]*Crisis* 17 (April 1919), 291; John C. Houk to G. N. Tillman, March 6, 1918, Houk Papers, container 92.

[36]Minutes of the Board of Directors, Sept. 8, 1919, NAACP Papers, container A-9; Knoxville *Sentinel*, Aug. 22, 1919, quoted in Herbert Jacob Seligmann, "The Press Abets the Mob," *Nation* 109 (Oct. 4, 1919), 460–61; Knoxville *Journal and Tribune*, Aug. 26, 1919. Significantly, none of those blacks recognized as "leaders" by the white community was among the original members of the Knoxville branch of the NAACP.

that the colored people of Knoxville have been stirred by some unusual and apparently sinister influence. . . ."[37] But as the account of the riot began to unravel itself from emotional hysteria and as it became evident that the rioters were whites rather than blacks, charges of outside agitation began to subside in favor of murmurs of shame and concern.

The trouble began when Mrs. Bertie Lindsay, a white woman, was shot in her bedroom early Saturday morning, August 30. Her cousin, Miss Ora Smith, who had been asleep in the same bed, described the attacker as a Negro. Later, police brought a black man, Maurice F. Mayes, for Miss Smith to identify, which she did. (Testimony at Mayes's trial revealed that, as a deputy sheriff, the defendant had incurred the enmity of several city police officers—including those making the arrest—because of Mayes's purported relationship with several white women.) As morning wore on, many people came to view the scene of the murder, and the Knoxville *Journal and Tribune* reported that "from early in the morning until late in the afternoon, little bunches of congregated men could be seen on practically every corner and near every store in that neighborhood, discussing the crime."[38]

The Knoxville municipal election was only a week away, and Mayor McMillan had always had the endorsement of most of the city's black politicians. Mayes, in fact, had been actively campaigning for the mayor's reelection on the day of his arrest, and there were even rumors that Mayes was McMillan's illegitimate son.[39] Sex, race-mixing, and fear that the mayor might interfere on Mayes's behalf inflamed feelings already heated by the racial explosions in Chicago and Washington.

[37] Chattanooga *Daily Times*, Sept. 2, 1919.

[38] Knoxville *Journal and Tribune*, Aug. 31, 1919, Sept. 27, 1921; interviews with Carl A. Cowan, June 16, 1970, and George McDade, May 29, 1972. McDade was one of Mayes's attorneys at the trial.

[39] Knoxville *Journal and Tribune*, Aug. 26, 31, Sept. 3, 5, 1915; interview with George McDade, May 29, 1972. Information concerning the rumors came from the comments of Charles G. Mynatt, a nephew of the prosecuting attorney in the Mayes trial, and Mary U. Rothrock, noted Tennessee historian. Their comments were relayed to the author by Dr. Stanley J. Folmsbee in a letter of Dec. 11, 1968.

245

Fearing trouble, Attorney General R. A. Mynatt and criminal judge Thomas A. R. Nelson instructed Sheriff W. T. Cate to remove Mayes from the county jail and take him by train to Chattanooga early Saturday afternoon. "Shortly after four o'clock a crowd began to gather around the county jail. This grew until at seven o'clock the streets were completely blocked and excitement was at a fever heat." The Memphis *Commercial Appeal* on August 31 estimated the crowd at fifteen hundred. Although delegates from the mob were allowed to search the jail to establish Mayes's absence, the crowd was not convinced. At 7:45 P.M. shots were fired, and shortly thereafter, battering rams and a dynamite blast burst the jail open to the mob.[40]

Having determined that Mayes had indeed been removed, the mob turned its attention to the release of twelve white inmates and the consumption of whiskey found in a storage room. The *Journal and Tribune* on Monday, September 1, asserted that some members of the mob had relatives in the jail and that others were former prisoners themselves. In fact, the sheriff's deputies stated that the Negro section of the jail, where Mayes would have been held, was not even touched and that no black inmates were seized or harmed in any way. The mob soon reduced the jail and the adjoining residence of the sheriff to rubble. The mob turned to vandalism, breaking porcelain toilet bowls, ripping out water pipes, tearing phones off the walls, and even stealing children's clothing from the home of the sheriff. Later estimates placed damage to the jail and nearby property at $50,000.

Reports came to the crowd at the jail that armed blacks were robbing several persons at the nearby intersection of Vine and Central avenues. This was the edge of the black section of town and a common gathering place for local Negroes on Saturday night. This news came just as a detachment of the machine gun company of the Fourth Tennessee Infantry arrived on the scene.[41] These national guardsmen "double timed" to the trouble

[40]Knoxville *Journal and Tribune*, Aug. 31, 1919.
[41]The national guardsmen of the Fourth Tennessee Infantry, under the command of

spot and set up two machine guns at the corner of Vine and Central. Running civilians surrounded the guardsmen as the mob began to leave the jail area and move to the Negro section. The *Journal and Tribune* described the subsequent action: "The crowd . . . raided every hardware store in that section, removing every weapon that would fire. Pawn shops were the next to be raided and many pistols, rifles, shotguns and thousands of rounds of ammunition were taken from these places."[42] The armed mob then returned to Vine and Central, where some blacks were barricaded on the upper floors of several buildings and others were milling around in the streets.

Although barricades were reported "a la Parisian," and blacks were supposed to have charged into the face of machine gun emplacements, most of the shooting was wild and sporadic. Even the eyewitness account of a white druggist, Joseph E. Carty, failed to establish which side first fired upon the other. Negro shooting was mainly by snipers, and Carty said that the presence of machine guns soon put the milling black crowd to flight. Lieutenant James W. Payne was killed when fellow soldiers opened up on snipers and caught him in the cross fire. Only one black man was reported killed during the night, discrediting the excited reports of full-scale charges. With the arrival of several hundred additional soldiers the next day, order was restored, despite rumors that out-of-town blacks and local veterans were preparing "to clean out the whites."[43]

Blacks were subjected to a considerable amount of buffeting and abuse as quiet was imposed. The mob violence had originated in the white community, among white citizens, but had buried itself in the harassment of blacks. Every Negro found outside the confines of his community was thoroughly searched and ques-

---

Adj. Gen. E. Baxter Sweeney, were encamped for training in the nearby suburb of Fountain City, now a part of Knoxville.

[42] Knoxville *Journal and Tribune*, Aug. 31, 1919.

[43] *Ibid.*, Sept. 1, 1919; interview with George McDade, May 29, 1972. Some of the buildings remaining in the area still show pockmarks from the battle.

tioned; the possession of any weapon brought immediate arrest. Four blacks were shot, though not fatally, by guardsmen who claimed that they had resisted investigation.[44] The guardsmen were largely from Memphis, and they had a reputation for racial antipathy. On an earlier occasion in Nashville, one of the Memphis companies had "stormed an ordnance center in an effort to get weapons to attack the Negro section of the capital city."[45] A black newspaper, the *Call* of Kansas City, Missouri, described the searching procedures practiced by such troops: "The indignities which colored women suffered at the hands of these soldiers would make the devil blush for shame. Low class white men took advantage of the helplessness of the colored men and began cursing and abusing them on the streets." A white leader of the Law and Order League also deplored behavior after the riot, saying pointedly that "the ruthlessness of the soldiers in handling the Negroes is the worst part."[46] Authorities made no effort to search whites, although city police did attempt to prevent their congregating on street corners.

Fear, but also determination, characterized the reaction of black Knoxvillians. Charles W. Cansler refused to let his family out of the house and slept with a loaded pistol under his pillow; when a group of whites thought to be members of the Klan threatened to parade through the black community, young blacks gathered with rocks and sticks in a show of resistance. Only the efforts of a black policeman, Joe Reynolds, prevented a renewal of the rioting and persuaded the whites to stay out of the area. Some clashes occurred, nevertheless, especially when soldiers attempted to enter black homes in a search for weapons.[47]

[44] Knoxville *Journal and Tribune*, Sept. 1, 1919.

[45] Memphis *Commercial Appeal*, Sept. 5, 1916; Nashville *Tennessean*, Sept. 1, 1919.

[46] *Call* (Kansas City), Oct. 4, 1919, quoted in Kerlin, *The Voice of the Negro*, 84; "Minutes Inter-Racial Conference Including Committee on After War Program & Representative of State YMCA Committee Held at Atlanta, Georgia, September 17, 1919," CIC Collection, Negro Collection, Atlanta University, subdivision 17-B-1.

[47] Interviews with two eyewitnesses, Mrs. J. Herman Daves, daughter of Charles W. Cansler, July 2, 1970, and Carl A. Cowan, one of the group of young blacks, June 16, 1970; Nashville *Banner*, Sept. 1, 1919.

Black Tennesseans were indignant. Novelist Richard Wright later recalled his fear, hatred, and determination as a youth in Memphis when he learned of Washington, Chicago, and Knoxville: ". . . though I did not witness any of it, I could not have been more thoroughly affected by it if I had participated in every clash. . . . I had already grown to feel that there existed men against whom I was powerless, men who could violate my life at will. I resolved that . . . if I were ever faced with a white mob . . . I would let go with my gun and kill as many of them as possible before they killed me." From Nashville, Edwin Mims of the Law and Order League recognized such feelings when he remarked: "I fear hatred on the part of the Knoxville negroes is the worst result of this riot."[48] The white press ran articles by conservative blacks in an effort to calm the situation. The Knoxville *Journal and Tribune* quoted Webster L. Porter, editor of the *East Tennessee News*, in his confident prediction that peaceful relations would soon return. "The friendly relationship between the races that has existed in our section," "can be attributed to the absence of just such deeds as has [sic] been committed, and the Negro citizenship is certainly desirous of retaining the same cordial feeling between the races as has always existed and that has gone so far in making our city one fit to live in." In true accommodationist fashion, Porter maintained that the criminal element was the cause of the trouble, not racial antipathy.[49]

Porter, however, spoke with an eye on the white leaders. Other blacks in Knoxville, roundly condemned by Porter as being in opposition "to every movement that is designed to promote the best interests of the races in the community," turned their attention to the civil rights program of the NAACP. Originally made up of a few teachers at Knoxville College, certain educated ministers, and several younger blacks, the newly chartered Knoxville

[48] Richard Wright, *Black Boy* (New York: Harper, 1945), 88–89; "Minutes Inter-Racial Conference . . . Atlanta, Georgia, September 17, 1919," CIC Collection, subdivision 17-B-1.

[49] *East Tennessee News*, n.d., quoted in Knoxville *Journal and Tribune*, Sept. 2, 1919.

branch became "unusually active" and took in a large number of new members.[50]

From other parts of the state, blacks expressed disbelief at the explosion in Knoxville. Isaac Fisher, ultraconservative black teacher at Fisk and editor of the *Fisk University News*, went straight to the source of the problem:

Despite the acute tensity of race relations which had begun to manifest itself in riots in Washington, Norfolk, and Chicago, we began whistling to keep up our courage, and confidently began boasting that no such riots could happen in the Southern part of our country. . . stating everywhere and insistently that our race relations here were so satisfactory that race riots were unthinkable . . . to our consternation we found that the laws of the mind are immutable and the concept of *race relations* brought back to the minds of men that with which it has been so long associated—i.e., ill-will conflict, antagonisms, resentment; and the Knoxville riot resulted.[51]

Indeed, both blacks and whites had glossed over the tensions of the past three years, taking public pronouncements as facts.

The immediate reactions of the state press varied. While the Chattanooga *Daily Times* focused on alleged outside agitation, the Nashville *Banner* maintained that because "the Knoxville area is really northern in its politics and race relations," the riot was part of the Northern problem and thus of no real concern to the South.[52] The emotional reactions soon gave way to cries for more emphasis on law enforcement and renewed efforts at interracial cooperation. Governor Roberts recognized that "a condition of unrest and potential lawlessness exists in Tennessee at present. The Negro situation," he said, "is serious. . . ." The confident assurance Roberts held in July was notably lacking as he explained to the citizens of the state "that he wanted to see no

[50]*East Tennessee News*, Jan. 6, 1921, clipping in NAACP Papers, container G-198; report of James G. Beck, secretary of the Knoxville branch, to the national office, Feb. 14, 1920, *ibid.*, container G-198.

[51]Isaac Fisher, "Wanted: An Immediate Local Program of Racial Goodwill and Law Enforcement," *Fisk University News* 10 (Oct. 1919), 15.

[52]Nashville *Banner*, Sept. 4, 1919.

more riots in Tennessee and that the laws of the state should be rigidly enforced." Meeting in Nashville on September 16, the Tennessee Law and Order League issued a statement calling for the "establishment of law and order leagues in all communities as soon as possible."[53] Governor Roberts seized upon this idea and turned it into a personal crusade. He stumped the entire state, proclaiming the week of November 9–16 to be Law and Order Week and urging its support by officials and civic organizations.

While whites hammered away at the need for law and order, traditional black leaders, although supporting Governor Roberts, stressed race relations. On September 26, a group of black men representing every section of Tennessee assembled in Nashville to form a People's Co-operative League of Tennessee, advocating "better understanding and relation between the races, better health, better schools, better homes, better farms, better citizenship." Described by one white liberal as being "the more conservative leaders," these blacks lauded the Law and Order League and expressed their willingness "to co-operate in every way possible for the suppression of crime and for the punishment of the guilty." The organization strongly resembled the Public Welfare Leagues founded in Nashville and Memphis during the years 1916–1917. Self-improvement and white encouragement were the goals of the appointed executive secretary, Robert E. Clay. By April 1920 he had established branches of the organization in thirty-seven counties.[54] In Memphis, Sutton Griggs spoke at a large meeting of blacks, warning the newly enfranchised black women "to beware of unsavory political alliances and vote only for the highest good of the city." This was a thinly disguised attempt to play down the fears which whites had expressed over increased bloc voting under the direction of Robert Church.[55]

[53] Knoxville *Journal and Tribune*, Oct. 8, 10, 1919; Chattanooga *Daily Times*, Sept. 17, 1919.

[54] *Christian Index*, Nov. 6, 1919; Chattanooga *Daily Times*, Sept. 28, 1919; Edwin Mims, "Law and Order in Tennessee," *Fisk University News* 10 (April, 1920), 9, 14, 15.

[55] Memphis *Commercial Appeal*, Oct. 7, 1919.

"Staid old Knoxville," meanwhile, reacted vigorously to the riot and its aftermath. While officials prepared cases against thirty-six men (all white) who had been charged with felonies during the riot, the Knoxville press urged strong action on the part of the court. The *Journal and Tribune* observed that "a more sickening act of insane folly was never before seen to disgrace Knoxville than was perpetrated last Saturday night and it is hoped the like of it will not ever again be witnessed. . . . Knoxville and Knox County have the opportunity of giving the rest of the country an example of the wholesome treatment of disturbing, destructive, and savage mobs. . . . "[56]

On October 4, 1919, despite the lack of positive evidence against him, Maurice F. Mayes was convicted of the murder of Mrs. Bertie Lindsay and sentenced to death. On October 14 the trial of the rioters began. The fact that the public was very much involved in this case became evident when it required eight days and 1,200 prospective jurors before twelve men were chosen for the jury. None of the civic leadership appeared among the twelve; there were nine farmers, two laborers, and one clerk.[57] The trial was concluded on October 25, with the acquittal of all but five of those charged in the rioting; the remaining five were beneficiaries of a mistrial.

Blacks and whites alike expressed disbelief. Judge Thomas A. R. Nelson vowed that the jury members involved in the acquittals should never be allowed to sit in judgment in Knox County again. Members of the Chamber of Commerce, meanwhile, intensified their successful efforts to establish a Law and Order League in Knoxville. No longer complacent, white leaders realized that their paternalistic attitudes had not allayed the racial fears and prejudices of the people. At first it had been easy to blame hoodlums and to dismiss the riot as mere vandalism.[58] The

---

[56] Knoxville *Journal and Tribune*, Sept. 2, 1919.
[57] *East Tennessee News*, Oct. 2, 1919, clipping in NAACP Papers, container D-61; Knoxville *Journal and Tribune*, Oct. 22, 1919.
[58] Arthur I. Waskow, *From Race Riot to Sit-In: 1919 and the 1960s, a Study in the*

jury opinion, however, clearly indicated that problems of race severely complicated the matter of law and order.

Beyond denouncing the release of the rioters, blacks responded by actively participating in the newly formed NAACP. While state organizations and local whites concentrated on the problem of law enforcement and race relations, the local branch of the NAACP pushed forward a program of tangible reform. A committee investigated the dives and dance halls of the city and made their findings public, declaring that these facilities were conducive to crime. Representatives also appeared before the city commission and received promises of a new park and playground for Negroes. In addition, a rest room for "Colored Women" was obtained in Market Hall. Previously, "there was only one with this sign on the outside, 'REST ROOM UP STAIRS FOR WHITE WOMEN ONLY.' " On petition from the association's Committee on Grievances, railroad officials also cleaned up "the unsanitary conditions of the Colored waiting room."[59] Such activities, in addition to a popular and spirited campaign to raise funds for a new trial for Maurice Mayes, marked a temporary, but significant, change in attitude among the usually conservative black Knoxvillians.

Almost exactly two years after the rioting of 1919, Knoxville officials had a chance to test the effectiveness of their law and order campaigns. On August 18, 1921 a young white school-teacher was allegedly raped and beaten by a black man in a community just outside Knoxville. A group of whites, estimated at eight hundred men and boys (including a seven-year-old carrying a twelve-gauge shotgun), "arrested" every stray black man they could find. Finally, the sheriff took one of the "suspects" into custody, and, openly mindful of the earlier precedent, "summoned every available deputy to the jail" and turned the bastille

---

Connections Between Conflict and Violence (Garden City, N. Y.: Doubleday, 1966), 108–9; Mims, "Law and Order in Tennessee," 13.

[59] Report of James G. Beck to the national office, Feb. 14, 1920, NAACP Papers, container G-198.

into an arsenal. The Knoxville *Journal and Tribune*, failing to realize the important role its inflammatory reporting had played two years earlier, published an account of the injuries suffered by the "very pretty blond" teacher and did not fail to note "the marks of the black fingers showing plainly on the girl's throat."[60]

On August 19 a crowd tried to storm the jail, but, despite a lack of support from city policemen, Sheriff Cate's men repulsed the mob, shooting twenty-seven white rioters in the process.[61] No evidence against the accused man was found, and he was shortly released. Law enforcement had improved and the courts were more conscious of the rights of blacks in 1921 than they had been in 1919, but the mere presence of the mob and the vigilante method of arrest indicated that race prejudice and fear had hardly been reduced.

The Knoxville riot, like almost all the postwar riots in Southern cities, was basically social: it was not a matter of economic competition or black political power. Instead, the 1919 outbreaks reflected wartime stress upon the entire caste system. Increased mobility, urban concentration, and the presence of black soldiers disrupted comfortable and controlled conditions and aroused latent white uneasiness. For months, the national and local press had stirred these fears and uncertainties to a boiling point by their emotional front-page treatment of the South's all-time bugaboo, interracial sex. The combination of basic social changes and an emotional catalyst repeatedly proved conducive to mob hysteria. The Knoxville riot was not a calculated conspiracy against blacks, but an irrational surface manifestation of deeper and more basic social conflict.

The brief period of rioting in Knoxville, the climax of three years of increased violence and racial tension, concerned many previously complacent Tennesseans. If the disruption had taken place in Memphis, East Tennesseans could easily have dismissed

---

[60] Knoxville *Journal and Tribune*, Aug. 19, 1921.
[61] *Ibid.*, Aug. 20, 21, 1921; *Crisis* 22 (Oct. 1921), 276.

the incident as being irrelevant to their situation; but if such trouble could occur in Knoxville, race relations throughout the state needed serious attention. The Tennessee Law and Order League campaigned with new urgency, appealed to conservative blacks, and, in many cases, broadened its program to include local reforms advocated by such black uplift organizations as the Public Welfare League. For a few months it seemed that the long-building problems of urbanization, poverty, and discrimination were to receive significant attention. Difficulties of postwar reconstruction and depression soon combined, however, with a relative quieting of racial violence to reduce the urgency of the "Negro problem." Tennessee essentially returned to the social status quo—two separate societies, drifting side by side and occasionally experiencing friction when circumstances brought them together. The efforts and hopes of the traumatic war years were almost forgotten, but not quite. The interracial discussions begun by the Public Welfare Leagues and the Law and Order Leagues became less action-oriented, but channels of communication that they established between the white liberals and black conservatives remained open. White racists persisted in their efforts to shackle and subordinate Negroes, while a small but growing group of young blacks rejected white paternalism as a solution to the "problem of black freedom."

CHAPTER XII.

A Slight Change in Direction

President Warren G. Harding's alliterative appeal for "not nostrums but normalcy" in postwar America had special meaning in Tennessee. After four years of sporadic racial violence, Tennesseans of both races sought relief. Tensions relaxed, overwhelming apathy returned, and the state's race relations drifted as loosely as did federal activities in Washington. "Normalcy," as practiced in Tennessee, however, did not mean a complete return to prewar conditions and attitudes. Despite the dominance of an apathetic majority, there were both whites and blacks who sustained their efforts to bring racial changes. The continued activities of these men and women, varying in purpose and intensity, produced a slight, but discernible, change in direction.

Although not the only voice to be heard, the Commission on Interracial Cooperation (CIC) dominated the speed and direction of Tennessee's drifting race relations during the 1920s. An outgrowth of the After-War Work of the YMCA in the South, the CIC was incorporated in Atlanta in late 1919 and officially entered Tennessee in 1920 when it absorbed the growing framework of the Law and Order League. The new organization's approach was to create regular opportunities for communication between black and white leaders. Accepting only the conservative blacks as spokesmen, the CIC reinstated these men to the positions of public leadership that many had lost during the violent war period. Operating very loosely and quite separately, the white liberals "advised" the organization's Colored Division in the traditional paternalistic fashion. Moved to action in order "to show the Negroes that the liberal Southern white man is really his best friend, and that the South is the best place in which he may live," these whites operated under the assumption that "even an approximation to ideal conditions [could] be gained only by gradual improvements."[1] Agitation of any kind only impeded progress in race relations. Their motto might have been: Prevent violence at all costs, and improve the black community when possible.

Tennessee's statewide organization was segregated in structure, rarely holding joint meetings except among the officers; the dual "commission" form had carried over directly from the earlier Law and Order and People's Co-operative leagues. The Colored Division's appointed leaders, William J. Hale (president) and Robert E. Clay (executive secretary), gave little time to coordinating the activities and encouraging the members of its branches. These men had a multitude of other commitments, and their lack of interest had important consequences among the black communities that would be moved only by their leaders. The vast majority of the local commissions were inactive, meeting irregularly and as a rule acting only when racial disruption threatened. One black participant later reflected that "the meetings were all alike: lip service was paid to 'how peaceful we are in this community.' "[2]

Black poet Langston Hughes commented on his experience with interracial conferences in his autobiography *The Big Sea*, and his description might have easily applied to Tennessee:

It was my first interracial conference. Since then, I've discovered that an awful lot of hooey revolves around interracial conferences in this country. In Europe people of all races meet and eat and drink and talk

---

[1]"Minutes of the Inter-Racial Conference Held at Blue Ridge, N. C., July 17, 1919," CIC Collection, Negro Collection, Atlanta University, subdivision 17-B-1; Nashville *Tennessean*, Sept. 17, 1919.

[2]Interview with Mr. and Mrs. J. Herman Daves, July 2, 1970. Neither Hale nor Clay ever corresponded with the Atlanta headquarters during the 1920s, leading CIC officer Mrs. Jesse Daniel Ames to inquire in 1931 if a state Colored Division even existed in Tennessee.

257

and dance and do whatever they are meeting to do without self-consciousness. But here, when there are Negroes and whites present together, there is often an amazing amount of gushing, of blundering, of commiserating, of talking pro and con, of theorizing and excusing. . . .[3]

Black response to the CIC was generally unenthusiastic, but favorable. There was no real opposition, and conservatives such as Webster L. Porter of Knoxville, George W. Franklin of Chattanooga, J. C. Napier of Nashville, and T. O. Fuller of Memphis were vocal in their support. No young Negroes, however, appeared among the leaders, and many were quietly skeptical. One young black college student from Chattanooga later described the CIC as being set up by whites "for the particular purpose" of gaining information about happenings and attitudes in the black communities and as "a way of encircling the folks that can raise the most hell."[4] Among the more active black supporters of the CIC's approach was the editor of the *Fisk University News*, Isaac Fisher. Fisher regularly attacked race "radicals," "bloc voting," and exclusive tendencies in both races. A graduate of Tuskegee, Fisher was thoroughly schooled in the accommodationism of Booker T. Washington and also in the belief that white help was a necessity in uplifting the Negro race. Such attitudes encouraged white liberals to feel what Will W. Alexander described as "that delightful sensation of doing something *for* someone."[5]

The CIC drew consistent praise for its often overrated accomplishment of "keeping channels of communication open." Yet its activities were often tangible as well. On the local level, many small improvements in living standards and public facilities took

[3]*The Big Sea: An Autobiography* (New York: Hill and Wang, 1963), 301.

[4]*East Tennessee News*, July 19, 1922, located in the newspaper file of the McClung Collection, Lawson-McGhee Library, Knoxville; 1922 *Minutes of the Inter-Racial Commission of Tennessee*, 1; interview with Dr. J. Monroe Bynes, July 13, 1972.

[5]Isaac Fisher, " 'Blocs'—Danger Signal," *Fisk University News* 14 (Nov. 1923), 1–4; Fisher, "The Value of Inter-Racial Work to Colored People," in Thomas Jackson Woofter, Jr., and Isaac Fisher, eds., *Cooperation in Southern Communities: Suggested Activities for County and City Inter-Racial Committees* (Atlanta: Commission on Inter-Racial Cooperation, 1921), 13–20; Will W. Alexander as quoted in Tindall, *Emergence of the New South*, 179.

place; state officials slowly recognized an increased responsibility for their black citizens, and strong and positive efforts prevented new outbreaks of racial violence.

Tennessee's various black communities made some concrete gains as a result of the activities of the CIC. During the year 1923–24, for example, three playgrounds with Negro supervisors (although meagerly funded) were made available for the black youth of Chattanooga, and the women of both races in that city formed a board to censor motion pictures being presented to the public. The city water system was extended into the black neighborhood at Franklin; and the Community Chest budget in Memphis included, for the first time, an appropriation of $25,000 for the Industrial Settlement Home now "fostered by the interracial committee." Basic reforms were less successful. Black members of the commission had been particularly anxious to obtain "better hospital facilities for colored patients, and opportunities . . . for colored doctors and nurses to take care of Negro patients in the hospitals," but they were able to accomplish few improvements in these areas.[6] Success would have involved a basic change in the caste society rather than simply the making of a donation of money or time to the "Negro problem."

Nashville's black and white leaders got the streetcar lines extended to Tennessee A & I, founded interracial discussion groups among Fisk, Peabody, and Vanderbilt students, and spearheaded a drive which led to a $160,000 legislative appropriation for expansion at A & I. Knoxville members, meanwhile, made fewer concrete gains. The NAACP branch there had previously achieved several small changes, and the two races had relaxed somewhat after the troubles in 1919. Complaints arose over the inadequate hospital facilities, bringing aid from the Rosenwald Fund for a

---

[6]Speech by Isaac Fisher, in the "Minutes of the Meeting of the Commission on Interracial Cooperation, Atlanta, March 29, 1921," CIC Collection, subdivision 17-B-1; *Progress in Race Relations: A Survey of the Work of the Commission on Interracial Cooperation for the Year 1923–1924*, 11–12; 1922 *Minutes of the Inter-Racial Commission of Tennessee*, 15–16; interview with De Witt C. Alfred, June 7, 1972.

259

Colored Annex to the General Hospital, but black doctors still could not practice in the facility. Knoxville streets in black neighborhoods remained unpaved, over one-third of the Negro homes had no sewage hook-up, and 60 percent of the houses did not have electricity. Commenting on the lack of initiative of Knoxville blacks, William Pickens of the NAACP declared in 1930 that "it seemed more profitable . . . to please the white population; it seemed more profitable to cater to the prejudice of the whites. . . ."[7] With such an attitude among blacks, whites felt no urgency to improve upon the reforms they had made after the 1919 riot.

In Memphis the CIC worked through a subcommittee of the white Chamber of Commerce and the group of ministers who headed the Public Welfare League. The Reverend T. O. Fuller chaired the Negro faction, and while admitting that its chief objective was "moulding sentiment" rather than action, Fuller's Inter-Racial League took credit for wide influence and accomplishment. He courted the local newspapers and was highly praised for his attack on Negro crime, but his claims of achieving new schools, new playground facilities, and access to the Tri-State Fair Grounds' summer recreation program needed tempering. White officials preferred to give credit and recognition to the conservative blacks, although political pressure from Robert Church was frequently the primary causative factor. Still, Fuller's organization claimed twelve hundred members, and was more active in the interracial program than any other black group in the state. The Memphis Inter-Racial League maintained a regular office and had a staff which, by the mid-1920s, included a full-time social worker whose salary was paid by white philanthropy.[8]

[7]*Progress in Race Relations, 1923–1924*, 14; *Progress in Race Relations, 1926*, 13; Cleveland *Gazette*, May 9, 1925; Knoxville *Journal*, Aug. 18, 1927; Knoxville *News-Sentinel*, June 20, 1928; Rothrock, ed., *The French Broad-Holston Country*, 320; Daves, *Social Study of the Colored Population of Knoxville*, 2–3; William Pickens, "Re-Visiting the South," *Crisis* 37 (April 1930), 127.

[8]*Progress in Race Relations, 1923–1924*, 12–13; Chicago *Broad Ax*, May 30, 1925; Thomas Oscar Fuller to Gov. Austin Peay, Dec. 17, 1925, and "Statement of the Activities

Competition between accommodationists like Fuller and Sutton Griggs and those politicians and NAACP supporters who wanted to use pressure led to more black activity in Memphis than existed elsewhere. A relative absence of white liberalism, however, put more responsibility for generating change upon blacks. Whites had to be cajoled, begged, frightened, and forced into making concessions and adaptations in their general tendency to ignore blacks. In Middle and East Tennessee, meanwhile, white liberalism took some of the lead, allowing the conservative blacks to maintain more traditional unassertive positions.

Although the white-controlled programs of the CIC tended to siphon off much of the black progressive impulse that had characterized the prewar years in Tennessee, some indigenous and separate black activities persisted. In Knoxville, for example, the Young Men's Civic and Welfare Club raised money for the local YMCA, the Negro schools, and an orphanage, and spearheaded a drive to build a Negro unit at the local tuberculosis sanitarium. In Chattanooga, beginning in 1919 and continuing for several years, the Band of Good Hope funded the Colored Day Nursery for neglected children and children whose parents worked. Black women in Nashville, meanwhile, formed the Reconstruction Service League and were particularly active in seeking money from the legislature to establish the Tennessee Vocational School for Colored Girls in 1921. This was a home for delinquent girls and was staffed completely by black personnel.[9]

The continued individual efforts by black organizations combined with the limited reforms of the CIC to improve conditions in the state's urban slums and led to a white political structure that became somewhat more sensitive to the lack of public services in black communities. The importance of the involvement of the CIC during the 1920s was that, despite its paternalistic approach, it

---

of the Interracial League, Memphis, Tennessee," Gov. Peay Papers, Tennessee State Library and Archives, container 86.

[9] Knoxville *Journal and Tribune*, Sept. 13, 1922; Knoxville *Journal*, Aug. 3, 1927; Chattanooga *Daily Times*, Jan. 30, 1922; *Crisis* 22 (Sept. 1921), 226.

eased the road for future advancement. White participation in black uplift in Tennessee was a necessity—a necessity born of black poverty and of total white control of public finances and law enforcement. The reluctant, discriminatory, and belated contributions of the 1920s accomplished a gradual break with the precedents of the first two decades of the century. Prior to World War I, the trend in race relations had been toward tightening the Jim Crow framework and neglecting the black population. By halting this process, and ever so slowly opening the eyes of whites to the needs of the Negroes, the prewar black progressives, the violence of the late 1910s, and the interest of the white liberals in the Law and Order League and the CIC combined to bring black Tennesseans onto the outer fringes of meaningful citizenship.

An obvious indication of small improvement and official recognition came with the hiring of a black man, James Hathaway Robinson, in 1929 as State Supervisor of Negro Welfare. As with George Edmund Haynes almost twenty years earlier, James Robinson concentrated upon black urban communities and saw his major task to be that of organizing "the existing social workers where we find them and to enlist them in our state-wide cause as co-operative influences." An important change in attitude, if not in accomplishment, had occurred, however. Haynes's work had been the product of private initiative and black progressivism, but the hiring of Robinson had been urged by the white-dominated CIC, supported at first by the General Education Board, and finally accepted as a legitimate, though marginal, responsibility of the state.[10]

The CIC, however, always focused most of its attention upon the prevention of racial violence. Therefore, its achievements in Tennessee were more tangible in this area than in winning full citizenship for Negroes. The CIC significantly reduced the number of lynchings by organizing citizens groups pledged to come to

[10]James H. Robinson, "The Negro Welfare Work of Tennessee," *Broadcaster* 2 (March 1930), 65–67; Robinson, "Negro Welfare in Tennessee," *Broadcaster* 3 (March 1931), 63–65.

the aid of harassed law enforcement officials, by publicly honoring those who resisted violence, and by using local interracial committees as a liaison between the races. Compared with the murders and rioting of the war years, Tennessee's record of eight mob-related deaths between 1922 and 1931 was an improvement. It was far from satisfactory, however, as the "official" records of other Southern states such as South Carolina, North Carolina, Alabama, and Virginia indicated even less violence. In Tennessee, it had been the law enforcement that had been improved, rather than the attitudes of the white people. This last fact was borne out by the numbers of "preventions" credited to the commission's work (four in 1930 alone).[11]

The CIC failed repeatedly in its efforts to get the Tennessee General Assembly to pass a measure that would automatically suspend sheriffs "in whose jurisdiction lynchings occur[red]." Reflecting a public oversensitivity to all the law-and-order propaganda, Republican Governor Alfred A. Taylor ran for reelection in 1922 on a platform that called for rescinding the State Police Law of 1919.[12] Taylor lost, but his successor showed little interest in using his office or the legislature to tighten law enforcement. White Tennesseans, with the exception of the "enlightened" professional classes, still were more concerned with the fear of Negro crime than with the contagion of violence. The CIC achieved measurable success in treating the symptoms of racial conflict, but its paternalism and condescension toward

[11]"They Shall Not Pass," program from the ceremony honoring Mrs. J. C. Butler of Huntington, Tenn., for her efforts in preventing a lynching on April 18, 1931, CIC Collection, subdivision 17C; Wilma Dykeman and James Stokely, *Seeds of Southern Change: The Life of Will Alexander* (Chicago: Univ. of Chicago Press, 1962), chs. 8–11; *Progress in Race Relations, 1926*, 14; Jesse Daniel Ames, "Suggested Points in Presenting Purpose of A.S.W.P.L.," Association of Southern Women for the Prevention of Lynching, 1932; Arthur F. Raper, *The Tragedy of Lynching* (Chapel Hill: Univ. of North Carolina Press, 1933), Appendix B; New York *Evening World*, May 29, 1929, clipping in NAACP Papers, container C-367.

[12]*Some Recent Trends in Race Relations* (Atlanta: Commission on Interracial Cooperation, 1931), 14; "The Record of Governor A. A. Taylor: His Vetoes and Other Messages," in *Speeches by Political Leaders of Tennessee*, compiled by the Univ. of Tennessee Library.

blacks did little to erase caste prejudice—the real source of surface eruptions.

Undoubtedly because it was led and controlled by whites, the
CIC received more publicity and functioned more continuously
during the 1920s than did any of the black-dominated organizations. Nevertheless, a large number of black Tennesseans rejected the gradualism and compromise of white-oriented programs. As early as February 22, 1907, the Nashville *Globe* had
warned that the "best friends" of the Negro could "be of great
service to us . . . but the first thing they should realize is that the
question will never be settled . . . on ante-bellum practices, no
matter how pleasant the relations were then."[13] By 1922 the
writer of this editorial was serving on the CIC in Tennessee, but a
new generation of young blacks, provoked by violence and motivated by the democratic propaganda of the war years, had taken
his place.

In addition to a growing number of younger blacks, a sizable
group of middle-aged black teachers, ministers, lawyers, and
businessmen also questioned the wisdom of having white paternalists fight the battles of caste and prejudice. Many of these black
men and women voiced a preference for the assertiveness of the
NAACP as opposed to the pleadings of the interracial leagues.
Handicapped, however, by the necessity for making a living in an
economy controlled by whites and by the tradition among black
Tennesseans of seeking white approval, Tennessee chapters of
the NAACP functioned only sporadically.

A certain Tennessee flavor had been noticeable in the organizational meeting of the NAACP in 1909—Ida Wells-Barnett, run out
of Memphis in the 1890s for her vocal stand against lynching,
participated vigorously in the discussions, hoping to make the
association as black and as action-oriented as possible.[14] For many
of the same reasons that forced Mrs. Wells-Barnett to flee, the
NAACP was slow to gain a following in the state. Blacks had

[13] Nashville *Globe*, Feb. 22, 1907.
[14] Ovington, *The Walls Came Tumbling Down*, 106.

become organization-minded, but they generally favored the white-tolerated gradualism of Booker T. Washington over the "agitational" approach taken by W. E. B. Du Bois and Ida Wells-Barnett.

The first show of sustained interest in the NAACP in Tennessee came from Memphis. In May 1914, Bert M. Roddy wrote the national office about forming a branch. A year later, Roddy had been able to enlist only seven other Negroes in the association's program.[15] These eight blacks subscribed regularly to the *Crisis*, but not until the outbreak of violence in 1917 did the community indicate significant interest. On June 11, 1917, less than three weeks after the burning of Ell Persons, Roddy held an organizational meeting of the Memphis NAACP, and fifty-three members paid their dues that evening. The vast majority of these recruits were business and professional men, along with a sprinkling of clergymen.[16] At the time even T. O. Fuller joined the ranks, although his enthusiasm dimmed somewhat when the national office of the association denounced Governor Rye for his negligence in law enforcement, and his membership soon lapsed.

Endorsements by Robert Church, the Lincoln League, and the *Western World Reporter* helped push membership into the hundreds during the next few months. The white press completely ignored the growth of the local NAACP, but the national office took optimistic note. Mindful of the Memphis success, secretary James Weldon Johnson planned an organizational trip to Knoxville, Nashville, and Chattanooga during the fall of 1917. Black's in the other cities, however, having experienced no violent outbreaks as yet, responded favorably to his preliminary overtures but took no action. Johnson called off his trip.[17]

[15] Bert M. Roddy to May Childs Nerney, secretary, May 29, 1914; Nerney to Roddy, June 6, 1914, April 18, 1915; Roddy to W. E. B. Du Bois, March 27, 1915, all in NAACP Papers, container G-199.

[16] "Application for Charter, June 11, 1917," James Weldon Johnson, acting secretary, to Roddy, June 26, 1917, NAACP Papers, container G-199.

[17] Nashville *Globe*, July 6, 1917. Johnson to Robert R. Church, Jr., June 19, 26, 1917; Johnson to Prof. W. H. Singleton of Chattanooga, June 20, 26, 1917; Singleton to Johnson,

Following the urging of Church, in April 1918 field secretary John R. Shillady again tried unsuccessfully to organize branches in Knoxville, Chattanooga, and Nashville. Shillady, who was white, also met with a reluctant Memphis Chamber of Commerce whose members, while professing new interest in the "Negro Problem," received him with "varying degress of disapproval." The local NAACP had irritated city officials with public complaints of police brutality and denunciations of recently enforced work and vagrancy laws. White leaders preferred to deal with the less militant and more easily led Public Welfare League.[18]

With the urging of James W. Johnson, Bob Church worked through his political contacts in Chattanooga and Nashville, and chapters finally were organized in these communities in the fall of 1918. In addition, common white and black outrage at the unprovoked shooting of a black man near Somerville in rural West Tennessee on April 9 had given the usually docile blacks of that area the courage to appeal to the NAACP for legal assistance. Three black physicians and nineteen black sharecroppers in Fayette County applied for a charter and paid their dues, but soon either lost interest or were forced to abandon their organization.[19] Otherwise, the NAACP in Tennessee was an urban phenomenon.

The more conservative approach of the Public Welfare and the Law and Order leagues seriously weakened the appeal of the local NAACP chapters in Memphis and, later, in Nashville. These two branches worked vigorously on occasion but did not carry out any

---

June 22, 1917; Johnson to Dr. Charles R. Wood of Knoxville, June 20, 1917; Dr. C. V. Roman of Nashville to Johnson, July 20, 1917; *Western World Reporter*, Dec. 14, 1917, clipping, all in NAACP Papers, container G-199.

[18]Church to Johnson, March 19, Oct. 25, 1918; Church to John R. Shillady, April 1, 1918; Walter White to Church, April 18, 1918; Memphis *Press*, March 29, 1918, clipping, all in NAACP Papers, container G-199; "Tours of the Secretary During the Drive," *Crisis* 26 (Aug. 1918), 174–75.

[19]Church to John R. Shillady, April 27, Oct. 24, 1918; C. S. Powell, Fayette County Negro physician, to W. E. B. Du Bois, April 15, 1918; Powell to Walter White, May 5, 1918; John R. Shillady to E. A. Fisher, secretary of Fayette County branch, Aug. 2, 1918; "Application for Charter, July 11, 1918"; Minutes of the Board of Directors, Jan. 24, 1924, all in NAACP Papers, containers G-198, C 199, A-9. Nashville *Banner*, Dec. 12, 1918.

sustained program. Of some importance was the Nashville chapter's stand in favor of the state police bill in 1919 and the donation of money to aid defenses of both Maurice Mayes and the alleged conspirators involved in the riots at Elaine, Arkansas, in the fall of 1919. Memphis members, meanwhile, launched an investigation into discrimination in the use of education funds in their city. Robert Church had been elected to the national board of directors, and the branch actually borrowed $1,000 from the national office for initiating a court challenge, but after six months the matter was dropped. In Memphis, Church became increasingly wrapped up in Republican politics and Bert Roddy concentrated upon launching his numerous business enterprises. While Sutton Griggs, Isaac Fisher, and their white colleagues lashed away at the "notorious organization," interest lagged in the state's two largest cities and membership fell off sharply.[20] By 1920, although the newly organized Knoxville chapter was reaching its peak of activity in fighting the Maurice Mayes case, the Chattanooga NAACP was also drifting toward stagnation, showing some interest in a series of peonage cases in Monticello, Georgia, but eventually going defunct in 1921.[21]

The chartering of a new NAACP chapter in Jackson, the state's fifth largest town, offered some encouragement to activist blacks in 1920. In that year, when Negroes in Tennessee were drifting away from the NAACP, fifty blacks, many of whom were either faculty members at Lane College or post office workers, launched

---

[20] Nashville *Banner*, March 22, 1919; Minutes of the Board of Directors, Sept. 8, and Nov. 10, 1919, NAACP Papers, container A-9; Charles Flint Kellogg, NAACP, 194. Bulletin of the Nashville branch, J. W. Grant, secretary, Dec. 28, 1920; Mary White Ovington, chairman of the board, to Grant, Jan. 10, 1921; Robert Church to John R. Shillady, April 2, 1918; Church to Walter White, May 21, 1918; White to Church, May 28, 1918; Bert M. Roddy to White, March 22, 1921, all in NAACP Papers, containers G-199, G-200. Chicago *Defender*, May 4, 1918, clipping in NAACP Papers, container G-199; Bolton Smith, "The Negro in War-Time," *Public* 21 (Aug. 31, 1918), 1110–13; *Crisis* 19 (Dec. 1919), 73; Memphis *Commercial Appeal*, March 13, 1921.

[21] W. D. Anderson, president of the Chattanooga branch, to Mary White Ovington, Dec. 14, 1920. For a discussion of the peonage cases near Monticello, Ga., see Daniel, *The Shadow of Slavery*, ch. 6.

an active program for recruiting members and "helping to make this Country a safe place to live in." For a year enthusiasm continued, but by late 1921 this chapter had also become inactive. The trend in Tennessee toward temporary abandonment of the NAACP was characteristic of what was happening in the nation as a whole. From a peak membership of 91,000 in 1919, the national rolls dropped to only 40,000 dues-paying members in 1921.[22] Part of the problem was the difficulty experienced by all groups that attempted to organize among blacks—money. The annual dues system made it necessary to convert the members all over again each year, which was difficult unless tangible results could be produced. That had been the problem with black organizations in Tennessee going back to the Colored Farmers' Alliance in the 1880s. Membership losses hurt the national association badly since it depended on dues more than philanthropy for support. As a result, efforts were constantly being made to revive the inactive branches in Tennessee.

Initial enthusiasm for the CIC further depressed interest in the NAACP in Tennessee. Although black leaders refrained from attacking the CIC directly, W. E. B. Du Bois did warn Southern blacks that the absence of the more radical stance of the NAACP would encourage whites to believe that Negroes were satisfied with their "progress." He also cautioned against filling interracial "committees with 'pussy footers' like Robert Moton or 'white-folks Niggers' like Isaac Fisher. Get more real black men," he said, "who dare to look you in the eye and speak the truth and who refuse to fawn and lie."[23] Supporters of the CIC, however, often sought to discredit the NAACP by name, fearing that any signs of racial militancy would only worsen race relations and disrupt their plan of gradual improvement.

[22] J. W. Lane, president of the Jackson branch, to James W. Johnson, Feb. 16, May 3, 1920; E. A. Lovett, secretary of the Jackson branch, to Mary White Ovington, March 19, 1920; Robert W. Bagnall, director of branches, to J. W. Lane, March 8, 1923; "Application for Charter, February 27, 1920," all in NAACP Papers, container G-198. Wilson Record, *Race and Radicalism: The NAACP and the Communist Party in Conflict* (Ithaca, N. Y.: Cornell Univ. Press, 1964), 31.

[23] Du Bois, "Inter-Racial Comity," *Crisis* 22 (May 1921), 6–7.

In addition to working vigorously for the defense of Maurice Mayes, the Knoxville chapter of the NAACP, led by the Reverend James H. Henderson and Knoxville College professor James L. Carey, investigated and offered legal counsel to other blacks in the area who were charged with violent crimes. They also applied directly to the city school board to improve high school facilities and to pay equal salaries to teachers of both races. Some more conservative Knoxville Negroes did not approve. Webster L. Porter, black editor of the *East Tennessee News* and *persona non grata* in much of the black community since his alleged criminal assault of a young girl several years earlier, carried on a campaign to discredit the NAACP and its leaders. Porter supported the CIC, however, and was considered a Negro leader by most whites; he enjoyed this conferred status immensely. His attacks on Carey were especially vicious, leading the Reverend Henderson to complain to the national office. As a result, a concerted effort was made by the NAACP to have Porter expelled from the Negro Press Association. Henderson maintained on one occasion that, as a result of Porter's smear tactics, "If Prof. Carey lived anywhere else in the South . . . he would have been lynched or driven out of town."[24]

Partially as a result of this split in leadership, as well as the unsuccessful conclusion of the Maurice Mayes campaign, the Knoxville chapter lapsed into inactivity during 1923. An active CIC and an absence of violence served to discourage revival of the chapter until 1934. Even then, however, Porter continued his attack. Writing several years after the demise of the Knoxville chapter, at a time when Carl A. Cowan and other young blacks

[24] Knoxville *Sentinel*, March 12, 1921. James L. Carey, president of the Knoxville branch, to Du Bois, Sept. 19, 1921; James. H. Henderson to Walter F. White, Jan. 8, Feb. 15, 1921; White to Henderson, Jan. 12, Feb. 18, 1921; William Pickens, field secretary, to several students at Knoxville College, Jan. 31, 1922; *East Tennessee News*, March 17, 1921, clipping, all in NAACP Papers, container G-198. Minutes of the Board of Directors, Feb. 14, 1921, *ibid.*, container A-9; interview with Mrs. Beulah H. Netherland, May 29, 1972.

were reorganizing, he lumped the NAACP into a group of "radical foreign organizations" which included the "Association of the Soviet Union," the Ku Klux Klan, and "the Order of Garveyism," and took great credit for killing the earlier effort.[25]

Porter was perhaps the most outspoken black critic of the NAACP in the entire state, but, once the shock of the war years subsided, other less blatant opposition had also helped discourage organizational efforts. White disapproval of the NAACP and reluctant praise for the CIC influenced black attitudes. The more conservative approach created no great ideological conflict for most Negroes. After all, black Tennesseans had long been accustomed to neglect by the system. Was not a "half-loaf" program of uplift better than no program at all?

Part of the open opposition of white Tennesseans came from the repeated efforts of the NAACP to secure the passage of the Dyer antilynching bill in Congress. Representative Leonidas Carstarphen Dyer of St. Louis, Missouri, introduced the measure in the summer of 1918, taking special note of the lynchings in Tennessee by writing to Governor Rye and sending him a copy of the bill. After the Knoxville riot, the NAACP specifically used the disturbance as an argument to win support from certain members of Congress. Such publicity drew the fire of whites. The Knoxville *Sentinel* editorialized against the NAACP and the antilynching legislation on the ground that it was "Stirring Up Trouble."[26]

Other white newspapers, particularly the Chattanooga *Daily Times* and the Memphis *Commercial Appeal*, vigorously attacked federal interference "with the rights of the state to enforce the laws against crime." Calling the Dyer bill "radical," "revolutionary," "vicious," and "pernicious," the *Daily Times* warned that federal officials who sought to investigate violence might them-

[25]*East Tennessee News*, July 26, 1934; typescript copy of an editorial in NAACP Papers, container G-198.

[26]Leonidas Carstarphen Dyer to Gov. Thomas C. Rye, June 6, 1918, Gov. Rye Papers, Tennessee State Library and Archives, container 33. James Weldon Johnson to Sen. Charles Curtis of Kansas, Sept. 3, 1919; Johnson to the editor of the Knoxville *Sentinel*, May 3, 1920, both in NAACP Papers, containers C-164, C-338.

selves become victims. Fighting the measure on the floor of the United States House of Representatives, Finnis James Garrett of the heavily black Ninth District asserted that the bill should be entitled "a bill to encourage rape." In the Senate, Tennessee's two solons, John Knight Shields and Kenneth Douglas McKellar, played key roles in filibustering against the passage of antilynching legislation. McKellar in particular played up the race issue.[27]

The national office of the NAACP encouraged branches in Tennessee to work for the Dyer bill, but, because of white hostility, such local action usually backfired. When a black newspaper, the Chattanooga *Defender*, started a publicity campaign to influence the congressman in its district to vote for the antilynching legislation, the *Daily Times* used the comments of conservative blacks in the city to belittle and reject the efforts of the black press. Blacks responded apathetically to personal appeals from James Weldon Johnson and William Pickens, and the Memphis branch, having been reorganized in 1923 by a group of prominent black women, had to cancel an appearance by Representative Dyer because, in their words, "We would have been embarrassed to have had a small crowd." Johnson had tried to use the campaign as a means of reviving the dormant Chattanooga branch, but was told: "It seems that the majority of our people don't understand this organization and its merits and worse still, they seem to be afraid to seek information."[28] The Dyer campaign coincided in Tennessee with the rise of the Ku Klux Klan in all the major cities. Fearing that radicalism among blacks would enhance the appeal of the Klan, conservative blacks argued persuasively against the wisdom of joining the NAACP.

Only two white voices in Tennessee openly supported the

[27] Chattanooga *Daily Times*, Jan. 28, 1922; Memphis *Commercial Appeal*, Nov. 29, 30, 1922, Nov. 4, 1928; Knoxville *Journal and Tribune*, Dec. 20, 1921; Mary Lu Nuckols, "The NAACP and the Dyer Anti-Lynching Bill: A Barometer of Emerging Negro Political Power" (M.A. thesis, Univ. of North Carolina, 1963), 36–37, 40, 50, 53.

[28] Chattanooga *Daily Times*, Jan. 29, 1922; interviews with Carl A. Cowan, June 16, 1970, Mr. and Mrs. J. Herman Daves, July 2, 1970, Mr. and Mrs. A. E. Lockert, July 10, 1970; clipping from the Memphis *Herald* (Negro), March 1924; Hattie F. Wilkerson,

Dyer bill during it ten-year tenure before Congress. The Knoxville *Journal and Tribune* was loyal to all Republican measures, and it spoke out frequently, especially seeking to rebut the fallacious but emotional argument that lynching was confined to black sex crimes. Meanwhile, Republican Congressman J. Will Taylor of Tennessee's Second District (which included Knoxville) voted for the Dyer bill on each occasion. A friend and close political ally of Robert Church, Taylor charged that federal legislation was needed because local officials had not been doing their duty, and he contended that lynching was a "disease so deep-rooted and malignant that it [would] not yield to ordinary treatment."[29]

With such limited support and such adamant opposition, the NAACP found it difficult to sustain interest among its Tennessee members once the threat of violence and dislocations of the war eased. As membership fell off and branches became dormant, the national office also lost enthusiasm. Neither Southern blacks nor Northern officers were to blame so much as the general racial climate of the South. The black activism appearing between 1917 and 1921 was in reality an aberration. Tensions caused by wartime fears, changes due to migration, and white encouragement of black organization and cooperation during the war had momentarily created a new atmosphere in race relations. Tennessee blacks had experienced a new prosperity and a new importance, but their heritage was one of apathy, accommodation, and caste. A "return to normalcy" meant a return to the dual society and its devotion to caste and white control. White liberals had become sensitive to the changes that had briefly stirred many blacks to action, but their proposals for uplift were implicitly tied to the willingness of the state's blacks to play their usual subordinate

president of the Memphis branch, to Robert W. Bagnall, Dec. 13, 1925; Mattie L. McMahan, former secretary of the Chattanooga branch, to Robert J. Spingarn, Dec. 19, 1923, all in NAACP Papers, containers G-198, G-199.

[29] Knoxville *Journal and Tribune*, Jan. 11, 26, 27, 28, 1922; Kelly, "Robert R. Church," 62–63.

role and to "reform" according to white standards and direction.

Bertram Doyle, a Fisk University professor, offered an observation that might serve as one explanation for the course of race relations in Tennessee during the 1920s. He proposed in 1937 that racial conflict such as that in 1917–1919 could only cease when "accommodation occurred." "In most cases," Doyle explained, "accommodation ensues when he [Negro] adopts the forms of behavior expected of him. That is to say, a reversion to the code of expected and accepted forms of behavior is generally calculated to solve situations where conflict exists in racial relations. For, by preserving the rank and precedence of persons, etiquette makes effective social action possible."[30] In his view, therefore, it was the willingness of black leaders to resume their subordinate roles and submit to the active guidance of white liberalism that slowly diminished public hostility.

Not all black Tennesseans were willing to have their individualism and initiative stripped in this fashion. And, although they were in a decided minority, their efforts were also important in establishing the slight change in direction of racial attitudes during the 1920s.

[30]Bertram Wilbur Doyle *The Etiquette of Race Relations in the South: A Study in Social Control* (Chicago: Univ. of Chicago Press, 1937), 170.

CHAPTER XIII.

In No Uncertain Terms

On February 4, 1925, students at Fisk University launched a strike against the administrative policies of the school's president, Fayette Avery McKenzie. This strike, or boycott, lasted over two months and led directly to McKenzie's resignation on April 16, 1925. The actions of the Fisk students and the support they received from Nashville's Negro community best illustrated the refusal of some black Tennesseans to consign their freedom and welfare to the paternalism of white liberals. The point of immediate conflict was education, yet, this new generation of "young Negroes," in their ability to stimulate the feelings and frustrations of practically an entire black community, touched a much more basic social question. Racial dignity, independence, and self-respect, questions debated by the Nashville *Globe* as early as 1906 and underlined by the events of World War I, again rose to the surface. Accommodation to white-imposed standards was easier, safer, and still the common approach, but on occasion during the 1920s typically conservative black Tennesseans showed a popular assertiveness and determination to effect change rarely seen earlier in the century.

Fisk students were seeking recognition of their status as men and women instead of accepting increased white paternalism in the form of curricular and extracurricular restriction. For black Nashvillians, however, the Fisk revolt was more than a student affair. The confrontation involved basic principles of student dignity and goals of Negro higher education, but it also involved the reciprocal responsibilities of the college and the local black community. The question was: What, if any, influence should the black students, patrons, and alumni have on the way their own schools were operated? Was Fisk to be a "Negro college" or "a college for Negroes?"[1] The issue was not new, but the response, both by students and community, reflected the impact of recent events and the occasionally more aggressive attitudes of the 1920s.

Long affiliated with the American Missionary Association, Fisk's president, Erastus Milo Cravath, had worked with the black community in Nashville as well as for the advancement of the university. Cravath died in 1900, however, and although his son, Paul Drennan Cravath, became chairman of the board of trustees, later presidents, in the words of the Globe, did "not come in contact with the Negro as those men did who took up this work at the close of the civil war." The seeds of discord between school and community were sown during the presidency of George Augustus Gates (1909–1915). The Globe had greeted Gates's appointment with a promise to "do all possible to make his administration a success" but soon voiced its disapproval of the new president's attitude toward blacks.[2]

The first conflict came in April 1911 when Gates was rude and abrupt to a visiting friend of Globe editor Henry Allen Boyd. Both Boyd and his guest, a representative of the Baltimore Afro-American Ledger, considered Gates's actions to be a racial affront—an expression of white condescension.[3] Two months later the relationship between the Fisk administration and the Nashville Globe deteriorated a step further. Much to the concern of conservative blacks in the community, the editors of the Globe again attacked Gates, this time for inviting whites to the June

[1] James A. Jones, president of Turner Normal College, Shelbyville, Tenn., to Nashville Globe, Nov. 22, 1912.
[2] Nashville Globe, April 2, Nov. 5, 1909; Nov. 15, 1912.
[3] Ibid., April 7, 1911.

commencement with the assurance that the audience would be strictly segregated. Pointing out that Gates had also replaced six of the twelve black faculty members with whites, the *Globe* raised the questions of "purpose" and "ownership" at Fisk: "The Negroes always looked upon Fisk University as theirs, . . . while it is under the Board of the American Missionary Society, it is a fact nevertheless that the famous Jubilee Singers, through their songs raised the money to build Jubilee Hall and a great portion of that to erect some of the other buildings, so in truth the Negroes of this country can say that Fisk University is theirs."[4]

Although other black newspapers throughout the country reprinted the *Globe*'s concerns, the aggressive young editors spoke for only a minority of black Nashvillians in 1911.[5] The relationship of white-operated Negro schools to the surrounding black community, however, kept cropping up. The *Globe* applauded such schools as Roger Williams (Nashville) and Turner Normal (Shelbyville) for being administered "exclusively" by and for Negroes. When George A. Gates sought to resign in 1912, following a railroad accident, the *Globe* immediately proclaimed that "the time is opportune when the administration of affairs at Fisk University should be placed in the hands of a Negro president." Acknowledging that many blacks "without courage and wise forethought" felt that it was "yet too early to place a Negro at the head of Fisk University," the editors still contended that there were black men who ranked as peers of any scholar or educator in the world and that Fisk deserved one of them as its next president.[6] The founders of institutions such as Fisk were gone, and their replacements were men of a different spirit. As a result, the *Globe* said, "the students who enter college under a white presi-

[4]C. C. Poindexter to George Edmund Haynes, July 6, 1911; Haynes to Poindexter, July 17, 1911; Haynes to R. T. Weatherby of Nashville, July 20, 1911, all in Haynes Papers, container 1909–1913. Nashville *Globe*, June 23, 1911.

[5]New York *Age*, n.d., quoted in the Nashville *Globe*, July 7, 1911. Also quoted in the *Globe* were comments critical of Gates from the Charleston (W. Va.) *Mountain Leader* and the Springfield *Illinois Chronicle*.

[6]Nashville *Globe*, June 28, Oct. 4, 1912.

dent and a white faculty, enter with the feeling of restlessness and discontent. That friendliness which should exist between teachers and pupils is missing, and as a consequence, there is a constant unrest on the part of the students."[7] But the board of trustees prevailed upon Gates to remain temporarily, and a new president was not installed until 1915.

The person eventually chosen as the new president of the institution was another white man, Fayette Avery McKenzie, described at the time as a "Puritan" who had been "born among the Underground Railway group in Pennsylvania." Perhaps as a concession to Nashville's black community, J. C. Napier was given a seat on the board of trustees at the same time that McKenzie was chosen president.[8] Black Nashvillians, however, having been awakened by the protests of the *Globe*, demonstrated a growing desire for the greater autonomy of Fisk. The feeling soon spread beyond the Fisk campus and came to apply to higher education in general. A white observer in 1916 noted that it was increasingly evident "that Negroes prefer to run their own school affairs." Dr. Charles V. Roman, the one black speaker at the installation of a white president, the elderly Dr. George Whipple Hubbard, at Nashville's famous Meharry Medical College, "was the only one who received a demonstrative ovation upon his appearance" before the predominantly black audience. Roman drew "tremendous applause" when he said in the course of his speech that he hoped "upon Dr. Hubbard's translation, his mantle would fall upon some worthy alumnus of Meharry." With respect to Fisk, several blacks in the community remarked to the white observer "that the time is not many years in the future when a Negro president will be demanded by the alumni and patrons of this institution."[9]

[7]*Ibid.*, Nov. 15, 1912.
[8]*Crisis* 11 (Nov. 1915), 16; 10 (Aug. 1915), 164.
[9]Walter E. Hogan, "Changing Conceptions of the Aim of Negro Education As Seen in the History of Colored Schools in Nashville, Tennessee" (M.A. thesis, George Peabody College for Teachers, 1917), 93–94.

Fayette McKenzie was hardly a man to calm the ambitions of concerned blacks. He was autocratic, austere, and aloof, and he made no special effort to gain the confidence of the students nor to stimulate the involvement of the interested black community in Nashville. McKenzie dedicated his administration to raising academic standards and to building a million-dollar endowment for the university. In line with these goals, he favored white department heads from white academic institutions, he sought personal associations mainly with teachers and administrators of the white schools in the city, and he assiduously cultivated the good will of the white business community.

Fisk was at a financial crossroads when McKenzie took office. His predecessor had faced a "drying up" of the old missionary sources of revenue and in turn had made a "strong plea for Southern friendship and financial support." Booker T. Washington had been appointed to the board of trustees in 1909 and had proved "exceedingly helpful" in bringing his paternalistic sources of revenue to Fisk. McKenzie came to Nashville as a representative of this new type of "scientific" philanthropy. His sources were many of the same ones tapped by Washington, and, in the view of W. E. B. Du Bois, the new money sought "to *use* the colored college for bringing the races nearer each other in the South."[10]

McKenzie's program of bringing the races together, however, had no place for black assertiveness. Paternalistic to the core, the Pennsylvania "Puritan" sought first to win white respect for Fisk and thereby to improve race relations and possibly gain some Southern financial support. He suppressed "radical" ideas, encouraged unassertive students, neglected the black community in Nashville, and completely acquiesced in the desires of white society. A contemporary black historian concluded that McKenzie probably "exceeded the limits of necessity in conforming to

[10]*Crisis* 28 (Oct. 1924), 251–52 (author's italics); Alrutheus A. Taylor, "Fisk University, 1866–1951" (unpublished manuscript, Amistad Research Center, Dillard Univ., New Orleans), 452; Meier, *Negro Thought in America*, 114.

the prevailing Southern ideas concerning the Negro."[11] Only such conservative blacks as Napier were ever entertained or taken into confidence by the new president. He preferred to associate with other whites, holding active membership in the Kiwanis Club and the Chamber of Commerce. And he arranged for white reserved seats at performances of the Jubilee Singers and for the girl's glee club to go through alleys and kitchen doors in order to sing before white men's clubs.[12]

To insure that students conformed to the Southern standard for well-behaved blacks, McKenzie suppressed the student paper, the Fisk *Herald*; tied the hands of the student council; refused to permit a student athletic association and abolished the baseball and track teams; governed the activities of the YMCA and other student-run organizations on campus with tight rules; censored all student orations and debates, and was reluctant to allow a student to represent Fisk in the international student conference in 1924. Students had to dress conservatively, with the women wearing dark hose, black hats, and matching uniforms. In 1920 McKenzie refused to allow a chapter of the NAACP on the campus, and he permitted only a censored version of the *Crisis* in the library. He wanted to keep organizations noncontroversial and limited to a number over which control could be exercised.[13]

Little organized opposition to McKenzie's activities came from either the Nashville black community or the students until after 1920. McKenzie instituted his program of "southernization" at Fisk during the years when enthusiastic black war efforts and statewide racial violence diverted attention away from the university. His admittedly autocratic way of dealing with blacks was

---

[11] Taylor, "Fisk University, 1866–1951," 454.

[12] Du Bois, "Fisk," *Crisis* 30 (May 1925), 41; Du Bois, "The Dilemma of the Negro," *American Mercury* 3 (Sept. 1924), 184; interview with George W. Gore, June 21, 1972.

[13] A list of grievances appeared in Du Bois, "Fisk," *Crisis* 30 (May 1925), 40–41; Nashville *Tennessean*, Feb. 8, 1925; Du Bois, "Fisk," *Crisis* 29 (April 1925), 248; Taylor, "Fisk University, 1866–1951," 457–63; McKenzie to Catherine D. Lealtad, Aug. 11, 1920, NAACP Papers, container G-200; Raymond Wolters, *The New Negro on Campus: Black College Rebellions of the 1920s* (Princeton: Princeton Univ. Press, 1975), ch. 1.

hardly noticeable or regarded as significant during a period when the wartime government acted similarly in its dealings with all Americans. McKenzie's attitude, however, was not an emergency measure; he argued that "under the very peculiar conditions at Fisk and in most colored schools, great authority and substantially the bulk of the initiative must be centered in the president."[14] On one occasion in 1918 male students refused to attend required study halls until the president "was inclined to treat them like men." McKenzie responded by denouncing their "Bolsheviki spirit" and expelling the leaders.[15]

After 1920 student complaints became more numerous. Many of the men at Fisk had served in the armed forces, some as part of the Negro officer-training program. These students and other young Nashville blacks who had become sensitive to racial discrimination during the war years came to resent the restrictiveness of conditions at Fisk. The *Christian Index* had printed a warning to whites in 1919 that they must now "take into account the aspirations for citizenship with all that the word connotes on the part of the younger generation of Negroes." Citizenship to many of Nashville's young blacks and to the students at Fisk during the early 1920s meant more student participation in all phases of the educational program.[16] McKenzie's autocratic policies took away means of self-expression, created second-class citizens, and relied upon fear instead of reason to bring social control.

In 1921 a trustee who came to hold religious meetings at Fisk was approached by several students concerning McKenzie's attitudes. He investigated their grievances and "reported to the

---

[14] McKenzie to vice-chairman of the board of trustees L. Hollingsworth Wood, April 8, 1919, quoted in Taylor, "Fisk University, 1866–1951," 457.

[15] McKenzie to Wood, May 30, 1918, Jan. 8, 1919, quoted in Taylor, "Fisk University, 1866–1951," 458.

[16] Interview with Meredith Gillespie Ferguson, president of Citizens Savings Bank and Trust Co. in Nashville, Nov. 10, 1971. Ferguson had finished college and was one of the young black veterans who came out of the war bent on demanding individual recognition and equality. *Christian Index*, July 31, 1919, quoted in Kerlin, *The Voice of the Negro*, 29.

president and trustees a condition of repression and tyranny, of insult and discrimination such as no men nor women should be subjected to." Officials gave no attention to his findings. Meanwhile, students, along with several representatives of the black community, talked to McKenzie about the fact that all the department heads and office staff were white. They suggested that a Negro understudy be assigned to each department head and also that, if the president was to be white, the dean should be black. A few black secretaries would show that the administration had confidence in the race. Nothing came of these overtures.[17] Repeated restrictions, especially in the realm of social affairs, brought the internal situation at Fisk to a slow boil by 1924.

Spring weather brought foliage to the giant oaks and maples on the Fisk campus and also increased student restiveness. Nashville had just gone through a winter of Ku Klux Klan rallies and renewed racial tension that was to prevail for another full year before calm and stability returned. Of particular importance to Fisk students was the case of Oswald Durant. In March 1923 Durant, an honor student at neighboring Meharry Medical College and a war veteran, had been accused of raping a white telephone operator. Despite his estranged wife's testimony that he had become sexually impotent since the war, Durant was quickly convicted and sentenced to life imprisonment. The lack of evidence and the light sentence, considering his color and the charges, led the entire black community to believe in Durant's innocence. Fisk students were active on Durant's behalf, and the local NAACP fought the case all through the fall and winter of 1923–24, eventually winning Durant's release and a new trial (which the prosecution never bothered to schedule) in 1925.[18]

While on campus to attend the graduation of his daughter Yolande in June, W. E. B. Du Bois became aware of the extent of

[17] Du Bois, "Fisk," *Crisis*, 29 (April 1925), 247–48; Ferguson interview, Nov. 10, 1970.
[18] Press releases of the NAACP, n.d., 1924 and May 29, 1925, NAACP Papers, container G-200; Taylor, "Fisk University, 1866–1951," 463; interview with Dr. J. Monroe Bynes, a classmate of Durant's at Meharry, July 13, 1972.

student unrest. Speaking at the alumni banquet and denying any prearranged connection between himself and the student grievances, Du Bois proceeded to blast McKenzie's administration both for its treatment of students and its refusal to pay any attention to alumni recommendations. Students applauded his speech and, in the eyes of conservative blacks, "demonstrated to the point of almost causing a riotous situation."[19]

McKenzie made no official response to the charges, but Nashville was in the process of trying to raise $50,000 for the college, and the seventy-five-year-old J. C. Napier was publicly irritated with Du Bois. He proclaimed that if Du Bois planned another such visit, "there are a sufficient number of well wishers who are interested in the welfare of Fisk University, . . . to accord him the warmest reception that he has ever had." Napier later wrote another member of the board of trustees that "the main actuating cause of Du Bois's assault—[was] personal malice due to matters connected with his daughter's expenses, etc. while a student."[20] Regardless of the reason for Du Bois's entry into the dispute, the deteriorating relationship between the Fisk administration and both the students and the Nashville black community stretched back over ten or fifteen years. Difficulties began after the death of Dr. Cravath, appeared publicly in the editorials of the Nashville *Globe* as early as 1911, and intensified with the stresses and changes of World War I.

When classes resumed in the fall of 1924, Du Bois stepped up his public attack, calling specifically for a new president at Fisk, "a reformed Board of Trustees (to include alumni) and a reconstitution of its faculty (to include more Negroes)." He did not demand that the new president be black, but many Nashville

[19]Chicago *Whip*, Aug. 2, 1924, clipping, Du Bois Papers, container 73.

[20]Napier's irritation was recorded by the sympathetic Knoxville *East Tennessee News*, July 24, 1924, clipping, Du Bois Papers, container 73; R. C. Edmondson to McKenzie, Dec. 18, 1924, Fayette Avery McKenzie Papers, container 2. Raymond Wolters has maintained that the alumni speech in June had been in a formative stage for many months and was an outgrowth of Du Bois's growing resentment against white-dominated, second-class education for blacks. See Wolters, *The New Negro on Campus*, ch. 2.

Negroes, at least, had longed for the coming of a black administration at Fisk for many years. Alumni, especially in the North, rushed to Du Bois's banner. A trustee committee received their charges of "glaring incompetency" against McKenzie but ignored them. Alumni attacks, meanwhile, poured fuel on the smoldering fire in Nashville. A "tin pan" riot and boycott of classes took place while the board of trustees was on campus during November Founder's Day exercises. A committee of seven students succeeded in getting a hearing before the board and presented their requests for more student organizations, fewer compulsory exercises, and greater consideration of student opinion. Despite McKenzie's opposition, the board of trustees suggested that less formal dress, a student council, and an athletic association would be in keeping with the aims of the school.[21]

While the internal affairs boiled at Fisk, racial events in Nashville kept pace. During the year a local black minister was killed by a police officer, a black businessman was shot down in his place of business by a white saloonkeeper who went completely unpunished, and during November two black women, one of them a student at Tennessee A & I, were beaten on streetcars by unchallenged white men. To cap this violence, on December 16, 1924, a black youth was taken from the county hospital by a band of white men and lynched.[22] The black community was up in arms, and Fisk students undoubtedly shared the fear and indignation.

Into this supercharged atmosphere President McKenzie injected the announcement in January 1925 that, except for allowing women to buy their own black hats "of a conservative style," the requests made by the students in November would be ignored both by himself and the board of trustees. A minor distur-

---

[21]The attacks appeared in *Crisis, American Mercury,* and *Sphinx* (the official organ of the Negro fraternity Alpha Phi Alpha). Du Bois, "Fisk," *Crisis* 29 (April 1925), 247–48; Taylor, "Fisk University 1866–1951," 465–66.

[22]Walter White's "Report on the Lynching in Nashville, 1924," NAACP Papers, container G-200.

bance took place on February 1, but after a chapel talk by McKenzie on the evening of February 4, the students staged a demonstration which consisted of yelling, beating ashcans, and breaking a few windows. McKenzie called in the Nashville police to quell the "riot." He gave the officers the names of the seven students who had headed the grievance committee earlier in the fall and charged them with committing a felony—an unbailable offense in Tennessee.[23] It soon came to light that some of these students were not even on campus at the time, leading to charges that McKenzie was continuing his tactics of getting rid of all those who led opposition to his policies.

Both the white and black communities immediately became involved in the dispute. Although the students repeatedly claimed that they were in favor of law and order and that the demonstration was not racial in any way, the issue of McKenzie's replacement split Nashville along racial lines.

Fisk students reacted to McKenzie's call for white policemen and his hard-line response of arrests and expulsions by declaring a general strike. Seniors, led by George Walter Streator, a native Nashvillian who later would serve as business manager of the *Crisis*, reporter for the New York *Times*, and successful labor organizer, wrote Howard University to see if they could transfer their credits at Fisk and graduate in June from the Washington school. Although rebuffed in this attempt, and despite McKenzie's public efforts to win parental support, the strikers' determination increased. Students sent a telegram to Paul D. Cravath, chairman of the board of trustees, asking for an investigation of the charges against McKenzie:

Every student would remain should he [McKenzie] be supplanted by a man of breadth of view and proper regard for the rights of students. His action in summarily arousing innocent students from sleep and rushing them off to jail and holding them there until the hour of trial and then abandoning the prosecution for lack of proof, is typical of his arrogant

[23]*Crisis* 29 (April 1925), 248–49.

and domineering treatment of every student who did not submit to his demands without question. May we not have a fair impartial investigation?[24]

McKenzie countered with two statements. The first, issued shortly after the strike was proclaimed, was an obvious attempt to play upon Southern fears of black revolt and outside agitation: "A challenge to school authority . . . was thrown down . . . by outside influences." In a plea for broader support, he announced on February 13 that "the situation is most disastrous, but if all will keep calm and will stand firm, perhaps greater things will come to Fisk than ever before. The citizens of Nashville, both colored and white, are rallying around me in a tremendous way, and if I can have the continued support of the outside public I believe I have a power behind me to secure *for* colored people vastly more than has ever been secured *for* them before."[25]

McKenzie claimed the support of both races, but he clearly directed his appeal to the white community. A firm stand to keep young blacks in their proper place, he apparently felt, would give Fisk increased financial support from the white citizens and, therefore, allow him to do even more for Negro education—along the lines he thought best. Almost without exception the Nashville white community rose to support his stand. In a letter to sympathetic trustee Thomas Jesse Jones, McKenzie described the constant demand placed upon him to speak at white civic clubs and reveled in the response he received from these audiences: "When I was introduced . . . everybody in the room rose to his feet and a great many yelled as well as a great many cheered with their hand clapping." Saying that he had declined at least one appearance because he feared "the danger of too much applause,"

[24] Nashville *Banner*, Feb. 5, 6, 7 (telegram), 1925; Nashville *Tennessean*, Feb. 8, 9, 1925; a brief Streator biography is in the New York *Times*, July 29, 1955.
[25] Nashville *Banner*, Feb. 8, 1925; *Letters and Telegrams from Parents of Fisk Students, Alumni, Students and Friends-at-large together with Certain Statements Relative to the Recent Disturbance at Fisk University, February 4, 1925* (Nashville, 1925), 43, pamphlet in Special Collections at Fisk University. Author's italics.

McKenzie appeared almost intoxicated with the power he felt he had in the white community:

Some how I feel that never before in the United States has a white in our work had such a hold upon a city as I now have upon Nashville. On the other hand, it is clearly obvious that if I fail to receive unconditional support . . . at the time of the flouting of my authority, not only will the white citizens and the money of Nashville be turned in other directions but the same will be true of the South as a whole and perhaps of a considerable part of the North.[26]

Both of Nashville's daily newspapers came to the unqualified support of the Fisk president, each editorializing with thinly veiled threats that a relaxation of law and order at the black school would mean withdrawal of white financial support. Deploring the student strike as a "mutiny and a disgrace," the *Banner* praised McKenzie because "he is not radical in his teachings . . . to the point of giving the youth under his direction false instructions as to their demanded *equality of rights* in all respects or to directing their steps along dangerous paths to a goal they can never attain."[27]

The members of the board of trustees also unanimously opposed the tactics of the students, but in the absence of their chairman they took no firm stand. Sentiment varied from adamant support of McKenzie to a willingness to appoint a new president to prevent a split that would destroy the school. Vice-Chairman L. Hollingsworth Wood and William H. Baldwin were among those who entertained thoughts of releasing McKenzie, while the president's staunchest supporters included Nashvillian Kate H. Trawick (wife of Arch M. Trawick) and Chicago lawyer Robert McMurdy. Mrs. Trawick became so incensed with the "out-of-town projectors of the trouble" that she threatened to resign. McMurdy, on the other hand, viewed Du Bois's stand as a challenge that had to be met. He recognized a sense of "great race

[26] McKenzie to Jones, Feb. 19, 1925, McKenzie Papers, container 2.
[27] Nashville *Banner*, Feb. 7, 1925; Nashville *Tennessean*, Feb. 6, 1925. Author's italics.

pride" among black Nashvillians, and he acknowledged that many of them felt "Dr. McKenzie is too friendly with the white people," but he opposed the assertiveness of Du Bois and the students: "Certainly we ought not to encourage this kind of application of race pride. If Dr. McKenzie had been friendly with the white people to the detriment of the colored people, or had surrendered their rights and privileges, the situation might be different, but I know the Doctor's ideas on the subject, . . . namely: That such favorably contacts as can be established tend to soften and ameliorate prejudices on both sides of the fence, particularly on our side."[28]

If the specific grievances at Fisk were not overtly racial, the paternalistic and restrictive philosophy which created them was. McKenzie had consciously curried favor with the white community; therefore, his decision to call white police onto the black campus was consistent with his personal and racial convictions. Under ordinary circumstances, the trouble might have remained an internal crisis at the university, but McKenzie's actions, coming at a time when the local black population was fully aroused by two years of police brutality and unpunished white violence, brought the large majority of the Negroes in Nashville to the side of the students. McKenzie was a staunch supporter of the CIC; the appeal of white paternalism temporarily paled. With the whites firmly and openly allied with the president and the blacks firmly and openly supporting the students, racial battle lines were drawn. The *Nation* summarized the delicate situation in these terms: "Unfortunately the race question has become involved at Fisk as well as the problem of academic discipline. To white Nashville the student revolt is a Negro uprising. To black Nashville President McKenzie has become a symbol of white domination. He seems, in an earnest effort to promote interracial

---

[28] McKenzie to Jones, Feb. 19, 1925; McMurdy to Cravath, April 16, 1925, both in McKenzie Papers, container 2. Trawick to Walter White, March 4, 1925, NAACP Papers, container C-367.

good will, to have lost contact with the race for which he was working."[29]

J. C. Napier at first strongly denounced the students, blaming the trouble on the agitations of Du Bois, but as Nashville blacks showed little support for such a stand, he fell quiet. Napier and Drs. Charles V. Roman and John Hale worked behind the scenes to get the students to call off the strike, but only W. W. Sumlin, an outspoken black physician, saw fit to challenge openly the growing local demands to oust McKenzie. Enjoying lavish attention from the white press, Sumlin had free use of the *Banner* and *Tennessean* to attack the students and those who supported them.[30] The publicity given to Sumlin clouded the real unanimity of the black community.

Two days after the disturbance of February 4 and consequent arrests, a group officially representing the Negro Board of Trade called a mass meeting to discuss the matter.[31] The leaders were men who had been part of the *Globe*'s "young Negro" faction some years earlier as well as representatives of the generation that had served in the war and become part of the "New Negro" movement of the 1920s. Among the former were Edward W. D. Isaac of the Nashville *Clarion* and the Baptist Young People's Board, T. Clay Moore, a local businessman and former president of the Fisk Alumni Association, and Dr. J. T. Phillips, a physician and a former alumni head. In the group of younger men were Noah Williams, a former army chaplain who opened his church, St. John's, to the public meeting, and Meredith Gillespie Fergu-

---

[29]"A Student Revolution," *Nation* 120 (March 18, 1925), 283.

[30]Nashville *Banner*, Feb. 5, 10, 12, 1925; Nashville *Tennessean*, Feb. 5, 10, 12, March 24, 1925; Ferguson interview, Nov. 10, 1970.

[31]The Negro Board of Trade paralleled the existing white Board of Trade (like a chamber of commerce) and had earlier declared its intention to become "instrumental in the amicable adjustment of any and all differences which may arise . . . between white man and black man." Such differences were certainly present in February 1925. Nashville *Globe*, March 15, Nov. 22, 1912. The Nashville Chamber of Commerce had frequent changes of name, being designated the Board of Trade from 1906 to 1913, the Commercial Club from 1913 to 1920, and the Chamber of Commerce after that time.

son, bookkeeper at the black-owned Citizens Savings Bank and an officer during World War I.[32]

The twenty-three-year-old student leader George Streator, therefore, found many black Nashvillians willing to support the strike. Support came in ways other than public meetings. Irritated at McKenzie's contempt for blacks requests, Ferguson and others worked full time in their efforts to aid those students who wanted to leave school. In order to stop the exodus, McKenzie obtained police guards to keep "outsiders" off the campus, got postal authorities to stop delivery and pickup of mail at the school, and asked local white merchants not to cash money orders sent by parents to pay for travel expenses. Even Napier was outraged by the mail restriction and managed personally to get the service restored. Ferguson, using his own savings, cashed student money orders, operating from his car in the street near the campus despite threats of arrest.[33]

On the night of February 9 an overflow crowd of 3,000 blacks heard Streator and the other student leaders plead their case. Resolutions drawn up by the Board of Trade were adopted, supporting the reasonableness of student complaints, denouncing McKenzie's use of local police at the school, requesting a full investigation by the Fisk board of trustees, and concluding that "it is our firm opinion that his [McKenzie's] usefulness as president of Fisk University is at an end." The preparation of these resolutions before the meeting indicated that a sizable element of the black population had already made up its mind: McKenzie should go. The meeting was a way of whipping up popular enthusiasm for the strike, and it also served to polarize further the Nashville citizenry along racial lines. When Dr. Sumlin tried to argue the case, he was shouted from the stage.[34]

Significantly, the student speakers denied that they were de-

---

[32] Nashville *Banner*, Feb. 6, 1925; Nashville *Globe*, April 2, Nov. 5, 1909; Ferguson interview, Nov. 10, 1970.
[33] Ferguson interview, Nov. 10, 1970.
[34] Nashville *Banner*, Feb. 10, 1925.

manding a black president and faculty, but they did seek a staff that "was in sympathy with the institution regardless of race, color, or creed." Likewise, T. Clay Moore, speaking for Nashville Negroes and the Board of Trade, reiterated that there was no *demand* for a black president. His speech left no doubts that many black Nashvillians would prefer a president of their own race, but he acknowledged that Fisk depended upon white money and "that the people among whom we live would not like it."[35] While blacks could no longer afford to sit quietly in the face of abuse, Moore recognized that Fisk could not be forced to hire a black president.

Rhetoric filled both the white and black press in the two months following the launching of the strike. Many parents sent their children back to the training school and high school departments, but even McKenzie's estimates put attendance at no more than 50 percent of the enrollment before February 4. Dr. Sumlin grew almost paranoid in his vituperative attacks in the white newspapers. In return, his car and garage were burned, he was denounced by the Negro Ministerial Alliance, insulted and refuted by both the black secular and religious press, and ejected from his post as president of the Rock City Academy of Medicine and banned "from the organization forever." Meredith G. Ferguson later estimated that the black community became "almost 100 percent" behind the student strikers and their demand for a new president. An outside observer, Walter F. White of NAACP, commented after a Nashville visit that he "gained the distinct impression that unless McKenzie is removed from the presidency of Fisk University, it is going to mean the end of the school's usefulness."[36]

[35]*Ibid.* Moore was quoted in the Nashville *Tennessean*, Feb. 9, 1925.

[36] McKenzie to Dr. Thomas Jesse Jones, Feb. 19, 1925; *Additional Letters from Parents of Fisk Students and from Alumni Together with Certain Other Statements Relative to the Recent Disturbance at Fisk University, February 4, 1925* (Nashville, 1925), 1, pamphlet, both in McKenzie Papers, container 2. Du Bois, "Fisk," *Crisis* 30 (May 1925), 40–41; Nashville *National Baptist Voice*, organ of the National Baptist Convention of America, April 4, 1925, Du Bois Papers, container 73; Nashville *Banner*, Feb. 12, 13, 17, 27, March

In the face of black local and national opposition which tended to grow with time rather than blow away, Fayette Avery McKenzie sent a brief and notably defensive letter of resignation to Paul D. Cravath on April 16, 1925. Six days later the board of trustees accepted his resignation.[37] An extremely proud and egotistical man, McKenzie had demanded unquestioned support for his stand. He clearly cared little about opposition in the black community, and he received full support from the white citizens of Nashville, but several members of the board of trustees had had reservations. The board now had the delicate task of replacing McKenzie with a man who could regain black confidence without antagonizing Nashville whites.

Talk of a black president for Fisk had floated about in Nashville for fifteen years, but Negroes had avoided demanding such a concession during the year-long crisis which led to McKenzie's resignation. Aware of this "hope" for a black administration and also of white caste-consciousness, the board appointed a white liberal, Herbert Adolphus Miller, an Ohio State University sociologist, to head the search for a new atmosphere and a new president for Fisk. Under Miller's direction, a student council, a student press, and an athletic association, as well as fraternities and sororities, were revived or instituted on the campus; strikers were fully restored to their previous academic status; and a search was begun for "competent" blacks of "experience, judgment, and education" to serve as deans and faculty members. In February 1926 Thomas Elsa Jones was named the new president. Jones, a white Quaker with a Ph.D. degree in sociology from Columbia University, brought to the college a more relaxed administration oriented to the black community.[38] Although Jones was not a

---

3, 1925; Nashville *Evening Tennessean*, March 24, 1925; "The Fisk Situation," a report to James Weldon Johnson by Walter White, NAACP Papers, container G-100.

[37]McKenzie to Cravath, April 16, 1925, McKenzie Papers, container 2; Nashville *Banner*, April 23, 1925.

[38]Taylor, "Fisk University, 1866–1951," 468; Herbert Adolphus Miller, "Report to Alumni Association of Fisk University," *Fisk University News* 15 (May 1925), 17–18; *Crisis*

Negro, he quickly won the support and friendship of Nashville blacks. In light of the potentially hostile local atmosphere and because such a white organization as the Chamber of Commerce had passed a resolution regretting McKenzie's resignation, "the logic of the circumstances" supported the board's decision to choose another white president.[39]

Jones proved to be an excellent choice to succeed the controversial McKenzie. Some of the faculty, including Isaac Fisher, resigned, but Northern philanthropy continued, white Nashvillians made good their $50,000 pledge to the school, student support was strong, and relationships with the black community were, once again, amiable. Students at other black institutions, perhaps noting the success of the Fisk maneuver, called strikes of their own, but the former strikers at the Nashville college sought ways of showing their pleasure at the changes made under Miller and Jones. During the 1926 commencement they "had their lives insured in a colored insurance company, the Supreme Life and Casualty Company of Columbus, Ohio, in favor of the university."[40]

Writing shortly after the conclusion of the Fisk controversy, Edwin Mims, a Vanderbilt professor and an organizer of the CIC, reflected upon changing black attitudes. "What is distinctly new in the immediate situation," he wrote, "is the voice of the Negro, North and South, speaking in no uncertain terms against injustice of all kinds."[41] University students, educated blacks, and Nashvillians, however, were not the only members of the race to speak

---

32 (July 1926), 128; Ferguson interview, Nov. 10, 1970; interview with Mr. and Mrs. Aeolian E. Lockert, July 16, 1970.

[39]"Resolutions for Dr. F. A. McKenzie," June 12, 1925, McKenzie Papers, container 2; Taylor, "Fisk University, 1866–1951," 469.

[40]Nashville *Banner*, June 4, 1925; Thomas Elsa Jones to Gov. Henry H. Horton, April 14, 1928, Gov. Horton Papers, Tennessee State Library and Archives, container 8; Brown, "The History of Negro Education in Tennessee," 70; Cleveland *Gazette*, May 16, 1925; Memphis *Commercial Appeal*, Oct. 26, 1927; *Crisis* 32 (July 1926), 128.

[41]Edwin Mims, *The Advancing South: Stories of Progress and Reaction* (New York: Doubleday, 1926), 267–68.

out "in no uncertain terms" and to show their discontent openly in Tennessee during the generally peaceful 1920s.

The Universal Negro Improvement Association (UNIA), founded in Jamaica in 1914 by Marcus Garvey and launched as a crusade for establishing black pride, had burst upon the American scene in 1920. Having established his first chapter in Harlem in 1917, Garvey held a gigantic convention in Madison Square Garden during August 1920, and the publicity he received gave notice of the association's appeal for black unity throughout the world. Garvey's message was that of black nationalism: rejection of the white world and the establishment of a black "empire" in Africa. The 1920 convention created a "nobility" and dispensed titles "upon the favored elite of the organization." While a number of prominent blacks, including Booker T. Washington's long-time secretary Emmett J. Scott initially were attracted to the association, the bulk of Garvey's support came from those black immigrants who had flooded the Northern cities during the war. [42] Depressed financially and spiritually at the end of the war, these blacks responded to the regal trappings and pride expressed by the Garvey movement.

Garveyism never got a wide public following among Southern Negroes. In Tennessee the blacks were caste-bound to white values, and this included an implicit rejection of their own blackness. Also characteristic of black Tennesseans was their dependence upon leaders; in this respect the leaders were, almost without exception, either wealthy or educated, two attributes which did not encourage response to the UNIA appeal for a return to Africa. Therefore, black nationalism played a negligible role in the lives of Tennessee blacks. Although Dr. Sumlin had tried to lump the student rebels at Fisk with the Garveyites as being

[42] The best discussion of the emergence of the Universal Negro Improvement Association in the United States is E. David Cronon, *Black Moses: The Story of Marcus Garvey and the Universal Negro Improvement Association* (Madison: Univ. of Wisconsin Press, 1955), ch. 3. The best source for a discussion of the racial ideology behind the UNIA is Amy Jacques Garvey, ed., *The Philosophy and Opinions of Marcus Garvey* (New York: Atheneum, 1970).

representatives of pretentious and dangerous "radicalism," the motivations of the two groups and their relative importance in Tennessee were very different.[43] The demand for the recognition of black individualism and human dignity within American society motivated the students and their supporters. This approach to change, championed by a revitalized NAACP, recurred frequently and eventually came to be accepted racial thinking in the state during the 1930s, 1940s, and 1950s. Black nationalism, meanwhile, experienced only one brief and minor flurry in the 1920s and then disappeared, staying dormant until resurrected by another generation of student "radicals" in the 1960s.

Apparently the only branch of the UNIA to be established in Tennessee appeared in Chattanooga around 1925. In that year Milton Minyard, a Chicago-based black man who claimed the title of "The First Mortal President Supreme General of the Hemiti Young Men's Industrial Association," came to work among the largely illiterate industrial laborers of the city. Previous attempts had been made to spread Garvey's message in Chattanooga, and Garvey himself, before being imprisoned in 1923, was supposed to have paid a visit. Mismanagement of funds and apathy had blocked the growth of the movement until Minyard brought an alleged Zulu prince named Romeo to the city in December 1925. After this visit, a more or less permanent group held regular meetings in a large stone house which had formerly been a private black orphanage. On August 4, 1927, after previously refusing the group permission to hold street meetings, the Chattanooga police raided the old orphanage. Minyard claimed that "the police did not relish the idea of our legionnaires wearing their uniforms in public. . . ." Chattanooga officials had indeed been sensitive to potential Garvey organizations for several years and had earlier attempted even to prevent black World War I veterans from wearing their uniforms when they returned home. The Baltimore *Afro-American* reported the

[43] Nashville *Banner*, Feb. 12, 1925.

Chattanooga conflict and also noted the harassment as a "typical Southern white reaction to colored organizations provided with military uniforms and weapons."[44]

A great deal of shooting had resulted from the police raid, and two blacks and one white officer were wounded. UNIA uniforms and a large supply of rifles were discovered during the attack, and rumors of black revolution immediately raced through the town. As if to substantiate Minyard's claim of white fear, the rumors alleged that thousands of blacks were involved in secret meetings aimed at conducting a violent uprising. An intensive investigation, however, turned up a lot of Garvey literature but few active members. One of the Negroes arrested claimed that over seven hundred Chattanoogans belonged to the organization, but black community leaders quickly denied that such was the case.[45]

For a few days the front pages of the local press were given over to accounts of the resistance of the Garveyites and the "Red" and "bolshevik" tendencies of the UNIA. At a time when newspapers were also giving attention to the appeals of two Boston anarchists, Nicola Sacco and Bartolomeo Vanzetti, fear of alien agitation was easily generated. Black leaders, especially J. F. Trimble of the Negro Business League, Dr. L. L. Patton of the dormant NAACP, and Dr. W. A. Thompson of the Inter-Racial League, expressed their "amazement" that such an organization could even exist in Chattanooga. Trimble blamed the trouble on "the illiterate negroes of the city" and maintained that "none of the colored fraternal orders, societies or churches have even been approached with 'red' propaganda." Whites praised "the good sense of the major part of the negroes of Chattanooga" and declared them "cold to the advances of Garvey's agents here."[46]

Eventually, the Chattanooga *Daily Times* ceased its fearful

[44]Chattanooga *Daily Times*, Aug. 6, 1927; Chattanooga *News*, Aug. 6, 1927; *Negro World*, Aug. 20, 1927; Baltimore *Afro-American*, Aug. 13, 1927, quoted in *Negro World*, Aug. 20, 1927; interview with De Witt C. Alfred, June 7, 1972.

[45]Chattanooga *Daily Times*, Aug. 5, 6, 7, 8, 1927; Chattanooga *News*, Aug. 5, 6, 1927.

[46]Chattanooga *Daily Times*, Aug. 6, 1927; Chattanooga *News*, Aug. 5, 1927.

reporting and editorialized, with relief, that the paucity of members showed that "the negroes as a whole had been in no way affected by the activities and propaganda of 'red' agitators. . . ." Almost exactly one year after the police raid, the old headquarters of the UNIA was leased by the city as an annex for a nearby black school.[47] The UNIA had disappeared from the city, Garvey had been deported to Jamaica, and the fears of August 27 had been forgotten.

Chattanooga had provided perhaps the greatest opportunity for the Garvey movement in Tennessee. A large number of immigrants had been coming to the city as a result of violence and peonage in the rural areas of north Georgia, and these migrants flooded an already sizable industrial labor pool. Nevertheless, the racism preached by Garvey ran counter to the ideological heritage of black Tennesseans. They accepted the value of emulating whites and being received by white society rather than rejecting it. The slightly changed direction of the black experience in the 1920s was partly the result of an expanded white awareness, but it was even more the consequence of a greater willingness of blacks to demand recognition of their rights. The process of change, however, was slow and uneven. Despite the organizational example set by the NAACP, the political awareness of Robert Church, the decisive episode at Fisk, and the appeal of the small cell of Garvey followers in Chattanooga, most blacks continued to stake their future on the hope for white enlightenment.

---

[47] Chattanooga *Daily Times*, Aug. 8, 1927.

Conclusion

Langston Hughes, reflecting in 1940 upon the black experience, sounded a persistent dilemma in Afro-American history. "For bread," he asked, "how much of the spirit must one give away?"[1] Certainly many black Tennesseans must have asked themselves this question when the dawning light of the twentieth century revealed the hovering, though still somewhat amorphous, presence of Jim Crow. The ideals of freedom and opportunity still burned brightly, and despite disillusionment associated with such setbacks as the collapse of the Freedmen's Bank and the absence of substantial economic progress, faith survived that the American dream was attainable.

A few black Tennesseans spoke out angrily from the beginning, rejecting expediency and charging whites with denying their human dignity and betraying the nation's promises. A larger number complained of the worsening conditions and actively petitioned for fair treatment from the controlling white system. But a majority, biting their lips, sighed and picked up their hoes or laundry baskets and went back to work. Although a significant thread of protest survived, most black Tennesseans came to accept another postponement (but not a cancellation) of the "dream." They took the public advice of Booker T. Washington, and they accepted accommodation as a realistic temporary alter-

---

[1] *The Big Sea*, 310.

native to racial conflict. But accommodation, whether it was conscious or merely apathetic, molded white attitudes, black expectations, and race relations and decisively influenced the future course of social development in Tennessee.

Tennesseans, and even Booker T. Washington, may have looked upon accommodation as a temporary approach, "yet," as Langston Hughes went on to observe, "how heavily the bricks of compromise settle into place!"[2] The discriminatory "half-loaf" appropriations given the Tennessee Agricultural and Industrial State Normal School, for example—appropriations for which blacks "rejoiced" and were "exceeding glad"[3]—set a precedent which for decades left the black school as the stepchild of the state's higher education system. In race relations, the willingness to accept segregation reinforced a practice of discrimination that gave ground ever so slowly, even with the gradual renewal of sympathetic white paternalism during the 1920s.

Dominated by a white caste system and resigned to slow progress, blacks again turned inward. Since the early days of slavery, Negroes had been denied the right to continue traditional African culture and yet also prevented from becoming integrated into American society. As a result, a distinct slave community had appeared, only to be partially uprooted by the promises of Reconstruction. As these promises faded after 1900, black Tennesseans responded by falling back upon and refining a persistent subculture.

The return of racial stability conditioned Tennesseans of both races to a gradual and paternalistically directed "progress" for blacks. The environment became quite static and, in retrospect, it is not surprising that the 1954 desegregation decision sent shock waves through the state. Whites protested that federal interference was unwarranted and unacceptable.[4] Traditional black lead-

[2] *Ibid.*

[3] Nashville *Globe*, March 12, 1909.

[4] White Tennessee reaction to the 1954 decision in *Brown* v. *Board of Education* is best discussed in Hugh Davis Graham, *Crisis in Print: Desegregation and the Press in Tennessee* (Nashville: Vanderbilt Univ. Press, 1967).

ers, meanwhile, welcomed the decision but moved to exploit it with deliberate caution. They, too, had settled somewhat heavily into a slow and compromising pace. "Bread" was still vulnerable, and the "spirit" was hesitant. Eventually, it would take a new generation of leaders, a generation not unlike the Fisk students of 1925 but prepared by another world war, a technological revolution, and a continuing urban crisis to make the necessary break with the habits of compromise and accommodation.

Bibliographical Essay

No large collection of manuscripts or single body of literature is available for the study of black Tennesseans at the turn of the century. Several archives contain important material, but the broad story has been assembled from thousands of scattered pieces of information. To cite all of these sources would be both unnecessary and impractical; this essay should be considered a supplement to the footnotes, not a complete discussion of all material consulted. One general note of explanation, however, is in order: sources in black history are especially fragmented and inconspicuous. Tremendous strides have been made in the last fifteen years in gathering and making these sources available to researchers, but the limited number of black institutions has meant fewer records of black activities, and the long neglect of white historians and archivists has discouraged adequate preservation of those valuable materials which have existed.

Pertinent manuscript collections are in short supply. The papers of George Edmund Haynes, James Carroll Napier, and William Edward Burghardt Du Bois at Fisk University are important collections, but they are not extensive. The Booker T. Washington papers, the Mary Church Terrell papers, and the National Association for the Advancement of Colored People records, all found in the Manuscript Division of the Library of Congress, are much more extensive but harder to use for specific areas of research. The papers of the Commission on Interracial Cooperation, located in the Negro Collection at Atlanta University, contain no great body of material relating directly to Tennessee, but the published minutes of the State Inter-Racial Commission of Tennessee and the *Progress in Race Relations* annual report found in the collection are helpful. Several small manuscript collections at the Tennessee State Library and Archives in Nashville contain information about black Tennesseans, but the papers of Fayette Avery McKenzie and the official correspondence of Tennessee's governors from 1900 to 1930 are clearly the most useful. The archives of the Tennessee Department of Insurance and Banking, Nashville, also hold the receivership records of the People's Savings Bank and Trust Company and the Fraternal and Solvent Savings Bank and Trust Company. These are invaluable sources of information in understanding the practices and handicaps of black financial institutions in the state. The John C. Houk papers in the McClung Collection at Knoxville's Lawson McGhee Library were helpful in discerning the fading general role of black Tennesseans in the state's Republican party.

Personal memoirs should be used with care, but in the absence of a large number of manuscript collections these sources have special value. George Washington Lee's *Beale Street: Where the Blues Began* (New York: Ballou, 1934) is the most valuable for this study. Lee combines his own experience with oral traditions and some investigation into Memphis's black past. Other memoirs include Charles W. Cansler, *Three Generations: The Story of a Colored Family of Eastern Tennessee* (Knoxville: privately printed, 1939), Thomas O. Fuller, *Twenty Years in Public Life, 1890–1910* (Nashville: National Baptist Publishing Board, 1910), Fred L. Hutchins, *What Happened in Memphis* (Memphis: privately printed, 1965), Mary Church Terrell, *A Colored Woman in a White World* (Washington, D.C.: National Association of Colored Women's Clubs, 1968), and the Federal Writers' Project, *These Are Our Lives* (Chapel Hill: Univ. of North Carolina Press, 1939). Annette E. and Roberta Church, *The Robert R. Churches of Memphis* (Ann Arbor: Edwards Brothers, 1974) is a valuable,

301

if selected, collection of documents and information about the careers and backgrounds of Robert R. Church, Sr. and Robert R. Church, Jr. Two biographical compilations, while excessively laudatory, provide key information: J. Bliss White, comp., *Biography and Achievements of the Colored Citizens of Chattanooga* (privately printed, 1904), and Green Polonius Hamilton, *The Bright Side of Memphis* (Memphis: privately printed, 1908). Two white memoirs deal extensively with the black experience in Tennessee: Benjamin Franklin Wilson, III, *The Negro As I Have Known Him, 1867–1943* (Nashville: Parthenon, 1946), and Samuel Leonard Smith, "All Along the Way From Sunrise on Satan Creek to the Evening Shadows at Peabody" (manuscript at George Peabody College for Teachers, Nashville). In addition, Evelyn Scott, *Background in Tennessee* (New York: Robert M. McBride, 1937) provides some valuable white impressions of black communities.

Although the quality and content of black journalism varied widely in the early 1900s, Negro newspapers and magazines fill many of the historical gaps left by an absence of manuscript collections and institutional records. Tennessee produced several black newspapers during this period, but most of them had short lives and copies were rarely preserved. Fortunately, a sizable run of the Nashville *Globe* does exist. Almost entirely ignored by historians, the *Globe* shunned most "canned" material and took an aggressive reporting and editorial stance. The *Globe* was responsive to national issues but gave considerable attention to the business, politics, and ideology of black Tennesseans. While concentrating upon Nashville and its environs, the *Globe* regularly reported the affairs of Negroes throughout the state. This newspaper's sensitivity to basic developments in the black community and its professional organization and appearance make it one of the most valuable sources for this study. Files of two other black newspapers published in Tennessee have been preserved. The *Christian Index*, the official organ of the Colored Methodist Episcopal Church, was especially conscious of social issues prior to 1920, and the Memphis *World*, although not founded until the early 1930s, contains several feature stories relating to earlier activities of that city's black population. Scattered extant copies and clippings from the Chattanooga *Defender*, the Memphis *Western World Reporter*, and the Knoxville *East Tennessee News* provide additional coverage. Other black newspapers such as the Indianapolis *Freeman* and the Cleveland *Gazette*, in addition to periodicals such as the *Crisis*, the *Messenger*, and the *Fisk University News*, carried either regular or frequent news items relating to black Tennesseans.

Nevertheless, existing black sources leave many holes in the record. To fill these gaps and provide necessary continuity and statewide perspective, the use of Tennessee's white press is both necessary and desirable. The big city dailies, while often biased and selective in their news reporting and editorial comment, serve best. Newspapers such as the Nashville *American*, the Memphis *Commercial Appeal*, the Chattanooga *Daily Times*, and the Knoxville *Journal and Tribune* provide important information when coordinated with available black materials.

Almost no contemporary scholarly works focused upon black Tennesseans at the turn of the century. By the 1920s, however, several studies of broad aspects of Negro life were taking the state into account. W. E. B. Du Bois's pathbreaking collection and publication of data at Atlanta University and Sutton Griggs's *The One Great Question: A Study of Southern Conditions at Close Range* (Nashville: Orion, 1907), of course, preceded the 1920s, and J. Herman Daves's *A Social Study of the Colored Population of Knoxville, Tennessee* (Knoxville: Free Colored Library, 1926) concentrated on one black community in the state, but most primary research in black history had a broader focus and began a few years after the founding of the Association for the Study of Negro Life and History in 1915. Some of these general studies which provide important information about Tennessee Negroes are Lorenzo J. Greene and Carter G. Woodson, *The Negro Wage Earner* (Washington, D. C.: Association for the Study of Negro

Life and History, 1930); Charles H. Wesley, *Negro Labor in the United States, 1850–1925* (New York: Vanguard, 1927); Paul K. Edwards, *The Southern Urban Negro as a Consumer* (New York: Prentice-Hall, 1932); Abram L. Harris, *The Negro as Capitalist* (Philadelphia: American Academy of Political and Social Science, 1936); Sterling D. Spero and Abram L. Harris, *The Black Worker: The Negro and the Labor Movement* (New York: Columbia Univ. Press, 1931); and Merah Steven Stuart, *An Economic Detour: A History of Insurance in the Lives of American Negroes* (New York: Malliet, 1940).

Government documents and publications are of only limited value. Official records and reports indicate that state agencies in Tennessee paid only scant attention to segregated black citizens. Statistics concerning public education are the most informative, but even these are not always complete and frequently are unreliable. The major source is the *Biennial Report of the Superintendent of Public Instruction*, a compilation of reports from county and city superintendents. In some years there were counties that did not submit reports, and on occasion double counting and other discrepancies are obvious. A detailed breakdown of Negro participation in public education was not made by the state superintendent until 1922. Attention given to black Tennesseans by the state Department of Agriculture is insignificant. The official journals of the state legislative bodies, meanwhile, recorded very little debate and discussion. Publications by various federal agencies occasionally had important bearing upon black Tennesseans—especially the Department of Agriculture's circulars relating to extension work among Negroes and the Department of Labor's bulletins compiled by the Women's Bureau. Charles E. Allred has extracted pertinent Tennessee statistics from the mass of federal data and published these in several studies. The collection most valuable for this book is *Tenure By Type of Farming Areas and Color in Tennessee* (written with Elmer E. Briner), University of Tennessee Agricultural Experiment Station, Rural Research Series Monograph, No. 85 (1938).

Oral history has become an increasingly used tool for filling in the lacunae in traditional research and gaining a more intimate perspective on the past. Although many of the same weaknesses found in personal memoirs also may be applied to oral sources, the hazards can be reduced. If conducted after careful preparation by the interviewer and checked against other available sources, the personal interview is invaluable in black history. I conducted nearly thirty interviews with black Tennesseans, and although the quality and usefulness of these sessions varied widely, they gave much needed insight into the Negro experience in Tennessee. Meredith G. Ferguson's involvement in the Fisk student strike, for example, provided key awareness of the students' determination and the administration's tactics. James T. Chandler, meanwhile, spoke personally of his "ground floor" experiences in the black insurance field, and Grady E. Walker talked informatively of rural life in Tennessee and the motivations behind black migration during and after World War I.

Tennessee has not often enough drawn the attention of historians, and there are still many areas in need of scholarly investigation. Some recent secondary works, however, deserve mention. David M. Tucker's *Lieutenant Lee of Beale Street* (Nashville: Vanderbilt Univ. Press, 1971) describes the activities of many of Memphis's black leaders during the 1920s. Samuel Henry Shannon's "Agricultural and Industrial Education at Tennessee State University During the Normal School Phase, 1912–1922" (Ph.D. diss., George Peabody College for Teachers, 1974) expands one aspect of the very general coverage of R. Grann Lloyd's *Tennessee Agricultural and Industrial State University* (Nashville: privately printed, 1962). Joseph H. Cartwright's *The Triumph of Jim Crow: Tennessee Race Relations in the 1880s* (Knoxville: Univ. of Tennessee Press, 1976) goes beyond Alrutheus Ambush Taylor's *The Negro in Tennessee, 1865–1880* (Washington, D. C.: Associated Publishers, 1941) and provides a good background for understanding the changing black political role after 1900. Other secondary works focusing upon Tennessee, but only indirectly informative about black Tennesseans, are William D. Miller, *Memphis During the Progressive Era, 1900–1917* (Memphis: Memphis State Univ. Press, 1957); Paul E. Isaac, *Prohibition and Politics: Turbulent Decades in Tennessee, 1886–1920* (Knoxville: Univ. of Tennessee Press, 1965); and Andrew D. Holt, *The Struggle for a State System of Public Schools in Tennessee, 1903–1936* (New York: Teachers College, Columbia Univ., 1938).

Studies of specific states or narrow topics cannot be written without extensive background reading. Numerous studies, many of them classics, provide the necessary perspective for research and writing in Southern and black history. Outstanding examples are Wilbur J. Cash, *The Mind of the South* (New York: Knopf, 1941); C. Vann Woodward, *Origins of the New South, 1877–1913* (Baton Rouge: Louisiana State Univ. Press, 1951); George Brown Tindall, *The Emergence of the New South, 1913–1945* (Baton Rouge: Louisiana State Univ. Press, 1967); and August Meier, *Negro Thought in America, 1880–1915: Racial Ideologies in the Age of Booker T. Washington* (Ann Arbor: Univ. of Michigan Press, 1963). Among the other works which provide either valuable perspective or specific information of use to this study of black Tennesseans are S. P. Fullinwider, *The Mind and Mood of Black America: 20th Century Thought* (Homewood, Ill.: Dorsey, 1969); Herbert R. Northrup, *Organized Labor and the Negro* (New York: Harper, 1944); William M. Tuttle, Jr., *Race Riot: Chicago in The Red Summer of 1919* (New York: Atheneum, 1972); Mary F. Berry, *Black Resistance/White Law: A History of Constitutional Racism in America* (New York: Appleton-Century-Crofts, 1971); Guichard Parris and Lester Brooks, *Blacks in the City: A History of the National Urban League* (Boston: Little, Brown, 1971); and Charles Flint Kellogg, *NAACP* (Baltimore: Johns Hopkins Univ. Press, 1967).

State and regional literature relating to black Southerners and Southern race relations has expanded significantly in the last fifteen years. These works have benefited from earlier pathfinding studies. Among the older volumes are Rayford W. Logan, *The Negro in American Life and Thought: The Nadir, 1877–1901* (New York: Dial, 1954); Albert D. Kirwan, *Revolt of the Rednecks: Mississippi Politics, 1876–1925* (Lexington: Univ. of Kentucky Press, 1951); Vernon L. Wharton, *The Negro in Mississippi, 1865–1890* (Chapel Hill: Univ. of North Carolina Press, 1947); George B. Tindall, *South Carolina Negroes, 1877–1900* (Columbia: Univ. of South Carolina Press, 1952); and Helen G. Edmonds, *The Negro and Fusion Politics in North Carolina* (Chapel Hill: Univ. of North Carolina Press, 1951). More recently, the field has blossomed with political studies such as Andrew Buni, *The Negro in Virginia Politics, 1902–1965* (Charlottesville: Univ. of Virginia Press, 1967); Margaret L. Callcott, *The Negro in Maryland Politics, 1870–1912* (Baltimore: Johns Hopkins Univ. Press, 1969); and at last the publication of Ralph J. Bunche, *The Political Status of the Negro in the Age of FDR* ed. and with an introduction by Dewey W. Grantham (Chicago: Univ. of Chicago Press, 1973). There are also important studies of black education such as Louis R. Harlan, *Separate and Unequal: Public School Campaigns and Racism in the Southern Seaboard States, 1901–1915* (Chapel Hill: Univ. of North Carolina Press, 1958), and Henry Allen Bullock, *A History of Negro Education in the South* (New York: Praeger, 1967). Concern with racism has inspired considerable research into Southern thought and society. Among the better works are Bruce Clayton, *The Savage Ideal: Intolerance and Intellectual Leadership in the South, 1890–1914* (Baltimore: Johns Hopkins Univ. Press, 1972), and Jack Temple Kirby, *Darkness at the Dawning: Race and Reform in the Progressive South* (Philadelphia: Lippincott, 1972). Recent studies of blacks in specific states include Lawrence D. Rice, *The Negro in Texas, 1874–1900* (Baton Rouge: Louisiana State Univ. Press, 1971), and Frenise A. Logan, *The Negro in North Carolina, 1876–1894* (Chapel Hill: Univ. of North Carolina Press, 1964). To the list I might now add this study of black Tennesseans.

Index

Abolitionism, in Tennessee, v
Accommodation, lingering effect of, 297–99
Agriculture: blacks in, 110–31; farm life and, 110–16; black farm organizations and, 116, 118, 119, 124, 125, 268; back-to-the-farm movements and, 120; federal aid to blacks in, 121–25; county fairs and, 125–26; black farm cooperatives and, 129–30. *See also* Land tenure
Alexander, Will Winton, 159, 258
Allen, Green, 40
Aluminum Company of America, 143
American Federation of Labor, 141, 159
American Home Investment Company, 191
American Interchurch College for Religious and Social Workers, 215
American Missionary Association, 63, 227, 275, 276
American National Bank (Nashville), 197, 198–99
Atlanta *Independent*, 16
Atlanta Life Insurance Company, 201
Ayres, Brown, 95

Baldwin, William H., 286
Baldwin, Mrs. William H., 215
Baltimore *Afro-American*, 294–95
Baltimore *Afro-American Ledger*, 275
Band of Good Hope (Chattanooga), 261
Banking, blacks in, 183–99. *See also* Fraternal Savings Bank and Trust Company; Fraternal and Solvent Savings Bank and Trust Company; One-Cent Savings Bank

Banking (*cont.*)
and Trust Company; Penny Savings Bank; People's Savings Bank and Trust Company; Solvent Savings Bank and Trust Company
Barbour, John L., 5
Bass, J. S., 92
Battle, Joseph Oliver, 15
Berry, D. Wellington, 211
Bethlehem Center (Nashville), 216, 218
Black nationalism, 293, 294
Bond, Horace Mann, 67
Bond, James, 67, 140
Bond, Julian, 67
Bond, Scott, 123
Bonner, Mark William, 201, 203
Booth, Benjamin F., 32
Boyd, Henry Allen: and Nashville *Globe*'s stands, 15, 96, 173; and support for Tennessee A & I, 96, 99, 100–101; and black financial institutions, 193, 201; and campaign for YMCA, 210; and racial insult at Fisk University, 275
Boyd, Richard Henry: and white discrimination, 1, 2, 20; and National Negro Business League, 5–6, 178; and financial support for Nashville *Globe*, 15; wins control of National Baptist Publishing Board, 18; and One-Cent Savings Bank, 26, 184, 185, 186, 193; supports streetcar boycott, 26–27, 33; and political activities, 47, 51, 52; and black farm improvement, 123, 125; manufactures Negro dolls, 175; dies in 1922, 193
Boyd, Robert Fulton, 92, 172

Broadcaster, 108
Brotherhood of Locomotive Firemen and Enginemen, 163
Brotherhood of Railroad Trainmen, 162
Brotherhood of Sleeping Car Porters, 162
Bryant, Ira T., 52, 201
"Bull Moose" party, 53
Burrus, John Houston, 91
Business: blacks in, 167–206; racial handicaps in, 167–71; 181–82; support of Nashville *Globe* for, 168, 171–79; in form of financial institutions, 173–74; in form of cooperative enterprises, 179–81. *See also* Banking; Insurance
Business and Professional League (Nashville), 177–78
Butler, Mrs. J. C., 263n
Bynes, J. Monroe, ix

Cahill Iron Works, 142
Campbell, H. T., 48
Campbell, Thomas M., 123
Cansler, Charles W., 75, 220, 221, 237, 243, 248
Carey, James L., 269
Carmack, Edward W., 1, 37, 68
Carr, Benjamin J., 100–102, 118n, 206
Carty, Joseph E., 247
Carver, George Washington, 118
Cash, Wilbur J., 135–36
Caste system: forces behind, vi–vii; tightened after 1900, 4; impact of, upon transportation, 6–9; impact of, upon legal due process, 9–10; semantics and, 71–72, 97, 101; impact of, upon school facilities, 85; state aid to black farmers, 126; at Du Pont Company, 144; impact of, upon black businessmen, 167–68, 171; in public parks, 224, 225; inhibits reform, 259; and etiquette of race relations, 272–73. *See also* Education; Educational philanthropy; Industry; Race relations; Streetcar boycott
Cate, W. T., 246, 254
Central Community Betterment League (Chattanooga), 219, 237
Chandler, James T., 204
Chattanooga: black economic position in, 3; lynching in, 10, 232; streetcar boycott in, 29–31; activities of National Negro Busi-

Chattanooga (*cont.*)
ness League in, 29, 179, 234; blacks in politics in, 38–39, 42–43, 53n; Ku Klux Klan in politics in, 42–43; school accommodations for blacks in, 74; efforts to locate Tennessee A & I in, 99, 100–101; health conditions among blacks in, 137–38, 219; blacks in iron industry in, 142–43, 160–61; black bank in, 183, 186; black progressivism in, 219–20; work of Commission on Interracial Cooperation in, 259, 261; activities of NAACP in, 265, 266, 267, 271, 295; presence of Universal Negro Improvement Association in, 294–96. *See also* Unions; World War I
Chattanooga *Blade*, 29, 31
Chattanooga *Daily Times*: opposes black streetcar boycott, 29; comments upon race riots in the North, 239–40; fears outside agitation, 242, 244–45, 250; opposes anti-lynching legislation, 270–71; fears "Garveyism" in Chattanooga, 295–96
Chattanooga *Defender*, 54, 242, 271
Chattanooga Plow Company, 142
Chicago race riot in 1919, 239, 240
Christian Index (Jackson), 28–29, 51, 234, 280
Church, Robert Reed, Jr.: political activity of, 11, 44–47, 50, 55–58, 222, 241, 251, 272, 296; sees value of political power, 239, 260; and Colored Citizens Association, 223; resentment of, against segregated streetcars, 36; relationship of, to Solvent Savings Bank, 191, 195, 196; support of, for World War I, 233; on worsening race relations in Memphis in 1919, 235; association of, with NAACP, 265, 266, 267
Church, Robert Reed, Sr.: background of, 188; and National Negro Business League, 178; and Solvent Savings Bank, 188, 189, 190, 122; and life insurance company proposal, 202; builds Church's Park, 228; death of, in 1912, 190
Citizens Savings Bank and Trust Company. *See* One-Cent Savings Bank and Trust Company
Clansman, The, 42
Claxton, Philander Priestly, 62, 69, 98

Clay, Robert E.: as assistant to State Agent for Negro Schools, 84; support of, for prohibition, 84; relationship of, to W. J. Hale and Tennessee A & I, 107; and the National Negro Business League, 178–79; on causes of racial conflict, 231; interracial work of, 157, 251
Cleveland *Gazette*, 195
Cole, Roman, 114
Colored Citizens Association (Memphis), 53, 222–25
Colored Chautauqua Association (Clarksville), 214
Colored Farmers' Alliance, 116, 268
Colored Farmers Association of East Tennessee, 119
Colored Joint Stock Company, 125
Colored State Teachers Association, 92
Colored Wheel, 116
Commission on Interracial Cooperation (CIC): as a conservative vehicle for change in race relations, 19; general activity of, in Tennessee, 256–64, 268–69, 270; in Chattanooga, 259, 261; in Franklin, 259; in Knoxville, 259–60, 261; in Memphis, 259, 260–61; in Nashville, 259, 261; emphasis of, upon reducing violence, 257, 262–63; supports improvement in black education, 76, 86, 106; and Tennessee Interracial Commission, 129; obscures indigenous black progressivism, 228
Community Federal Savings and Loan Association, 199
Compulsory school attendance: racial implications, 73–75
Conference for Education in the South, 61–64. *See also* Southern Education Board
Coolidge, Calvin, 54
Cortelyou, George B., 28
Cowan, Carl A., 269–70
Cravath, Erastus Milo, 275, 282
Cravath, Paul Drennan, 275, 284
Crisis, 178, 265, 279, 284
Crump, Edward Hull: political power of, in Memphis, 45–46; support from black voters for, 45–46; relationship of, to progressivism, 222, 223, 224
Crump, J. A., 138

Dabney, Charles William, 62, 64, 69
Davidson County Court, 100–101
Davidson County Negro Farmers Alliance, 124
Davis, Clifford, 44
Delta Penny Savings Bank, 194, 202
Democratic party. *See* Politics
Dillard, James Hardy, 95
Dixie Portland Cement Company, 142–43
Dixon, Nace, 39, 41
Douglass, Frederick, 185
Douglass Park (Memphis), 224–25
Doyle, Bertram, 273
Du Bois, William Edward Burghardt: quote from, ix-x; as symbol of protest, 6, 265; educational philosophy of, 93–94; and *Moon Weekly Illustrated*, 140; on blacks and trade unions, 159; on black business enterprise, 176–77, 180, 190, 196; on value of NAACP, 268; on "scientific" philanthropy at Fisk University, 278; role of, in Fisk student strike, 281–83, 286–87
Du Bois, Yolande, 281
Du Pont Company: black workers at, during World War I, 143–44
Durant, Oswald, 281
Dyer, Leonidas C.: as author of antilynching bill, 270, 271
Dyer antilynching bill, 270–72
Dyersburg, 201

Early, John H., 9
Earthman, E. S., 40
Eddings, W. J., 30
Education, public: blacks and, 59–87; educational philanthropy in, 79–87. *See also* Southern Education Board
Educational philanthropy: and blacks in Tennessee, 61–64, 79–87; in private schools for blacks, 61, 74, 93; in public schools for blacks, 79–87; white attitudes toward, 63–65
Edwards, Georgia, 7–8, 11
Edwards, J. L., 40
Ellington, W. A., 237
Evans, Henry Clay, 41
Ewing, Taylor G., 143

Fairs, black county, 125–26

Farley, John W., 56
Farm life, for blacks, 110–16
Farmer's Institute (Nashville), of 1909, 118
Fayette County, 41, 59–60, 77, 130, 266
Federal aid to black farmers: by Hatch Act of 1887, 121; by Smith-Lever Act of 1914, 122; by Federal Farm Loan Act of 1916, 124–25; by Smith-Hughes Act of 1917, 124
Ferguson, Meredith Gillespie, 280n, 288–89, 290
Firemen, blacks as, 141
Fisher, Isaac, 250, 258, 267, 268, 292
Fisk *Herald*, 279
Fisk University: normal training at, 92; business program at, 170; student strike at, 274–92
Fourth Tennessee Infantry: and Knoxville riot, 246–48
Franklin, George W., Jr., 176, 258
Fraternal and Solvent Savings Bank and Trust Company: activities of, 193–97; collapses, 194; impact of collapse of, 194–96, 204. *See also* Fraternal Savings Bank and Trust Company; Solvent Savings Bank and Trust Company
Fraternal Savings Bank and Trust Company: activities of, 190–91; merges with Solvent Savings Bank and Trust Company, 193. *See also* Fraternal and Solvent Savings Bank and Trust Company
Frazier, James B., 6, 7
Freedmen's Savings Bank and Trust Company: operations of, in Tennessee, 174; legacy of, among black Tennesseans, 183–85, 186, 194, 297
Fuller, Thomas Oscar: opposes streetcar boycott, 24, 31; heads Memphis Welfare League, 228; supports World War I, 233; supports Commission on Interracial Cooperation, 258, 260; joins NAACP, 265

Gailer, Thomas F., 236
Garrett, Finnis James, 271
Garvey, Marcus: activities of, 293, 296; support in Tennessee for, 294–96
Gates, George Augustus, 215, 275–76
General Education Board: and aid to education, 79–81, 86–87, 106; and farm demonstration program, 121, 124; and State Supervisor of Negro Welfare, 262

George Peabody College for Teachers, 91, 96
Gompers, Samuel, 159
Grant, J. W., 132, 217
Green, Henry M.: in Knoxville politics, 39, 41; advocacy of, for better health care, 220; as author of *Pellagra in Monograph*, 220
Green, I. E., 170
Griggs, Sutton Elbert: early opposition by, to caste restrictions, 12–13; protest novels of, 12; as supporter of streetcar boycott, 25, 27; and black education, 67, 74; accepts black inferiority, 13, 14, 15, 18; and cooperation with T. O. Fuller, 24, 261; close ties of, with white paternalists, 195, 228; opposes black political activism, 46, 251; opposes the NAACP, 267; leaves Tennessee, 46
Griggsby, Charles, 38, 39

Hale, John, 288
Hale, William Jasper: and proposed location of Tennessee A & I in Chattanooga, 100–101; as president of Tennessee A & I, 101–108; alleged relationship of, to Robert L. Jones, 101–102; as president of Tennessee's Colored Division of Commission on Interracial Cooperation, 257; relationship of, to Booker T. Washington, 102, 108
Hamilton County Court, 101
Harding, Warren G., 54, 256
Hardy, H. C., 127
Harlan, John Marshall, 10
Harris, Solomon Parker, 39, 41, 217
Harrison, W. H., 4, 18
Hart, Dock A., 15, 96, 118n
Hart, W. M., 10
Hawkins, W. D., 178
Hayes, Thomas H.: as officer in National Negro Business League, 178; as business entrepreneur, 190–91, 200, 201; conviction of, in collapse of Fraternal and Solvent Bank, 194; support of, for World War I, 233
Haynes, George Edmund: advises against migration from farms, 120, 232; work of, with National Urban League in Tennessee, 214–21, 226–29, 262

Hays, Will, 57
Haywood County, 70
Henderson, James H., 269
Hill, Richard, 49, 172
Homemakers' Club (Knoxville), 213
Hoover, Herbert, 57
Hortense (Dickson County), 119
Houk, John C., 108, 129
Howard University, 284
Howse, Hilary E., 17, 101
Hubbard, George Whipple, 277
Hughes, J. K., 82n
Hughes, Langston, 257–58, 297, 298
Hutchins, Styles L., 10

Industrial Settlement Home (Memphis), 226, 259
Industry: blacks in lumber, 133; blacks in phosphate, 133–34; blacks in coal, 134–35; blacks in iron, 141–43, 160–61; increase in black women laborers in, 165
Insurance companies, black experience with, 199–205
International Molders' Union of North America, 160–61
Isaac, Edward W. D., 25, 118n, 288

Jackson: opposition to segregated streetcars in, 28; activities of NAACP in, 267–68. See also Lane College; West Tennessee Negro Farmers' Institute
Jeanes (Anna T.) Foundation, 79, 80, 82–83, 86–87, 95, 124
"Jeanes Teachers," 80, 82–83, 87, 107, 121
Johnson, Andrew N., 168, 177, 212
Johnson, Calvin F., 221
Johnson, Ed, 10, 232
Johnson, Mrs. J. J., 213
Johnson, James Weldon, 265–66, 271
Johnson, Jack, 17
Jones, James A., 23, 218, 233–34, 238
Jones, Robert L., 69, 96, 101–102
Jones, Thomas Elsa, 291–92
Jones, Thomas Jesse, 285
Jones, William N., 227
Jubilee Singers, 276, 279

Keith, Hardy L., 217
Keller, H. H., 143
Kellor, Frances A., 215
Kitrelle, A. N., 196

Knapp, Bradford, 124
Knapp, Seaman A., 121
Knights and Daughters of Labor, 195
Knoxville: opposition to segregated streetcars in, 33; impact of municipal reform in, 39; blacks in politics in, 39, 42; educational facilities for blacks in, 74, 75, 78; black progressivism in, 213, 219, 220–21, 230; race riot in, 244–55; activities of NAACP in, 244, 249–50, 253, 265, 266, 267, 269–70; work of Commission on Interracial Cooperation in, 259–60, 261. See also Race relations; World War I
Knoxville Chamber of Commerce, 252
Knoxville College, 74, 90, 95, 249
Knoxville Journal and Tribune, 157, 252, 254, 272
Knoxville Negro Board of Trade, 211
Knoxville race riot of 1919: setting for, 244–45; violent conflict during, 246–48; impact of, 248–55; reaction in Knoxville to, 252–54; reaction of NAACP to, 249–50, 253, 270
Knoxville Sentinel, 63, 244, 270
Ku Klux Klan: in Tennessee politics, 42–44; some white opposition to, 242; activities in Knoxville of, 244, 248; activities in Nashville of, 281; impact of, upon support for Dyer antilynching bill, 271

La Follette (Campbell County), 238
Land tenure, black farmers and: land ownership form of, 111, 113, 127; sharecropping form of, 111–13, 127, 130; wage labor form of, 113, 127
Lane, Franklin K., 8
Lane, James Franklin, 118
Lane, Mrs. James Franklin, 214
Lane, James W., 233
Lane College, 116, 267
Lankford, W. H., 5
Lawyers, black: handicaps facing, 174–75
Lebanon Bureau of Domestic Labor, 140
Lee, George Washington, 46, 195–96
Life and Casualty Insurance Company, 201
Lily white Republicanism, 4, 47–51, 54, 55–58
Lincoln League, 56–58, 224, 265. See also Robert R. Church, Jr.

Lindsay, Bertie, 245
Locke, W. Alonzo, 196
Lockert, Aeolian E., 144n
Lodge Force bill, 41
Louisville and Nashville Railroad, 7
Lynching: in Chattanooga in 1906, 10, 232; during World War I, 232, 234–38; reduction of, in 1920s, 262–63; proposed legislation against, 270–72; in Nashville in 1924, 283
Lyon, A. A. 241

McAdoo, William Gibbs, 163–64
McAlister, Hill, 45
McCulloch, James E., 215–16
McGhee, Rosa, ix
McIlheron, Jim, 236n
McKellar, Kenneth D., 271
McKenzie, Fayette Avery: and Fisk University student strike, 274, 277–92; resigns as president of Fisk University, 291
McKissack, Moses, 179–80, 203
McMillan, John E., 243–44, 245
McMurdy, Robert, 286–87
McNair, G. W., 120
Madison Square Garden, 293
Manning, J. W., 108
Martin, J. B., 46, 190–91
Maryville College: black students at, 4, 61n, 63
Maury County, 133–34
Mayes, Maurice: and Knoxville race riot, 245–46, 252, 253, 267, 269
Mayfield, Robert L.: challenges segregation in transportation, 7, 11; challenges exclusion of blacks from juries, 9; difficulties of, as attorney, 9–10, 175; supports Democrats, 51, 52; supports "State Police" bill, 238
Meharry Medical College, 277, 281
Melton, W. H., 48, 56
Memphis: opposition to segregated streetcars in, 24, 25, 31–33; blacks in politics in, 42–47, 53, 55–58, 222–23, 241, 251; educational facilities for blacks in, 74–75, 78; impact of black migration upon, 144, 191, 221–22, 227, 228; activities of NAACP in, 195, 242, 265, 266, 267, 271; black insurance companies in, 200–201, 202–204; black progressives

Memphis (cont.)
in, 221–28, 230; lynching in, 227; work of Commission on Interracial Cooperation in, 259, 260–61. See also Race relations; Racial violence; Unions; World War I
Memphis Association for the Protection of Colored Women, 226–27
Memphis Chamber of Commerce: relationship of, to black progressives, 228; support of, for World War I labor and vagrancy laws, 235, 260; views of, on the Commission on Interracial Cooperation, 260; views of, on the NAACP, 266
Memphis Colored Citizen, 48
Memphis Commercial Appeal: support of, for improved black schools, 65–66; opposes Lincoln League activities, 56; deplores out-migration of blacks, 128; opposes antilynching legislation, 270
Memphis Inter-Racial League, 260
Memphis Negro Board of Trade, 211
Memphis Public Welfare League, 260, 266
Memphis Street Railway Company, 21
Memphis Times, 18, 228
Memphis Triangle, 46
Messenger, 43
Methodist Episcopal Church, South, 216
Metropolitan Life Insurance Company, 200
Migration, black: from farm to cities, 119–20, 123, 126–31; economic motivation of, 132–36, 143–58; white reaction to, 128–29, 132; black reaction to, 119, 120, 132, 179; governmental concern for, during World War I, 123; impact of World War I upon, 143–58; impact of, upon housing in Memphis, 191; tension created by, 232, 254
Miller, Herbert Adolphus, 291, 292
Miller, Randolph M., 29–30, 31, 175
Mims, Edwin, 249, 292
Mind of the South, 136
Minyard, Milton, 294–95
Mississippi Beneficial Life Insurance Company (Mississippi Life), 202–203
Montgomery County, 117
Moon Weekly Illustrated, 140
Mooney, C. P. J., 43, 224, 225
Moore, T. Clay, 288, 290
Morgan, Harcourt A., 122

Morrill Act of 1862, 89, 91, 122
Morrill Act of 1890: failure to provide funds from, to black Tennesseans, 90, 91, 95, 122; funds from, applied to Tennessee A & I, 97, 98, 102, 103, 106
Morrison, Mary, 32
Moton, Robert, 268
Municipal reform, commission system of: impact of, upon black officeholders, 4, 11, 38–39, 40, 41
Murphy, John Paul, 90–91
Mynatt, R. A., 246
Mynders, Seymour A., 69

Napier, James Carroll: relationship of, to Booker T. Washington, 5, 6, 52, 176, 178; protests against segregation in transportation, 6–7, 26–27; as a loyal Republican, 47–48, 50, 52; on board of trustees of Jeanes Foundation, 82, 95; as leader in drive to establish Tennessee A & I, 88, 95, 98, 100; active role of, in National Negro Business League, 176–78; role of, with One-Cent Savings Bank and Trust Company, 26, 186, 192, 193; accepts white paternalism, 216, 258; expectations of, from black support of World War I, 234; opposition of, to racial violence, 237, 238; relationship of, to Fisk University, 277, 279, 282, 288, 289
Nashville: reasons for active black community in, 89; activities of National Negro Business League in, 5, 25, 172, 176–78; streetcar boycott in, 24–28, 33–35; blacks in politics in, 39, 42, 51–53; educational facilities for blacks in, 74; relationship of, to founding of Tennessee A & I, 88–89, 93–101; blacks as firemen in, 141; black banks in, 184–87, 189, 191–93, 197–99; insurance companies and blacks in, 200, 201, 203, 205; black progressivism in, 208, 209–19, 220, 223, 230; lynching in, 227; activities of NAACP in, 238, 265, 266–67; work of Commission on Interracial Cooperation in, 259, 261; blacks in, and Fisk University student strike, 274–92; whites in, and Fisk University student strike, 284–92. See also Unions; World War I
Nashville American, 21–22, 62–63, 64, 65

Nashville Banner, 250, 286, 288
Nashville Chamber of Commerce, 292
Nashville, Chattanooga and St. Louis Railway, 7–8
Nashville Clarion, 24, 27–28, 179, 288
Nashville Colored Ministers' Alliance, 233
Nashville Commercial Daily, 236
Nashville Globe: general racial philosophy of, 15–17, 89, 138, 274; support of, for streetcar boycott, 14, 25, 35; political independence of, 17, 42, 49, 50, 51–53; and improved and equal education for blacks, 66, 70, 72, 75, 79, 93–94, 95, 96–98; supports improved black farming instead of migration, 117–18, 120; attacks replacement of black firemen, 141; support of, for black businesses, 15, 168, 171–79, 187, 202; as catalyst for progressive reform in Nashville, 209–13, 217; resistance of, to white violence, 239; and interracial cooperation, 264; and Fisk University's relationship to the Nashville black community, 275–77, 282
Nashville Negro Board of Trade: as a progressive force, 211–13; 217; supports students in Fisk University student strike, 288, 289, 290
Nashville Negro Ministerial Alliance, 290
Nashville Railway and Light Company, 34
Nashville Tennessean, 239, 288
Nashville Transit Company, 28
Nation, 287–88
National Association for the Advancement of Colored People (NAACP): general activity of, in Tennessee, 19, 241–42, 264–72, 296; in Memphis, 195, 242, 265, 266, 267, 271; in Chattanooga, 265, 266, 267, 271, 295; in Nashville, 238, 265, 266–67; in Knoxville, 244, 249–50, 253, 265, 266, 267, 269–70; in Somerville, 266; in Jackson, 267–68; opposes Smith-Lever Act, 122; protests against violence to black railroad workers, 164; supports "State Police" bill, 238; creates tension among whites, 241–42; investigates peonage, 267; chapter of, denied at Fisk University, 279; defends Oswald Durant, 281; works for passage of Dyer antilynching bill, 270–72; revitalization of, in 1930s, 269–70, 294

National Association for Thrift Among Colored People, 226
National Baptist Convention: splits in 1915, 18–19
National Baptist Publishing Board, Incorporated, 18n
National Baptist Publishing Board, Unincorporated, 18n, 24, 34
National Farm Loan Association, 124
National Federation of Colored Women's Clubs, 213
National League on Urban Conditions Among Negroes (Urban League): as a progressive force in Tennessee, 214–21, 226–29; and school of social work, 215–16; and Nashville League on Conditions Among Negroes, 217; and Nashville Public Welfare League, 217–18; and Chattanooga Central Community Betterment League, 219; and Memphis Welfare League, 227–28. See also George Edmund Haynes; Progressivism
National Medical Association, 239
National Negro Bankers Association, 197
National Negro Business League: business philosophy of, 176, 178; chapters of, in Tennessee, 25, 29, 176–79; national meeting of, in Nashville in 1903, 5, 172, 176; national meeting of, in Chattanooga in 1917, 179, 234
National Negro Farmers and Rural Teachers Congress, 125
National Playground Association, 224
Negro Booster Club (Nashville), 212
Negro dolls, 175
Negro Southern Baseball League, 180
Nelson, Thomas, A. R., 246, 252
New York Age, 56
New York Times, 284
Nichols, H. S., 122
Norris, Isaac F., 92

Odgen, Robert Curtis, 62n, 63, 64
Ogden Movement. See Conference for Education in the South
Old Folks and Orphans' Home (Memphis), 214
Oldfield, J. J. J., 54
Oliver, Robert B., and Brothers, 161–62

One-Cent Savings Bank and Trust Company: activities of, 184–87, 189, 192–93, 198–99; Boyd family influence in, 173; becomes Citizens Savings Bank and Trust Company, 26, 192; refuses merger with closed People's Bank, 198; survives run in 1931, 198–99
Overton, Watkins, 46
Ovington, Mary White, ix

Pace, Harry Herbert, 189, 190, 201, 223
Paine, Rowlett, 44, 45–46
Parden, Noah W., 10
Patterson, Malcolm R.: political support of, by blacks, 17, 51, 96, 117; attention of, to black farmers, 117; comments by, on black migration, 128; release of black youths from prison by, 210
Patton, L. L., 295
Payne, James W., 247
Pearson, Josephine A., 241
Peay, Austin, 45, 54, 106
Peck, Thomas, 118
Penny Savings Bank, 183, 186
People's Co-operative League of Tennessee, 251
People's Savings Bank and Trust Company: activities of, 124, 186–87, 192, 197–99; collapses, 197–99
People's Steam Laundry, 169
Perry, Heman E., 202–203
Persons, Ell, 227, 236n, 265
Phillips, J. T., 288
Phyllis Wheatley Club, 213, 217
Pickens, William, 260, 271
Politics: blacks in, in Tennessee, 37–58, 222–23, 241, 251; in Chattanooga, 38–39, 42–43, 58n; in Knoxville, 39, 42; in Memphis, 42–47, 53, 55–58, 222–23, 241, 251; in Nashville, 39, 42, 51–53; and Republican party, 4, 11, 47–51, 54, 55–58; and support for Democrats, 17, 51–55, 96, 100, 117; and woman suffrage, 54, 241; and reaction to Ku Klux Klan, 42–44; statutory restrictions on, 40–41
Porter, Webster L., 55, 249, 258, 269, 270
Porter, William, 48
Price, A. G., 169
Progressivism, black: most active in

Progressivism (cont.)
Nashville, 208, 209–19, 220, 223, 230; in Chattanooga, 219–20; in Knoxville, 213, 219, 220–21, 230; in Memphis, 221–28, 230; and charity work, 212–14, 226; and business efficiency, 212; and education, 213, 228; and health care, 212, 218, 219, 220, 224–25; and morality in youth, 209–10, 214, 226; and penal reform, 210, 218; and political pressure, 222–25; and recreational facilities, 212, 218, 224, 225, 228; relationship of, with white progressivism, 215, 217–18, 220, 227–29; role of women's organizations in, 213–14; and social work, 215–16; and Nashville *Globe*'s emphasis upon local action, 209, 211, 217. *See also* National League on Urban Conditions Among Negroes
Provident Life Insurance Company, 201
Prudential Life Insurance Company, 200

Race relations: geographical differences in, within the state, 2–3, 89, 221, 223, 227, 243–44; at the heart of Tennessee's violence, 250, 251, 254–55; after World War I, 256–73. *See also* Educational philanthropy; Racial violence
Racial violence: and black Tennesseans, 208, 227, 231–55, 283; role of newspapers in, 240–41, 254; diminishes in 1920s, 262–63. *See also* Knoxville race riot of 1919; Lynching
Railway Employees Protective Association, 200
Randolph, A. Philip, 43
Reconstruction, in Tennessee, v
Reconstruction Finance Corporation, 199
Reconstruction Service League, 261
"Red Summer" of 1919, 239
Reformers' League (Mt. Pleasant), 214
Reid, Eugene L., 38
Republican party. *See* Politics
Reynolds, Joe, 248
Rising Sun Manufacturing Company, 143
Rivers v. *State* (1906), 9
Roane Iron Company, 142
Roberts, Albert H.: black political support for, 54; strong advocacy of, for law and order, 238, 239, 250–51; reaction of, to

Roberts, Albert H. (cont.)
Chicago race riot, 240, 243
Roberts, Eugene P., 215
Robinson, George T., 23, 138
Robinson, J. G., 19
Robinson, James Hathaway, 262
Robinson, Walter, 58n
Rock City Academy of Medicine (Nashville), 290
Roddy, Bert M.: as organizer of Three States Better Farming Association, 124–25; active role of, in National Negro Business League, 178; as business entrepreneur, 180–81, 190; as leader in Colored Citizens Association, 223; gives support for World War I, 233; shows early interest in NAACP, 265, 267
Roddy's Citizens' Co-operative Stores, 180–81
Roger Williams University, 4, 92, 105, 276
Roman, Charles Victor, 67, 216, 277, 288
Roosevelt, Theodore, 48, 49
Rosenwald, Julius, 83
Rosenwald (Julius) Fund: education work of, in Tennessee, 79, 80, 83–85, 86–87, 107; aid of, to Industrial Settlement Home, 226; contribution of, toward hospital facilities for blacks in Knoxville, 259–60
Rye, Tom C., 235, 237, 238, 270

Sacco, Nicola, 295
Saunders, Clarence, 180
Scales, Searcy, 179–80
Schieffelin, William Jay, 215
Scott, Edward F., 189
Scott, Emmett J., 293
Scott, Evelyn, v
Scott, J. Jay, 176, 189–90
Scott, Lathan (Lation?), 236n
Segregation. *See* Caste system
Sequatchie County, 73
Settle, Josiah T., 32, 48, 49–50
Shields, John Knight, 32, 271
Shillady, John R., 266
Shipp, Joseph F., 10
Singleton, Benjamin "Pap," 126
Slater (John F.) Fund, 79, 80–81, 86–87

Slatter, Horace, 53
Smith, Alfred E., 54–55
Smith, Bolton, 242
Smith, Ora, 245
Smith, Samuel Leonard, 79–82, 84–85
Smith-Hughes Act of 1917, 124
Smith-Lever Act of 1914, 122
Socialist party, 53
Solvent Savings Bank and Trust Company: activities of, 188–91, 202; and Roddy's Citizens' Co-operative Stores, 180, 181; as a major center of black leadership, 222, 223; merges with Fraternal Savings Bank and Trust Company, 193. See also Fraternal and Solvent Savings Bank and Trust Company
South Central Life Insurance Company, 202
Southern Education Board, 62–64, 69–70, 75–76, 79, 88, 93, 96. See also Conference for Education in the South
Southern Life Insurance Company, 202–203
Spear, Allan H., vi
Spence, Mary E., 35
Standard Life Insurance Company, 201, 202–203
State Agent for Negro Schools, 79
State Police (Constabulary) Law of 1919, 238–39
Stevens, T. E., 42n
Streator, George Walter, 284, 289
Streetcar Law (Segregation) of 1905: as part of tightening caste system, 4; legislative background for, 20–22
Streetcar segregation: black opposition to, 8–9, 14, 20–36; opposition in Memphis to, 24, 25, 31–33; opposition in Jackson to, 28; opposition in Knoxville to, 33; boycott against, in Nashville, 24–28, 33–35; boycott against, in Chattanooga, 29–31
Stuart, Merah Steven, 46, 167n, 205
Sumlin, W. W., 288, 289, 290, 293
Sunday School Publishing Board, National Baptist Convention of United States of America, 198
Supreme Life and Casualty Insurance Company, 292

Taft, William Howard, 49, 52
Talley, Thomas Washington, 118
Tate, H. D., 121–22
Taylor, Alfred A., 54, 263
Taylor, G. Tom, 128
Taylor, J. Will, 272
Taylor, Preston: background of, 26n; as organizer of Union Transportation Company, 25, 26–27, 34–35; works to locate Tennessee A & I in Nashville, 99; addresses Farmers' Institute, 118; as leader in National Negro Business League, 176, 177; founded Railway Employees Protective Association, 200; as an original investor in Universal Life Insurance Company, 203
Ten-Men Investment Club (Memphis), 180
Tennessee Agricultural and Industrial State Normal School (Tennessee A & I): founding and early years of, 88–109; relationship of Nashville to founding of, 88–89, 93–101; relationship of Chattanooga to founding of, 99, 100–101, 105; early student life at, 103–104; early opposition from Fisk University supporters to, 105; discrimination against, in funding of, 71, 298; negligible funds for, under Smith-Lever Act, 122; aid from General Education Board to, 106; support from Commission on Interracial Cooperation for, 106; caste semantics and, 71–72; greatest areas of student support in Tennessee for, 105, 106; impact of, 77, 104–105, 115; becomes a four-year "teachers college," 108–109
Tennessee Coal and Iron Company, 142
Tennessee Colored State Poultry Association, 125
Tennessee Home League (Chicago), 157
Tennessee Interracial Commission, 129
Tennessee Law and Order League: activities of, 235–39, 244, 251, 252, 255; absorbed by Commission on Interracial Cooperation, 256; impact of, 262, 266
Tennessee Normal, Agricultural and Mechanical Association, 96
Tennessee State Association of Teachers in Colored Schools, 108

Tennessee Vocational School for Colored Girls, 261
Thompson, John, 117–18
Thompson, W. H., 295
Three States Better Farming Association, 125
Tobacco, black growers of, 117
Transfer Omnibus Motor Car Company, 30–31
Trawick, Arch M., 218
Trawick, Kate H., 286
Tri-State Bank, 196
Tri-State Casket and Coffin Company, 190, 191, 195
Trigg, Joseph M., 39
Trimble, J. F., 295
Turner Normal College, 23, 276
Tuskegee "machine," 176
Tyree, Bishop Evans, 140
Tyree, Hiram, 38–39, 40, 41

Unicoi County, 73
Union Protective Assurance Company (Union Protective Life Insurance Company), 200–201
Union Transportation Company, 14, 27–28, 33–35
Unions: blacks in, 141, 142, 157, 158–65; for barbers, 141; in iron industry, 142, 157, 160–61; for railroad workers, 161–65; in skilled trades, 159–60
United States Cast Iron Pipe Works, 142
Universal Life Insurance Company: activities of, 200, 202, 203–204, 205; ties of, to Fraternal and Solvent Savings Bank and Trust Company, 196, 204; ties of, to People's Savings Bank and Trust Company, 197
Universal Negro Improvement Association, 293–96
Urbanization: among blacks in Tennessee, 135–66; and standard of living, 136–39, 165, 221–22; and discrimination in housing, 137, 138n; and vulnerability of blacks to loan sharks, 138–39; and passage of vagrancy laws, 139–40
Uya, Okon E., ix

Vanzetti, Bartolomeo, 295

Vaughn, C. D., 16n

Washington, Booker T.: philosophical influence of, in Tennessee, vii, 4–5, 30, 176, 178, 229, 237, 265, 297, 298; loss of symbolic leadership of, with death in 1915, 18–19; philosophy of, as a "search for order," 208–209; economic philosophy of, 205–206; interest of, in aiding black businesses, 5, 168, 176, 178; accepts white paternalism, 216, 225; urges protest against segregated transportation, 6; and Theodore Roosevelt, 48; and Southern education crusade, 66, 75–76; as model and supporter of W. J. Hale, 102, 108; makes plea for juvenile correction facilities, 210; as member of board of trustees of Fisk University, 278
Washington, D. C., race riot of 1919, 239
Walker, Joseph Edison, 202–203, 204
Ward, Alfred F., 191, 193, 194
Ware, W. P., 126, 130
Watkins, Mrs. A., 20
Wells, Madison, 218
Wells-Barnett, Ida, 264, 265
West Tennessee Civic and Political League, 46–47, 224
West Tennessee Negro Farmers' Institute, 116, 119, 123
Western World Reporter (Memphis), 265
Wheatley National Bank Association, 196
Wheeling Molding Foundry, 157
White, J. W., 183n
White, Walter F., 290
White primary, 4
Whitecapping, 65, 114, 115n, 119, 133, 232
Wilkerson, Wayman: in Memphis-area politics, 46, 56, 57; as leader in National Negro Business League, 176; as a founder and officer in Fraternal Savings Bank, 189, 190–91, 195
Wilkerson, Mrs. Wayman, 195
Williams, Noah, 288
Williams, William Taylor B., 74
Willis, H. N., 183n
Wilson, John Thomas, 203
Wilson County, 81–82
Woman suffrage, 241
Wood, L. Hollingsworth, 286

Worley, Parks, 84, 241
World War I: economic impact of, 143–58, 163–64; and industrial labor recruiters, 157; black economic support of, 233; heavy black army enlistment during, 232–33; impact upon race relations of, 210, 231, 234–38, 254

Wright, Richard, 249

Young Men's Business Club (Memphis), 227
Young Men's Civic and Welfare Club (Knoxville), 261

Twentieth-Century America Series
DEWEY W. GRANTHAM, GENERAL EDITOR

Each volume in this series will focus on some aspect of the politics of social change in recent American history, utilizing new approaches to clarify the response of Americans to the dislocating forces of our own day—economic, technological, racial, demographic, and administrative.

VOLUMES PUBLISHED:

The Reaffirmation of Republicanism: Eisenhower and the Eighty-third Congress by Gary W. Reichard

The Crisis of Conservative Virginia: The Byrd Organization and the Politics of Massive Resistance by James W. Ely, Jr.

Black Tennesseans, 1900–1930 by Lester C. Lamon

This book has been set on the Variable Input Phototypesetter in eleven-point Caledonia with two-point line spacing. Phototypositor Columbus was used for display. The book was designed by Bill Cason, composed by Moran Industries, Inc., Baton Rouge Louisiana, printed offset by Thomson-Shore, Inc., Dexter, Michigan, and bound by John H. Dekker & Sons, Inc., Grand Rapids, Michigan. The paper on which the book is printed bears the watermark of the S. D. Warren Company and is designed for an effective life of at least three hundred years.

THE UNIVERSITY OF TENNESSEE PRESS
KNOXVILLE